WORLD OF WARCRAFT®

BOOK ONE

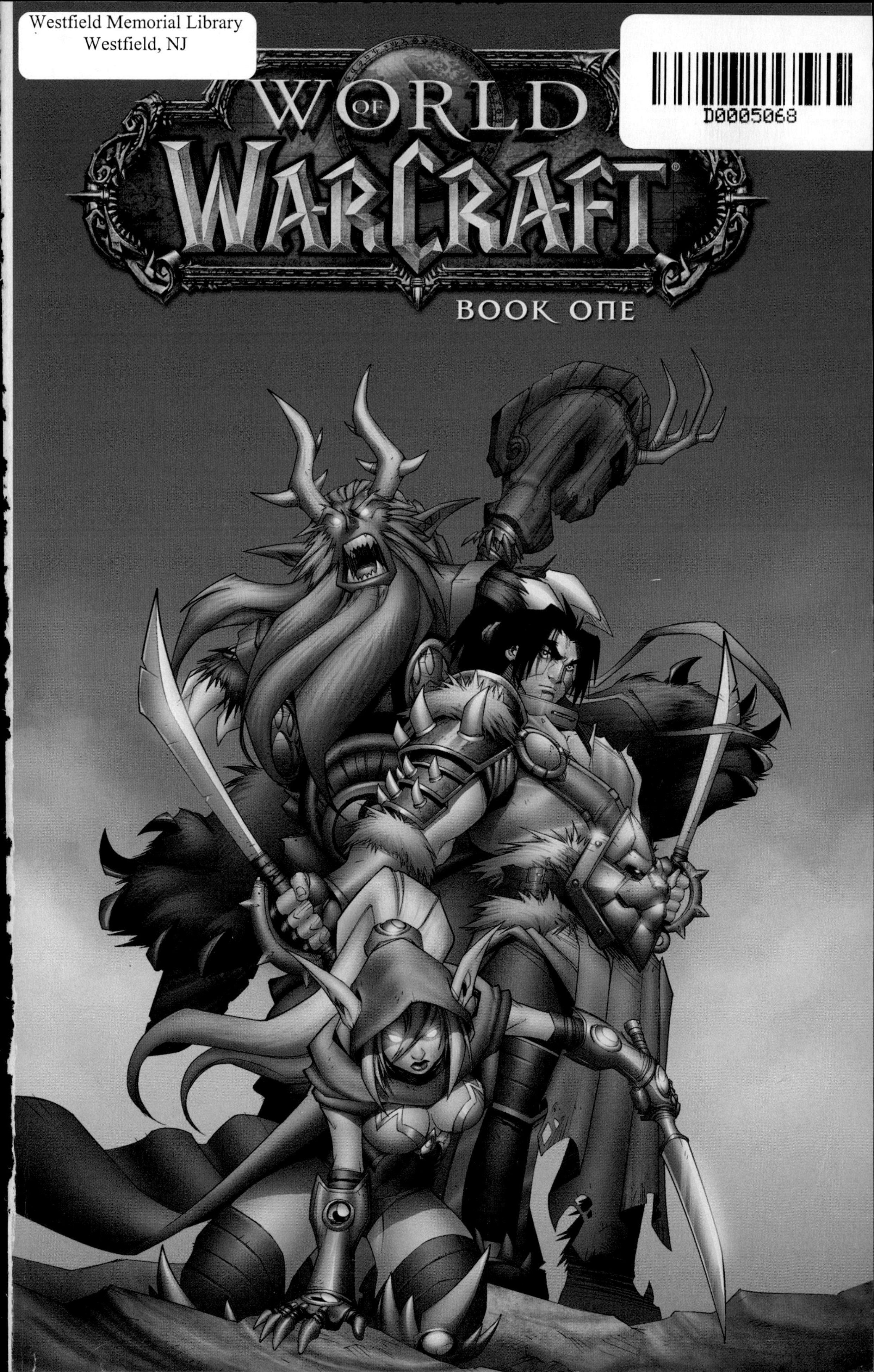

Writer: Walter Simonson
Penciler: Ludo Lullabi
Inker: Sandra Hope
with Richard Friend (#2)
with Philip Moy (#5&7)
Colors: Randy Mayor
with Carrie Strachan (#5&6)
Letters: Nick Napolitano (#1-2), Steve Wands (#3-7)

Collected Edition Cover and Original Series covers by Samwise Didier
Original Series covers by Jim Lee
Original Series Cover #7 by Ludo Lullabi and Sandra Hope
Special thanks to Jean Wacquet and Olivier Jalabert

For Blizzard Entertainment:

Chris Metzen, Senior VP—Creative Development
Shawn Carnes, Manager—Creative Development
Micky Neilson, Story Consultation and Development
Glenn Rane, Art Director
Cory Jones, Director—Global Business Development and Licensing
Jason Bischoff, Associate Licensing Manager

Additional Development:
Samwise Didier, Evelyn Fredericksen, Ben Brode, Sean Wang

Blizzard Special Thanks: Brian Hsieh, Gina Pippin

For DC Comics:

Jim Lee, Editorial Director
John Nee, Senior VP—Business Development
Hank Kanalz, VP—General Manager, WildStorm and Editor
Kristy Quinn, Assistant Editor
Ed Roeder, Art Director
Paul Levitz, President & Publisher
Georg Brewer, VP—Design & DC Direct Creative
Richard Bruning, Senior VP—Creative Director
Patrick Caldon, Executive VP—Finance & Operations
Chris Caramalis, VP—Finance
John Cunningham, VP—Marketing
Terri Cunningham, VP—Managing Editor
Alison Gill, VP—Manufacturing
David Hyde, VP—Publicity
Paula Lowitt, Senior VP—Business & Legal Affairs
MaryEllen McLaughlin, VP—Advertising & Custom Publishing
Gregory Noveck, Senior VP—Creative Affairs
Sue Pohja, VP—Book Trade Sales
Steve Rotterdam, Senior VP—Sales & Marketing
Cheryl Rubin, Senior VP—Brand Management
Jeff Trojan, VP—Business Development, DC Direct
Bob Wayne, VP—Sales

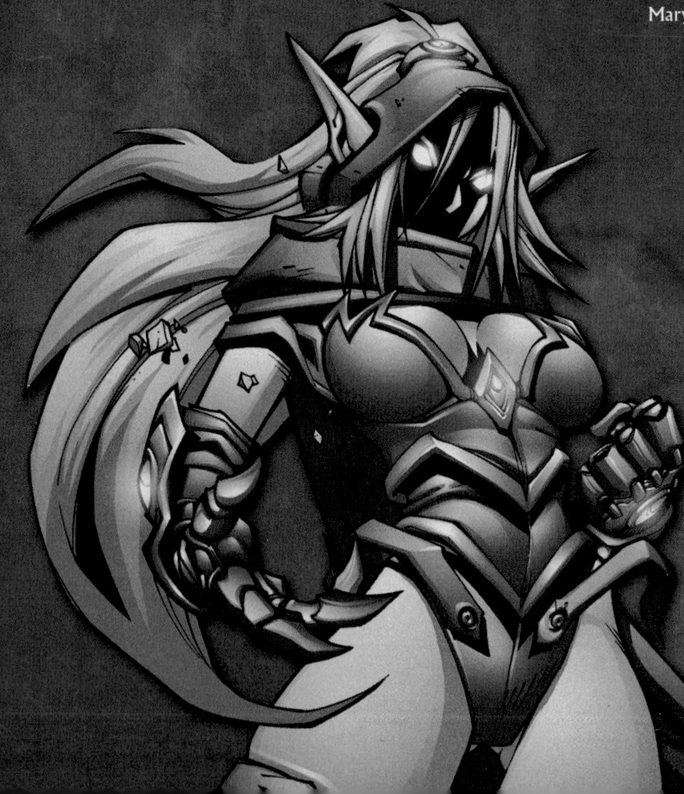

WORLD OF WARCRAFT Book One, published by WildStorm Productions, an imprint of DC Comics, 888 Prospect St, Suite 240, La Jolla, CA 92037.

Hardcover ISBN: 978-1-4012-1836-2
Softcover ISBN: 978-1-4012-2076-1

Chasing Thunder

A foreword by Chris Metzen

I've been a comics fan all my life. Okay—that's probably an understatment...<cough> I've got a twenty-dollar-a-week habit and...well, I may need help. Thing is—those soulless bastards in the comics industry not only draw me in with monthly issues of high adventure and cleverly unfolding drama—but now they're tempting me with these really sweet, premium collected editions of stuff I ALREADY own...and I CAN'T say NO! The horror...the horror....

In all seriousness, I was honored to be asked to write a foreword to this very special book. It's a crazy thing...holding this book in my hands. Considering how heavily the world of comics has informed the creation of the Warcraft universe, this book feels like the completion of a grand circle to me.

While Warcraft is a high-octane "swords & sorcery" setting, I don't think it's any secret that its unique flavor is steeped heavily in comics lore. It's absolutely saturated by the colorful themes and motifs that continually play out in the complex yet glorious universes inhabited by our favorite spandex-clad heroes. I know, I know...you might be wondering what magical broadswords and demon-forged fel reavers have to do with secret identities and skin-tight costumes. A few examples pop to mind:

...like just how influential the heart and soul of Captain America was in developing the true vibe of Warcraft paladins (*Avenger's Shield*, anyone?)

...or how much Alex Ross's mythic renderings of Superman in KINGDOM COME and JUSTICE influenced the draenei's heroic poses and animation sets

...or how "The Dreaming" from SANDMAN and "The Green" from SWAMP THING both

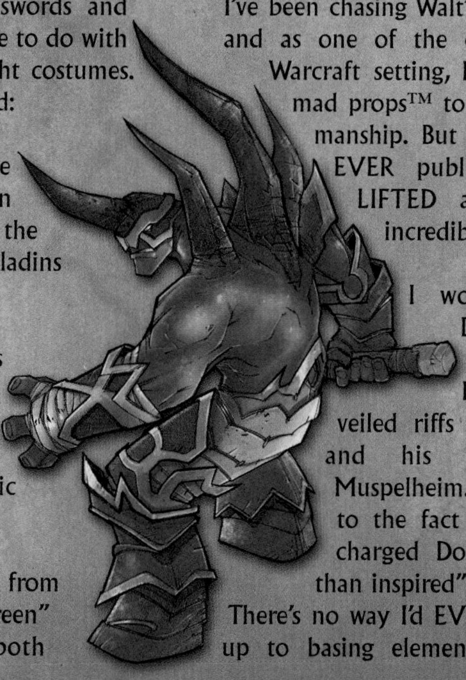

helped to shape the Warcraft druids' mystical Emerald Dream (d'uh)...and who could forget the diabolical Dr. Boom and his Boom-Bots lurking out in the crumbling wastes of Netherstorm???

While I could name a hundred more (and increasingly wack) examples of how comics concepts bleed into World of Warcraft—there's one specific comic that's been hardwired into Warcraft's DNA from the very start. It remains my favorite comic book run ever—and perhaps my single greatest inspiration as a storyteller.

Walter Simonson's unforgettable run on *The Mighty Thor*.

If you haven't read Walt's full run on *Thor*, it would be hard for me to explain just how truly epic it is (which means go pick up the trades!). The art, script, and sheer scope of imagination all blended together to create an incredibly rich, mythic tapestry that was more than a story...it was a sojourn through a vital, fantastical WORLD steeped in unabashed HEROISM.

I've been chasing Walt's vision since I was kid, and as one of the chief architects of the Warcraft setting, I feel obligated to give mad props™ to his unparalleled craftsmanship. But c'mon—it's not like I'd EVER publicly admit to having LIFTED any ideas from that incredible run...

I wouldn't be CAUGHT DEAD suggesting that Sargeras and his Burning Legion are just veiled riffs on the demon Surtur and his legions from fiery Muspelheim. NEVER would I cop to the fact that Thrall's lightning-charged Doomhammer was "more than inspired" by the mighty Mjolnir! There's no way I'd EVEN CONSIDER owning up to basing elements of the night elves' architecture on the uber-Viking city of Asgard (Samwise is going to kill me for that one). World trees, giant wolves named Fenris, Viking warlords, armies of the vengeful dead…COINCIDENCE, nothing more! Imagine then—after years of working on the Warcraft series and hoping that a comic based on it might someday take shape— the CHAMPIONS at WildStorm convinced Walter Simonson to step boldly into the lands of Azeroth…

The fact of it still makes me giddy.

…okay, so I've geeked out pretty hard here…but the rip-roaring tale of gladiators, demigods, and mistaken identities you're about to read (or re-read, Heaven forbid) is proof enough of the man's genius. Still, it must be said, no comics story ever really gets off the ground until the artwork falls into place. Over the years, we've been very particular about the kind of art that defines the Warcraft style. We looked at a lot of amazing artists in hopes of finding just the right visionary to bring this series to life. Strangely enough, we found him far across the sea—in the fabled lands of distant France.

Ludo Lullabi.

The man with the musical name absolutely floored us with his initial sketches of the lands and characters of this setting. His style absolutely sang to the hyper-proportioned, over-the-top visual bombast that is Warcraft. And while his drawing style was an immediate fit for this project, I've also been amazed at his dynamic framework and sequential storytelling. The rhythm of his frames and page layouts flow perfectly with Walt's plotlines. It's like a friggin' symphony of words and flashing blades…

All told, this comic series has been an amazing fusion of incredible talents and epic ideas. I want to thank Jim, Hank, Walter, and all of our amazing brothers and sisters at WildStorm for taking the wild leap of faith with us—and proving that a Warcraft comic book could even work.

What were the odds anyway, right?

— Chris Metzen

Vice President of Creative Development
Blizzard Entertainment

CHAPTER 0

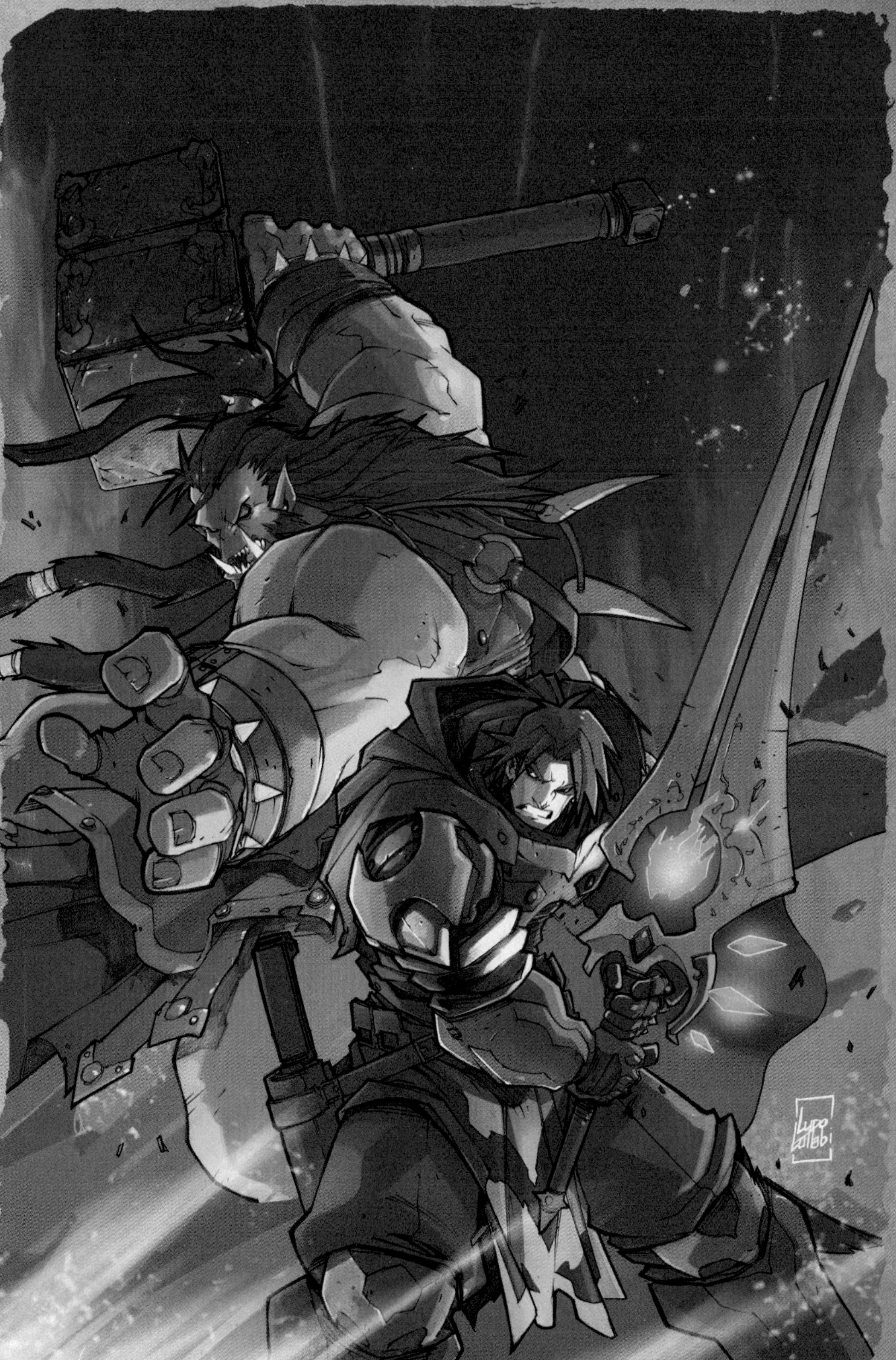

Blizzcon Exclusive Cover by Ludo Lullabi

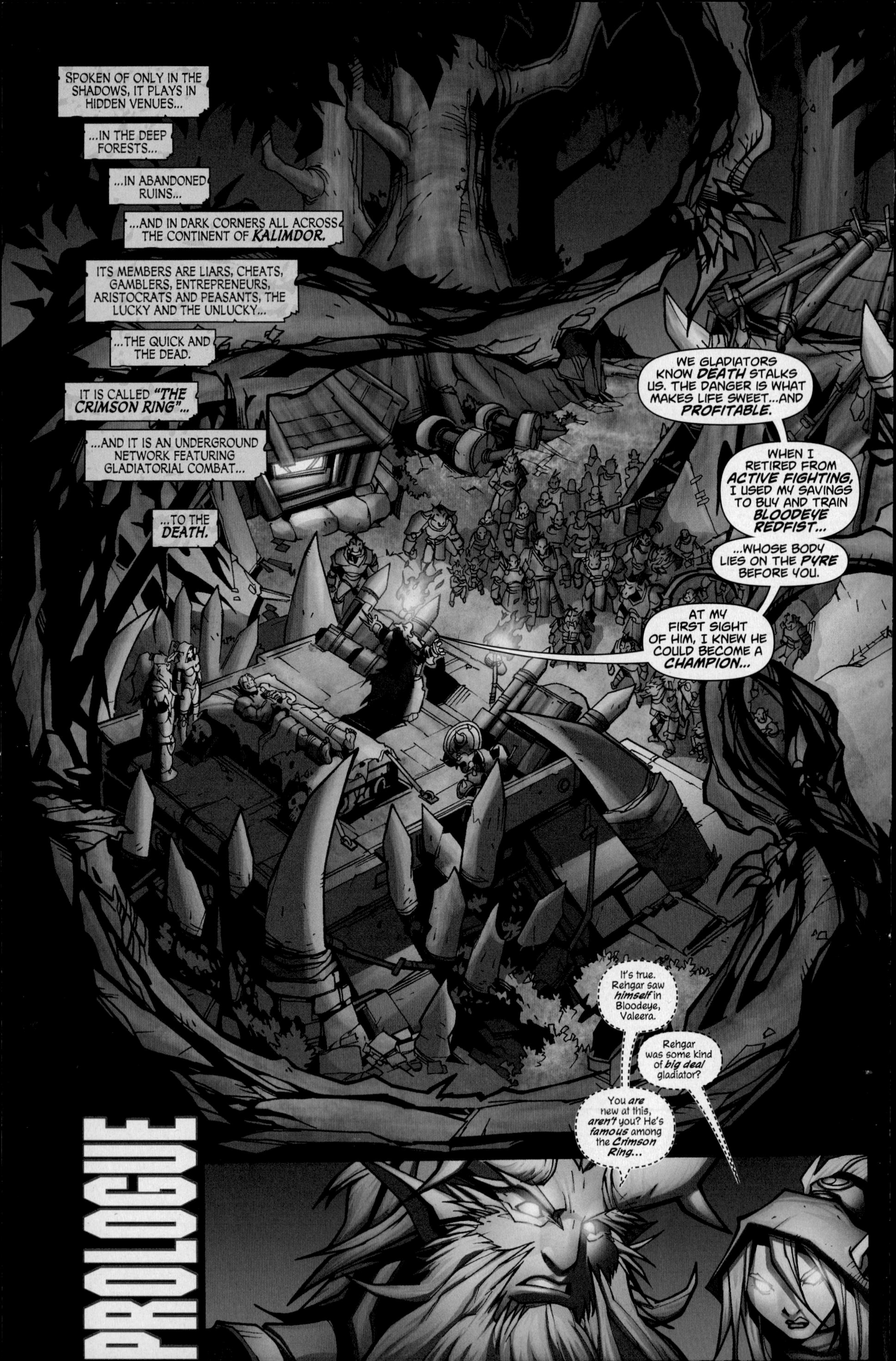
SPOKEN OF ONLY IN THE SHADOWS, IT PLAYS IN HIDDEN VENUES...
...IN THE DEEP FORESTS...
...IN ABANDONED RUINS...
...AND IN DARK CORNERS ALL ACROSS THE CONTINENT OF KALIMDOR.
ITS MEMBERS ARE LIARS, CHEATS, GAMBLERS, ENTREPRENEURS, ARISTOCRATS AND PEASANTS, THE LUCKY AND THE UNLUCKY...
...THE QUICK AND THE DEAD.
IT IS CALLED "THE CRIMSON RING"...
...AND IT IS AN UNDERGROUND NETWORK FEATURING GLADIATORIAL COMBAT...
...TO THE DEATH.
WE GLADIATORS KNOW DEATH STALKS US. THE DANGER IS WHAT MAKES LIFE SWEET...AND PROFITABLE.
WHEN I RETIRED FROM ACTIVE FIGHTING, I USED MY SAVINGS TO BUY AND TRAIN BLOODEYE REDFIST...
...WHOSE BODY LIES ON THE PYRE BEFORE YOU.
AT MY FIRST SIGHT OF HIM, I KNEW HE COULD BECOME A CHAMPION...
It's true. Rehgar saw himself in Bloodeye, Valeera.
Rehgar was some kind of big deal gladiator?
You are new at this, aren't you? He's famous among the Crimson Ring...
PROLOGUE

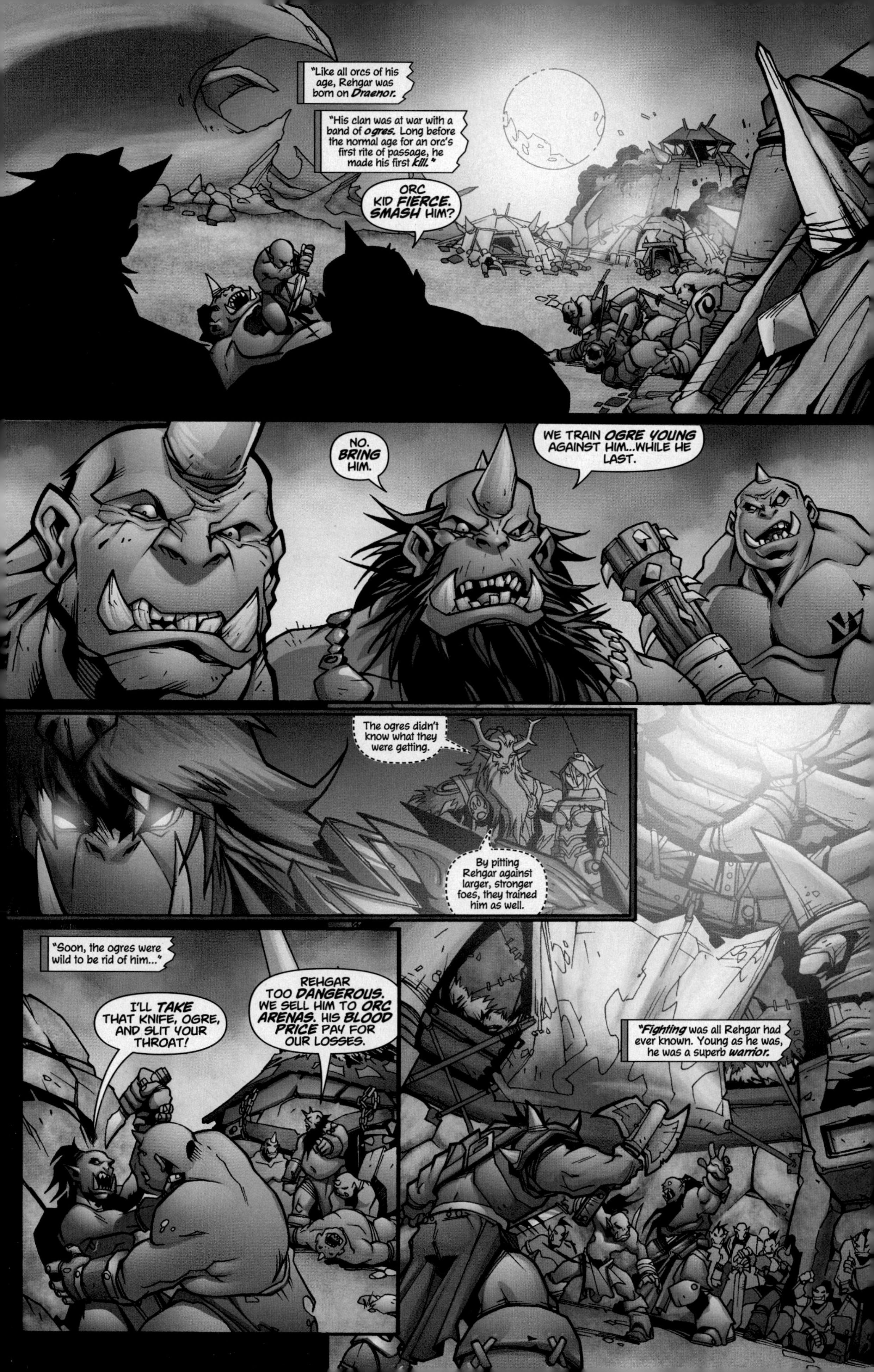
"Like all orcs of his age, Rehgar was born on Draenor.
"His clan was at war with a band of ogres. Long before the normal age for an orc's first rite of passage, he made his first kill."
ORC KID FIERCE. SMASH HIM?
NO. BRING HIM.
WE TRAIN OGRE YOUNG AGAINST HIM...WHILE HE LAST.
The ogres didn't know what they were getting.
By pitting Rehgar against larger, stronger foes, they trained him as well.
"Soon, the ogres were wild to be rid of him..."
I'LL TAKE THAT KNIFE, OGRE, AND SLIT YOUR THROAT!
REHGAR TOO DANGEROUS. WE SELL HIM TO ORC ARENAS. HIS BLOOD PRICE PAY FOR OUR LOSSES.
"Fighting was all Rehgar had ever known. Young as he was, he was a superb warrior.

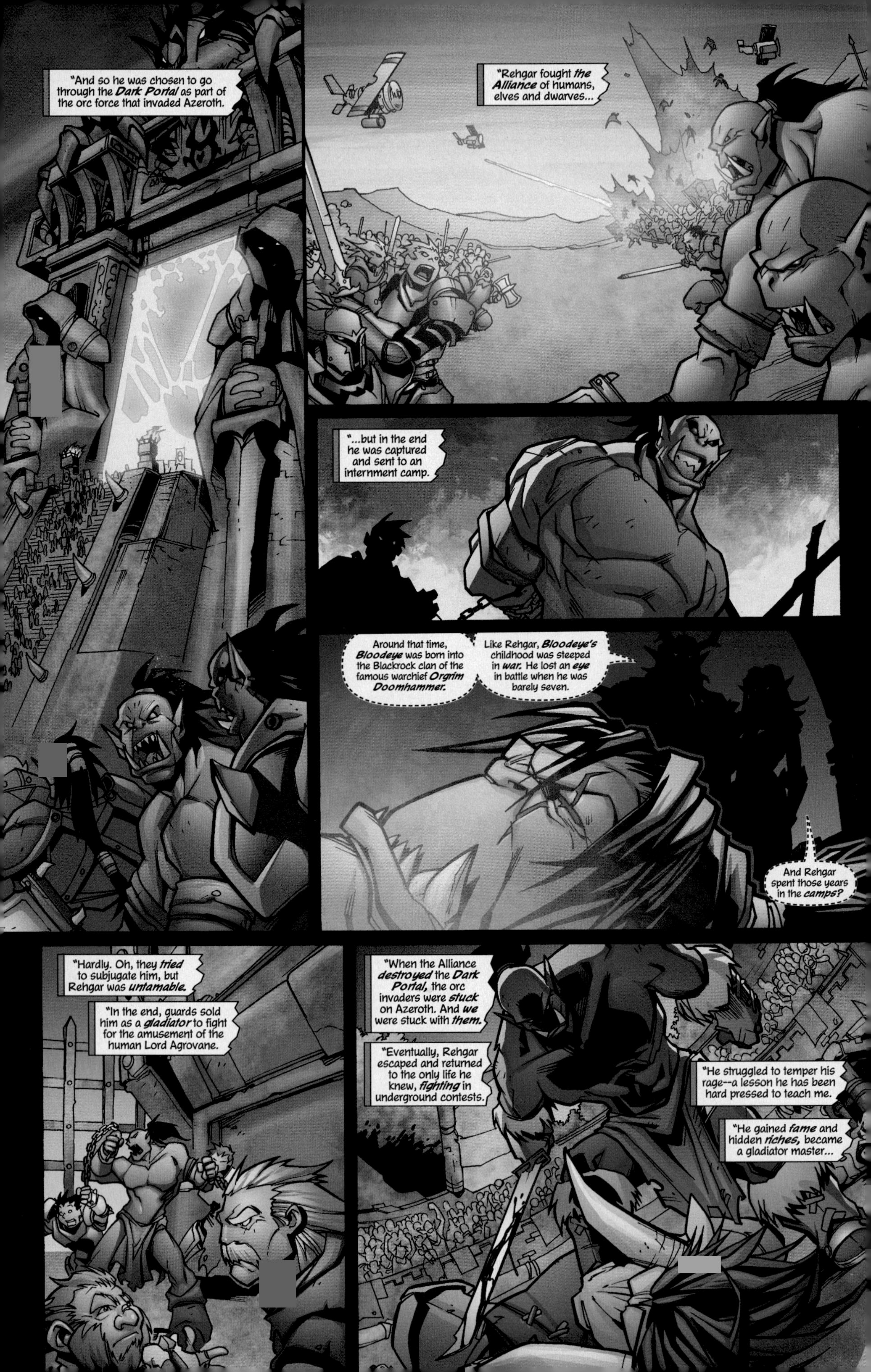
"And so he was chosen to go through the *Dark Portal* as part of the orc force that invaded Azeroth.
"Rehgar fought *the Alliance* of humans, elves and dwarves...
"...but in the end he was captured and sent to an internment camp.
Around that time, *Bloodeye* was born into the Blackrock clan of the famous warchief *Orgrim Doomhammer.*
Like Rehgar, *Bloodeye's* childhood was steeped in *war.* He lost an *eye* in battle when he was barely seven.
And Rehgar spent those years in the *camps?*
"Hardly. Oh, they *tried* to subjugate him, but Rehgar was *untamable.*
"In the end, guards sold him as a *gladiator* to fight for the amusement of the human Lord Agrovane.
"When the Alliance *destroyed* the *Dark Portal,* the orc invaders were *stuck* on Azeroth. And *we* were stuck with *them.*
"Eventually, Rehgar escaped and returned to the only life he knew, *fighting* in underground contests.
"He struggled to temper his rage--a lesson he has been hard pressed to teach me.
"He gained *fame* and hidden *riches,* became a gladiator master...

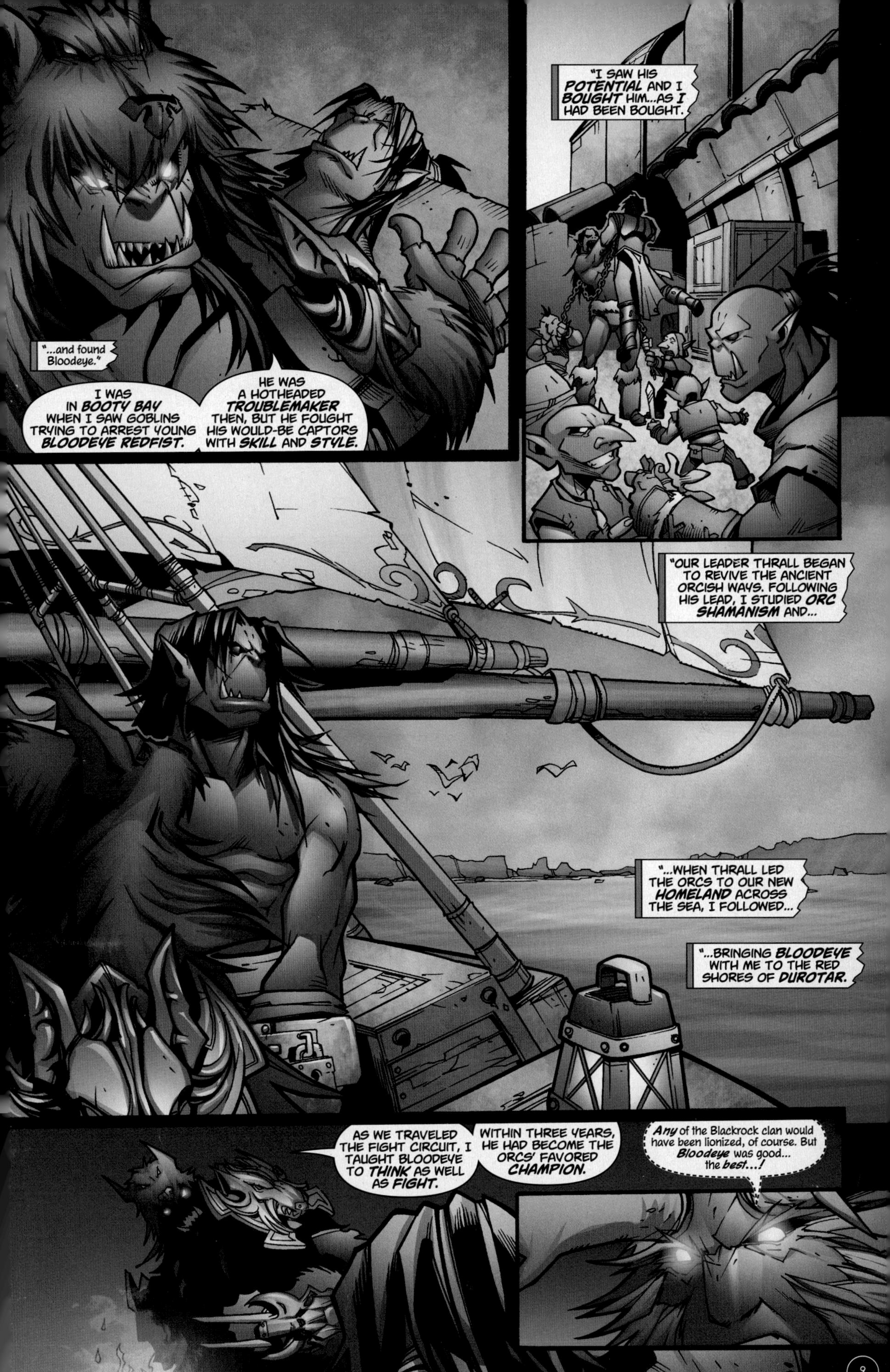
"...and found Bloodeye."
I WAS IN BOOTY BAY WHEN I SAW GOBLINS TRYING TO ARREST YOUNG BLOODEYE REDFIST.
HE WAS A HOTHEADED TROUBLEMAKER THEN, BUT HE FOUGHT HIS WOULD-BE CAPTORS WITH SKILL AND STYLE.
"I SAW HIS POTENTIAL AND I BOUGHT HIM...AS I HAD BEEN BOUGHT.
"OUR LEADER THRALL BEGAN TO REVIVE THE ANCIENT ORCISH WAYS. FOLLOWING HIS LEAD, I STUDIED ORC SHAMANISM AND...
"...WHEN THRALL LED THE ORCS TO OUR NEW HOMELAND ACROSS THE SEA, I FOLLOWED...
"...BRINGING BLOODEYE WITH ME TO THE RED SHORES OF DUROTAR.
AS WE TRAVELED THE FIGHT CIRCUIT, I TAUGHT BLOODEYE TO THINK AS WELL AS FIGHT.
WITHIN THREE YEARS, HE HAD BECOME THE ORCS' FAVORED CHAMPION.
Any of the Blackrock clan would have been lionized, of course. But Bloodeye was good... the best...!

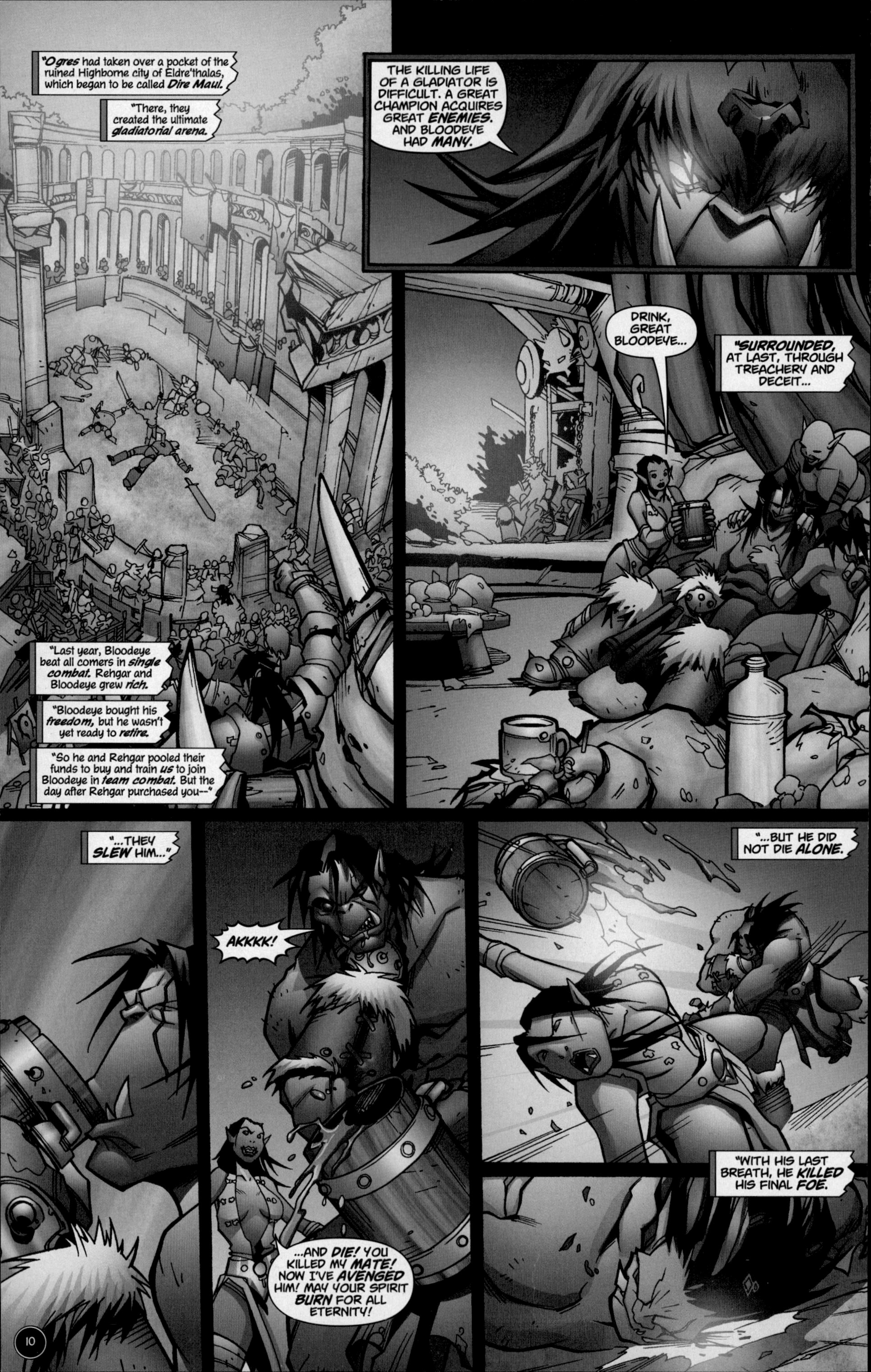

"Ogres had taken over a pocket of the ruined Highborne city of Eldre'thalas, which began to be called Dire Maul.
"There, they created the ultimate gladiatorial arena.
THE KILLING LIFE OF A GLADIATOR IS DIFFICULT. A GREAT CHAMPION ACQUIRES GREAT ENEMIES. AND BLOODEYE HAD MANY.
"Last year, Bloodeye beat all comers in single combat. Rehgar and Bloodeye grew rich.
"Bloodeye bought his freedom, but he wasn't yet ready to retire.
"So he and Rehgar pooled their funds to buy and train us to join Bloodeye in team combat. But the day after Rehgar purchased you--"
DRINK, GREAT BLOODEYE...
"SURROUNDED, AT LAST, THROUGH TREACHERY AND DECEIT...
"...THEY SLEW HIM..."
AKKKK!
...AND DIE! YOU KILLED MY MATE! NOW I'VE AVENGED HIM! MAY YOUR SPIRIT BURN FOR ALL ETERNITY!
"...BUT HE DID NOT DIE ALONE.
"WITH HIS LAST BREATH, HE KILLED HIS FINAL FOE.

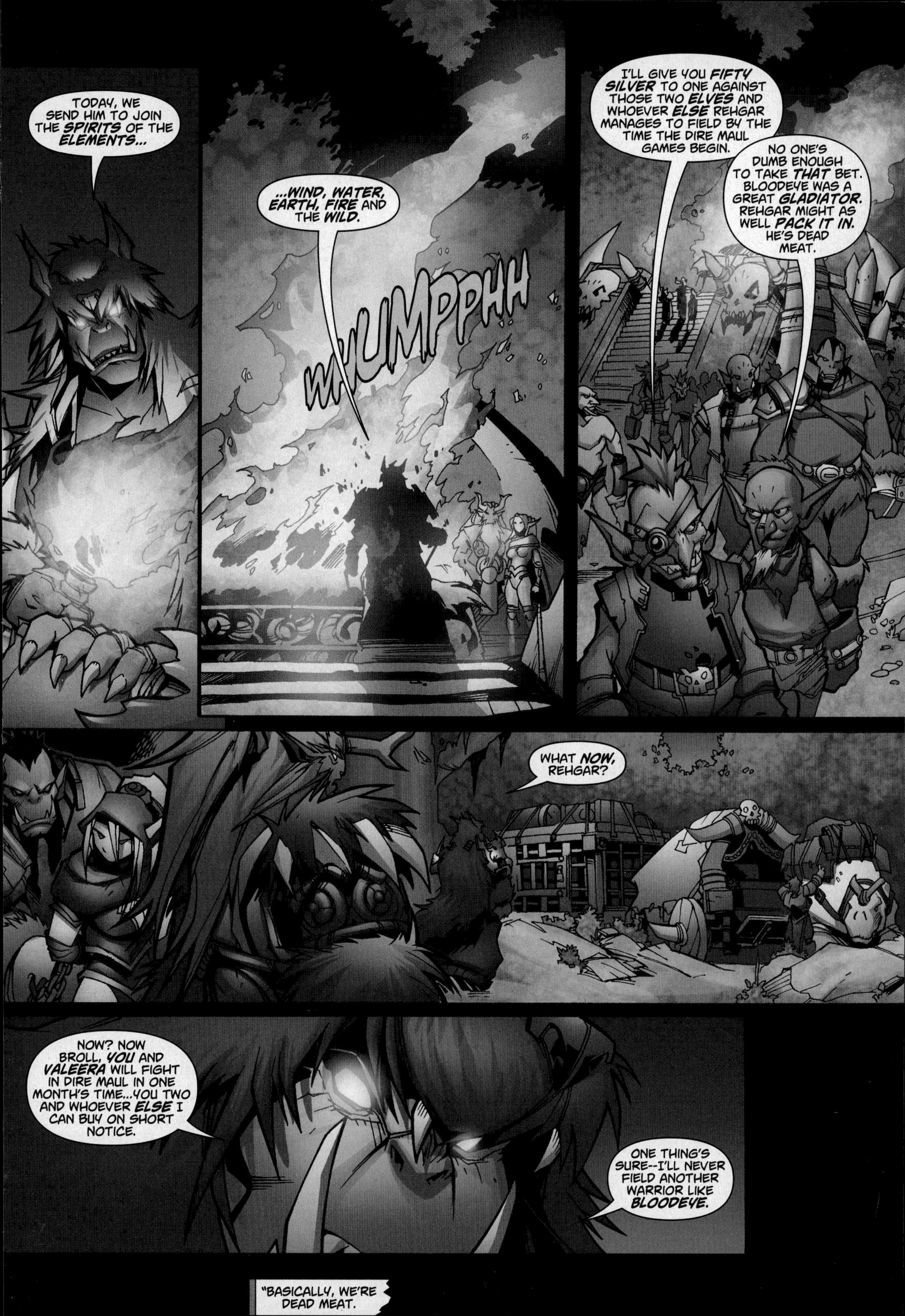
TODAY, WE SEND HIM TO JOIN THE SPIRITS OF THE ELEMENTS...
...WIND, WATER, EARTH, FIRE AND THE WILD.
WHUMPPHH
I'LL GIVE YOU FIFTY SILVER TO ONE AGAINST THOSE TWO ELVES AND WHOEVER ELSE REHGAR MANAGES TO FIELD BY THE TIME THE DIRE MAUL GAMES BEGIN.
NO ONE'S DUMB ENOUGH TO TAKE THAT BET. BLOODEYE WAS A GREAT GLADIATOR. REHGAR MIGHT AS WELL PACK IT IN. HE'S DEAD MEAT.
WHAT NOW, REHGAR?
NOW? NOW BROLL, YOU AND VALEERA WILL FIGHT IN DIRE MAUL IN ONE MONTH'S TIME...YOU TWO AND WHOEVER ELSE I CAN BUY ON SHORT NOTICE.
ONE THING'S SURE--I'LL NEVER FIELD ANOTHER WARRIOR LIKE BLOODEYE.
"BASICALLY, WE'RE DEAD MEAT.

CHAPTER I

Issue #1 Cover
by Samwise Didier

Issue #1 Cover
by Jim Lee and David Baron

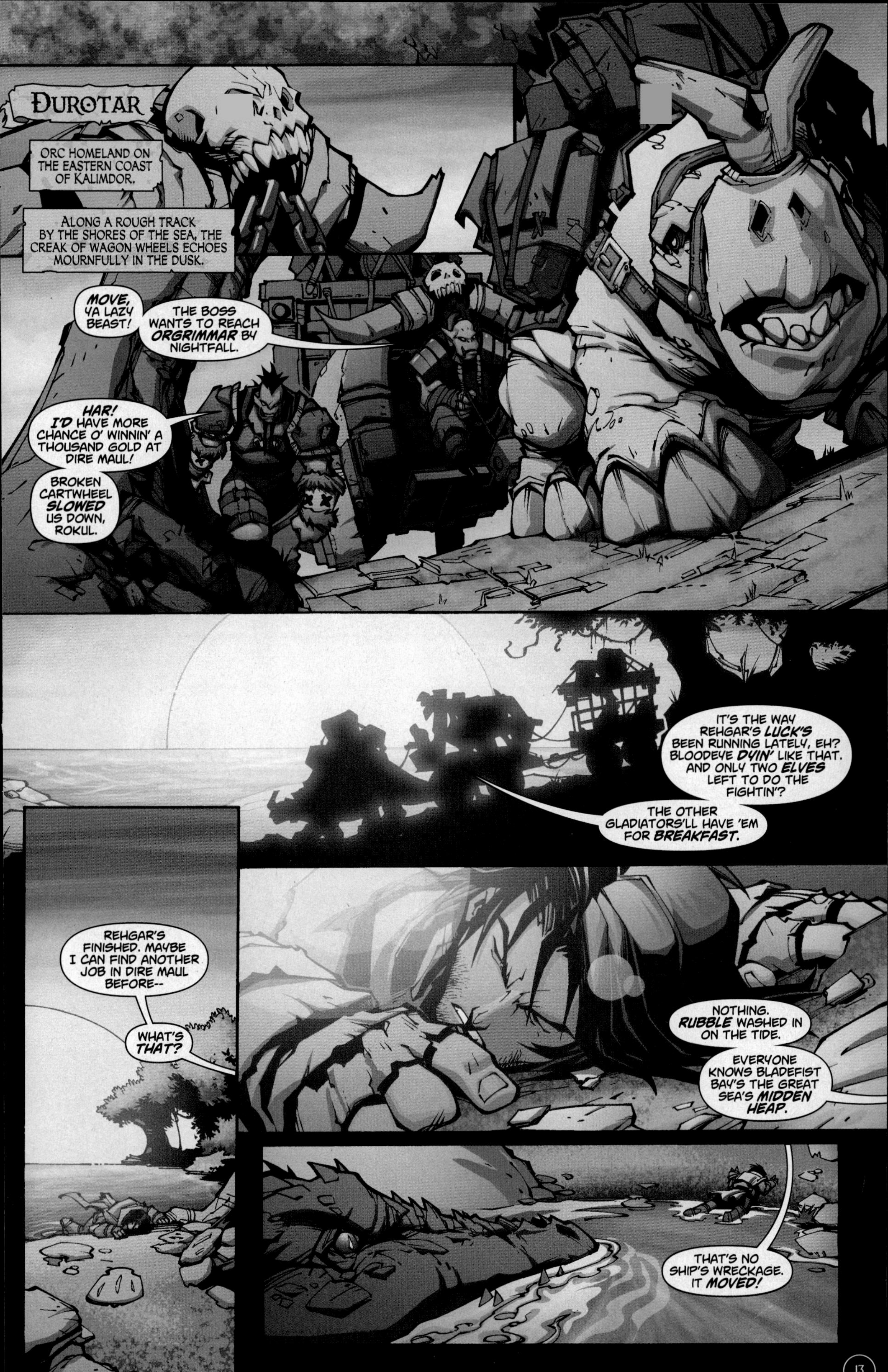
DUROTAR
ORC HOMELAND ON THE EASTERN COAST OF KALIMDOR.
ALONG A ROUGH TRACK BY THE SHORES OF THE SEA, THE CREAK OF WAGON WHEELS ECHOES MOURNFULLY IN THE DUSK.
MOVE, YA LAZY BEAST!
THE BOSS WANTS TO REACH ORGRIMMAR BY NIGHTFALL.
HAR! I'D HAVE MORE CHANCE O' WINNIN' A THOUSAND GOLD AT DIRE MAUL!
BROKEN CARTWHEEL SLOWED US DOWN, ROKUL.
IT'S THE WAY REHGAR'S LUCK'S BEEN RUNNING LATELY, EH? BLOODEYE DYIN' LIKE THAT. AND ONLY TWO ELVES LEFT TO DO THE FIGHTIN'?
THE OTHER GLADIATORS'LL HAVE 'EM FOR BREAKFAST.
REHGAR'S FINISHED. MAYBE I CAN FIND ANOTHER JOB IN DIRE MAUL BEFORE--
WHAT'S THAT?
NOTHING. RUBBLE WASHED IN ON THE TIDE.
EVERYONE KNOWS BLADEFIST BAY'S THE GREAT SEA'S MIDDEN HEAP.
THAT'S NO SHIP'S WRECKAGE. IT MOVED!

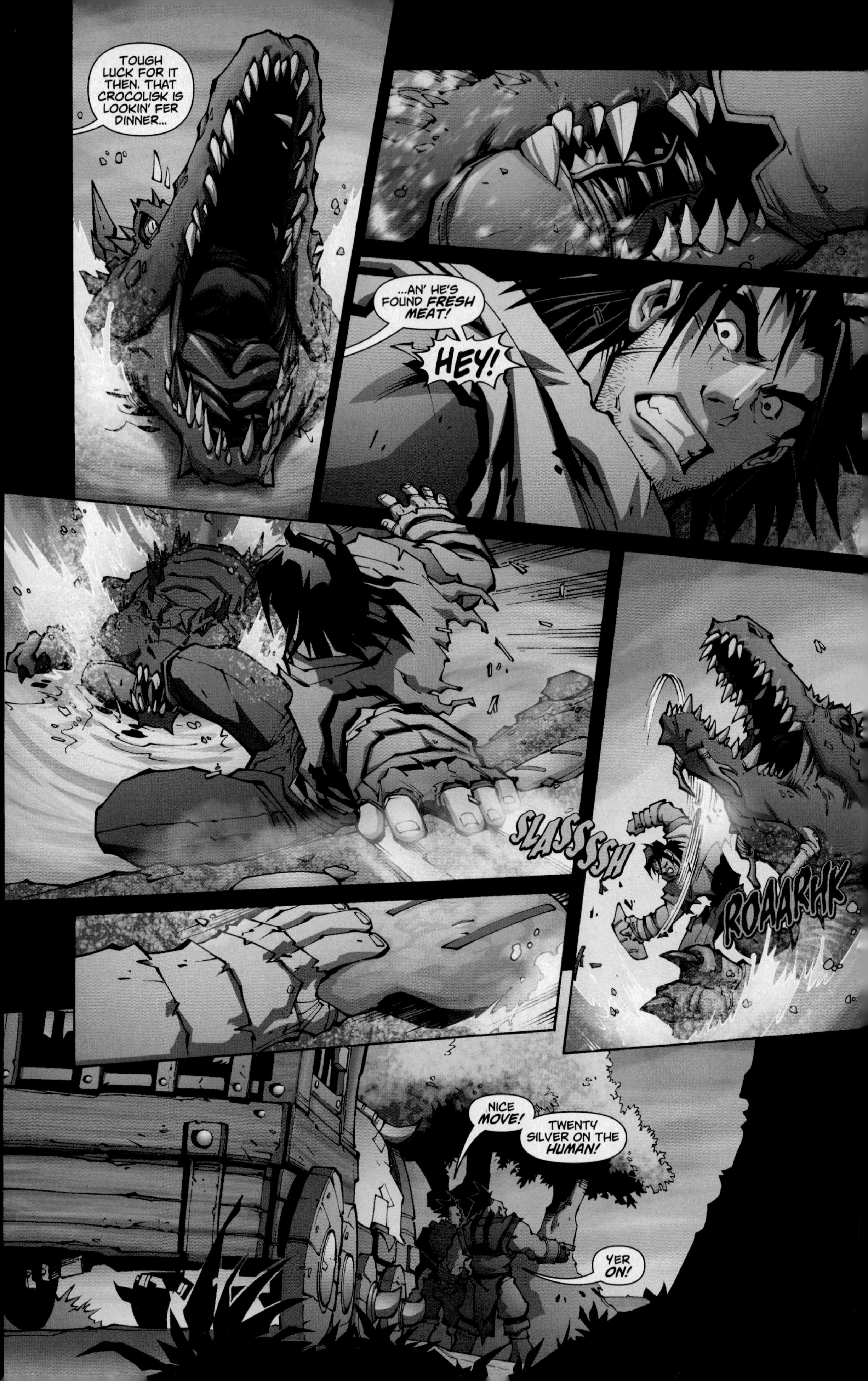
TOUGH LUCK FOR IT THEN. THAT CROCOLISK IS LOOKIN' FER DINNER...
...AN' HE'S FOUND FRESH MEAT!
HEY!
SLASSSSSH
ROAARHK
NICE MOVE!
TWENTY SILVER ON THE HUMAN!
YER ON!

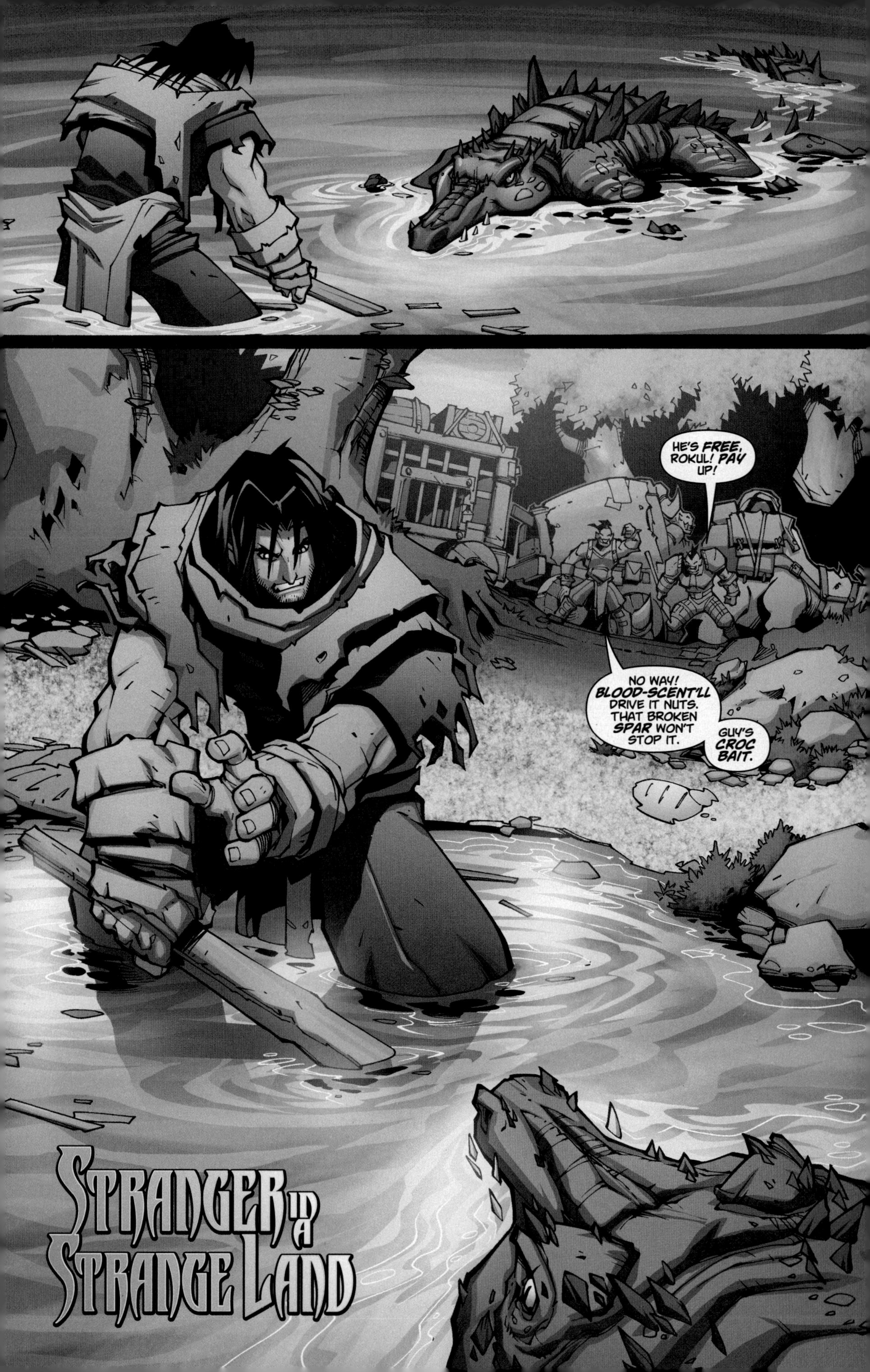
HE'S FREE, ROKUL! PAY UP!
NO WAY! BLOOD-SCENT'LL DRIVE IT NUTS. THAT BROKEN SPAR WON'T STOP IT.
GUY'S CROC BAIT.
STRANGER IN A STRANGE LAND

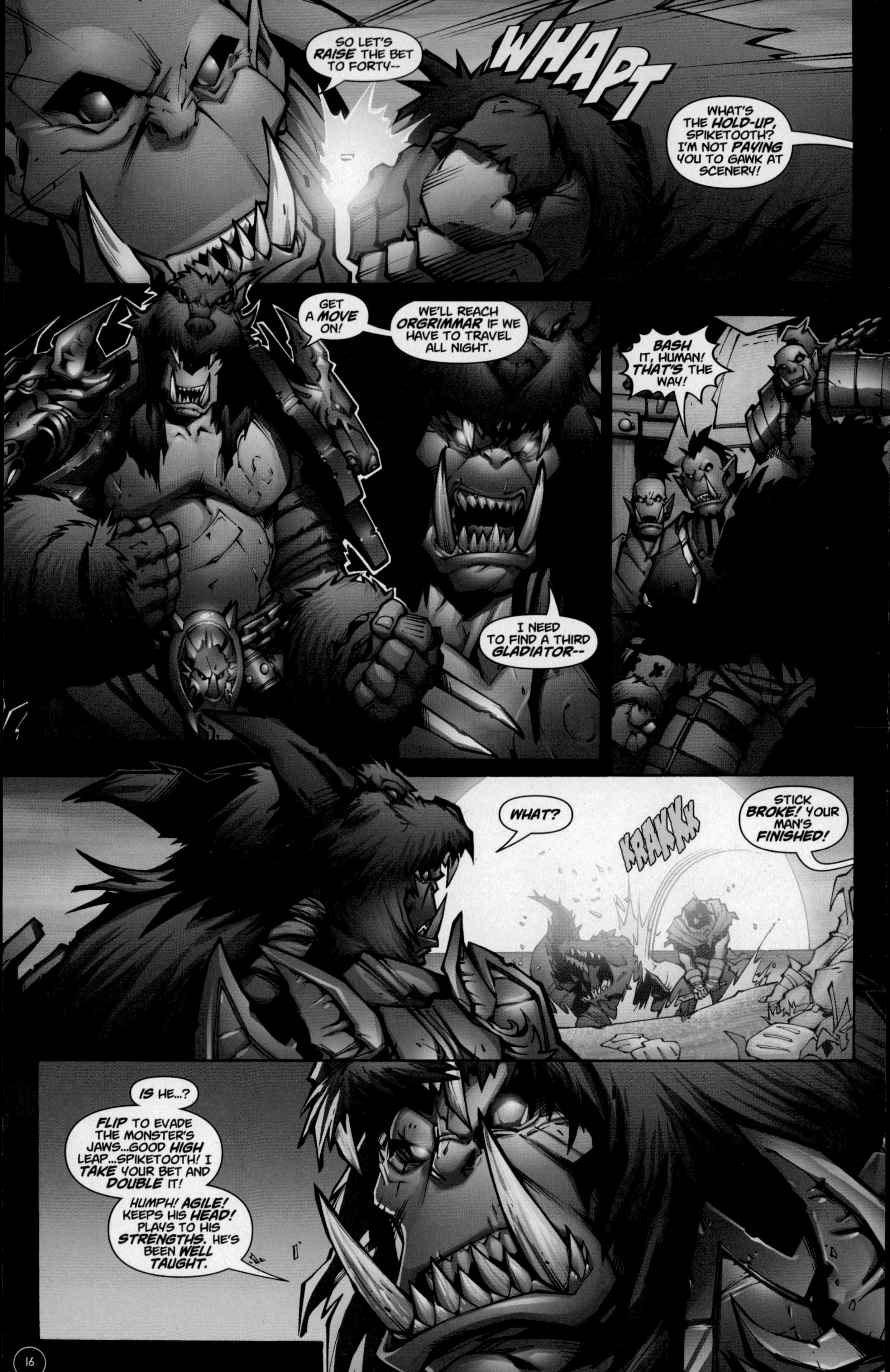
SO LET'S RAISE THE BET TO FORTY--
WHAPT
WHAT'S THE HOLD-UP, SPIKETOOTH? I'M NOT PAYING YOU TO GAWK AT SCENERY!
GET A MOVE ON!
WE'LL REACH ORGRIMMAR IF WE HAVE TO TRAVEL ALL NIGHT.
I NEED TO FIND A THIRD GLADIATOR--
BASH IT, HUMAN! THAT'S THE WAY!
WHAT?
KRAKKK
STICK BROKE! YOUR MAN'S FINISHED!
IS HE...?
FLIP TO EVADE THE MONSTER'S JAWS...GOOD HIGH LEAP...SPIKETOOTH! I TAKE YOUR BET AND DOUBLE IT!
HUMPH! AGILE! KEEPS HIS HEAD! PLAYS TO HIS STRENGTHS. HE'S BEEN WELL TAUGHT.

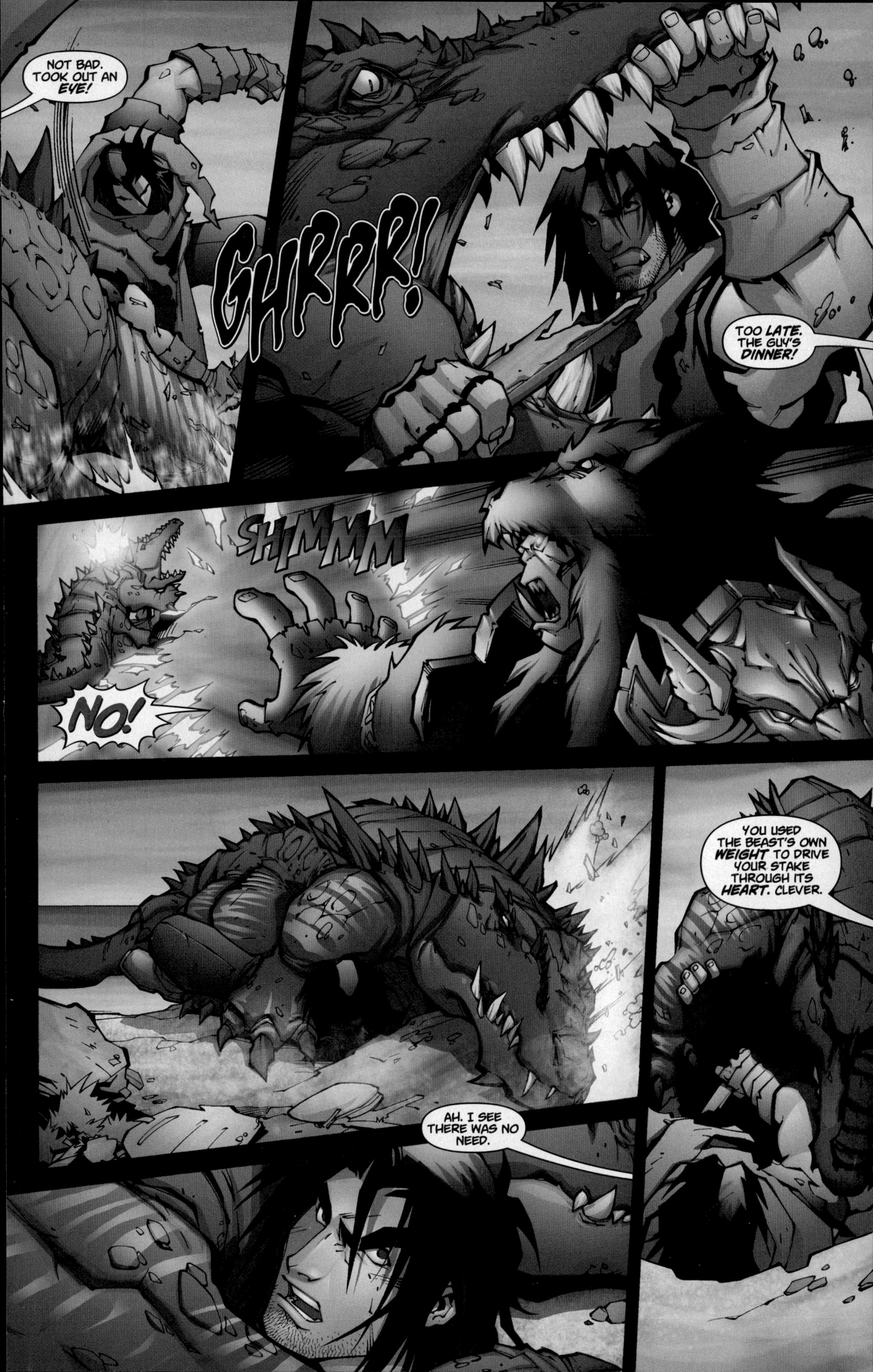
NOT BAD. TOOK OUT AN EYE!
GHRRR!
TOO LATE. THE GUY'S DINNER!
SHIMMM
NO!
YOU USED THE BEAST'S OWN WEIGHT TO DRIVE YOUR STAKE THROUGH ITS HEART. CLEVER.
AH. I SEE THERE WAS NO NEED.

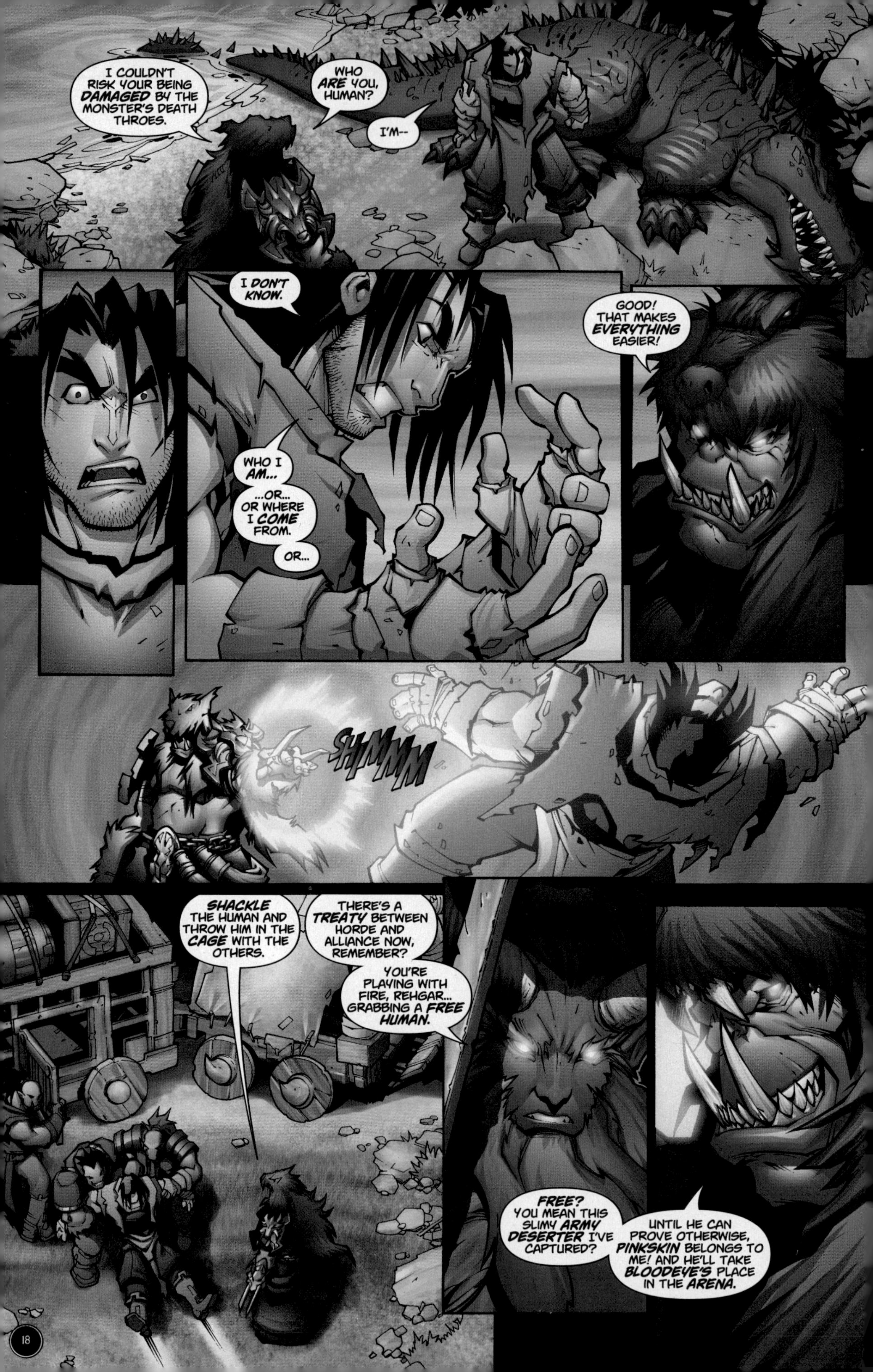
I COULDN'T RISK YOUR BEING DAMAGED BY THE MONSTER'S DEATH THROES.
WHO ARE YOU, HUMAN?
I'M--
I DON'T KNOW.
WHO I AM...
...OR...
OR WHERE I COME FROM.
OR...
GOOD! THAT MAKES EVERYTHING EASIER!
SHIMMM
SHACKLE THE HUMAN AND THROW HIM IN THE CAGE WITH THE OTHERS.
THERE'S A TREATY BETWEEN HORDE AND ALLIANCE NOW, REMEMBER?
YOU'RE PLAYING WITH FIRE, REHGAR... GRABBING A FREE HUMAN.
FREE? YOU MEAN THIS SLIMY ARMY DESERTER I'VE CAPTURED?
UNTIL HE CAN PROVE OTHERWISE, PINKSKIN BELONGS TO ME! AND HE'LL TAKE BLOODEYE'S PLACE IN THE ARENA.

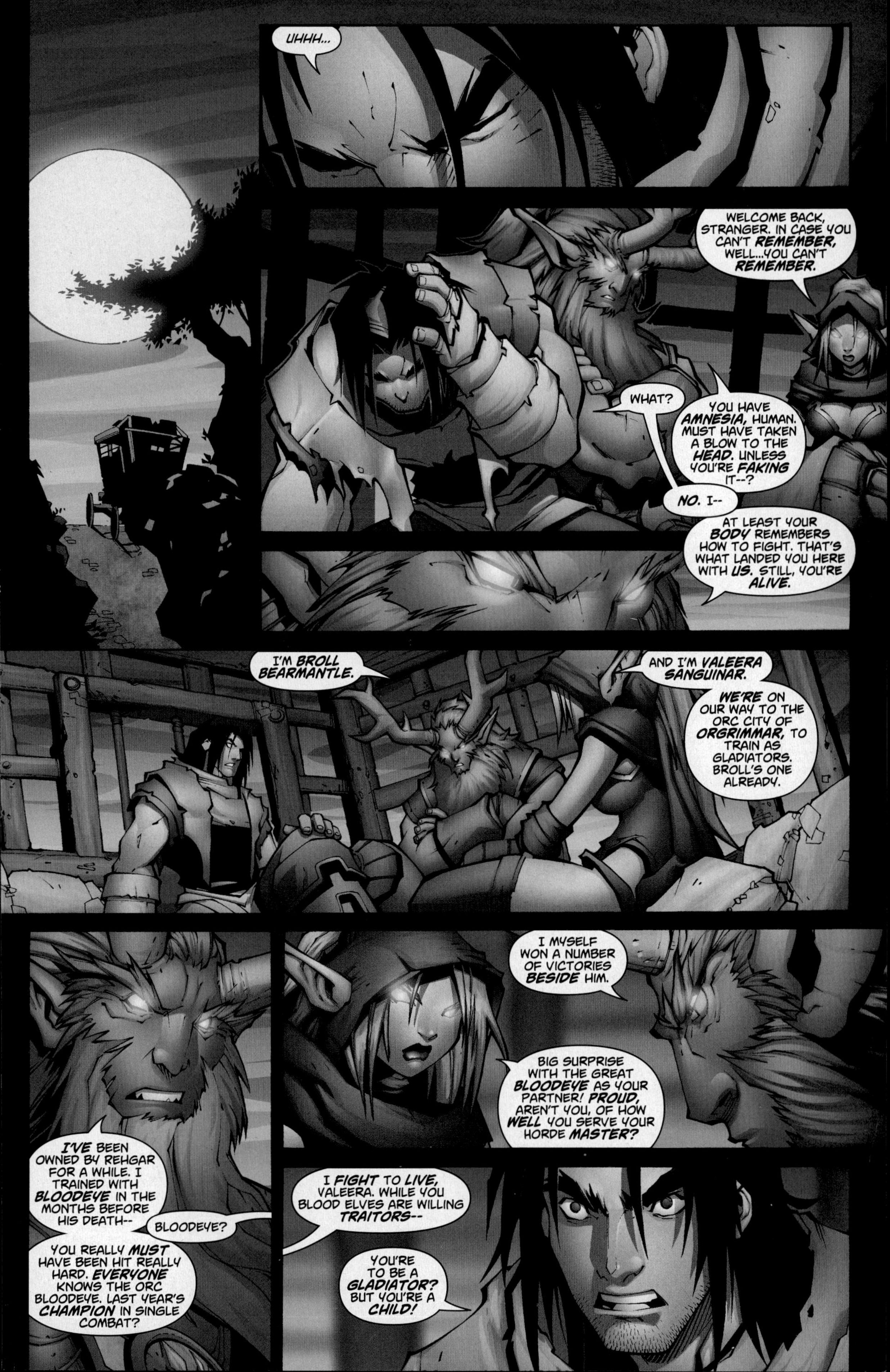
UHHH...
WELCOME BACK, STRANGER. IN CASE YOU CAN'T REMEMBER, WELL...YOU CAN'T REMEMBER.
WHAT?
YOU HAVE AMNESIA, HUMAN. MUST HAVE TAKEN A BLOW TO THE HEAD. UNLESS YOU'RE FAKING IT--?
NO. I--
AT LEAST YOUR BODY REMEMBERS HOW TO FIGHT. THAT'S WHAT LANDED YOU HERE WITH US. STILL, YOU'RE ALIVE.
I'M BROLL BEARMANTLE.
AND I'M VALEERA SANGUINAR.
WE'RE ON OUR WAY TO THE ORC CITY OF ORGRIMMAR, TO TRAIN AS GLADIATORS. BROLL'S ONE ALREADY.
I'VE BEEN OWNED BY REHGAR FOR A WHILE. I TRAINED WITH BLOODEYE IN THE MONTHS BEFORE HIS DEATH--
BLOODEYE?
YOU REALLY MUST HAVE BEEN HIT REALLY HARD. EVERYONE KNOWS THE ORC BLOODEYE. LAST YEAR'S CHAMPION IN SINGLE COMBAT?
I MYSELF WON A NUMBER OF VICTORIES BESIDE HIM.
BIG SURPRISE WITH THE GREAT BLOODEYE AS YOUR PARTNER! PROUD, AREN'T YOU, OF HOW WELL YOU SERVE YOUR HORDE MASTER?
I FIGHT TO LIVE, VALEERA. WHILE YOU BLOOD ELVES ARE WILLING TRAITORS--
YOU'RE TO BE A GLADIATOR? BUT YOU'RE A CHILD!

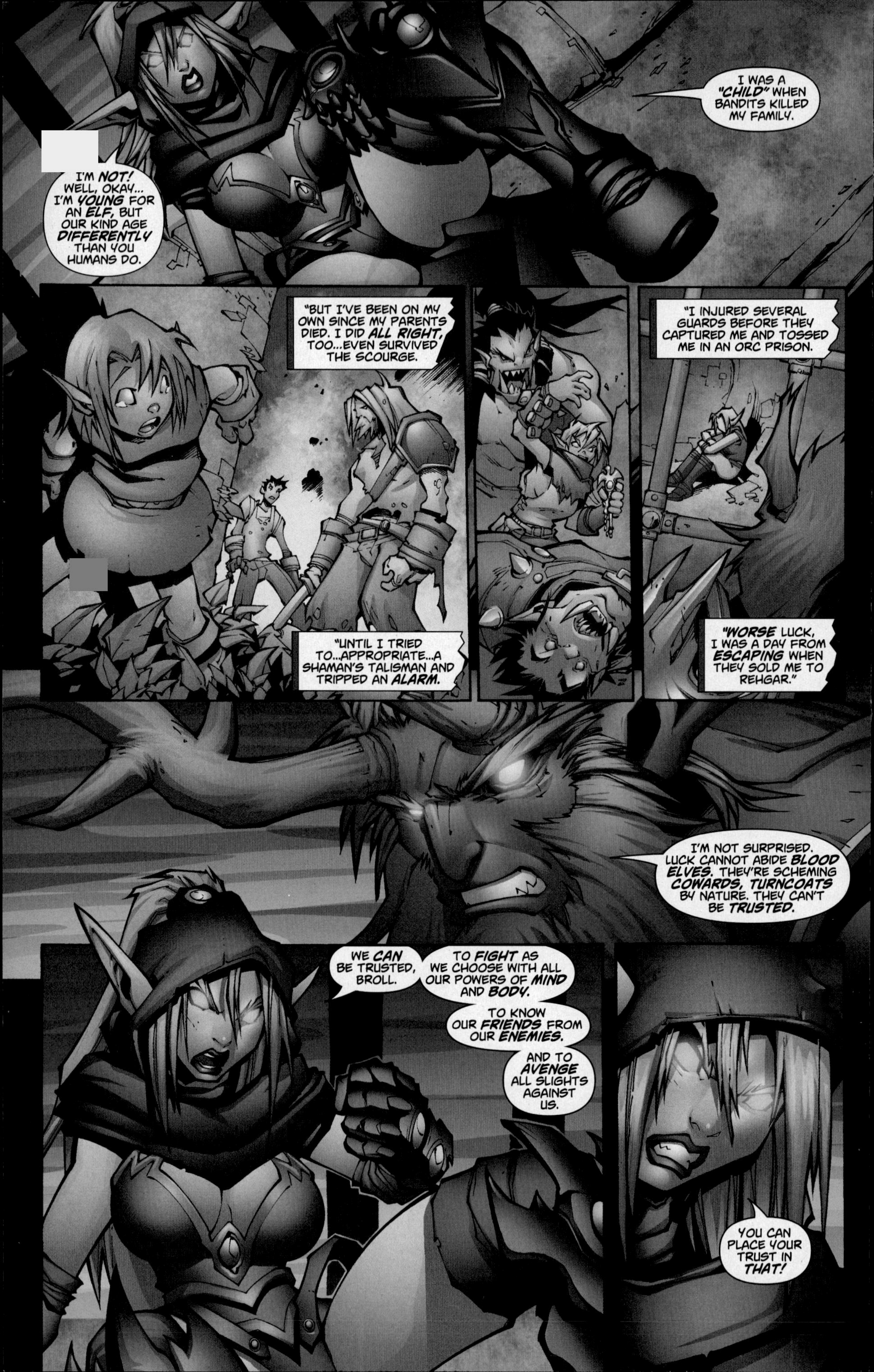
I'M NOT! WELL, OKAY... I'M YOUNG FOR AN ELF, BUT OUR KIND AGE DIFFERENTLY THAN YOU HUMANS DO.
I WAS A "CHILD" WHEN BANDITS KILLED MY FAMILY.
"BUT I'VE BEEN ON MY OWN SINCE MY PARENTS DIED. I DID ALL RIGHT, TOO...EVEN SURVIVED THE SCOURGE.
"UNTIL I TRIED TO...APPROPRIATE...A SHAMAN'S TALISMAN AND TRIPPED AN ALARM.
"I INJURED SEVERAL GUARDS BEFORE THEY CAPTURED ME AND TOSSED ME IN AN ORC PRISON.
"WORSE LUCK, I WAS A DAY FROM ESCAPING WHEN THEY SOLD ME TO REHGAR."
I'M NOT SURPRISED. LUCK CANNOT ABIDE BLOOD ELVES. THEY'RE SCHEMING COWARDS, TURNCOATS BY NATURE. THEY CAN'T BE TRUSTED.
WE CAN BE TRUSTED, BROLL.
TO FIGHT AS WE CHOOSE WITH ALL OUR POWERS OF MIND AND BODY.
TO KNOW OUR FRIENDS FROM OUR ENEMIES.
AND TO AVENGE ALL SLIGHTS AGAINST US.
YOU CAN PLACE YOUR TRUST IN THAT!

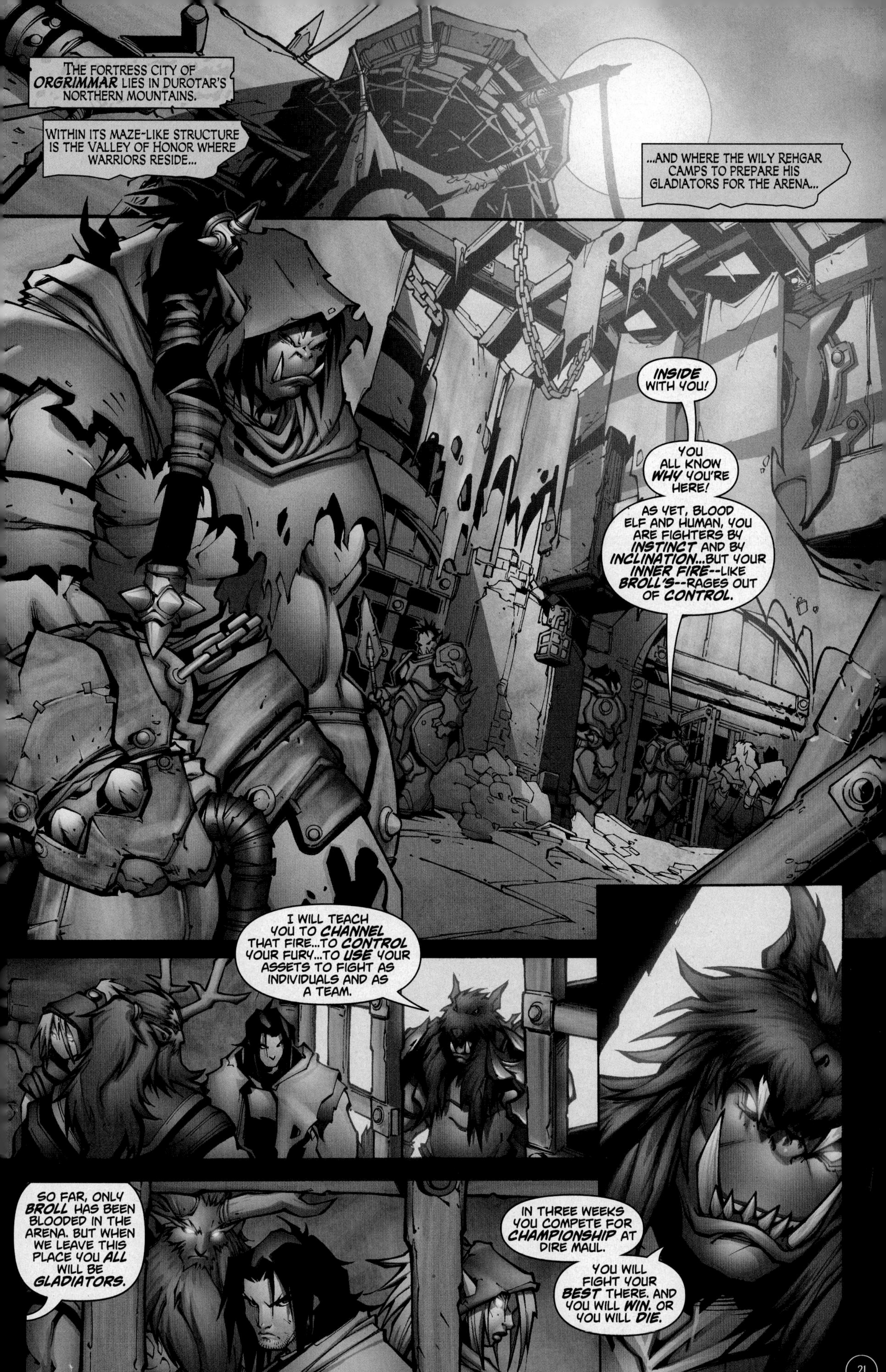
THE FORTRESS CITY OF ORGRIMMAR LIES IN DUROTAR'S NORTHERN MOUNTAINS.
WITHIN ITS MAZE-LIKE STRUCTURE IS THE VALLEY OF HONOR WHERE WARRIORS RESIDE...
...AND WHERE THE WILY REHGAR CAMPS TO PREPARE HIS GLADIATORS FOR THE ARENA...
INSIDE WITH YOU!
YOU ALL KNOW WHY YOU'RE HERE!
AS YET, BLOOD ELF AND HUMAN, YOU ARE FIGHTERS BY INSTINCT AND BY INCLINATION...BUT YOUR INNER FIRE--LIKE BROLL'S--RAGES OUT OF CONTROL.
I WILL TEACH YOU TO CHANNEL THAT FIRE...TO CONTROL YOUR FURY...TO USE YOUR ASSETS TO FIGHT AS INDIVIDUALS AND AS A TEAM.
SO FAR, ONLY BROLL HAS BEEN BLOODED IN THE ARENA. BUT WHEN WE LEAVE THIS PLACE YOU ALL WILL BE GLADIATORS.
IN THREE WEEKS YOU COMPETE FOR CHAMPIONSHIP AT DIRE MAUL.
YOU WILL FIGHT YOUR BEST THERE. AND YOU WILL WIN. OR YOU WILL DIE.

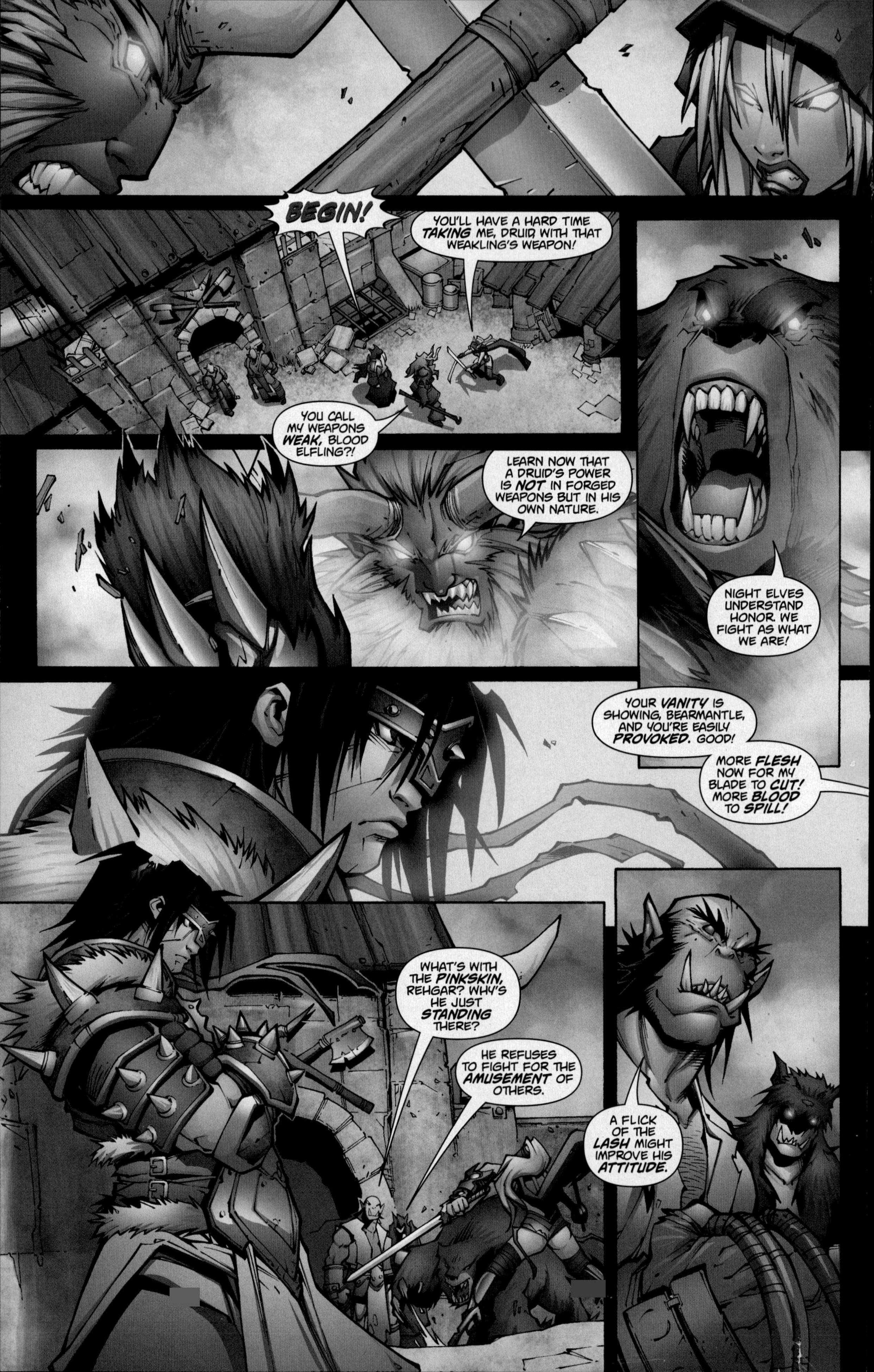
BEGIN!
YOU'LL HAVE A HARD TIME TAKING ME, DRUID WITH THAT WEAKLING'S WEAPON!
YOU CALL MY WEAPONS WEAK, BLOOD ELFLING?!
LEARN NOW THAT A DRUID'S POWER IS NOT IN FORGED WEAPONS BUT IN HIS OWN NATURE.
NIGHT ELVES UNDERSTAND HONOR. WE FIGHT AS WHAT WE ARE!
YOUR VANITY IS SHOWING, BEARMANTLE, AND YOU'RE EASILY PROVOKED. GOOD!
MORE FLESH NOW FOR MY BLADE TO CUT! MORE BLOOD TO SPILL!
WHAT'S WITH THE PINKSKIN, REHGAR? WHY'S HE JUST STANDING THERE?
HE REFUSES TO FIGHT FOR THE AMUSEMENT OF OTHERS.
A FLICK OF THE LASH MIGHT IMPROVE HIS ATTITUDE.

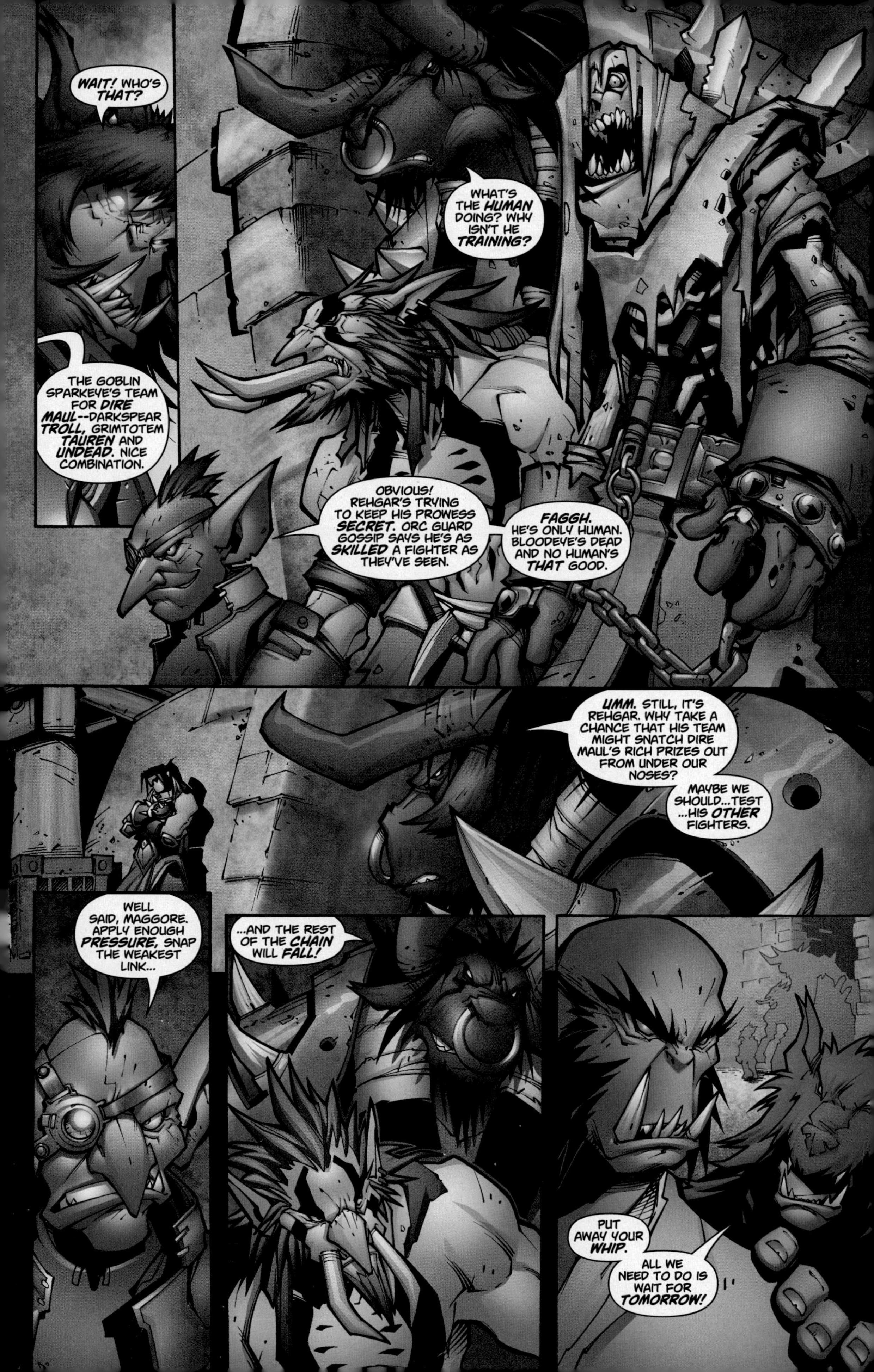
WAIT! WHO'S THAT?
WHAT'S THE HUMAN DOING? WHY ISN'T HE TRAINING?
THE GOBLIN SPARKEYE'S TEAM FOR DIRE MAUL--DARKSPEAR TROLL, GRIMTOTEM TAUREN AND UNDEAD. NICE COMBINATION.
OBVIOUS! REHGAR'S TRYING TO KEEP HIS PROWESS SECRET. ORC GUARD GOSSIP SAYS HE'S AS SKILLED A FIGHTER AS THEY'VE SEEN.
FAGGH. HE'S ONLY HUMAN. BLOODEYE'S DEAD AND NO HUMAN'S THAT GOOD.
UMM. STILL, IT'S REHGAR. WHY TAKE A CHANCE THAT HIS TEAM MIGHT SNATCH DIRE MAUL'S RICH PRIZES OUT FROM UNDER OUR NOSES?
MAYBE WE SHOULD...TEST ...HIS OTHER FIGHTERS.
WELL SAID, MAGGORE. APPLY ENOUGH PRESSURE, SNAP THE WEAKEST LINK...
...AND THE REST OF THE CHAIN WILL FALL!
PUT AWAY YOUR WHIP.
ALL WE NEED TO DO IS WAIT FOR TOMORROW!

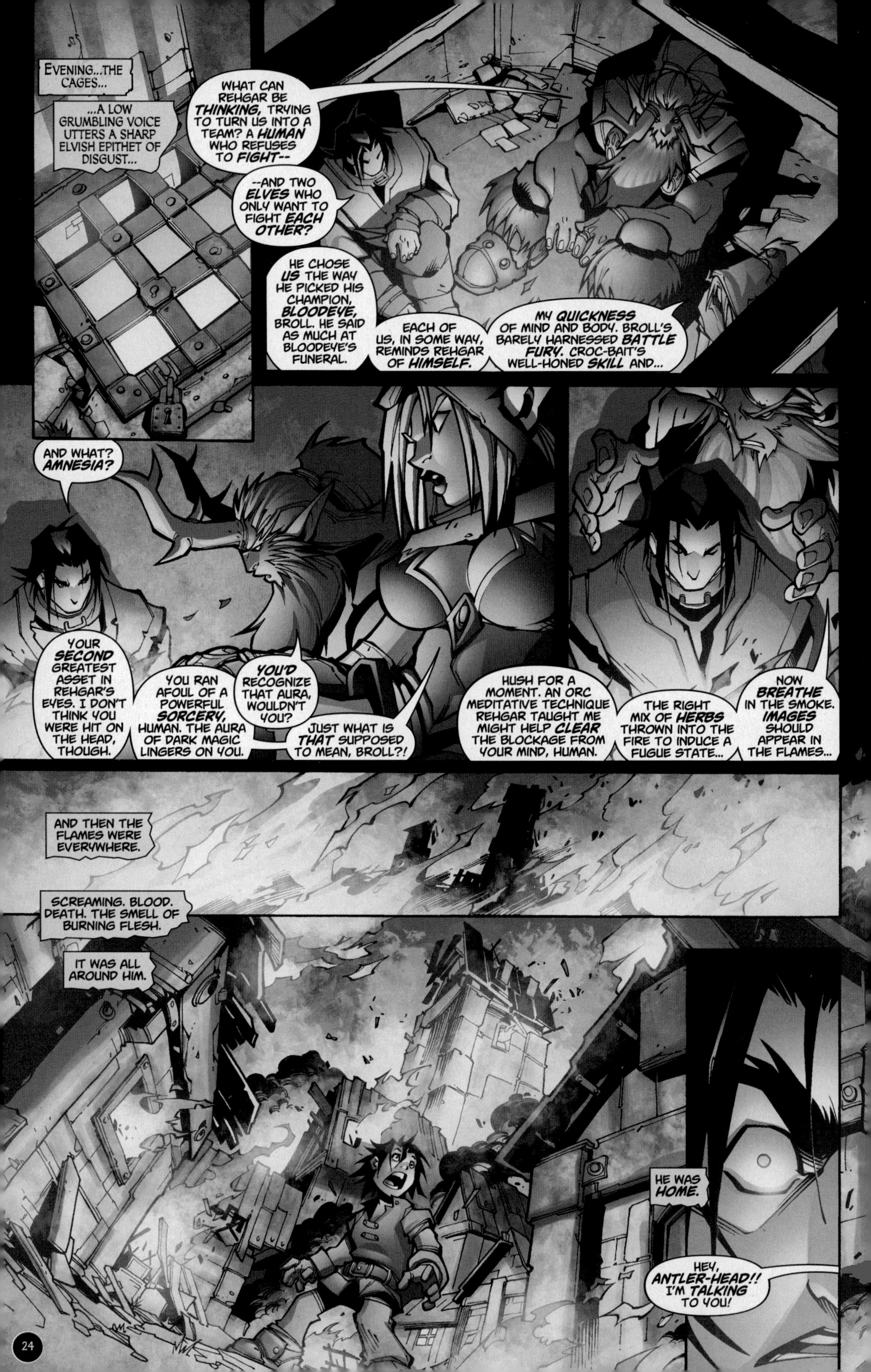
EVENING...THE CAGES...
...A LOW GRUMBLING VOICE UTTERS A SHARP ELVISH EPITHET OF DISGUST...
WHAT CAN REHGAR BE THINKING, TRYING TO TURN US INTO A TEAM? A HUMAN WHO REFUSES TO FIGHT--
--AND TWO ELVES WHO ONLY WANT TO FIGHT EACH OTHER?
HE CHOSE US THE WAY HE PICKED HIS CHAMPION, BLOODEYE, BROLL. HE SAID AS MUCH AT BLOODEYE'S FUNERAL.
EACH OF US, IN SOME WAY, REMINDS REHGAR OF HIMSELF.
MY QUICKNESS OF MIND AND BODY. BROLL'S BARELY HARNESSED BATTLE FURY. CROC-BAIT'S WELL-HONED SKILL AND...
AND WHAT? AMNESIA?
YOUR SECOND GREATEST ASSET IN REHGAR'S EYES. I DON'T THINK YOU WERE HIT ON THE HEAD, THOUGH.
YOU RAN AFOUL OF A POWERFUL SORCERY, HUMAN. THE AURA OF DARK MAGIC LINGERS ON YOU.
YOU'D RECOGNIZE THAT AURA, WOULDN'T YOU?
JUST WHAT IS THAT SUPPOSED TO MEAN, BROLL?!
HUSH FOR A MOMENT. AN ORC MEDITATIVE TECHNIQUE REHGAR TAUGHT ME MIGHT HELP CLEAR THE BLOCKAGE FROM YOUR MIND, HUMAN.
THE RIGHT MIX OF HERBS THROWN INTO THE FIRE TO INDUCE A FUGUE STATE...
NOW BREATHE IN THE SMOKE. IMAGES SHOULD APPEAR IN THE FLAMES...
AND THEN THE FLAMES WERE EVERYWHERE.
SCREAMING. BLOOD. DEATH. THE SMELL OF BURNING FLESH.
IT WAS ALL AROUND HIM.
HE WAS HOME.
HEY, ANTLER-HEAD!! I'M TALKING TO YOU!

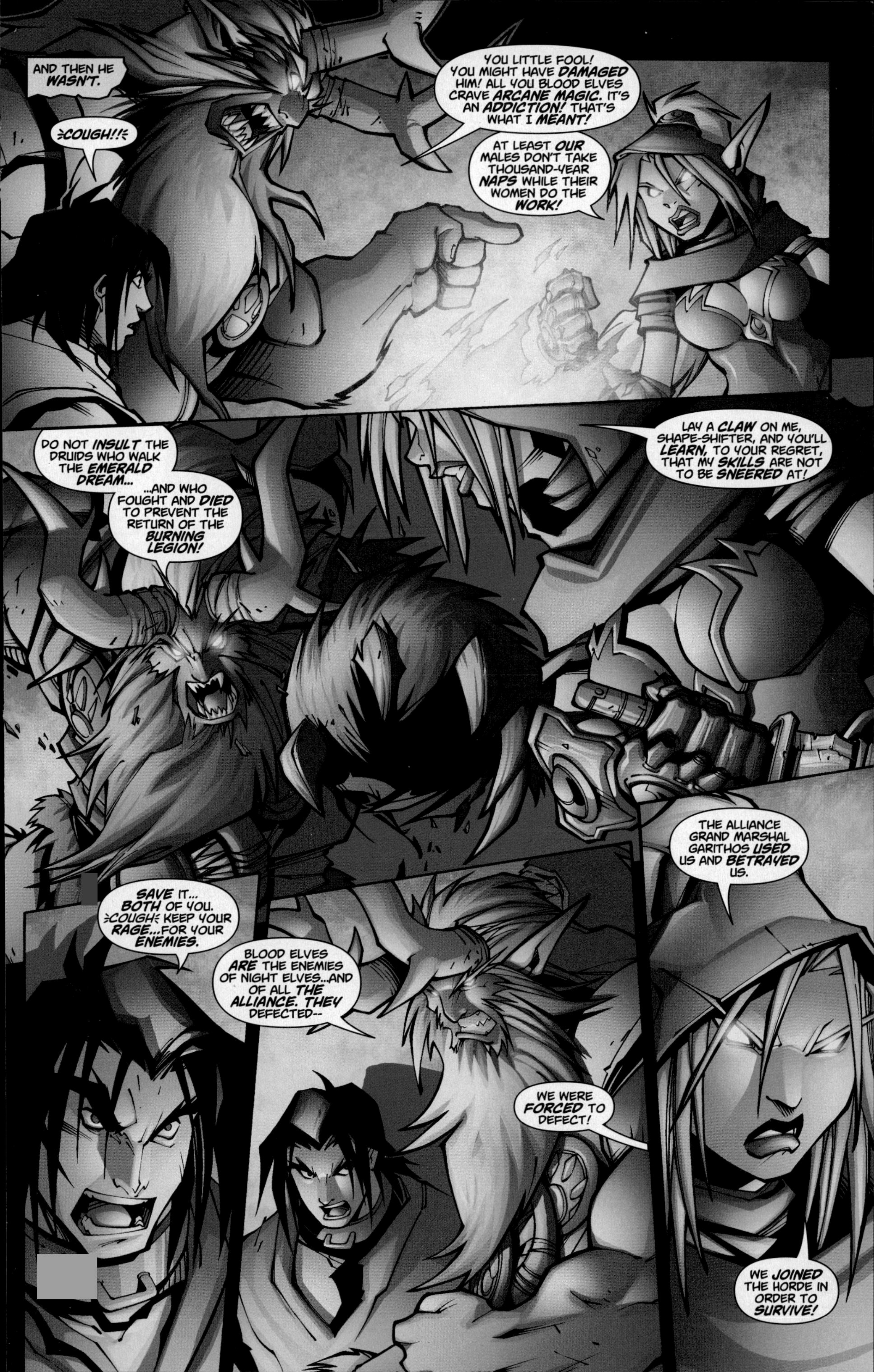

AND THEN HE WASN'T.
COUGH!!
YOU LITTLE FOOL! YOU MIGHT HAVE DAMAGED HIM! ALL YOU BLOOD ELVES CRAVE ARCANE MAGIC. IT'S AN ADDICTION! THAT'S WHAT I MEANT!
AT LEAST OUR MALES DON'T TAKE THOUSAND-YEAR NAPS WHILE THEIR WOMEN DO THE WORK!
DO NOT INSULT THE DRUIDS WHO WALK THE EMERALD DREAM...
...AND WHO FOUGHT AND DIED TO PREVENT THE RETURN OF THE BURNING LEGION!
LAY A CLAW ON ME, SHAPE-SHIFTER, AND YOU'LL LEARN, TO YOUR REGRET, THAT MY SKILLS ARE NOT TO BE SNEERED AT!
SAVE IT... BOTH OF YOU. COUGH KEEP YOUR RAGE...FOR YOUR ENEMIES.
BLOOD ELVES ARE THE ENEMIES OF NIGHT ELVES...AND OF ALL THE ALLIANCE. THEY DEFECTED--
WE WERE FORCED TO DEFECT!
THE ALLIANCE GRAND MARSHAL GARITHOS USED US AND BETRAYED US.
WE JOINED THE HORDE IN ORDER TO SURVIVE!

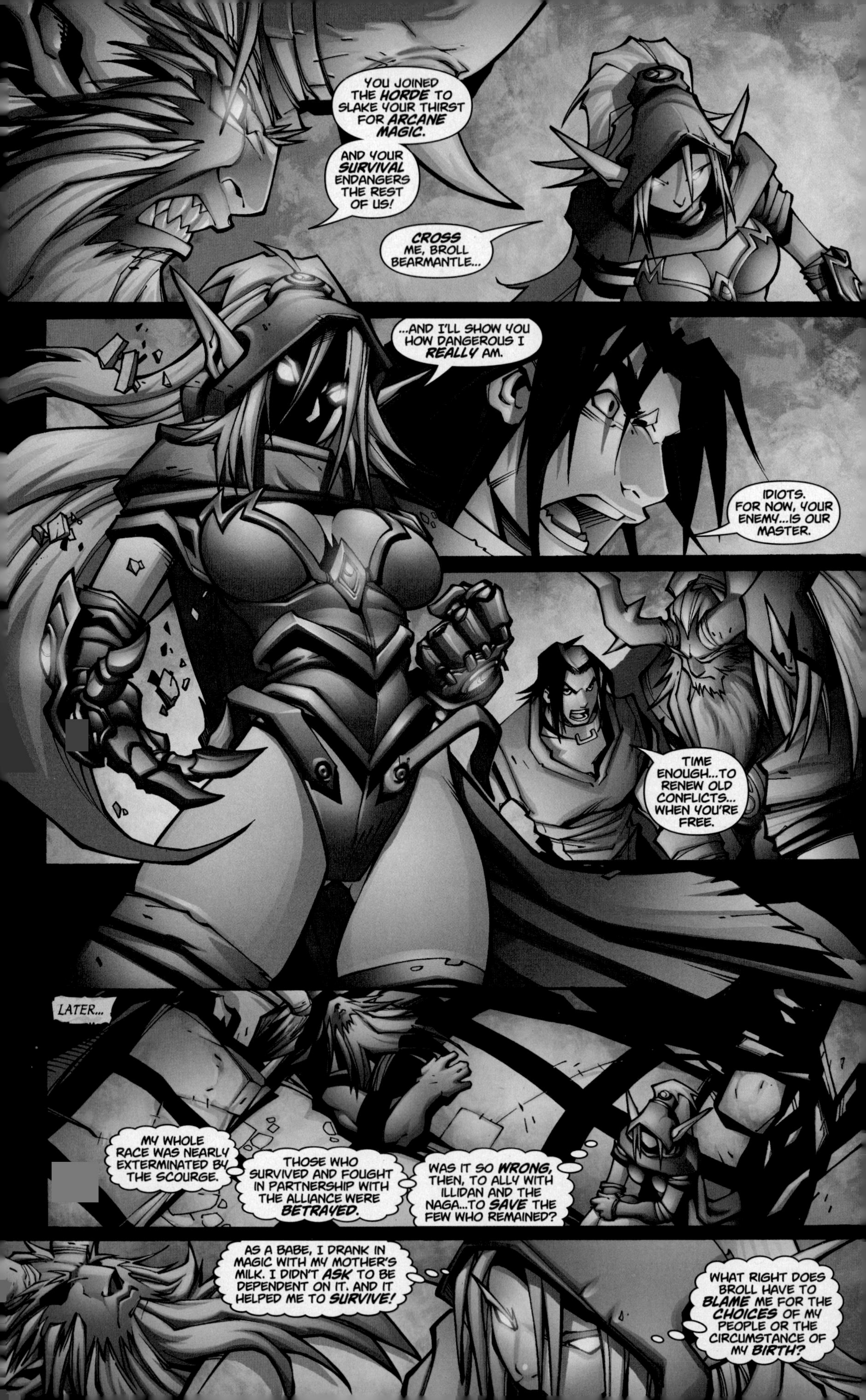
YOU JOINED THE HORDE TO SLAKE YOUR THIRST FOR ARCANE MAGIC.
AND YOUR SURVIVAL ENDANGERS THE REST OF US!
CROSS ME, BROLL BEARMANTLE...
...AND I'LL SHOW YOU HOW DANGEROUS I REALLY AM.
IDIOTS. FOR NOW, YOUR ENEMY...IS OUR MASTER.
TIME ENOUGH...TO RENEW OLD CONFLICTS... WHEN YOU'RE FREE.
LATER...
MY WHOLE RACE WAS NEARLY EXTERMINATED BY THE SCOURGE.
THOSE WHO SURVIVED AND FOUGHT IN PARTNERSHIP WITH THE ALLIANCE WERE BETRAYED.
WAS IT SO WRONG, THEN, TO ALLY WITH ILLIDAN AND THE NAGA...TO SAVE THE FEW WHO REMAINED?
AS A BABE, I DRANK IN MAGIC WITH MY MOTHER'S MILK. I DIDN'T ASK TO BE DEPENDENT ON IT. AND IT HELPED ME TO SURVIVE!
WHAT RIGHT DOES BROLL HAVE TO BLAME ME FOR THE CHOICES OF MY PEOPLE OR THE CIRCUMSTANCE OF MY BIRTH?

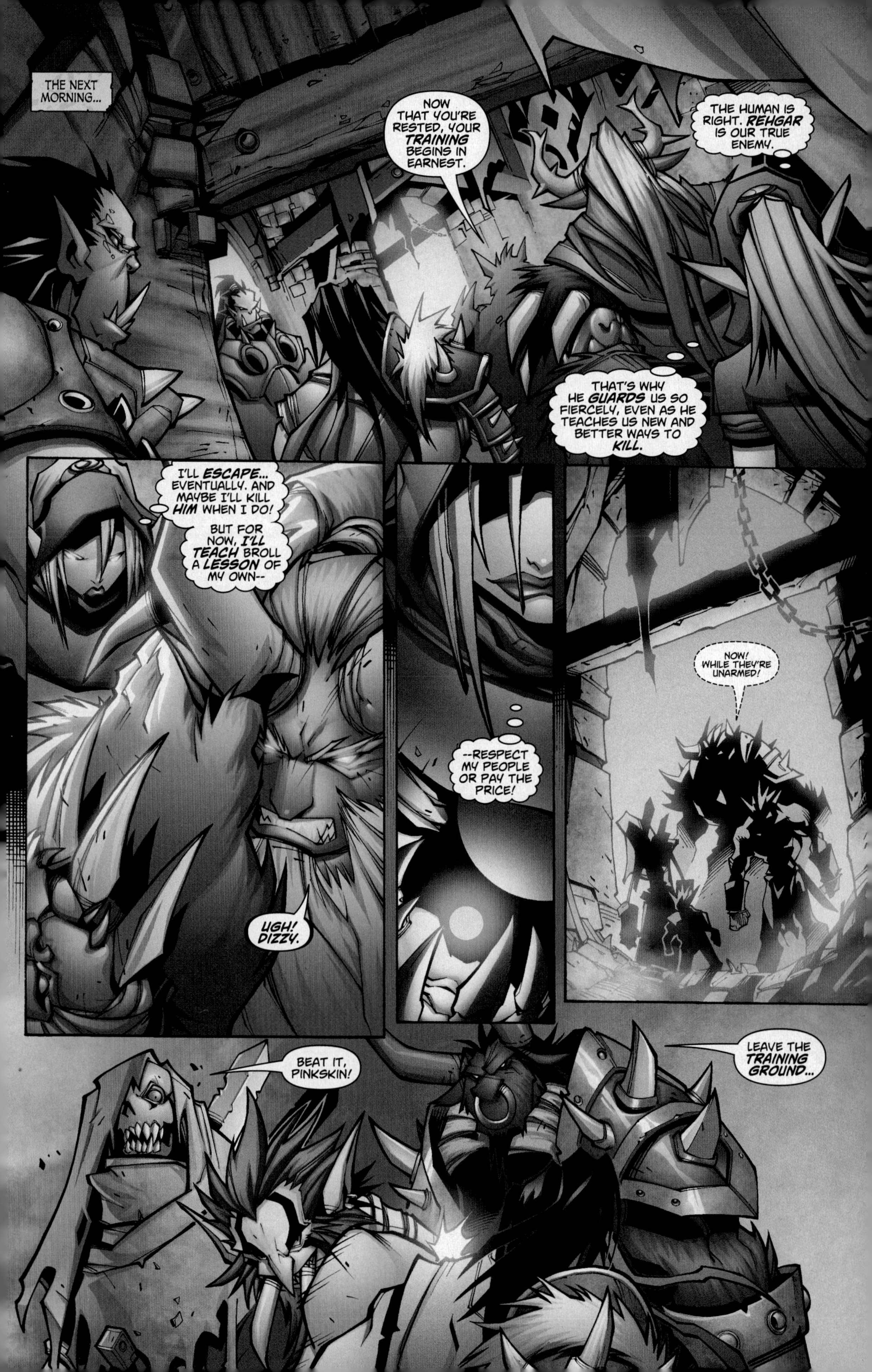
THE NEXT MORNING...
NOW THAT YOU'RE RESTED, YOUR TRAINING BEGINS IN EARNEST.
THE HUMAN IS RIGHT. REHGAR IS OUR TRUE ENEMY.
THAT'S WHY HE GUARDS US SO FIERCELY, EVEN AS HE TEACHES US NEW AND BETTER WAYS TO KILL.
I'LL ESCAPE... EVENTUALLY. AND MAYBE I'LL KILL HIM WHEN I DO!
BUT FOR NOW, I'LL TEACH BROLL A LESSON OF MY OWN--
UGH! DIZZY.
--RESPECT MY PEOPLE OR PAY THE PRICE!
NOW! WHILE THEY'RE UNARMED!
BEAT IT, PINKSKIN!
LEAVE THE TRAINING GROUND...

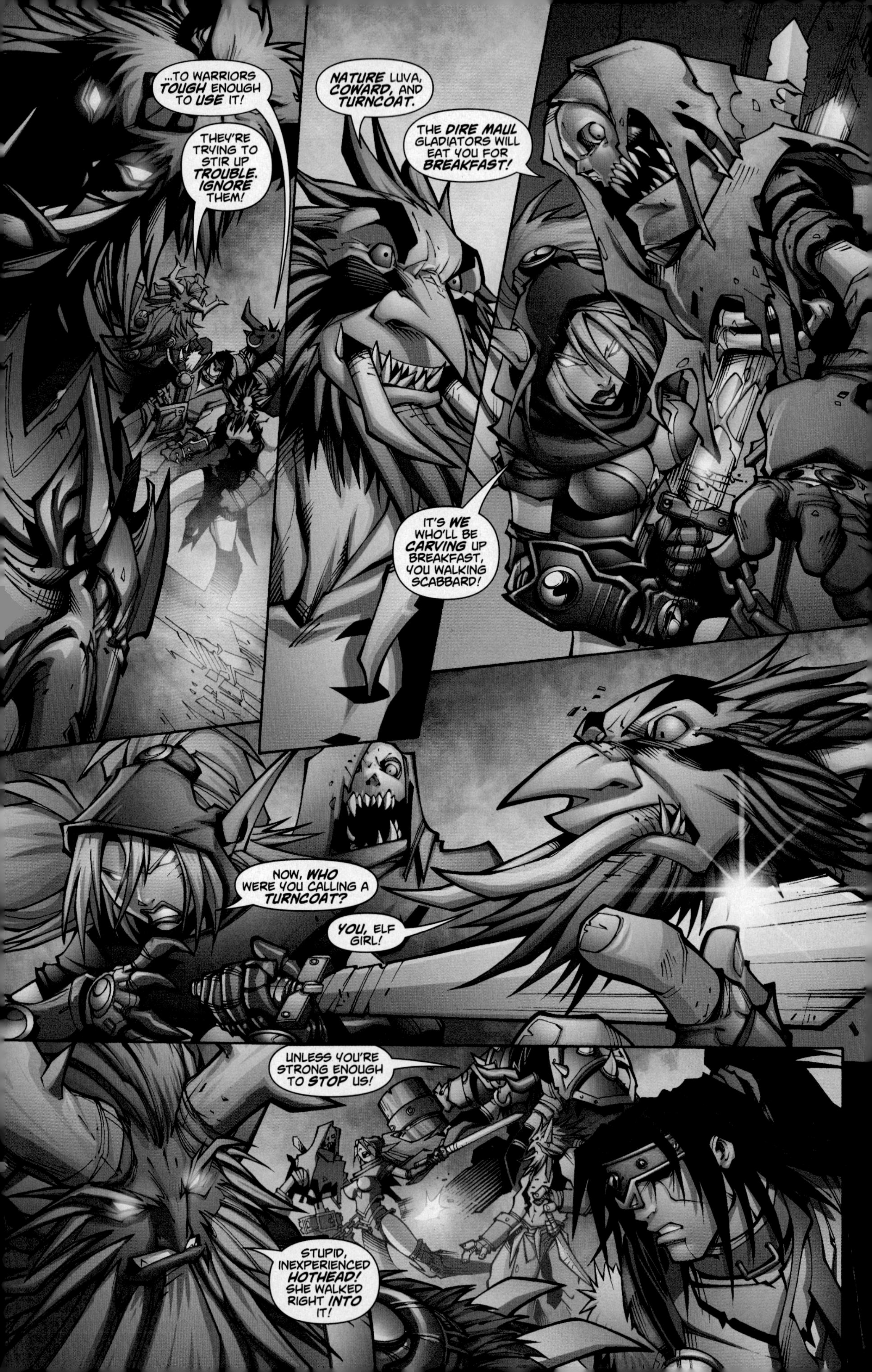
...TO WARRIORS TOUGH ENOUGH TO USE IT!
THEY'RE TRYING TO STIR UP TROUBLE. IGNORE THEM!
NATURE LUVA, COWARD, AND TURNCOAT.
THE DIRE MAUL GLADIATORS WILL EAT YOU FOR BREAKFAST!
IT'S WE WHO'LL BE CARVING UP BREAKFAST, YOU WALKING SCABBARD!
NOW, WHO WERE YOU CALLING A TURNCOAT?
YOU, ELF GIRL!
UNLESS YOU'RE STRONG ENOUGH TO STOP US!
STUPID, INEXPERIENCED HOTHEAD! SHE WALKED RIGHT INTO IT!

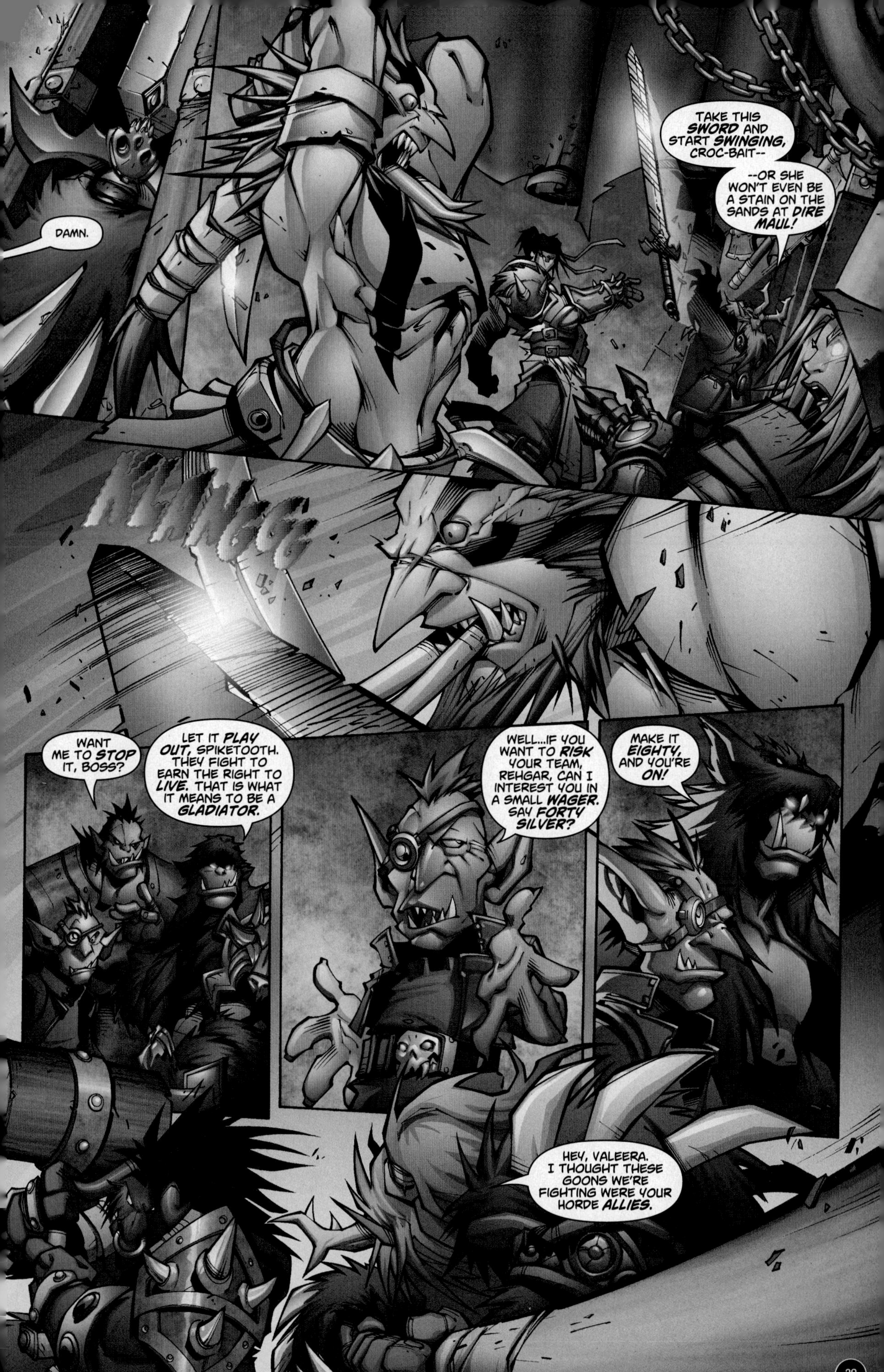

DAMN.
TAKE THIS SWORD AND START SWINGING, CROC-BAIT--
--OR SHE WON'T EVEN BE A STAIN ON THE SANDS AT DIRE MAUL!
WANT ME TO STOP IT, BOSS?
LET IT PLAY OUT, SPIKETOOTH. THEY FIGHT TO EARN THE RIGHT TO LIVE. THAT IS WHAT IT MEANS TO BE A GLADIATOR.
WELL...IF YOU WANT TO RISK YOUR TEAM, REHGAR, CAN I INTEREST YOU IN A SMALL WAGER. SAY FORTY SILVER?
MAKE IT EIGHTY, AND YOU'RE ON!
HEY, VALEERA. I THOUGHT THESE GOONS WE'RE FIGHTING WERE YOUR HORDE ALLIES.

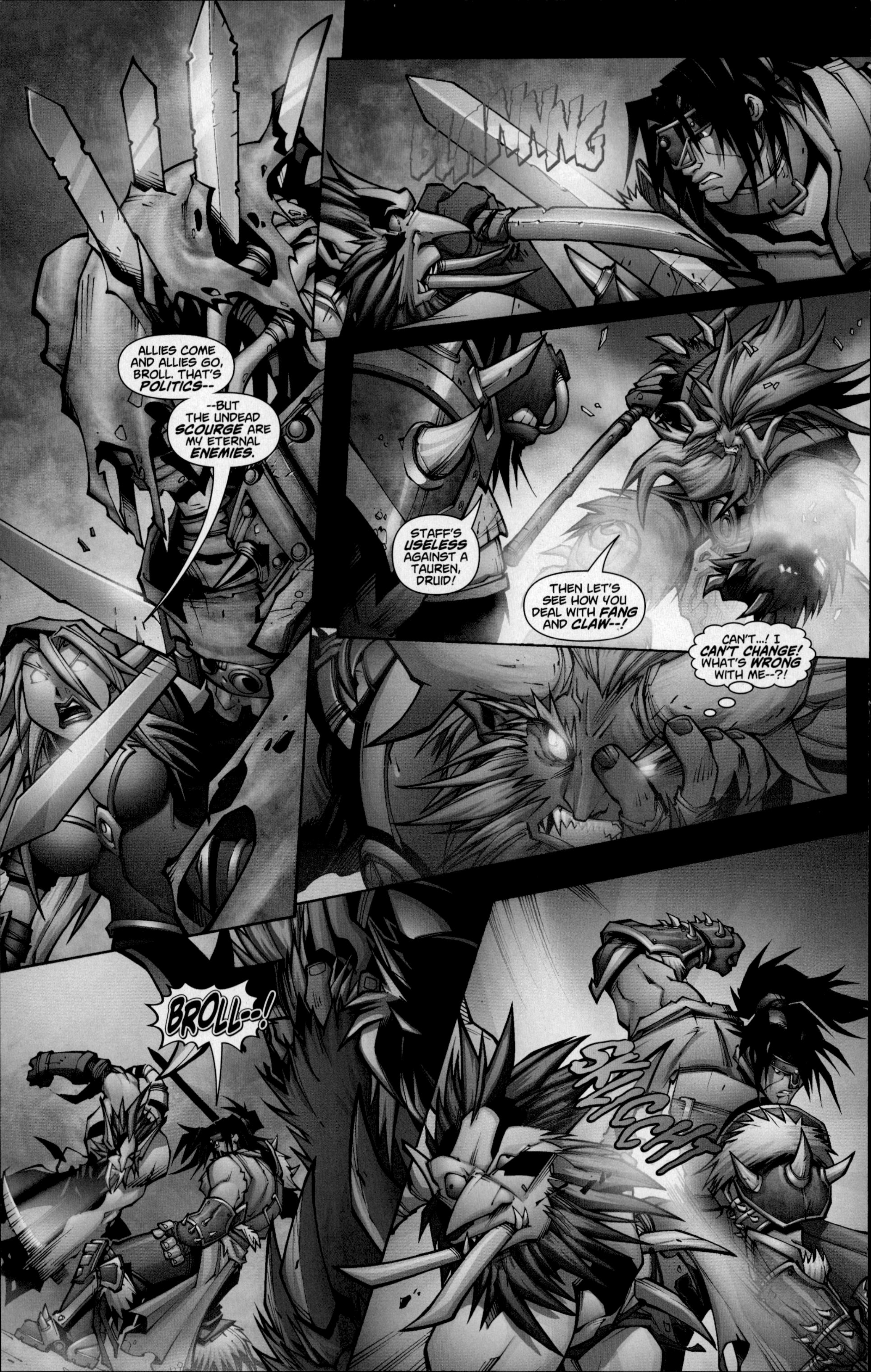
ALLIES COME AND ALLIES GO, BROLL. THAT'S POLITICS--
--BUT THE UNDEAD SCOURGE ARE MY ETERNAL ENEMIES.
STAFF'S USELESS AGAINST A TAUREN, DRUID!
THEN LET'S SEE HOW YOU DEAL WITH FANG AND CLAW--!
CAN'T...! I CAN'T CHANGE! WHAT'S WRONG WITH ME--?!
BROLL--!

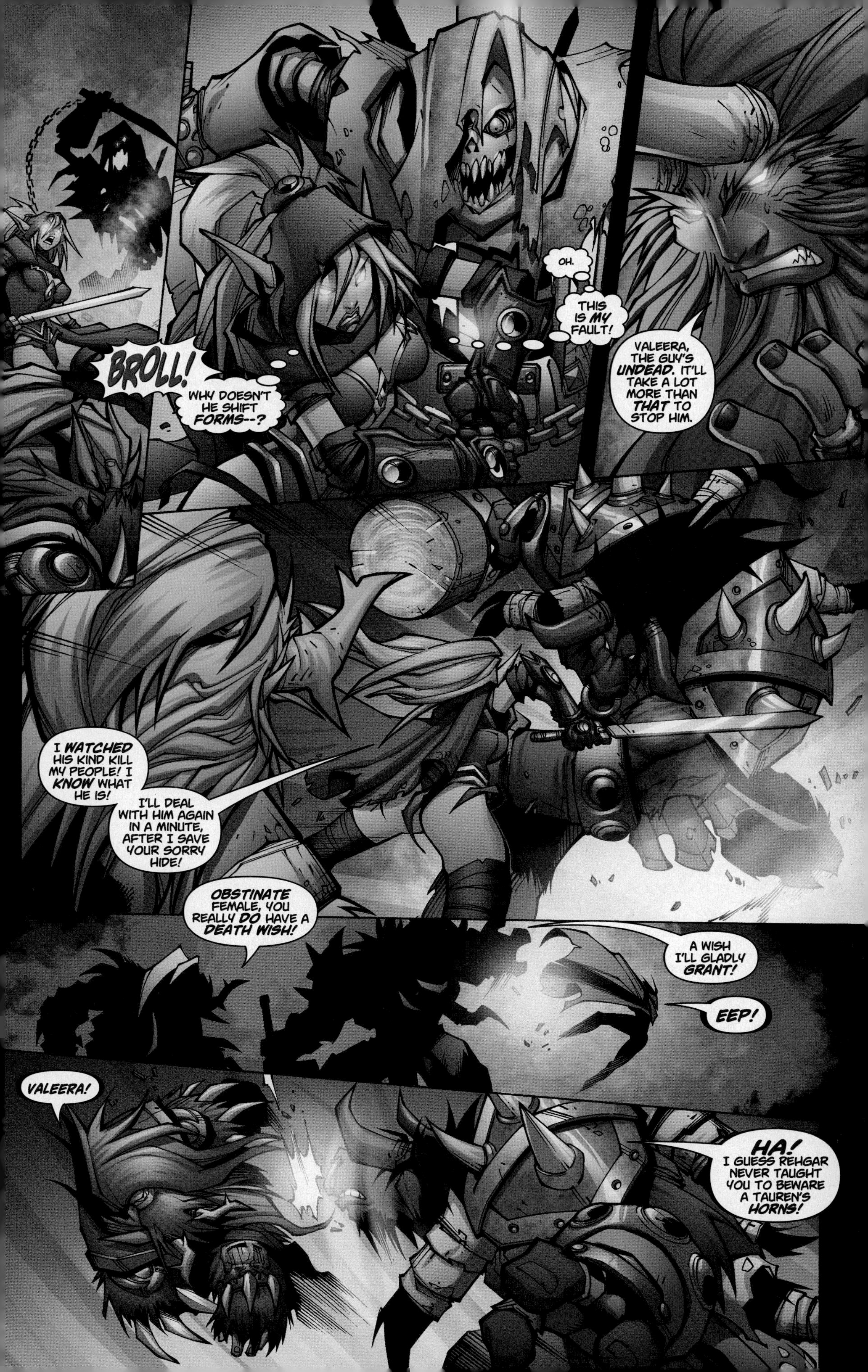
BROLL!
WHY DOESN'T HE SHIFT FORMS--?
OH.
THIS IS MY FAULT!
VALEERA, THE GUY'S UNDEAD. IT'LL TAKE A LOT MORE THAN THAT TO STOP HIM.
I WATCHED HIS KIND KILL MY PEOPLE! I KNOW WHAT HE IS!
I'LL DEAL WITH HIM AGAIN IN A MINUTE, AFTER I SAVE YOUR SORRY HIDE!
OBSTINATE FEMALE, YOU REALLY DO HAVE A DEATH WISH!
A WISH I'LL GLADLY GRANT!
EEP!
VALEERA!
HA! I GUESS REHGAR NEVER TAUGHT YOU TO BEWARE A TAUREN'S HORNS!

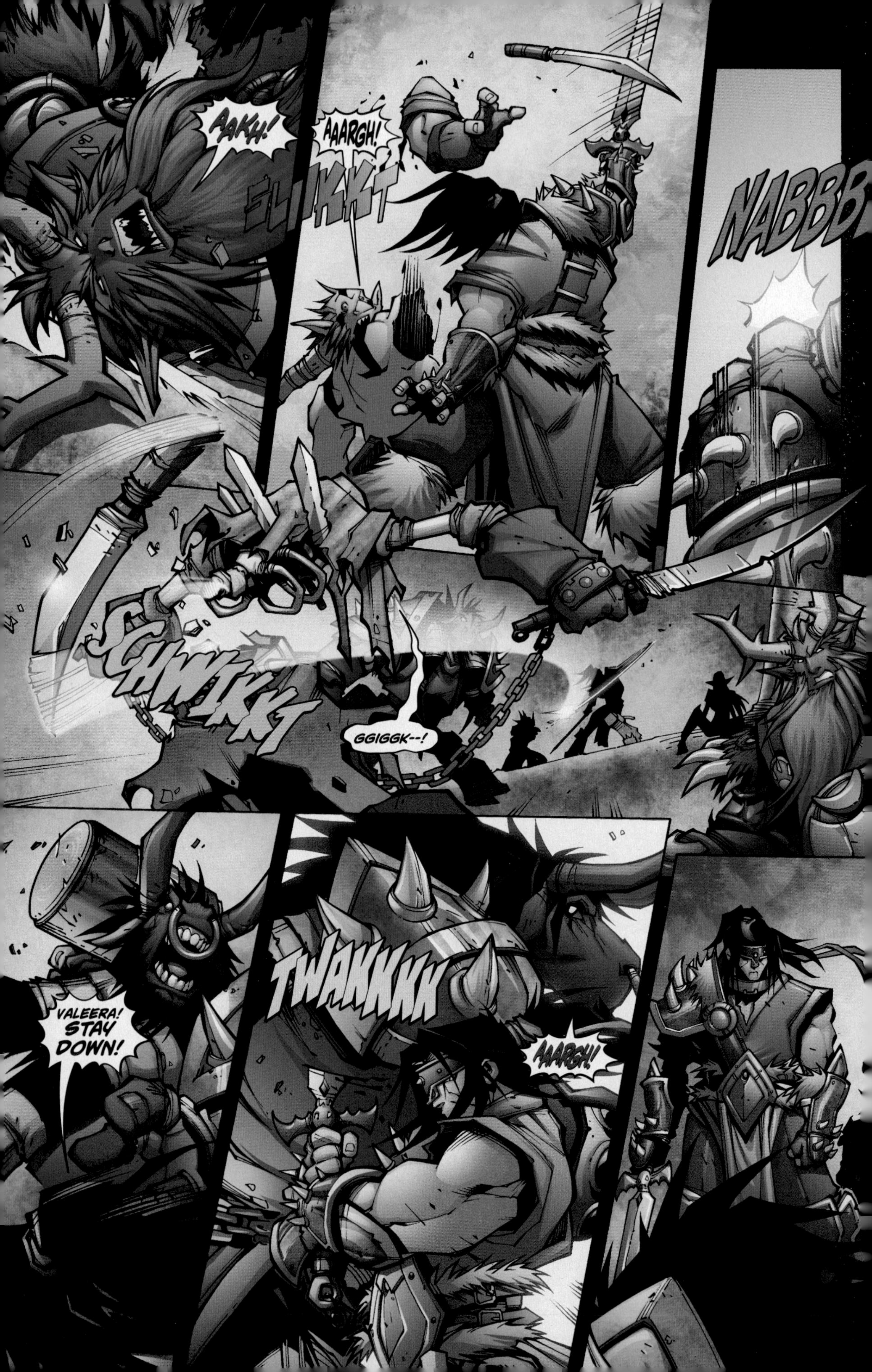
AAKH!
AAARGH!
FLIKKT
NABBB
SCHWIKKT
GGIGGK--!
VALEERA! STAY DOWN!
TWAKKKK
AAARGH!

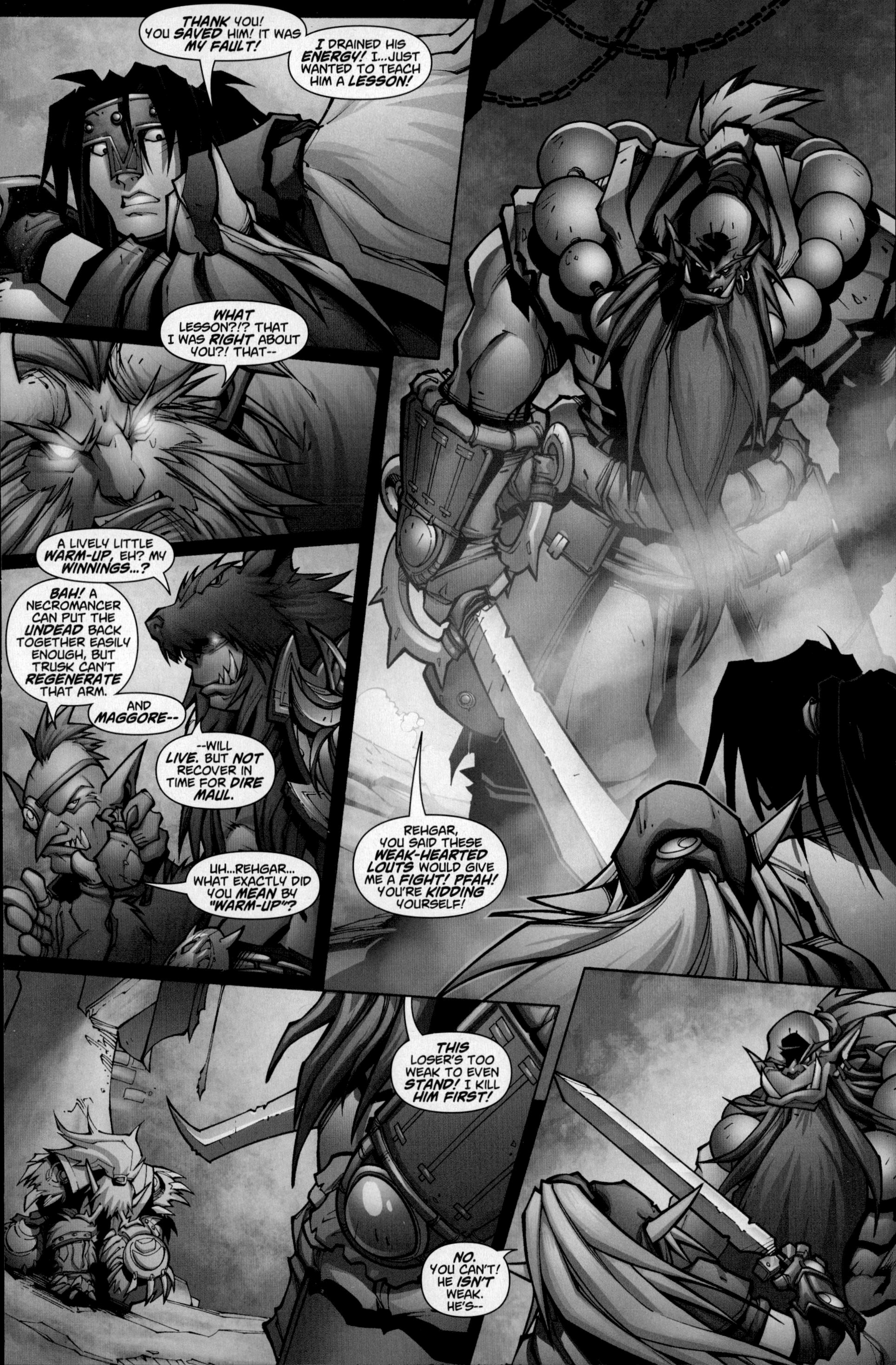
THANK YOU! YOU SAVED HIM! IT WAS MY FAULT!
I DRAINED HIS ENERGY! I...JUST WANTED TO TEACH HIM A LESSON!
WHAT LESSON?!? THAT I WAS RIGHT ABOUT YOU?! THAT--
A LIVELY LITTLE WARM-UP, EH? MY WINNINGS...?
BAH! A NECROMANCER CAN PUT THE UNDEAD BACK TOGETHER EASILY ENOUGH, BUT TRUSK CAN'T REGENERATE THAT ARM.
AND MAGGORE--
--WILL LIVE. BUT NOT RECOVER IN TIME FOR DIRE MAUL.
UH...REHGAR... WHAT EXACTLY DID YOU MEAN BY "WARM-UP"?
REHGAR, YOU SAID THESE WEAK-HEARTED LOUTS WOULD GIVE ME A FIGHT! PFAH! YOU'RE KIDDING YOURSELF!
THIS LOSER'S TOO WEAK TO EVEN STAND! I KILL HIM FIRST!
NO. YOU CAN'T! HE ISN'T WEAK. HE'S--

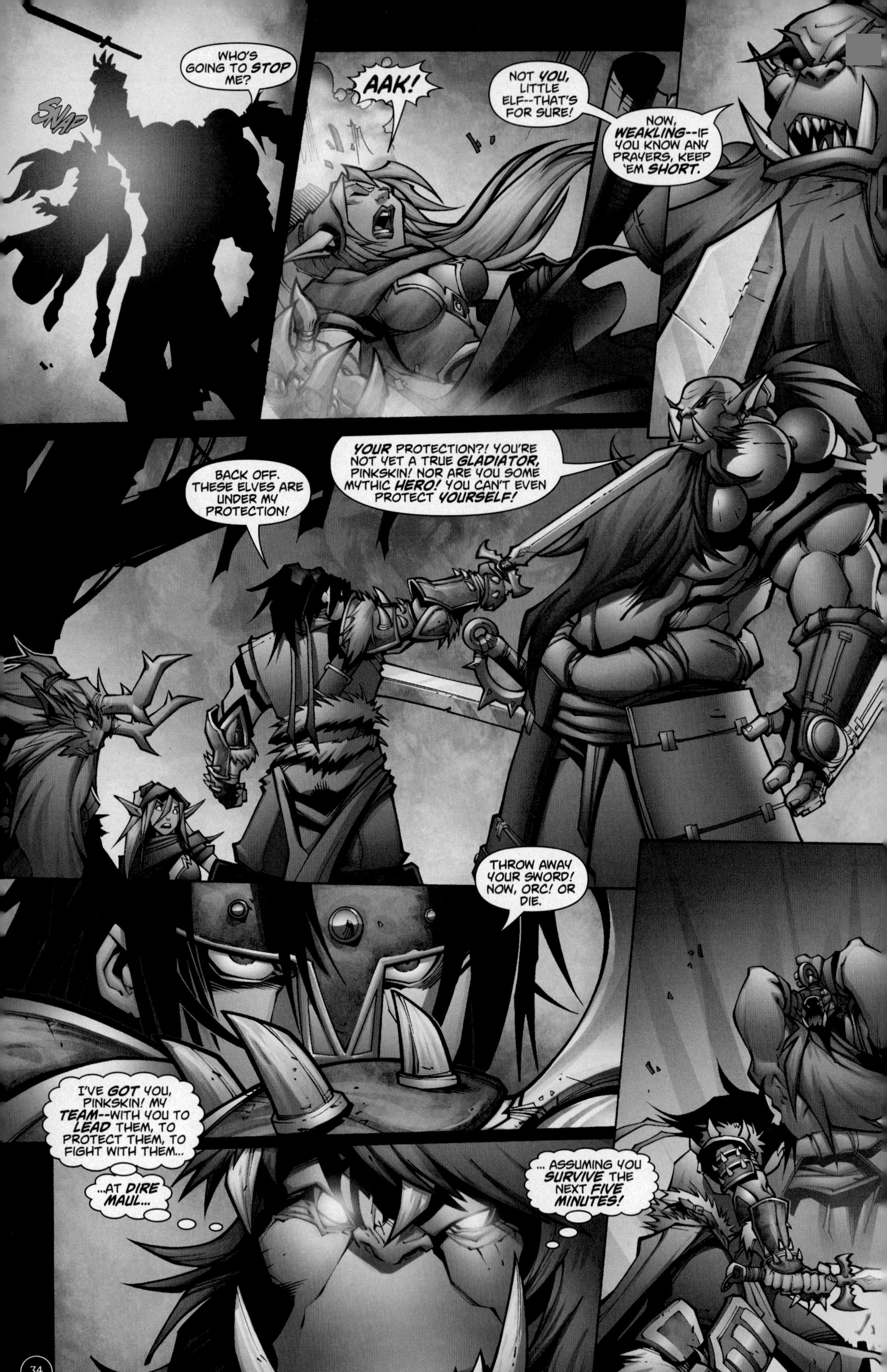

WHO'S GOING TO STOP ME?
SNAP
AAK!
NOT YOU, LITTLE ELF--THAT'S FOR SURE!
NOW, WEAKLING--IF YOU KNOW ANY PRAYERS, KEEP 'EM SHORT.
BACK OFF. THESE ELVES ARE UNDER MY PROTECTION!
YOUR PROTECTION?! YOU'RE NOT YET A TRUE GLADIATOR, PINKSKIN! NOR ARE YOU SOME MYTHIC HERO! YOU CAN'T EVEN PROTECT YOURSELF!
THROW AWAY YOUR SWORD! NOW, ORC! OR DIE.
I'VE GOT YOU, PINKSKIN! MY TEAM--WITH YOU TO LEAD THEM, TO PROTECT THEM, TO FIGHT WITH THEM...
...AT DIRE MAUL...
... ASSUMING YOU SURVIVE THE NEXT FIVE MINUTES!

CHAPTER 2

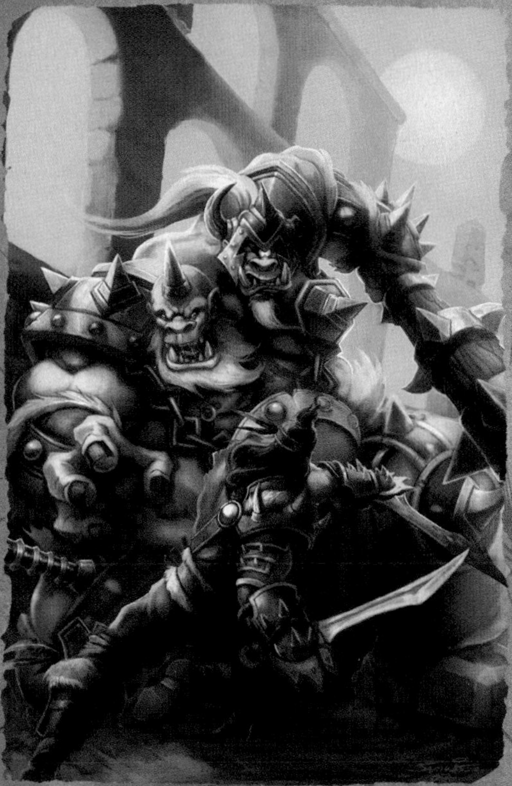

Issue #2 Cover
by Samwise Didier

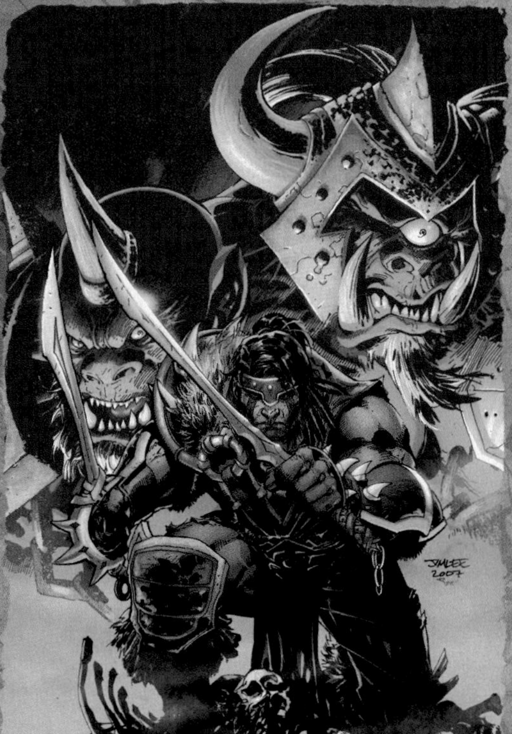

Issue #2 Cover
by Jim Lee and Alex Sinclair

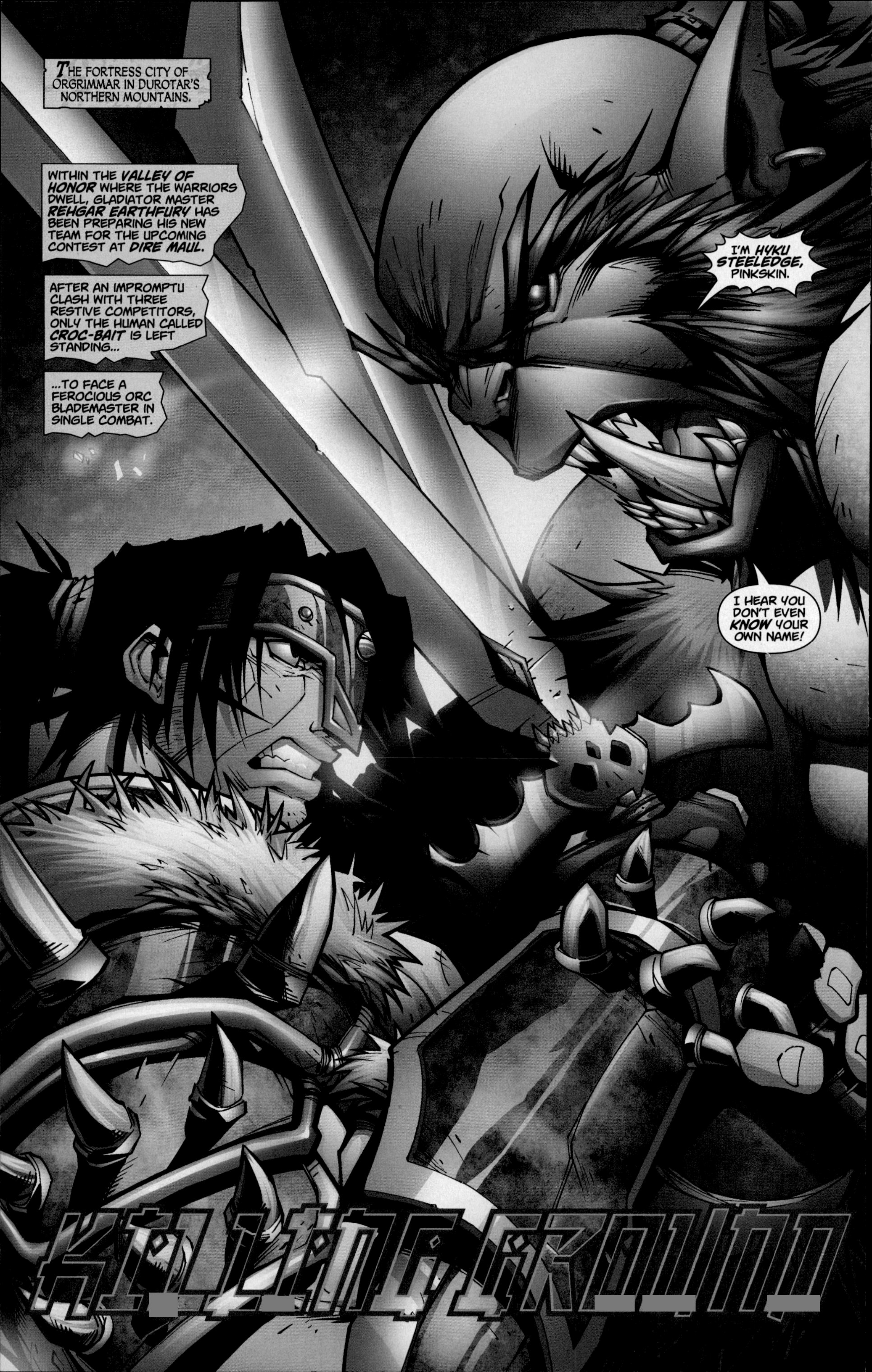
THE FORTRESS CITY OF ORGRIMMAR IN DUROTAR'S NORTHERN MOUNTAINS.
WITHIN THE VALLEY OF HONOR WHERE THE WARRIORS DWELL, GLADIATOR MASTER REHGAR EARTHFURY HAS BEEN PREPARING HIS NEW TEAM FOR THE UPCOMING CONTEST AT DIRE MAUL.
AFTER AN IMPROMPTU CLASH WITH THREE RESTIVE COMPETITORS, ONLY THE HUMAN CALLED CROC-BAIT IS LEFT STANDING...
...TO FACE A FEROCIOUS ORC BLADEMASTER IN SINGLE COMBAT.
I'M HYKU STEELEDGE, PINKSKIN.
I HEAR YOU DON'T EVEN KNOW YOUR OWN NAME!
KILLING GROUND

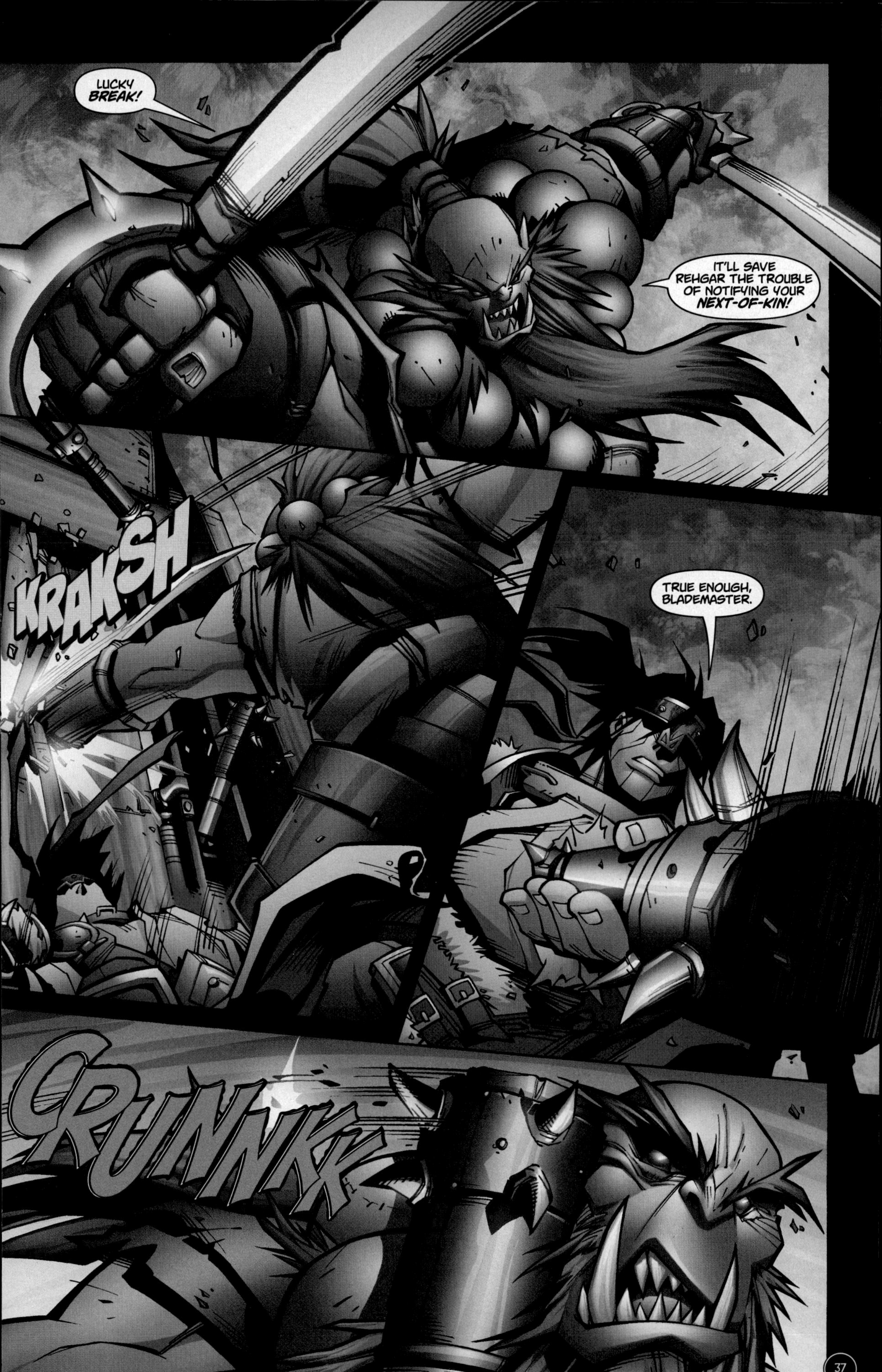
LUCKY BREAK!
IT'LL SAVE REHGAR THE TROUBLE OF NOTIFYING YOUR NEXT-OF-KIN!
KRAKSH
TRUE ENOUGH, BLADEMASTER.
CRUNNKK

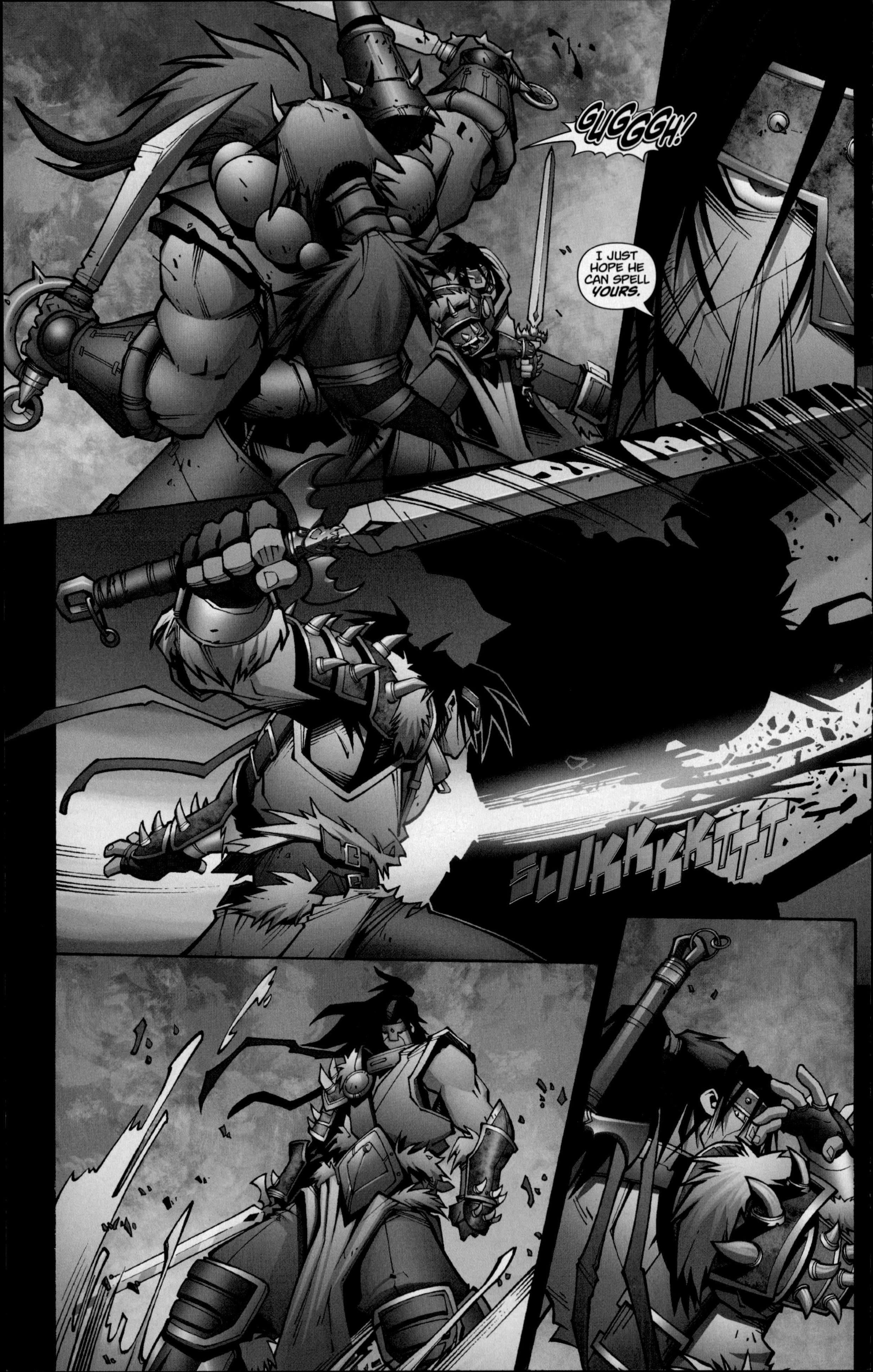
GUGGGH!
I JUST HOPE HE CAN SPELL YOURS.
SLIIKKKKTTT

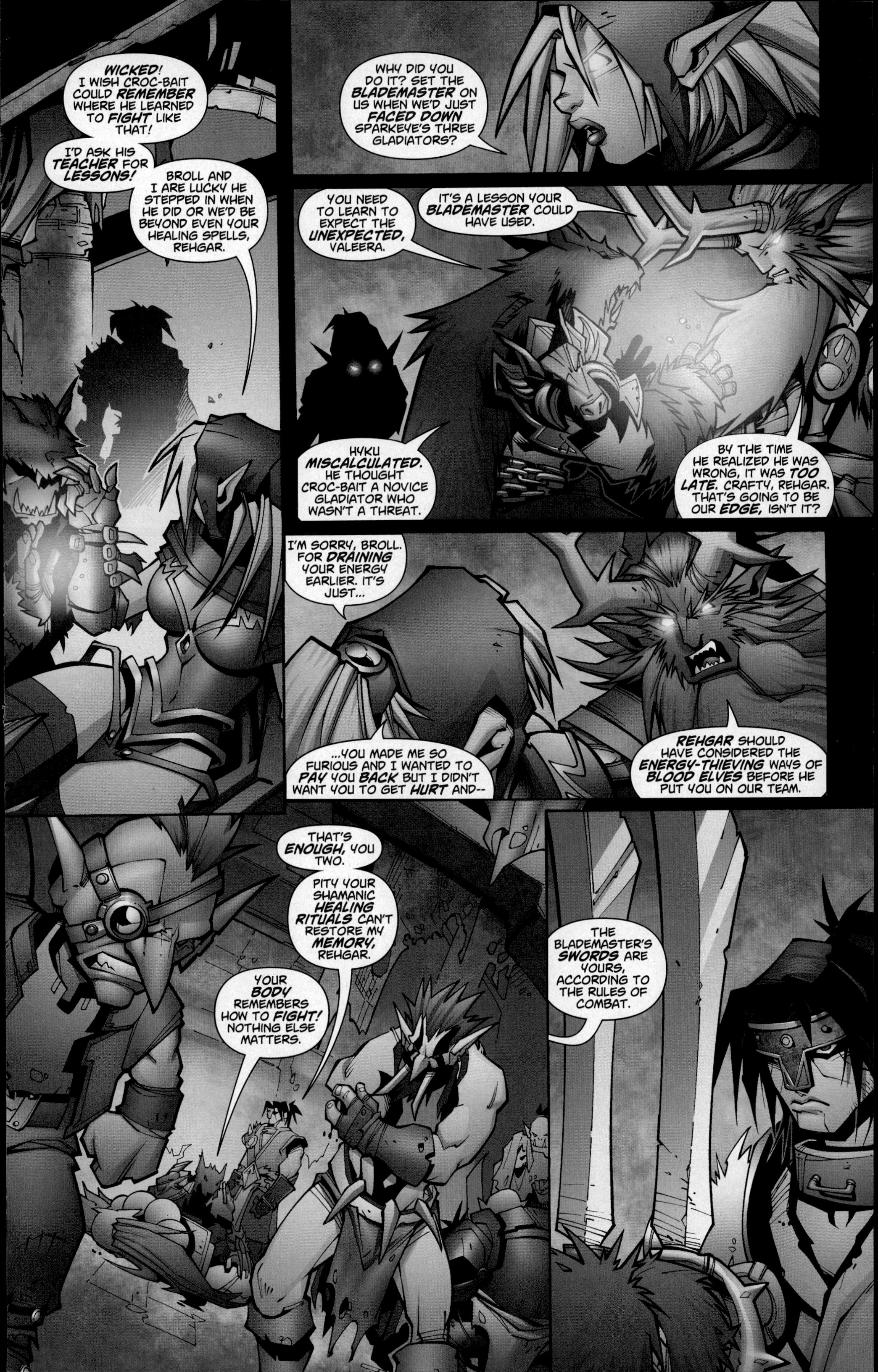
WICKED! I WISH CROC-BAIT COULD REMEMBER WHERE HE LEARNED TO FIGHT LIKE THAT!
I'D ASK HIS TEACHER FOR LESSONS!
BROLL AND I ARE LUCKY HE STEPPED IN WHEN HE DID OR WE'D BE BEYOND EVEN YOUR HEALING SPELLS, REHGAR.
WHY DID YOU DO IT? SET THE BLADEMASTER ON US WHEN WE'D JUST FACED DOWN SPARKEYE'S THREE GLADIATORS?
YOU NEED TO LEARN TO EXPECT THE UNEXPECTED, VALEERA.
IT'S A LESSON YOUR BLADEMASTER COULD HAVE USED.
HYKU MISCALCULATED. HE THOUGHT CROC-BAIT A NOVICE GLADIATOR WHO WASN'T A THREAT.
BY THE TIME HE REALIZED HE WAS WRONG, IT WAS TOO LATE. CRAFTY, REHGAR. THAT'S GOING TO BE OUR EDGE, ISN'T IT?
I'M SORRY, BROLL. FOR DRAINING YOUR ENERGY EARLIER. IT'S JUST...
...YOU MADE ME SO FURIOUS AND I WANTED TO PAY YOU BACK BUT I DIDN'T WANT YOU TO GET HURT AND--
REHGAR SHOULD HAVE CONSIDERED THE ENERGY-THIEVING WAYS OF BLOOD ELVES BEFORE HE PUT YOU ON OUR TEAM.
THAT'S ENOUGH, YOU TWO.
PITY YOUR SHAMANIC HEALING RITUALS CAN'T RESTORE MY MEMORY, REHGAR.
YOUR BODY REMEMBERS HOW TO FIGHT! NOTHING ELSE MATTERS.
THE BLADEMASTER'S SWORDS ARE YOURS, ACCORDING TO THE RULES OF COMBAT.

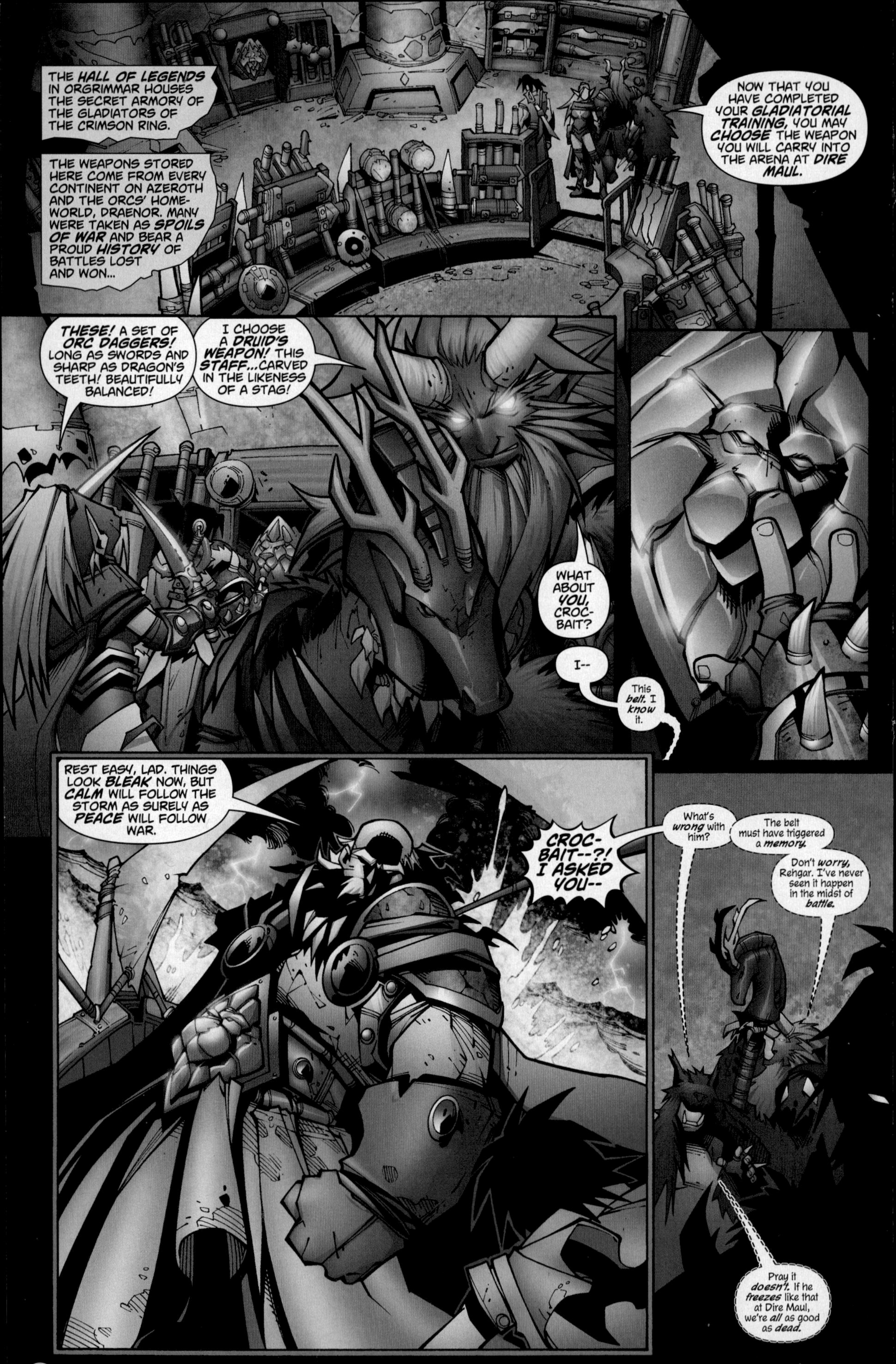
THE HALL OF LEGENDS IN ORGRIMMAR HOUSES THE SECRET ARMORY OF THE GLADIATORS OF THE CRIMSON RING.
THE WEAPONS STORED HERE COME FROM EVERY CONTINENT ON AZEROTH AND THE ORCS' HOME-WORLD, DRAENOR. MANY WERE TAKEN AS SPOILS OF WAR AND BEAR A PROUD HISTORY OF BATTLES LOST AND WON...
NOW THAT YOU HAVE COMPLETED YOUR GLADIATORIAL TRAINING, YOU MAY CHOOSE THE WEAPON YOU WILL CARRY INTO THE ARENA AT DIRE MAUL.
THESE! A SET OF ORC DAGGERS! LONG AS SWORDS AND SHARP AS DRAGON'S TEETH! BEAUTIFULLY BALANCED!
I CHOOSE A DRUID'S WEAPON! THIS STAFF...CARVED IN THE LIKENESS OF A STAG!
WHAT ABOUT YOU, CROC-BAIT?
I--
This belt. I know it.
REST EASY, LAD. THINGS LOOK BLEAK NOW, BUT CALM WILL FOLLOW THE STORM AS SURELY AS PEACE WILL FOLLOW WAR.
CROC-BAIT--?! I ASKED YOU--
What's wrong with him?
The belt must have triggered a memory.
Don't worry, Rehgar. I've never seen it happen in the midst of battle.
Pray it doesn't. If he freezes like that at Dire Maul, we're all as good as dead.

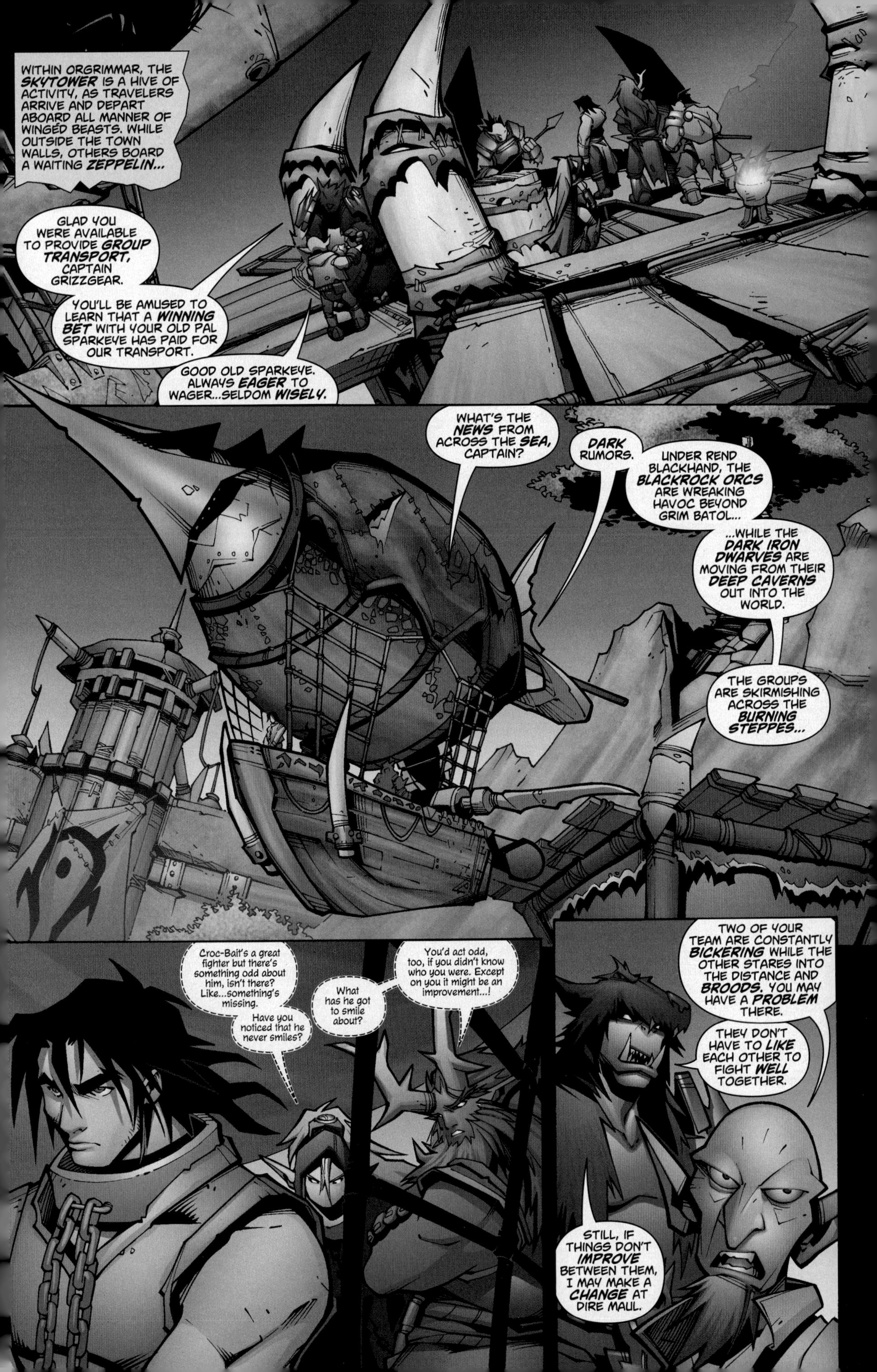
WITHIN ORGRIMMAR, THE SKYTOWER IS A HIVE OF ACTIVITY, AS TRAVELERS ARRIVE AND DEPART ABOARD ALL MANNER OF WINGED BEASTS. WHILE OUTSIDE THE TOWN WALLS, OTHERS BOARD A WAITING ZEPPELIN...
GLAD YOU WERE AVAILABLE TO PROVIDE GROUP TRANSPORT, CAPTAIN GRIZZGEAR.
YOU'LL BE AMUSED TO LEARN THAT A WINNING BET WITH YOUR OLD PAL SPARKEYE HAS PAID FOR OUR TRANSPORT.
GOOD OLD SPARKEYE. ALWAYS EAGER TO WAGER...SELDOM WISELY.
WHAT'S THE NEWS FROM ACROSS THE SEA, CAPTAIN?
DARK RUMORS.
UNDER REND BLACKHAND, THE BLACKROCK ORCS ARE WREAKING HAVOC BEYOND GRIM BATOL...
...WHILE THE DARK IRON DWARVES ARE MOVING FROM THEIR DEEP CAVERNS OUT INTO THE WORLD.
THE GROUPS ARE SKIRMISHING ACROSS THE BURNING STEPPES...
Croc-Bait's a great fighter but there's something odd about him, isn't there? Like...something's missing.
Have you noticed that he never smiles?
What has he got to smile about?
You'd act odd, too, if you didn't know who you were. Except on you it might be an improvement...!
TWO OF YOUR TEAM ARE CONSTANTLY BICKERING WHILE THE OTHER STARES INTO THE DISTANCE AND BROODS. YOU MAY HAVE A PROBLEM THERE.
THEY DON'T HAVE TO LIKE EACH OTHER TO FIGHT WELL TOGETHER.
STILL, IF THINGS DON'T IMPROVE BETWEEN THEM, I MAY MAKE A CHANGE AT DIRE MAUL.

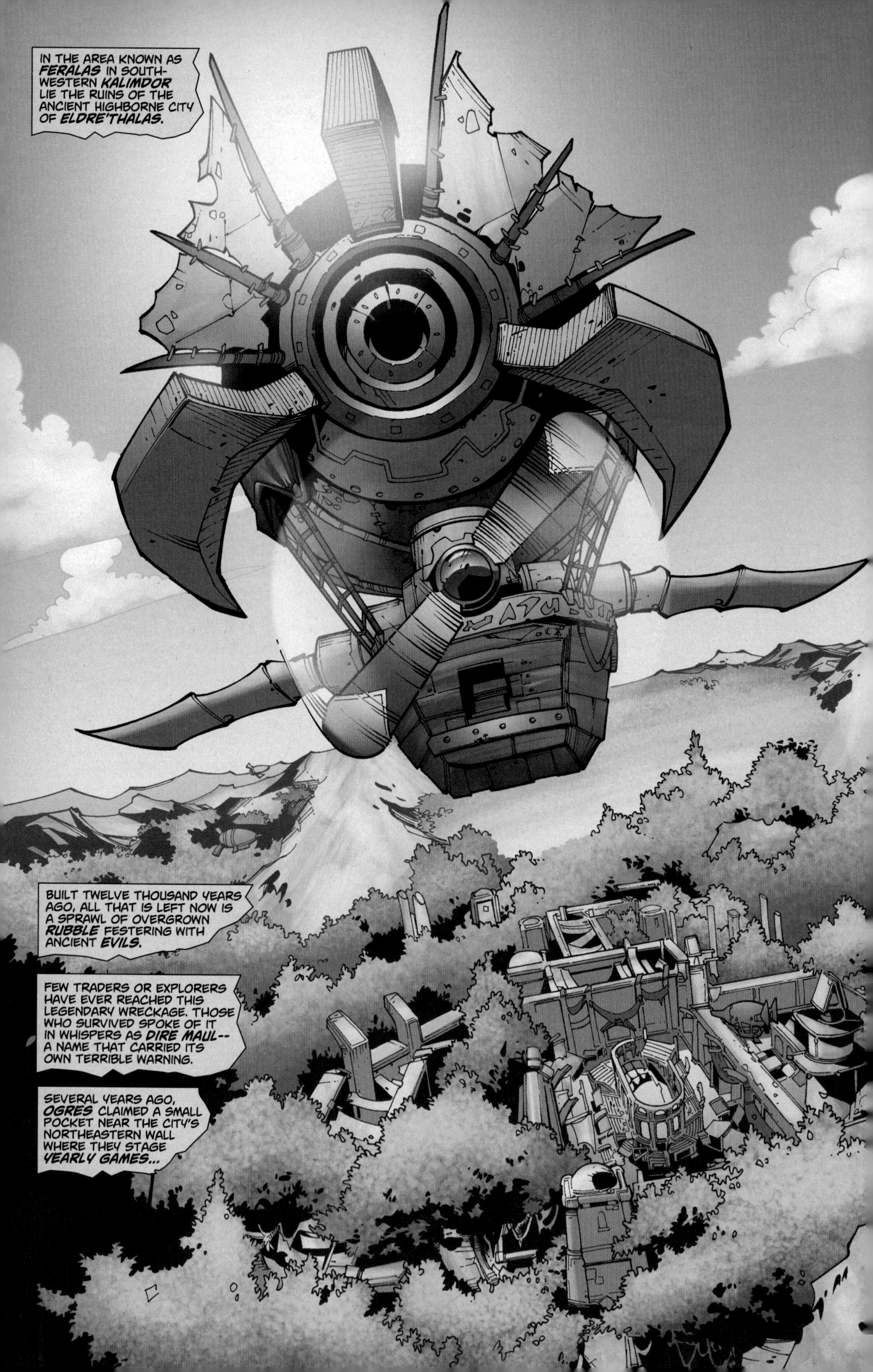
IN THE AREA KNOWN AS FERALAS IN SOUTH-WESTERN KALIMDOR LIE THE RUINS OF THE ANCIENT HIGHBORNE CITY OF ELDRE'THALAS.
BUILT TWELVE THOUSAND YEARS AGO, ALL THAT IS LEFT NOW IS A SPRAWL OF OVERGROWN RUBBLE FESTERING WITH ANCIENT EVILS.
FEW TRADERS OR EXPLORERS HAVE EVER REACHED THIS LEGENDARY WRECKAGE. THOSE WHO SURVIVED SPOKE OF IT IN WHISPERS AS DIRE MAUL-- A NAME THAT CARRIED ITS OWN TERRIBLE WARNING.
SEVERAL YEARS AGO, OGRES CLAIMED A SMALL POCKET NEAR THE CITY'S NORTHEASTERN WALL WHERE THEY STAGE YEARLY GAMES...

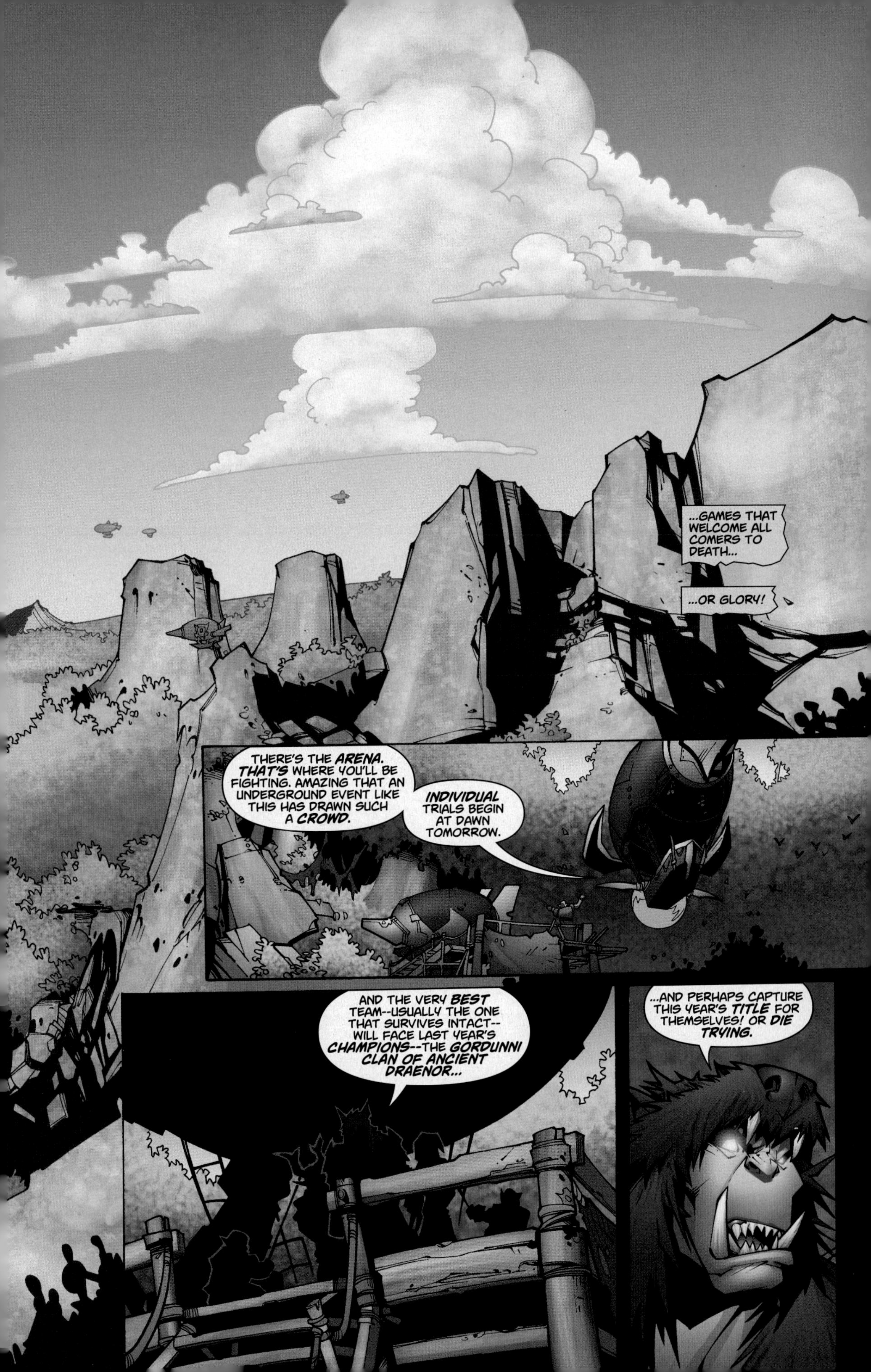
...GAMES THAT WELCOME ALL COMERS TO DEATH...
...OR GLORY!
THERE'S THE ARENA. THAT'S WHERE YOU'LL BE FIGHTING. AMAZING THAT AN UNDERGROUND EVENT LIKE THIS HAS DRAWN SUCH A CROWD.
INDIVIDUAL TRIALS BEGIN AT DAWN TOMORROW.
AND THE VERY BEST TEAM--USUALLY THE ONE THAT SURVIVES INTACT--WILL FACE LAST YEAR'S CHAMPIONS--THE GORDUNNI CLAN OF ANCIENT DRAENOR...
...AND PERHAPS CAPTURE THIS YEAR'S TITLE FOR THEMSELVES! OR DIE TRYING.

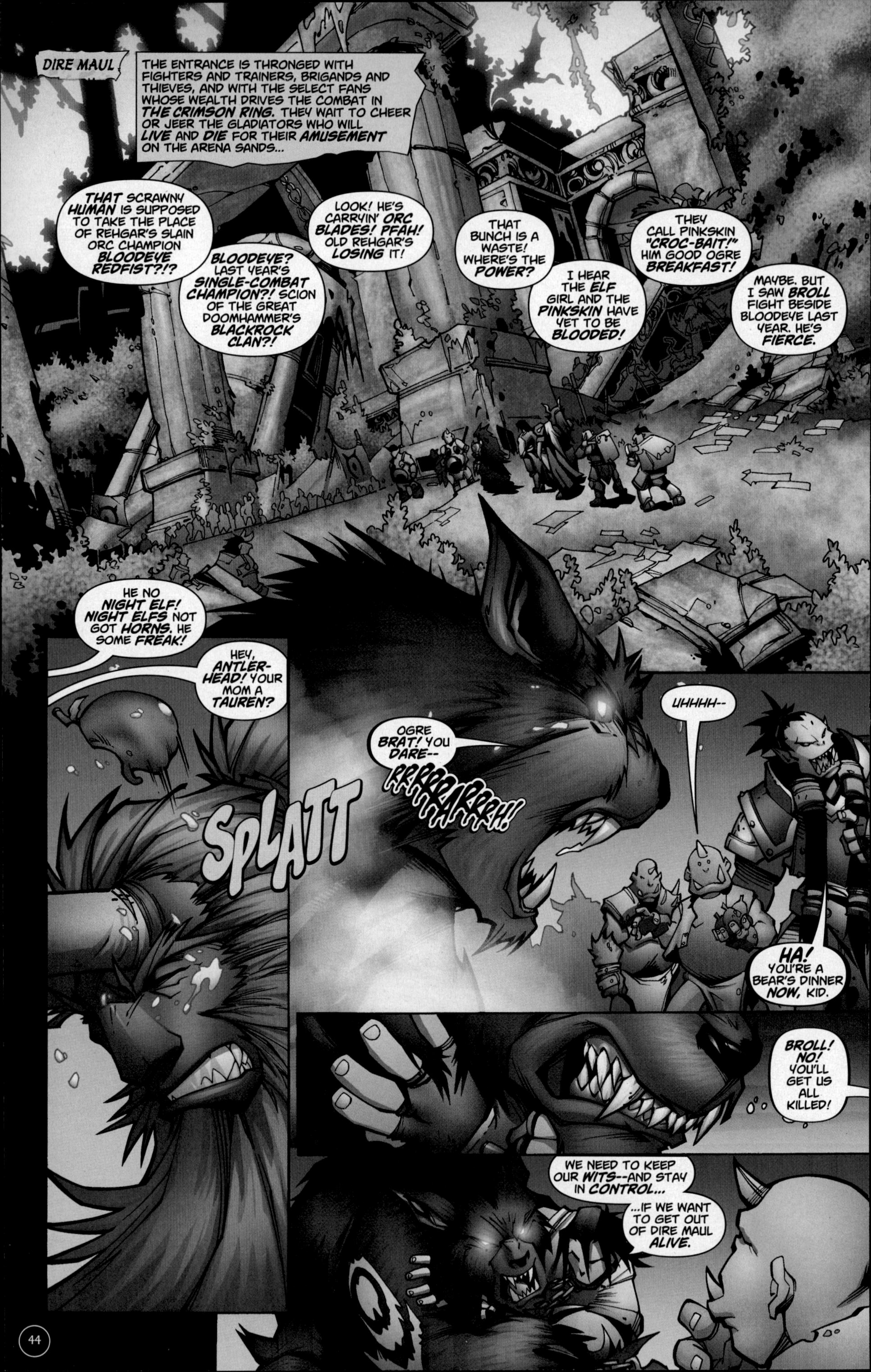
DIRE MAUL
THE ENTRANCE IS THRONGED WITH FIGHTERS AND TRAINERS, BRIGANDS AND THIEVES, AND WITH THE SELECT FANS WHOSE WEALTH DRIVES THE COMBAT IN THE CRIMSON RING. THEY WAIT TO CHEER OR JEER THE GLADIATORS WHO WILL LIVE AND DIE FOR THEIR AMUSEMENT ON THE ARENA SANDS...
THAT SCRAWNY HUMAN IS SUPPOSED TO TAKE THE PLACE OF REHGAR'S SLAIN ORC CHAMPION BLOODEYE REDFIST?!?
BLOODEYE? LAST YEAR'S SINGLE-COMBAT CHAMPION?! SCION OF THE GREAT DOOMHAMMER'S BLACKROCK CLAN?!
LOOK! HE'S CARRYIN' ORC BLADES! PFAH! OLD REHGAR'S LOSING IT!
THAT BUNCH IS A WASTE! WHERE'S THE POWER?
I HEAR THE ELF GIRL AND THE PINKSKIN HAVE YET TO BE BLOODED!
THEY CALL PINKSKIN "CROC-BAIT!" HIM GOOD OGRE BREAKFAST!
MAYBE. BUT I SAW BROLL FIGHT BESIDE BLOODEYE LAST YEAR. HE'S FIERCE.
HE NO NIGHT ELF! NIGHT ELFS NOT GOT HORNS. HE SOME FREAK!
HEY, ANTLER-HEAD! YOUR MOM A TAUREN?
SPLATT
OGRE BRAT! YOU DARE--
RRRRRRARRRH!
UHHHH--
HA! YOU'RE A BEAR'S DINNER NOW, KID.
BROLL! NO! YOU'LL GET US ALL KILLED!
WE NEED TO KEEP OUR WITS--AND STAY IN CONTROL...
...IF WE WANT TO GET OUT OF DIRE MAUL ALIVE.

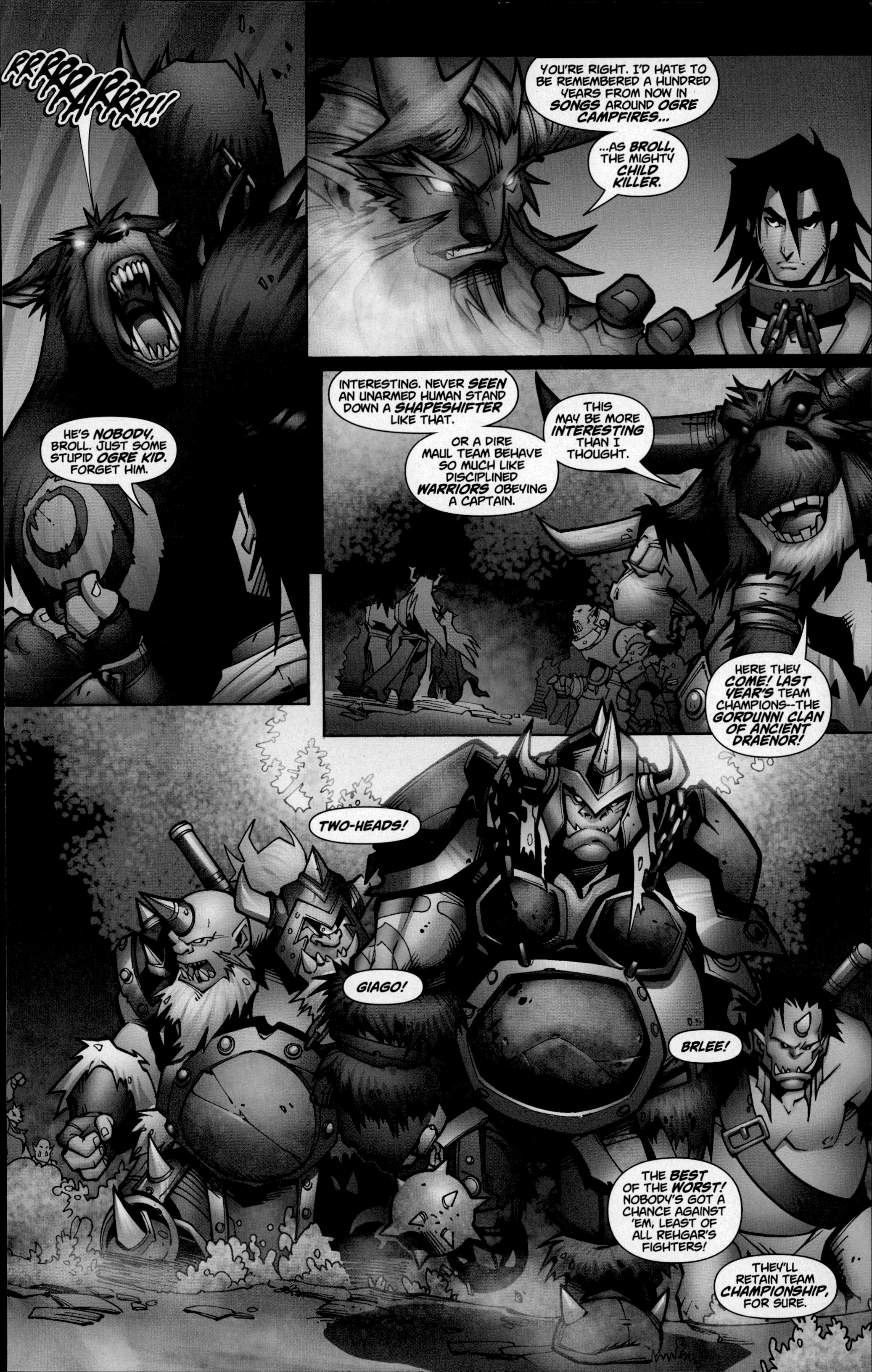
RRRRRRARRRRH!
YOU'RE RIGHT. I'D HATE TO BE REMEMBERED A HUNDRED YEARS FROM NOW IN SONGS AROUND OGRE CAMPFIRES...
...AS BROLL, THE MIGHTY CHILD KILLER.
HE'S NOBODY, BROLL. JUST SOME STUPID OGRE KID. FORGET HIM.
INTERESTING. NEVER SEEN AN UNARMED HUMAN STAND DOWN A SHAPESHIFTER LIKE THAT.
OR A DIRE MAUL TEAM BEHAVE SO MUCH LIKE DISCIPLINED WARRIORS OBEYING A CAPTAIN.
THIS MAY BE MORE INTERESTING THAN I THOUGHT.
HERE THEY COME! LAST YEAR'S TEAM CHAMPIONS--THE GORDUNNI CLAN OF ANCIENT DRAENOR!
TWO-HEADS!
GIAGO!
BRLEE!
THE BEST OF THE WORST! NOBODY'S GOT A CHANCE AGAINST 'EM, LEAST OF ALL REHGAR'S FIGHTERS!
THEY'LL RETAIN TEAM CHAMPIONSHIP, FOR SURE.

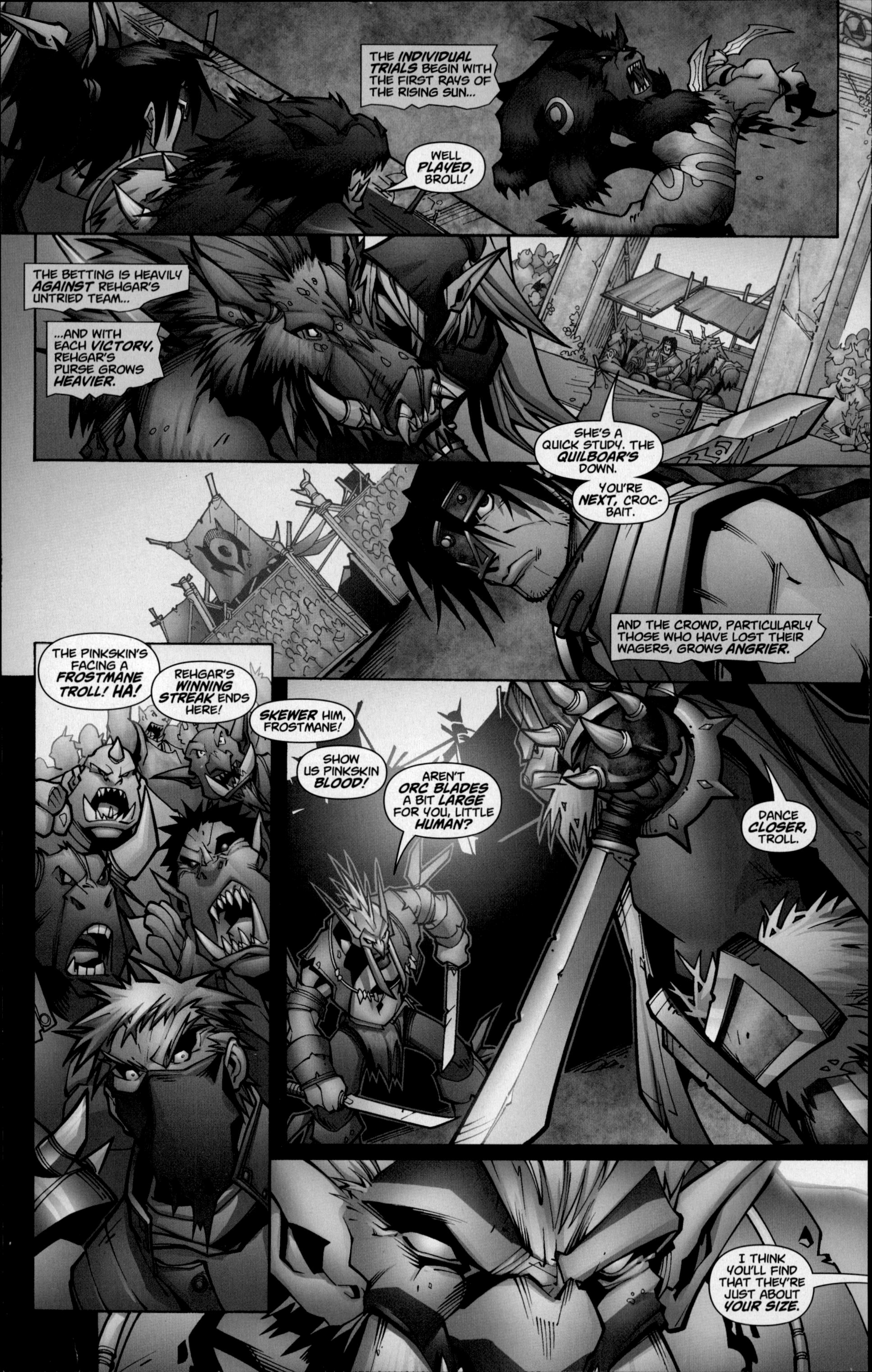
THE INDIVIDUAL TRIALS BEGIN WITH THE FIRST RAYS OF THE RISING SUN...
WELL PLAYED, BROLL!
THE BETTING IS HEAVILY AGAINST REHGAR'S UNTRIED TEAM...
...AND WITH EACH VICTORY, REHGAR'S PURSE GROWS HEAVIER.
SHE'S A QUICK STUDY. THE QUILBOAR'S DOWN.
YOU'RE NEXT, CROC-BAIT.
AND THE CROWD, PARTICULARLY THOSE WHO HAVE LOST THEIR WAGERS, GROWS ANGRIER.
THE PINKSKIN'S FACING A FROSTMANE TROLL! HA!
REHGAR'S WINNING STREAK ENDS HERE!
SKEWER HIM, FROSTMANE!
SHOW US PINKSKIN BLOOD!
AREN'T ORC BLADES A BIT LARGE FOR YOU, LITTLE HUMAN?
DANCE CLOSER, TROLL.
I THINK YOU'LL FIND THAT THEY'RE JUST ABOUT YOUR SIZE.

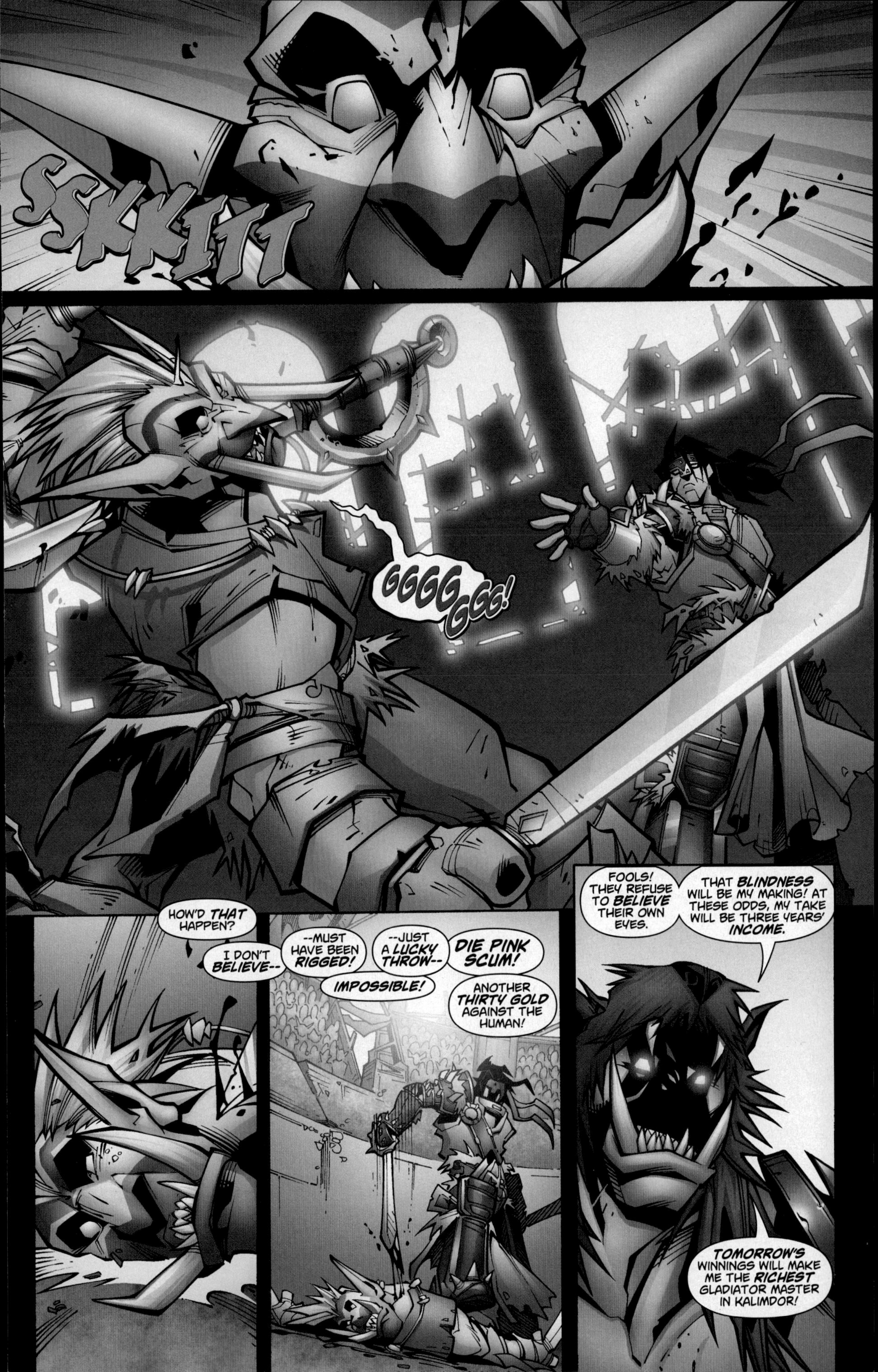
SSKKITT
GGGGGGG!
HOW'D THAT HAPPEN?
I DON'T BELIEVE--
--MUST HAVE BEEN RIGGED!
--JUST A LUCKY THROW--
DIE PINK SCUM!
IMPOSSIBLE!
ANOTHER THIRTY GOLD AGAINST THE HUMAN!
FOOLS! THEY REFUSE TO BELIEVE THEIR OWN EYES.
THAT BLINDNESS WILL BE MY MAKING! AT THESE ODDS, MY TAKE WILL BE THREE YEARS' INCOME.
TOMORROW'S WINNINGS WILL MAKE ME THE RICHEST GLADIATOR MASTER IN KALIMDOR!

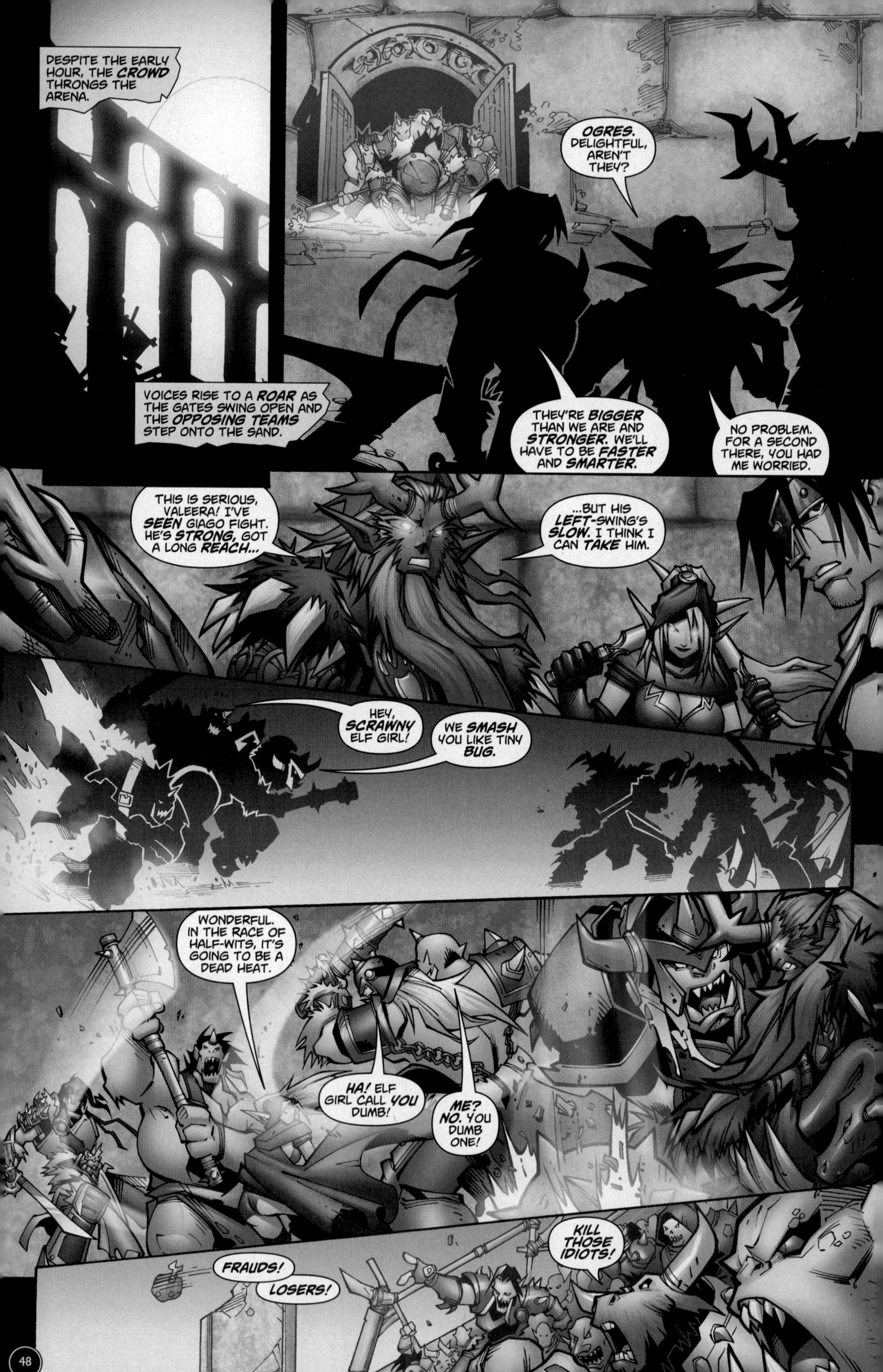

DESPITE THE EARLY HOUR, THE CROWD THRONGS THE ARENA.
VOICES RISE TO A ROAR AS THE GATES SWING OPEN AND THE OPPOSING TEAMS STEP ONTO THE SAND.
OGRES. DELIGHTFUL, AREN'T THEY?
THEY'RE BIGGER THAN WE ARE AND STRONGER. WE'LL HAVE TO BE FASTER AND SMARTER.
NO PROBLEM. FOR A SECOND THERE, YOU HAD ME WORRIED.
THIS IS SERIOUS, VALEERA! I'VE SEEN GIAGO FIGHT. HE'S STRONG, GOT A LONG REACH...
...BUT HIS LEFT-SWING'S SLOW. I THINK I CAN TAKE HIM.
HEY, SCRAWNY ELF GIRL!
WE SMASH YOU LIKE TINY BUG.
WONDERFUL. IN THE RACE OF HALF-WITS, IT'S GOING TO BE A DEAD HEAT.
HA! ELF GIRL CALL YOU DUMB!
ME? NO. YOU DUMB ONE!
KILL THOSE IDIOTS!
FRAUDS!
LOSERS!

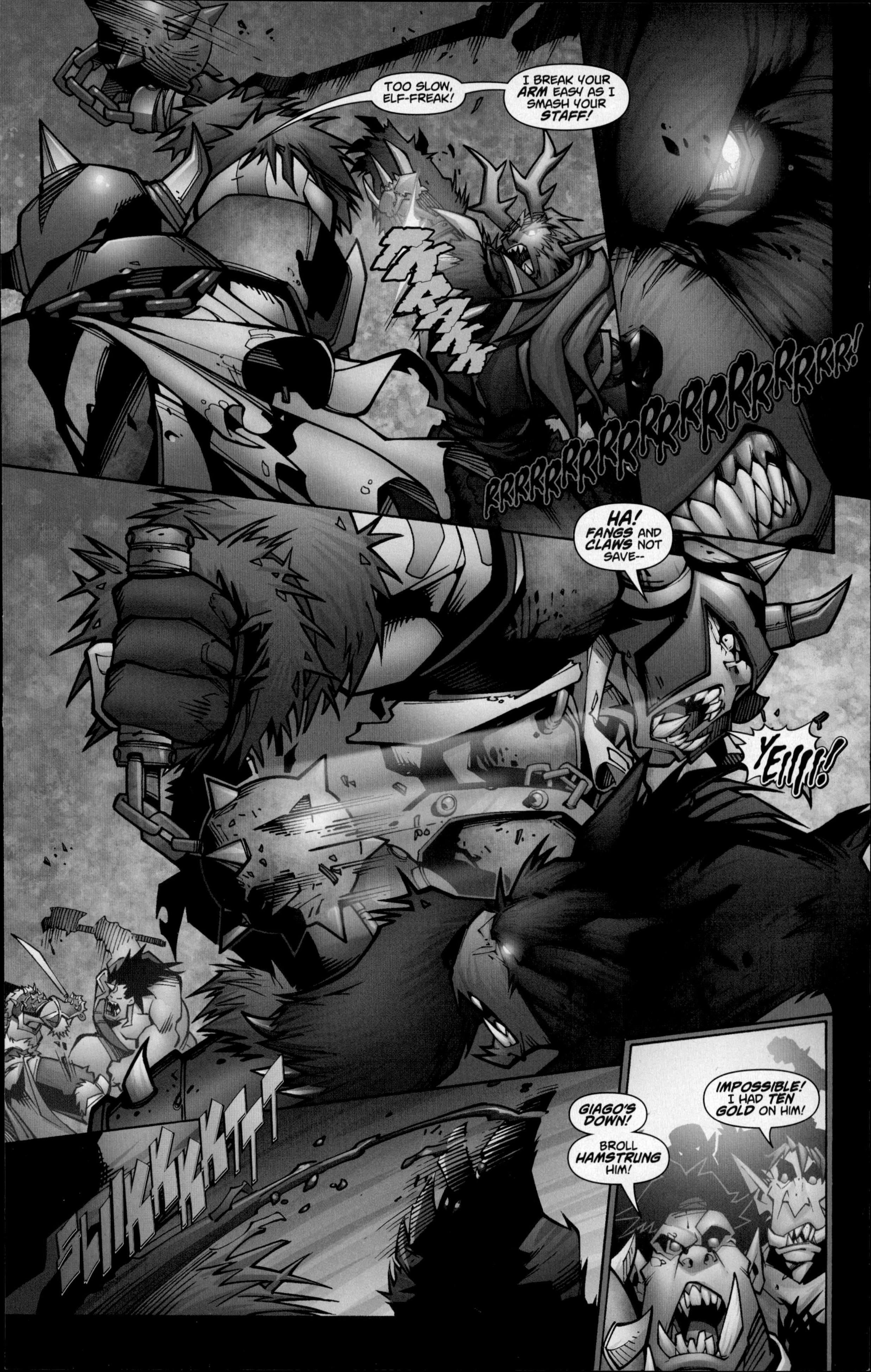

TOO SLOW, ELF-FREAK!
I BREAK YOUR ARM EASY AS I SMASH YOUR STAFF!
TKRAKK
RRRRRRRRRRRRRRRRRRRRRR!
HA! FANGS AND CLAWS NOT SAVE--
YEIIII!
SLTIKKKKTTT
GIAGO'S DOWN!
BROLL HAMSTRUNG HIM!
IMPOSSIBLE! I HAD TEN GOLD ON HIM!

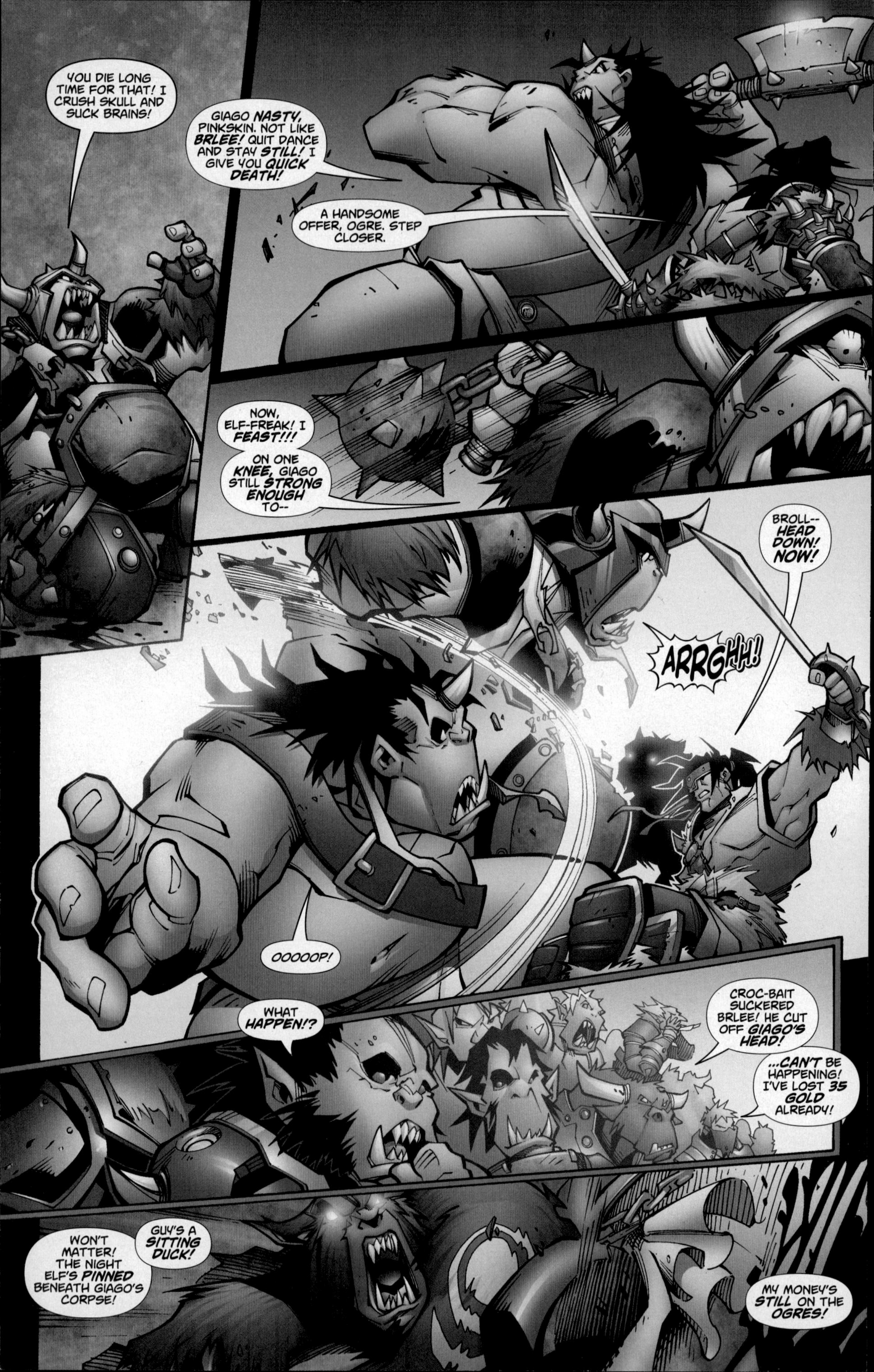
YOU DIE LONG TIME FOR THAT! I CRUSH SKULL AND SUCK BRAINS!
GIAGO NASTY, PINKSKIN. NOT LIKE BRLEE! QUIT DANCE AND STAY STILL! I GIVE YOU QUICK DEATH!
A HANDSOME OFFER, OGRE. STEP CLOSER.
NOW, ELF-FREAK! I FEAST!!!
ON ONE KNEE, GIAGO STILL STRONG ENOUGH TO--
BROLL-- HEAD DOWN! NOW!
ARRGHH!
OOOOOP!
WHAT HAPPEN!?
CROC-BAIT SUCKERED BRLEE! HE CUT OFF GIAGO'S HEAD!
...CAN'T BE HAPPENING! I'VE LOST 35 GOLD ALREADY!
WON'T MATTER! THE NIGHT ELF'S PINNED BENEATH GIAGO'S CORPSE!
GUY'S A SITTING DUCK!
MY MONEY'S STILL ON THE OGRES!

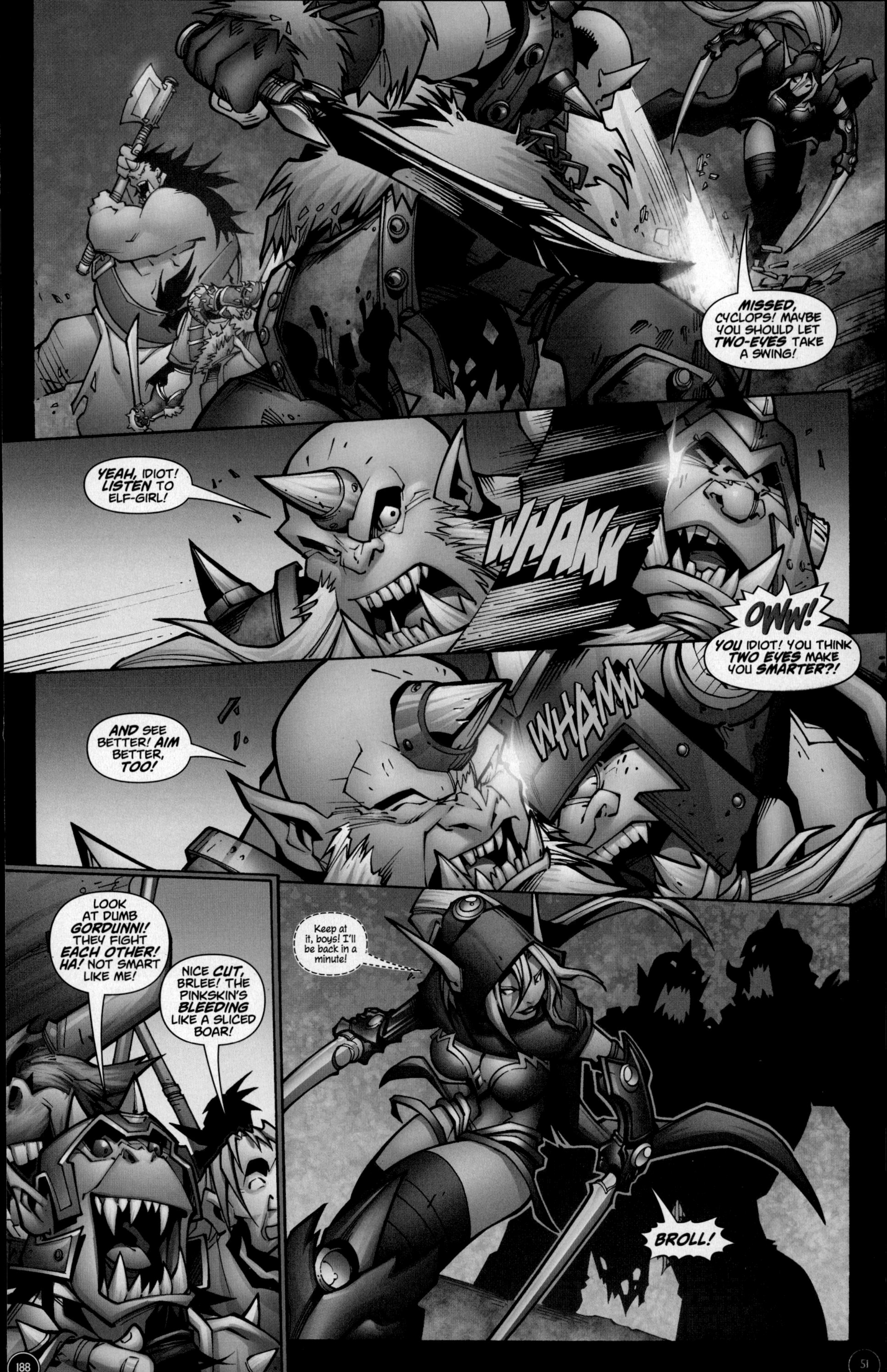

MISSED, CYCLOPS! MAYBE YOU SHOULD LET TWO-EYES TAKE A SWING!
YEAH, IDIOT! LISTEN TO ELF-GIRL!
WHAKK
OWW!
YOU IDIOT! YOU THINK TWO EYES MAKE YOU SMARTER?!
WHAMM
AND SEE BETTER! AIM BETTER, TOO!
LOOK AT DUMB GORDUNNI! THEY FIGHT EACH OTHER! HA! NOT SMART LIKE ME!
NICE CUT, BRLEE! THE PINKSKIN'S BLEEDING LIKE A SLICED BOAR!
Keep at it, boys! I'll be back in a minute!
BROLL!

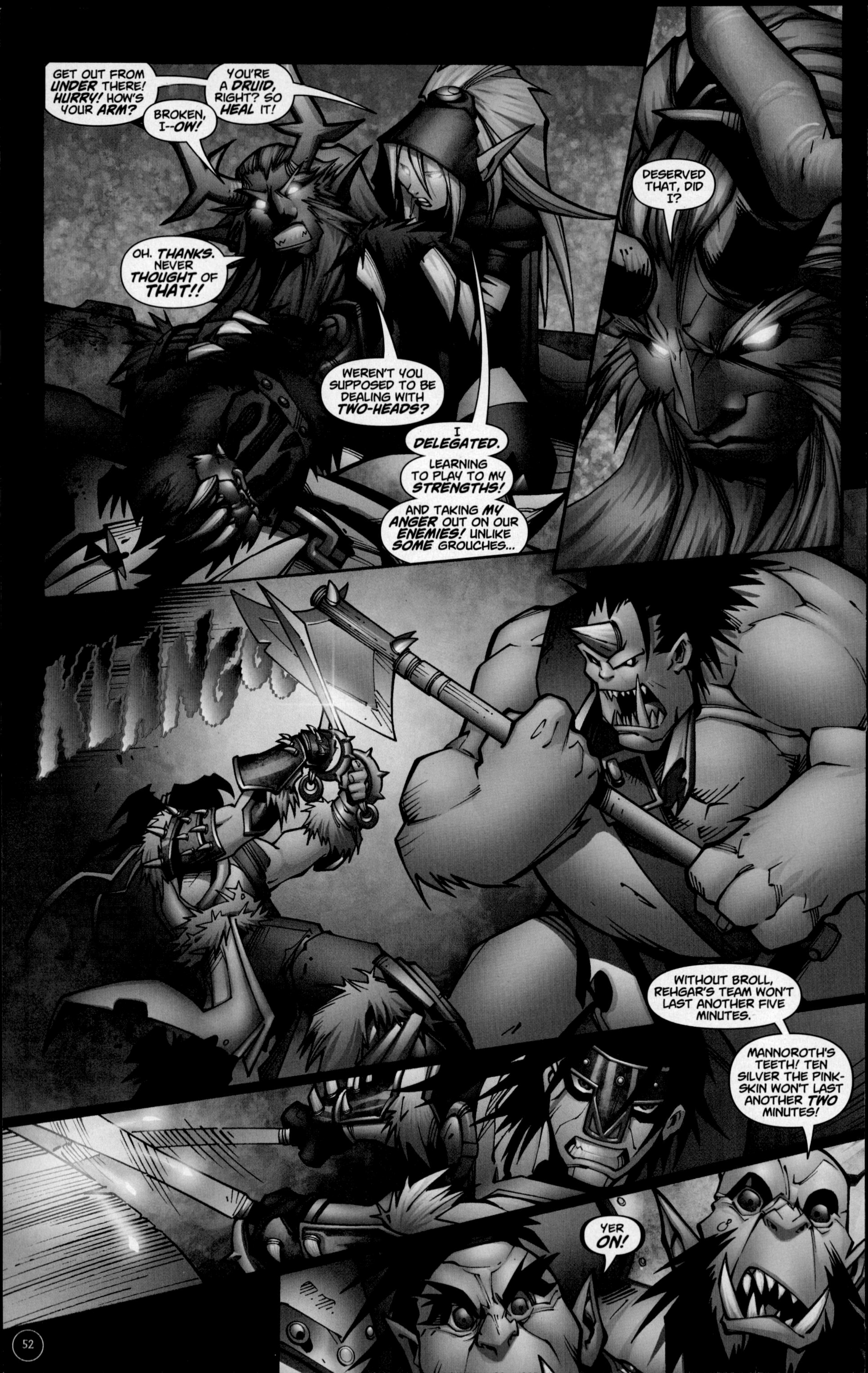
GET OUT FROM UNDER THERE! HURRY! HOW'S YOUR ARM?
BROKEN, I--OW!
YOU'RE A DRUID, RIGHT? SO HEAL IT!
OH. THANKS. NEVER THOUGHT OF THAT!!
DESERVED THAT, DID I?
WEREN'T YOU SUPPOSED TO BE DEALING WITH TWO-HEADS?
I DELEGATED.
LEARNING TO PLAY TO MY STRENGTHS!
AND TAKING MY ANGER OUT ON OUR ENEMIES! UNLIKE SOME GROUCHES...
WITHOUT BROLL, REHGAR'S TEAM WON'T LAST ANOTHER FIVE MINUTES.
MANNOROTH'S TEETH! TEN SILVER THE PINK-SKIN WON'T LAST ANOTHER TWO MINUTES!
YER ON!

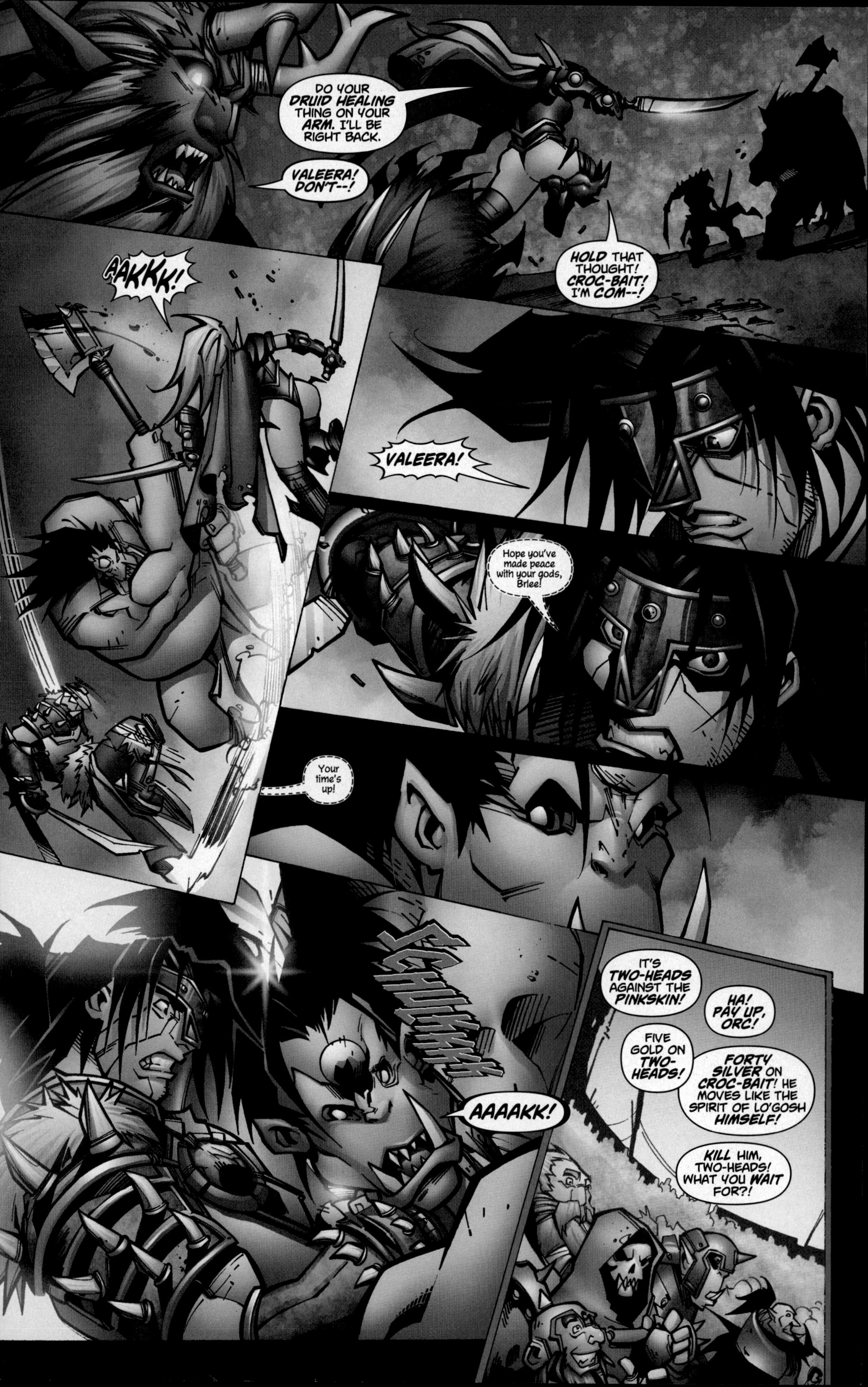
DO YOUR DRUID HEALING THING ON YOUR ARM. I'LL BE RIGHT BACK.
VALEERA! DON'T--!
HOLD THAT THOUGHT! CROC-BAIT! I'M COM--!
AAKKK!
VALEERA!
Hope you've made peace with your gods, Brlee!
Your time's up!
SCHUKKKK
AAAAKK!
IT'S TWO-HEADS AGAINST THE PINKSKIN!
HA! PAY UP, ORC!
FIVE GOLD ON TWO-HEADS!
FORTY SILVER ON CROC-BAIT! HE MOVES LIKE THE SPIRIT OF LO'GOSH HIMSELF!
KILL HIM, TWO-HEADS! WHAT YOU WAIT FOR?!

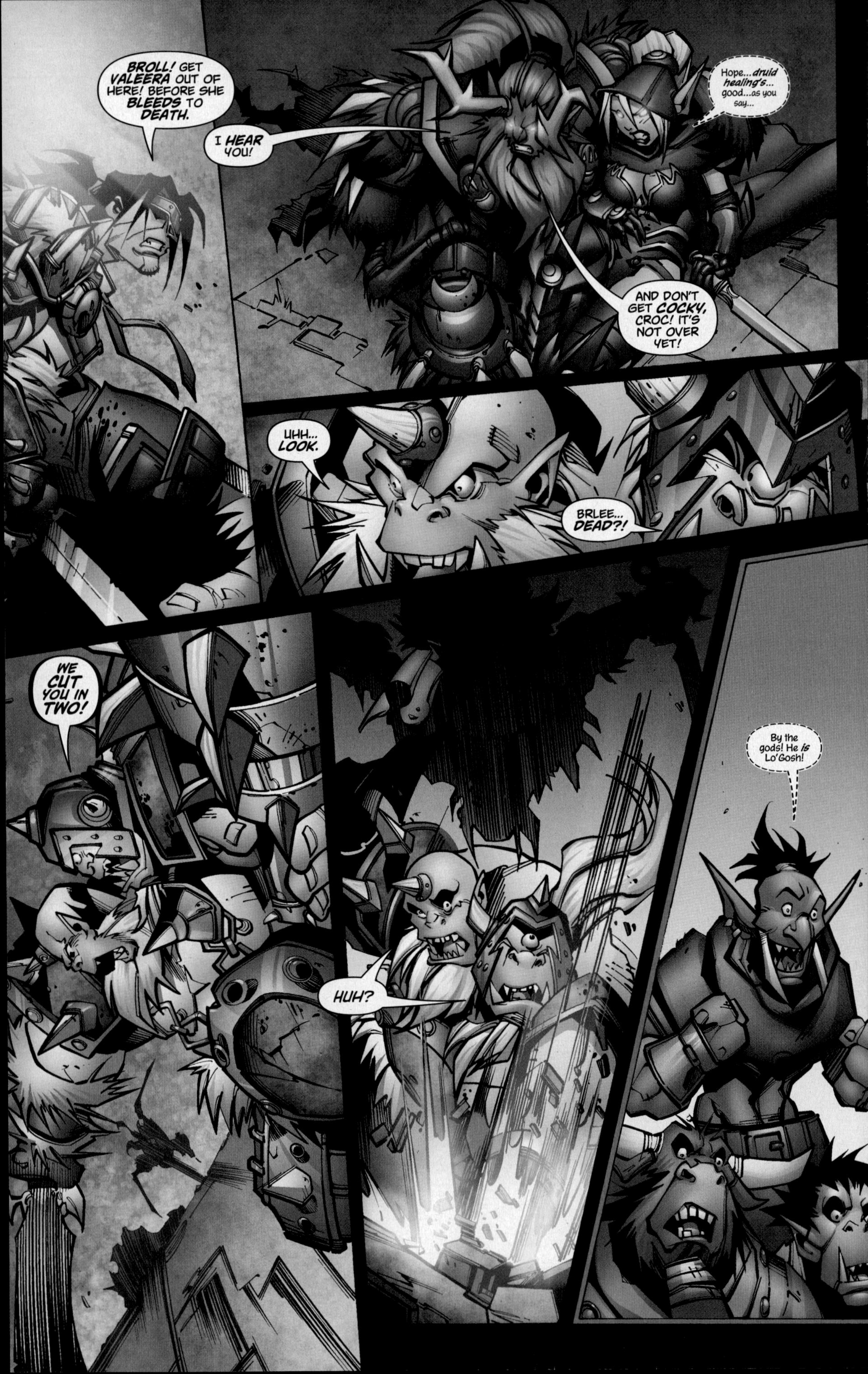
BROLL! GET VALEERA OUT OF HERE! BEFORE SHE BLEEDS TO DEATH.
I HEAR YOU!
Hope...druid healing's... good...as you say...
AND DON'T GET COCKY, CROC! IT'S NOT OVER YET!
UHH... LOOK.
BRLEE... DEAD?!
WE CUT YOU IN TWO!
HUH?
By the gods! He is Lo'Gosh!

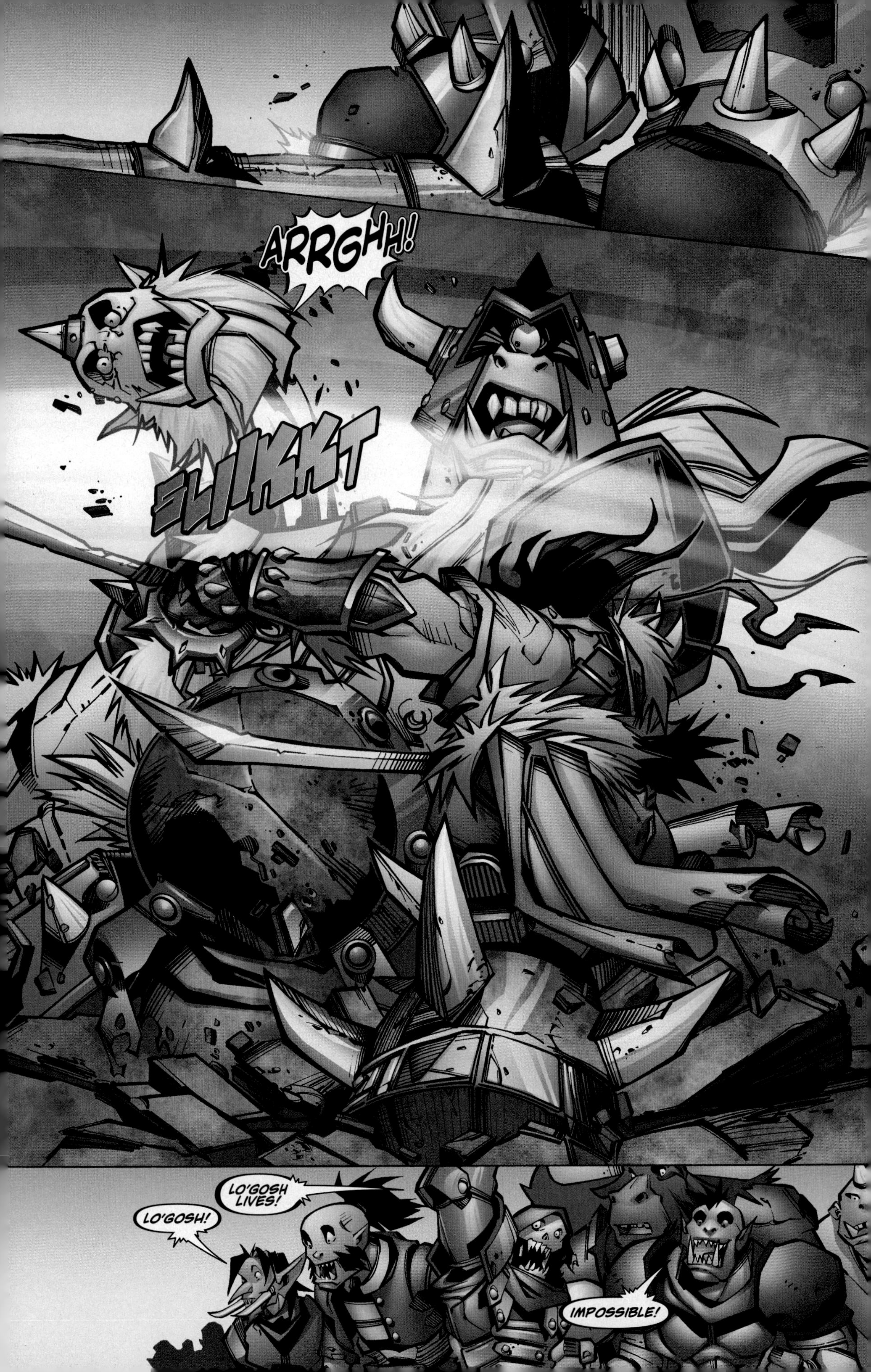
ARRGHH!
SLIIKKT
LO'GOSH!
LO'GOSH LIVES!
IMPOSSIBLE!

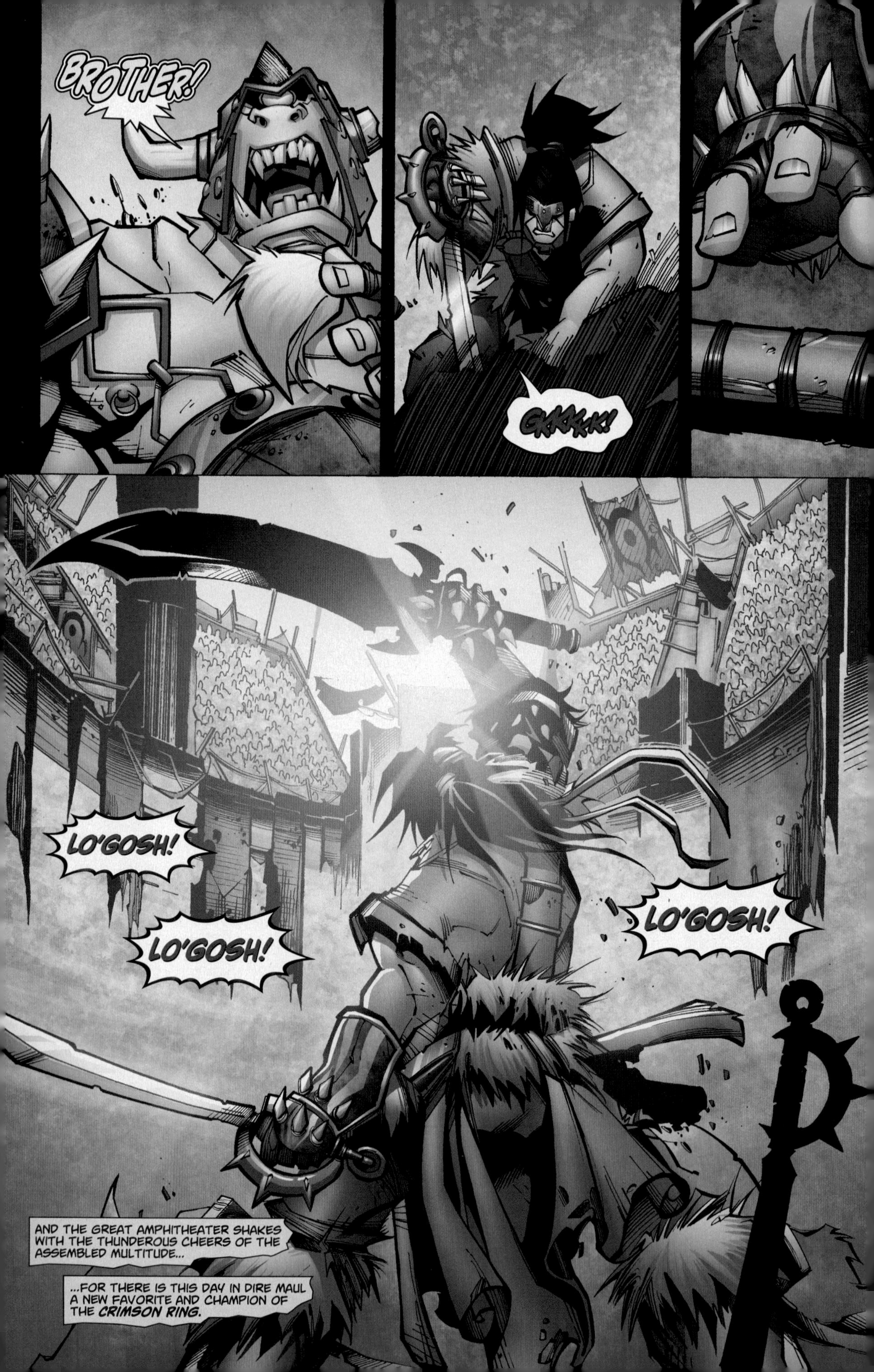
BROTHER!
GKKKK!
LO'GOSH!
LO'GOSH!
LO'GOSH!
AND THE GREAT AMPHITHEATER SHAKES WITH THE THUNDEROUS CHEERS OF THE ASSEMBLED MULTITUDE...
...FOR THERE IS THIS DAY IN DIRE MAUL A NEW FAVORITE AND CHAMPION OF THE *CRIMSON RING*.

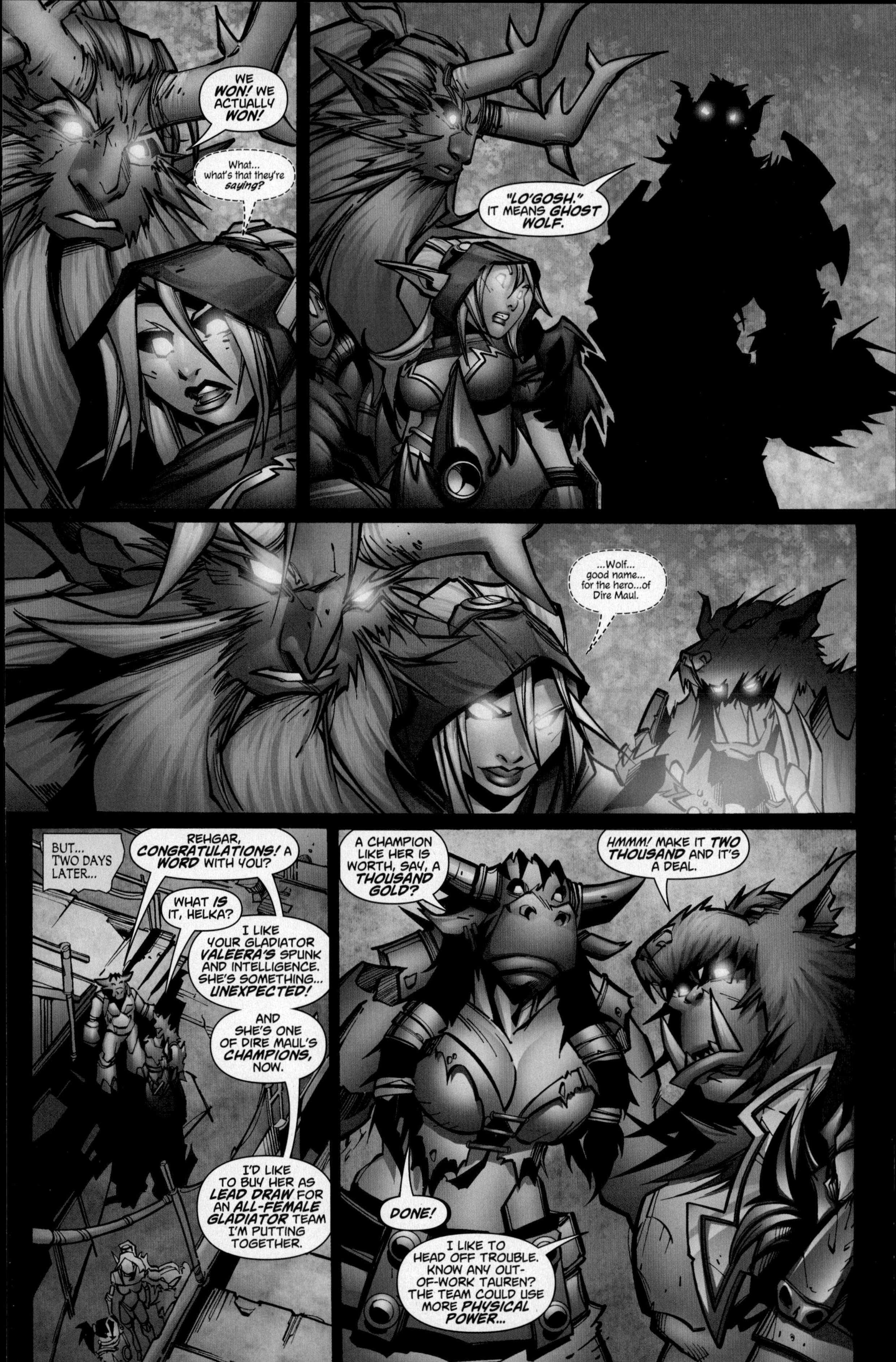
WE WON! WE ACTUALLY WON!
What... what's that they're saying?
"LO'GOSH." IT MEANS GHOST WOLF.
...Wolf... good name... for the hero...of Dire Maul.
BUT... TWO DAYS LATER...
REHGAR, CONGRATULATIONS! A WORD WITH YOU?
WHAT IS IT, HELKA?
I LIKE YOUR GLADIATOR VALEERA'S SPUNK AND INTELLIGENCE. SHE'S SOMETHING... UNEXPECTED!
AND SHE'S ONE OF DIRE MAUL'S CHAMPIONS, NOW.
I'D LIKE TO BUY HER AS LEAD DRAW FOR AN ALL-FEMALE GLADIATOR TEAM I'M PUTTING TOGETHER.
A CHAMPION LIKE HER IS WORTH, SAY, A THOUSAND GOLD?
HMMM! MAKE IT TWO THOUSAND AND IT'S A DEAL.
DONE!
I LIKE TO HEAD OFF TROUBLE. KNOW ANY OUT-OF-WORK TAUREN? THE TEAM COULD USE MORE PHYSICAL POWER...

Sketches By Ludo Lullabi

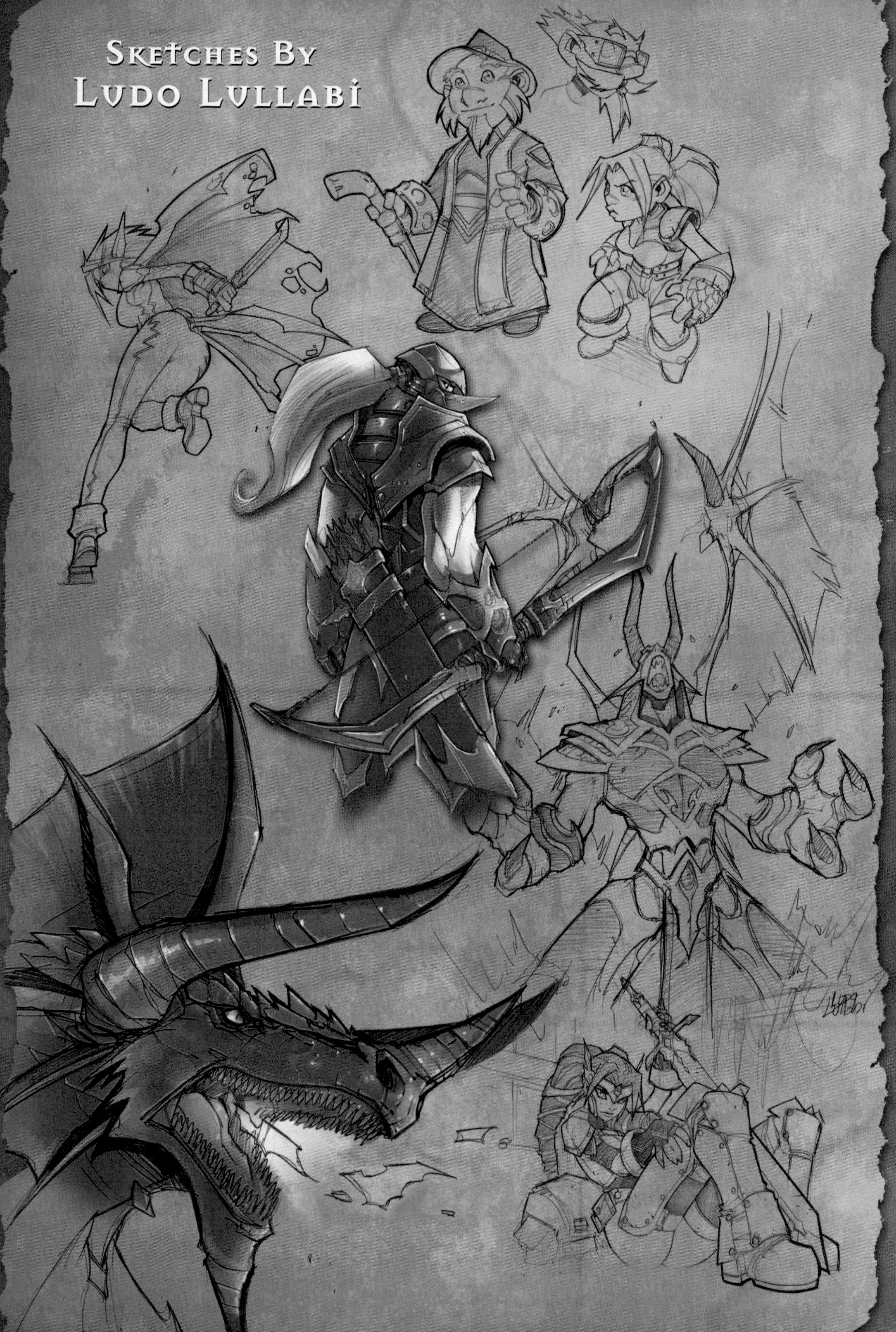

CHAPTER 3

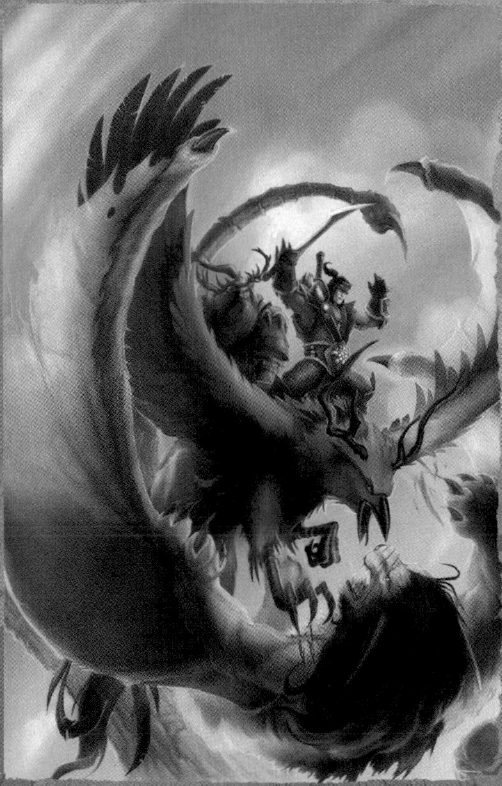

Issue #3 Cover
by Samwise Didier

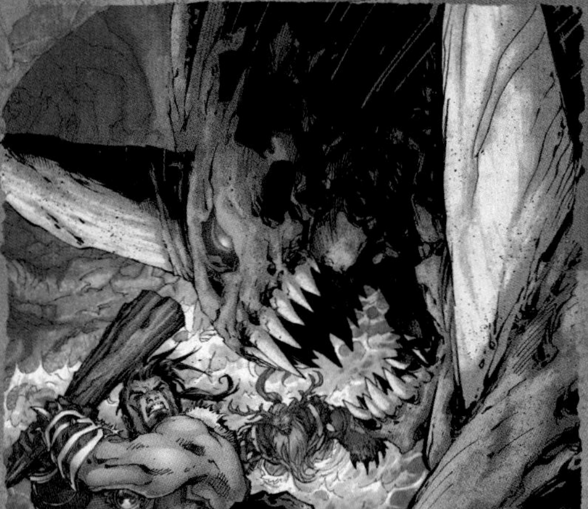

Issue #3 Cover
by Jim Lee and Alex Sinclair

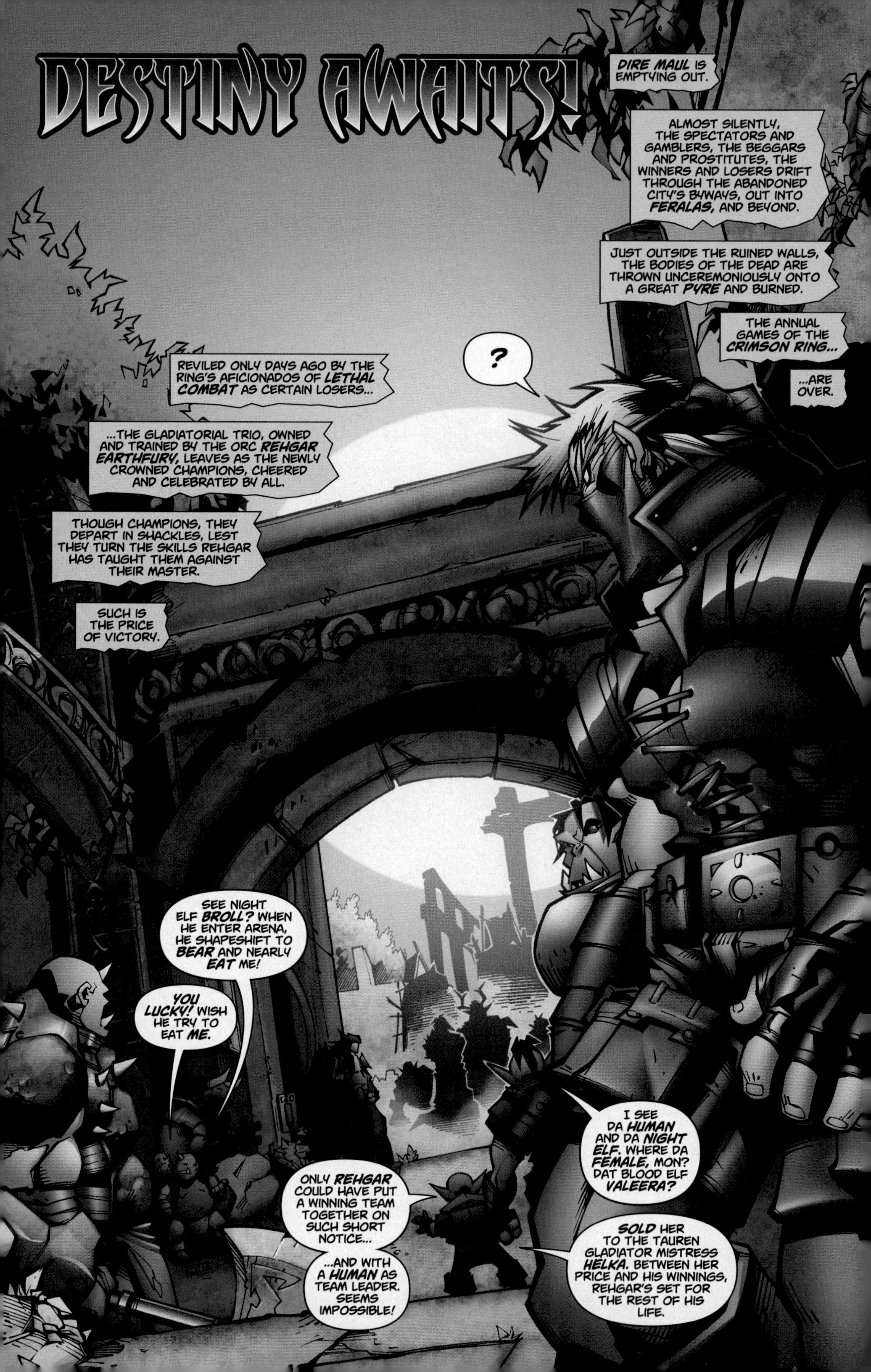
DESTINY AWAITS!
DIRE MAUL IS EMPTYING OUT.
ALMOST SILENTLY, THE SPECTATORS AND GAMBLERS, THE BEGGARS AND PROSTITUTES, THE WINNERS AND LOSERS DRIFT THROUGH THE ABANDONED CITY'S BYWAYS, OUT INTO FERALAS, AND BEYOND.
JUST OUTSIDE THE RUINED WALLS, THE BODIES OF THE DEAD ARE THROWN UNCEREMONIOUSLY ONTO A GREAT PYRE AND BURNED.
THE ANNUAL GAMES OF THE CRIMSON RING...
...ARE OVER.
?
REVILED ONLY DAYS AGO BY THE RING'S AFICIONADOS OF LETHAL COMBAT AS CERTAIN LOSERS...
...THE GLADIATORIAL TRIO, OWNED AND TRAINED BY THE ORC REHGAR EARTHFURY, LEAVES AS THE NEWLY CROWNED CHAMPIONS, CHEERED AND CELEBRATED BY ALL.
THOUGH CHAMPIONS, THEY DEPART IN SHACKLES, LEST THEY TURN THE SKILLS REHGAR HAS TAUGHT THEM AGAINST THEIR MASTER.
SUCH IS THE PRICE OF VICTORY.
SEE NIGHT ELF BROLL? WHEN HE ENTER ARENA, HE SHAPESHIFT TO BEAR AND NEARLY EAT ME!
YOU LUCKY! WISH HE TRY TO EAT ME.
I SEE DA HUMAN AND DA NIGHT ELF. WHERE DA FEMALE, MON? DAT BLOOD ELF VALEERA?
ONLY REHGAR COULD HAVE PUT A WINNING TEAM TOGETHER ON SUCH SHORT NOTICE...
...AND WITH A HUMAN AS TEAM LEADER. SEEMS IMPOSSIBLE!
SOLD HER TO THE TAUREN GLADIATOR MISTRESS HELKA. BETWEEN HER PRICE AND HIS WINNINGS, REHGAR'S SET FOR THE REST OF HIS LIFE.

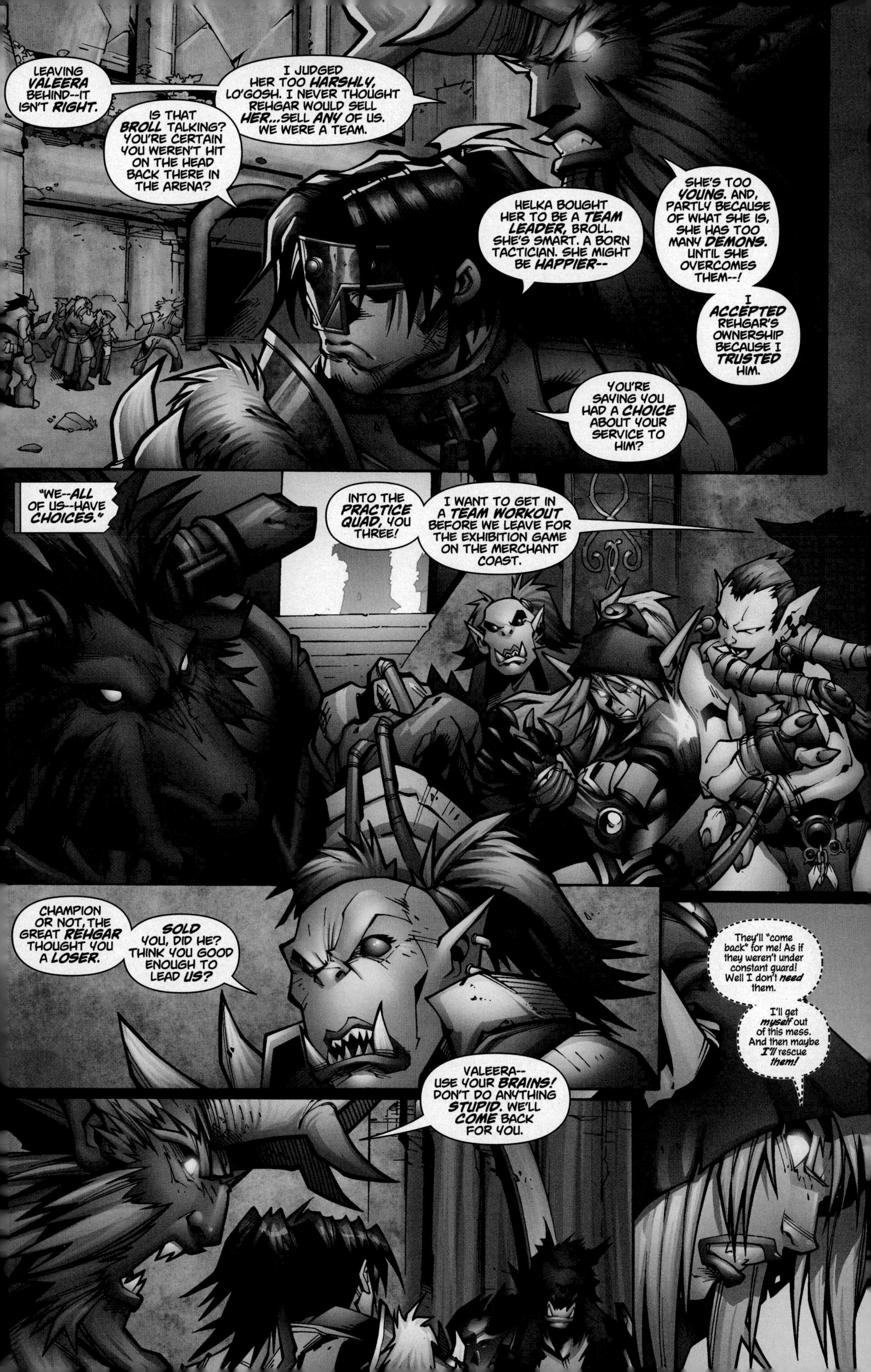
LEAVING VALEERA BEHIND--IT ISN'T RIGHT.
I JUDGED HER TOO HARSHLY, LO'GOSH. I NEVER THOUGHT REHGAR WOULD SELL HER...SELL ANY OF US. WE WERE A TEAM.
IS THAT BROLL TALKING? YOU'RE CERTAIN YOU WEREN'T HIT ON THE HEAD BACK THERE IN THE ARENA?
HELKA BOUGHT HER TO BE A TEAM LEADER, BROLL. SHE'S SMART. A BORN TACTICIAN. SHE MIGHT BE HAPPIER--
SHE'S TOO YOUNG. AND, PARTLY BECAUSE OF WHAT SHE IS, SHE HAS TOO MANY DEMONS. UNTIL SHE OVERCOMES THEM--!
I ACCEPTED REHGAR'S OWNERSHIP BECAUSE I TRUSTED HIM.
YOU'RE SAYING YOU HAD A CHOICE ABOUT YOUR SERVICE TO HIM?
"WE--ALL OF US--HAVE CHOICES."
INTO THE PRACTICE QUAD, YOU THREE!
I WANT TO GET IN A TEAM WORKOUT BEFORE WE LEAVE FOR THE EXHIBITION GAME ON THE MERCHANT COAST.
CHAMPION OR NOT, THE GREAT REHGAR THOUGHT YOU A LOSER.
SOLD YOU, DID HE? THINK YOU GOOD ENOUGH TO LEAD US?
They'll "come back" for me! As if they weren't under constant guard! Well I don't need them.
I'll get myself out of this mess. And then maybe I'll rescue them!
VALEERA-- USE YOUR BRAINS! DON'T DO ANYTHING STUPID. WE'LL COME BACK FOR YOU.

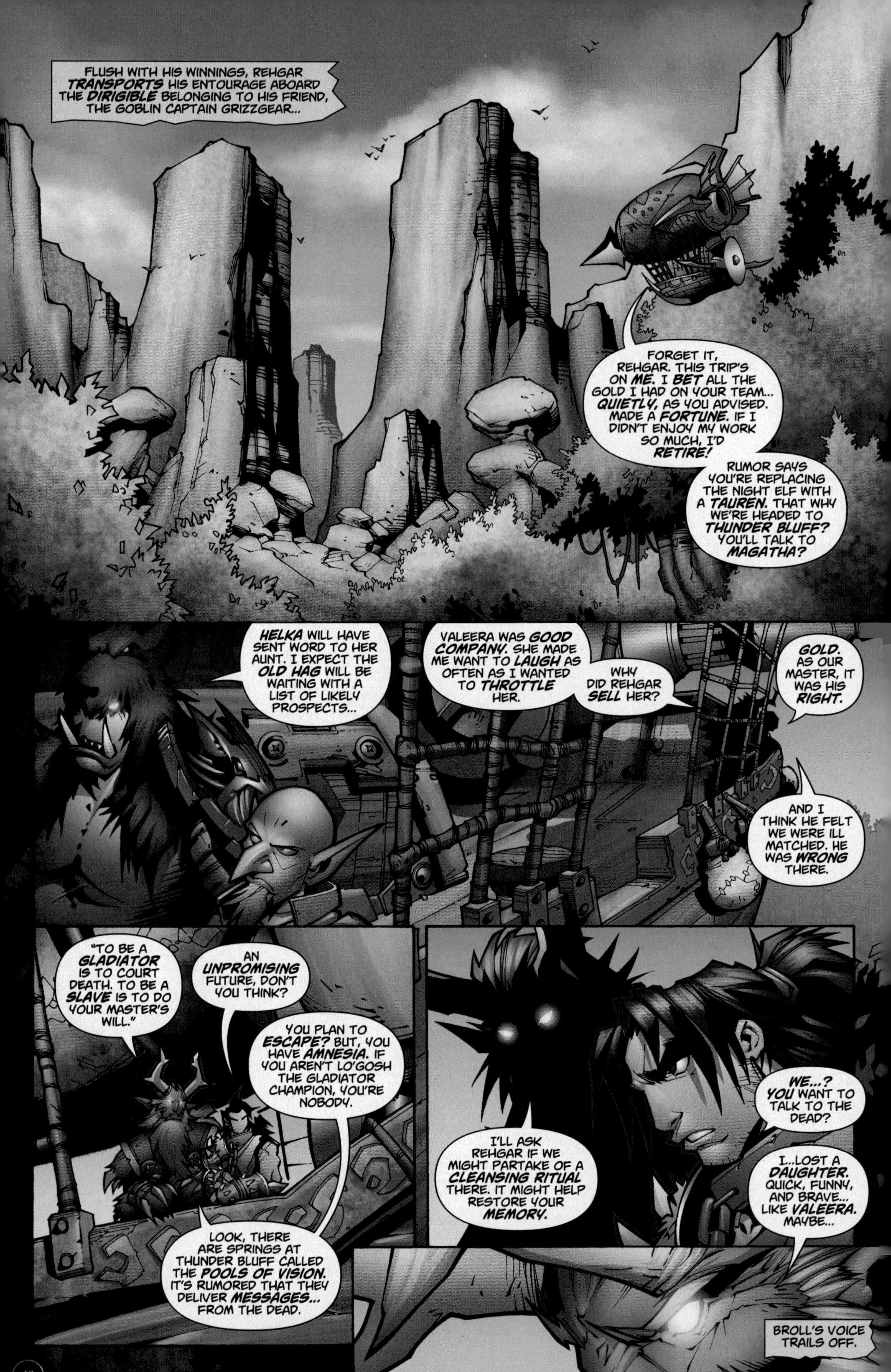
FLUSH WITH HIS WINNINGS, REHGAR TRANSPORTS HIS ENTOURAGE ABOARD THE DIRIGIBLE BELONGING TO HIS FRIEND, THE GOBLIN CAPTAIN GRIZZGEAR...
FORGET IT, REHGAR. THIS TRIP'S ON ME. I BET ALL THE GOLD I HAD ON YOUR TEAM... QUIETLY, AS YOU ADVISED. MADE A FORTUNE. IF I DIDN'T ENJOY MY WORK SO MUCH, I'D RETIRE!
RUMOR SAYS YOU'RE REPLACING THE NIGHT ELF WITH A TAUREN. THAT WHY WE'RE HEADED TO THUNDER BLUFF? YOU'LL TALK TO MAGATHA?
HELKA WILL HAVE SENT WORD TO HER AUNT. I EXPECT THE OLD HAG WILL BE WAITING WITH A LIST OF LIKELY PROSPECTS...
VALEERA WAS GOOD COMPANY. SHE MADE ME WANT TO LAUGH AS OFTEN AS I WANTED TO THROTTLE HER.
WHY DID REHGAR SELL HER?
GOLD. AS OUR MASTER, IT WAS HIS RIGHT.
AND I THINK HE FELT WE WERE ILL MATCHED. HE WAS WRONG THERE.
"TO BE A GLADIATOR IS TO COURT DEATH. TO BE A SLAVE IS TO DO YOUR MASTER'S WILL."
AN UNPROMISING FUTURE, DON'T YOU THINK?
YOU PLAN TO ESCAPE? BUT, YOU HAVE AMNESIA. IF YOU AREN'T LO'GOSH THE GLADIATOR CHAMPION, YOU'RE NOBODY.
LOOK, THERE ARE SPRINGS AT THUNDER BLUFF CALLED THE POOLS OF VISION. IT'S RUMORED THAT THEY DELIVER MESSAGES... FROM THE DEAD.
I'LL ASK REHGAR IF WE MIGHT PARTAKE OF A CLEANSING RITUAL THERE. IT MIGHT HELP RESTORE YOUR MEMORY.
WE...? YOU WANT TO TALK TO THE DEAD?
I...LOST A DAUGHTER. QUICK, FUNNY, AND BRAVE... LIKE VALEERA. MAYBE...
BROLL'S VOICE TRAILS OFF.

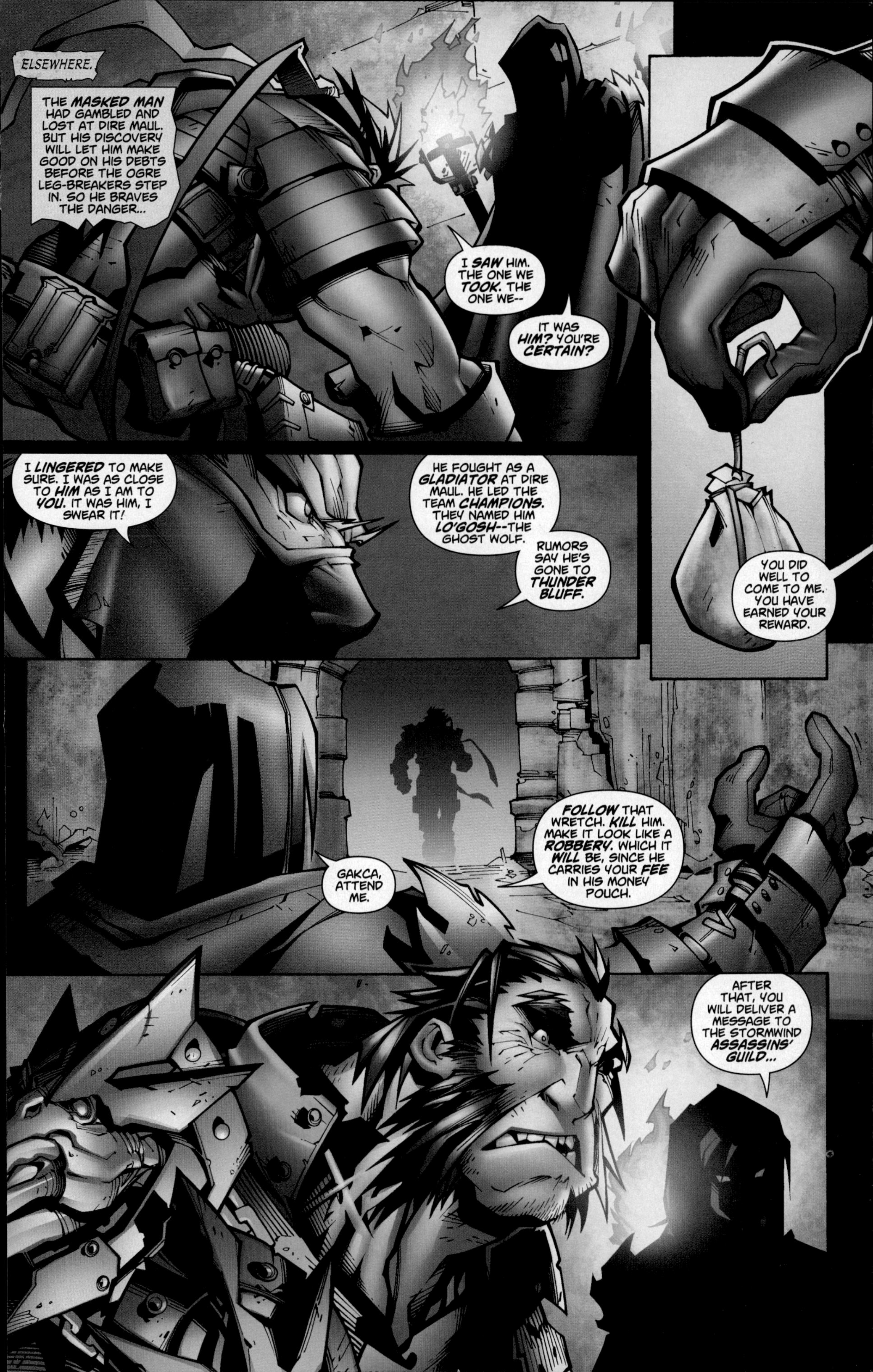
ELSEWHERE.
THE MASKED MAN HAD GAMBLED AND LOST AT DIRE MAUL. BUT HIS DISCOVERY WILL LET HIM MAKE GOOD ON HIS DEBTS BEFORE THE OGRE LEG-BREAKERS STEP IN. SO HE BRAVES THE DANGER...
I SAW HIM. THE ONE WE TOOK. THE ONE WE--
IT WAS HIM? YOU'RE CERTAIN?
I LINGERED TO MAKE SURE. I WAS AS CLOSE TO HIM AS I AM TO YOU. IT WAS HIM, I SWEAR IT!
HE FOUGHT AS A GLADIATOR AT DIRE MAUL. HE LED THE TEAM CHAMPIONS. THEY NAMED HIM LO'GOSH--THE GHOST WOLF.
RUMORS SAY HE'S GONE TO THUNDER BLUFF.
YOU DID WELL TO COME TO ME. YOU HAVE EARNED YOUR REWARD.
GAKCA, ATTEND ME.
FOLLOW THAT WRETCH. KILL HIM. MAKE IT LOOK LIKE A ROBBERY. WHICH IT WILL BE, SINCE HE CARRIES YOUR FEE IN HIS MONEY POUCH.
AFTER THAT, YOU WILL DELIVER A MESSAGE TO THE STORMWIND ASSASSINS' GUILD...

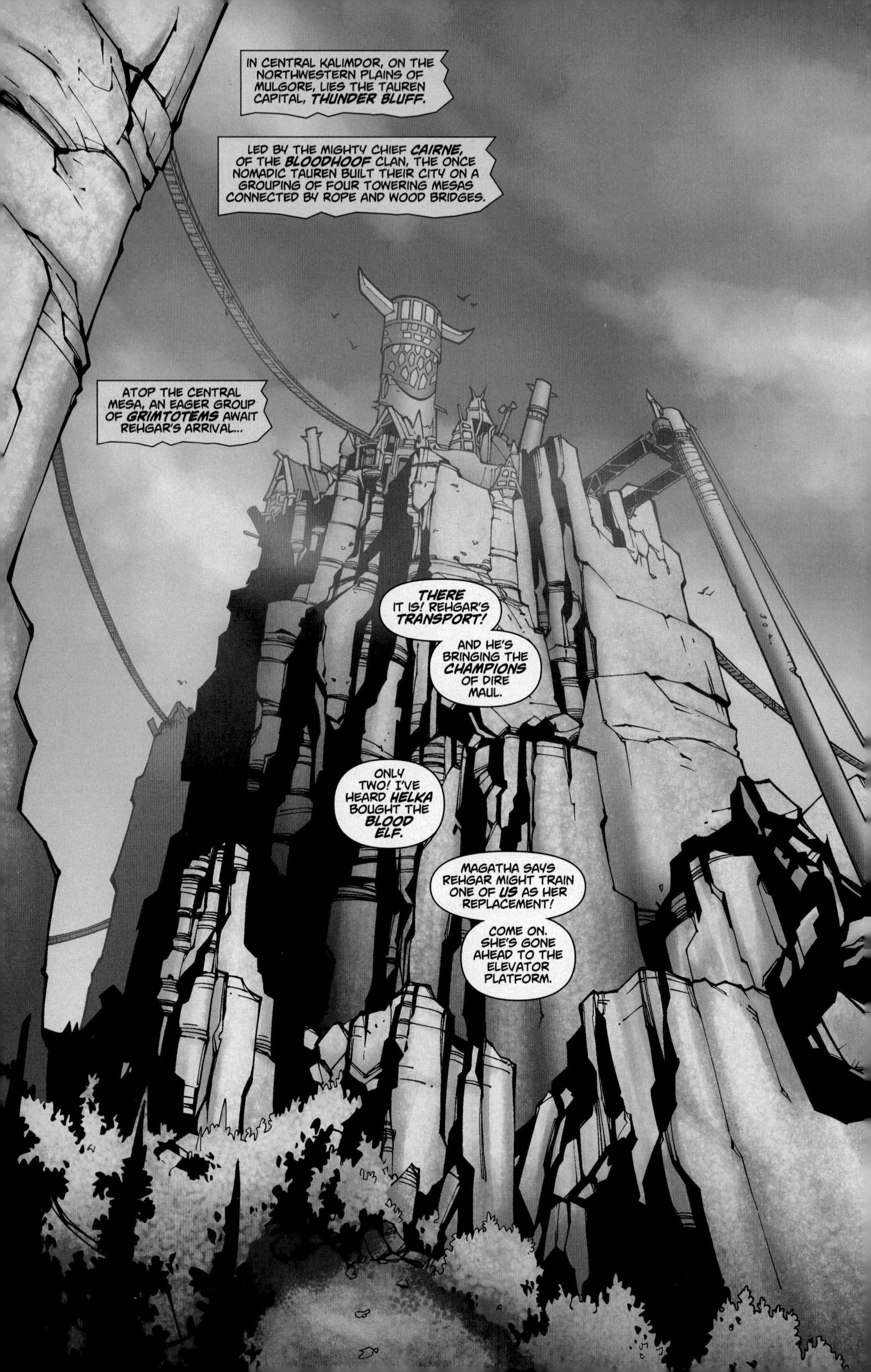
IN CENTRAL KALIMDOR, ON THE NORTHWESTERN PLAINS OF MULGORE, LIES THE TAUREN CAPITAL, THUNDER BLUFF.
LED BY THE MIGHTY CHIEF CAIRNE, OF THE BLOODHOOF CLAN, THE ONCE NOMADIC TAUREN BUILT THEIR CITY ON A GROUPING OF FOUR TOWERING MESAS CONNECTED BY ROPE AND WOOD BRIDGES.
ATOP THE CENTRAL MESA, AN EAGER GROUP OF GRIMTOTEMS AWAIT REHGAR'S ARRIVAL...
THERE IT IS! REHGAR'S TRANSPORT!
AND HE'S BRINGING THE CHAMPIONS OF DIRE MAUL.
ONLY TWO! I'VE HEARD HELKA BOUGHT THE BLOOD ELF.
MAGATHA SAYS REHGAR MIGHT TRAIN ONE OF US AS HER REPLACEMENT!
COME ON. SHE'S GONE AHEAD TO THE ELEVATOR PLATFORM.

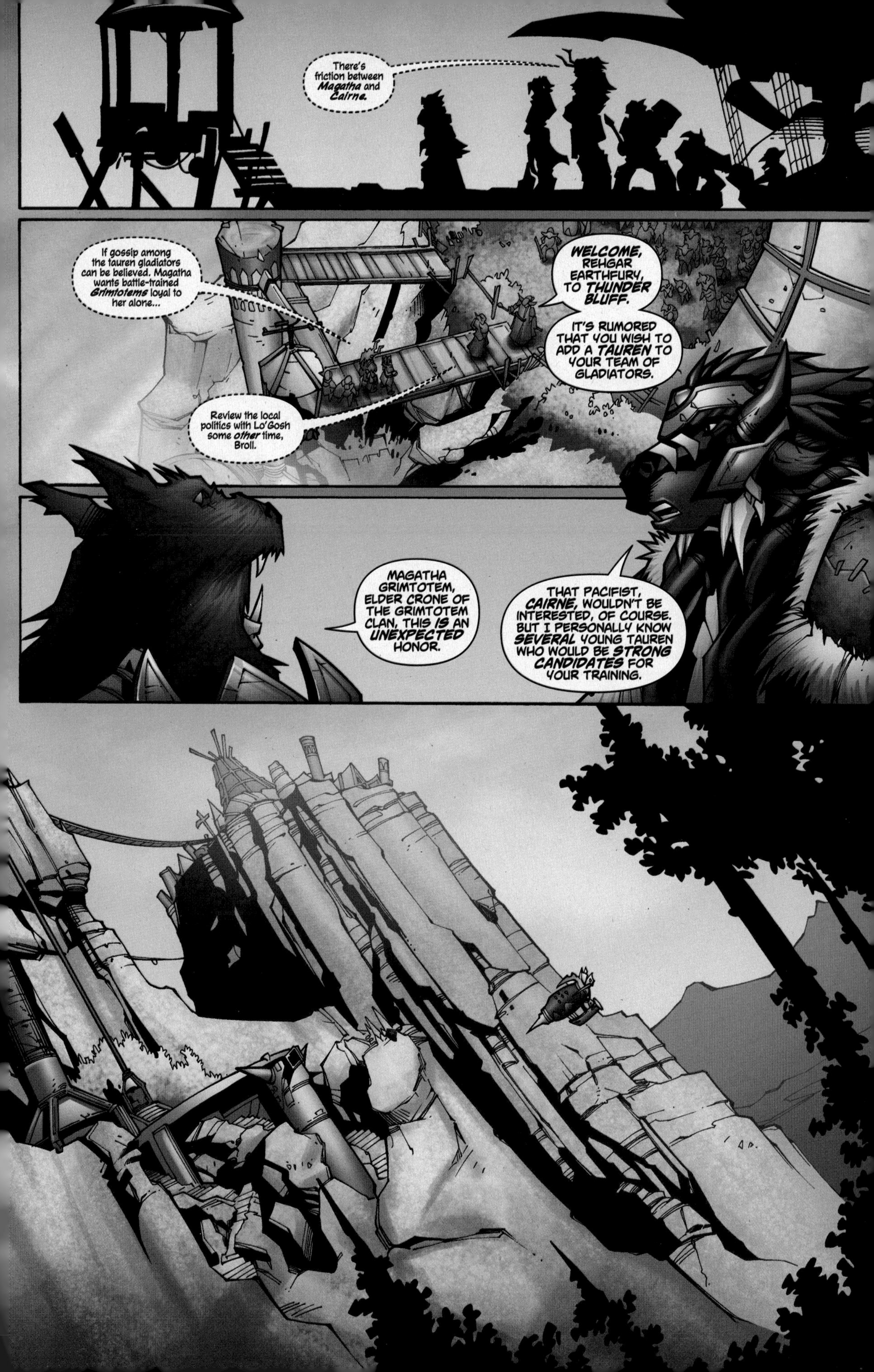
There's friction between Magatha and Cairne.
If gossip among the tauren gladiators can be believed. Magatha wants battle-trained Grimtotems loyal to her alone...
Review the local politics with Lo'Gosh some other time, Broll.
WELCOME, REHGAR EARTHFURY, TO THUNDER BLUFF.
IT'S RUMORED THAT YOU WISH TO ADD A TAUREN TO YOUR TEAM OF GLADIATORS.
MAGATHA GRIMTOTEM, ELDER CRONE OF THE GRIMTOTEM CLAN, THIS IS AN UNEXPECTED HONOR.
THAT PACIFIST, CAIRNE, WOULDN'T BE INTERESTED, OF COURSE. BUT I PERSONALLY KNOW SEVERAL YOUNG TAUREN WHO WOULD BE STRONG CANDIDATES FOR YOUR TRAINING.

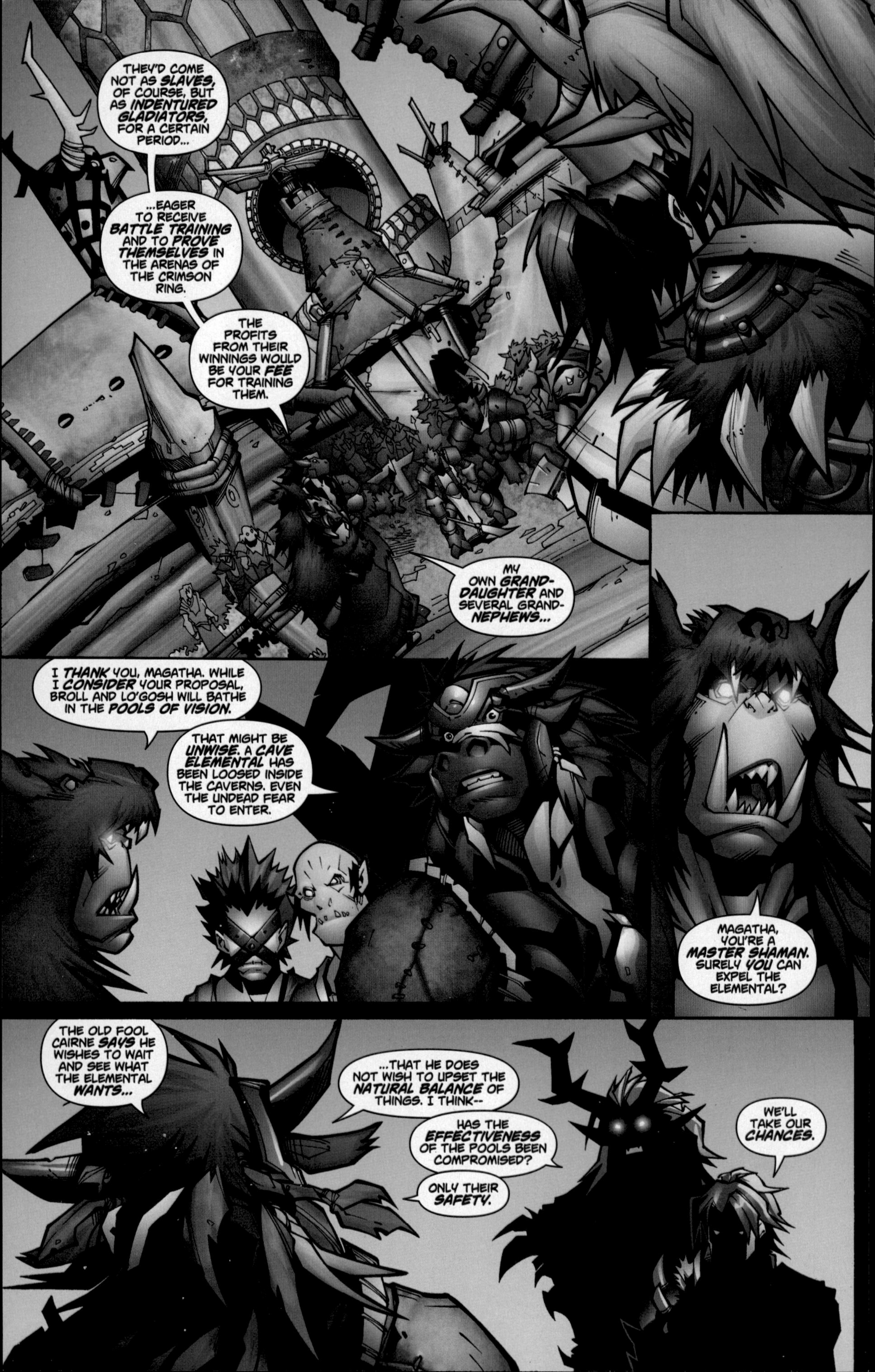
THEY'D COME NOT AS SLAVES, OF COURSE, BUT AS INDENTURED GLADIATORS, FOR A CERTAIN PERIOD...
...EAGER TO RECEIVE BATTLE TRAINING AND TO PROVE THEMSELVES IN THE ARENAS OF THE CRIMSON RING.
THE PROFITS FROM THEIR WINNINGS WOULD BE YOUR FEE FOR TRAINING THEM.
MY OWN GRAND-DAUGHTER AND SEVERAL GRAND-NEPHEWS...
I THANK YOU, MAGATHA. WHILE I CONSIDER YOUR PROPOSAL, BROLL AND LO'GOSH WILL BATHE IN THE POOLS OF VISION.
THAT MIGHT BE UNWISE. A CAVE ELEMENTAL HAS BEEN LOOSED INSIDE THE CAVERNS. EVEN THE UNDEAD FEAR TO ENTER.
MAGATHA, YOU'RE A MASTER SHAMAN. SURELY YOU CAN EXPEL THE ELEMENTAL?
THE OLD FOOL CAIRNE SAYS HE WISHES TO WAIT AND SEE WHAT THE ELEMENTAL WANTS...
...THAT HE DOES NOT WISH TO UPSET THE NATURAL BALANCE OF THINGS. I THINK--
HAS THE EFFECTIVENESS OF THE POOLS BEEN COMPROMISED?
ONLY THEIR SAFETY.
WE'LL TAKE OUR CHANCES.

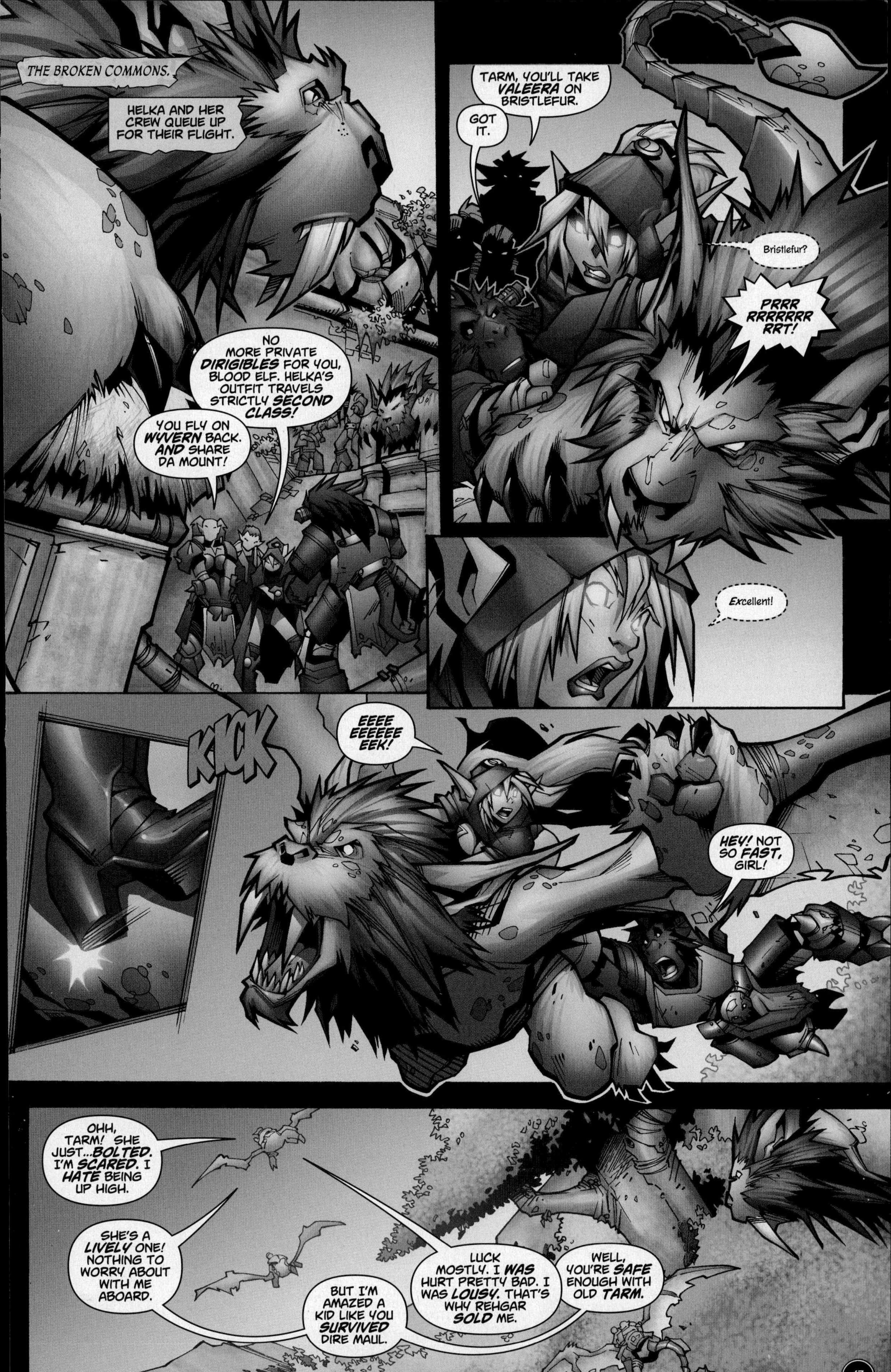

THE BROKEN COMMONS.
HELKA AND HER CREW QUEUE UP FOR THEIR FLIGHT.
NO MORE PRIVATE DIRIGIBLES FOR YOU, BLOOD ELF. HELKA'S OUTFIT TRAVELS STRICTLY SECOND CLASS!
YOU FLY ON WYVERN BACK. AND SHARE DA MOUNT!
TARM, YOU'LL TAKE VALEERA ON BRISTLEFUR.
GOT IT.
Bristlefur?
PRRR RRRRRRR RRT!
Excellent!
KICK
EEEE EEEEEE EEK!
HEY! NOT SO FAST, GIRL!
OHH, TARM! SHE JUST...BOLTED. I'M SCARED. I HATE BEING UP HIGH.
SHE'S A LIVELY ONE! NOTHING TO WORRY ABOUT WITH ME ABOARD.
BUT I'M AMAZED A KID LIKE YOU SURVIVED DIRE MAUL.
LUCK MOSTLY. I WAS HURT PRETTY BAD. I WAS LOUSY. THAT'S WHY REHGAR SOLD ME.
WELL, YOU'RE SAFE ENOUGH WITH OLD TARM.

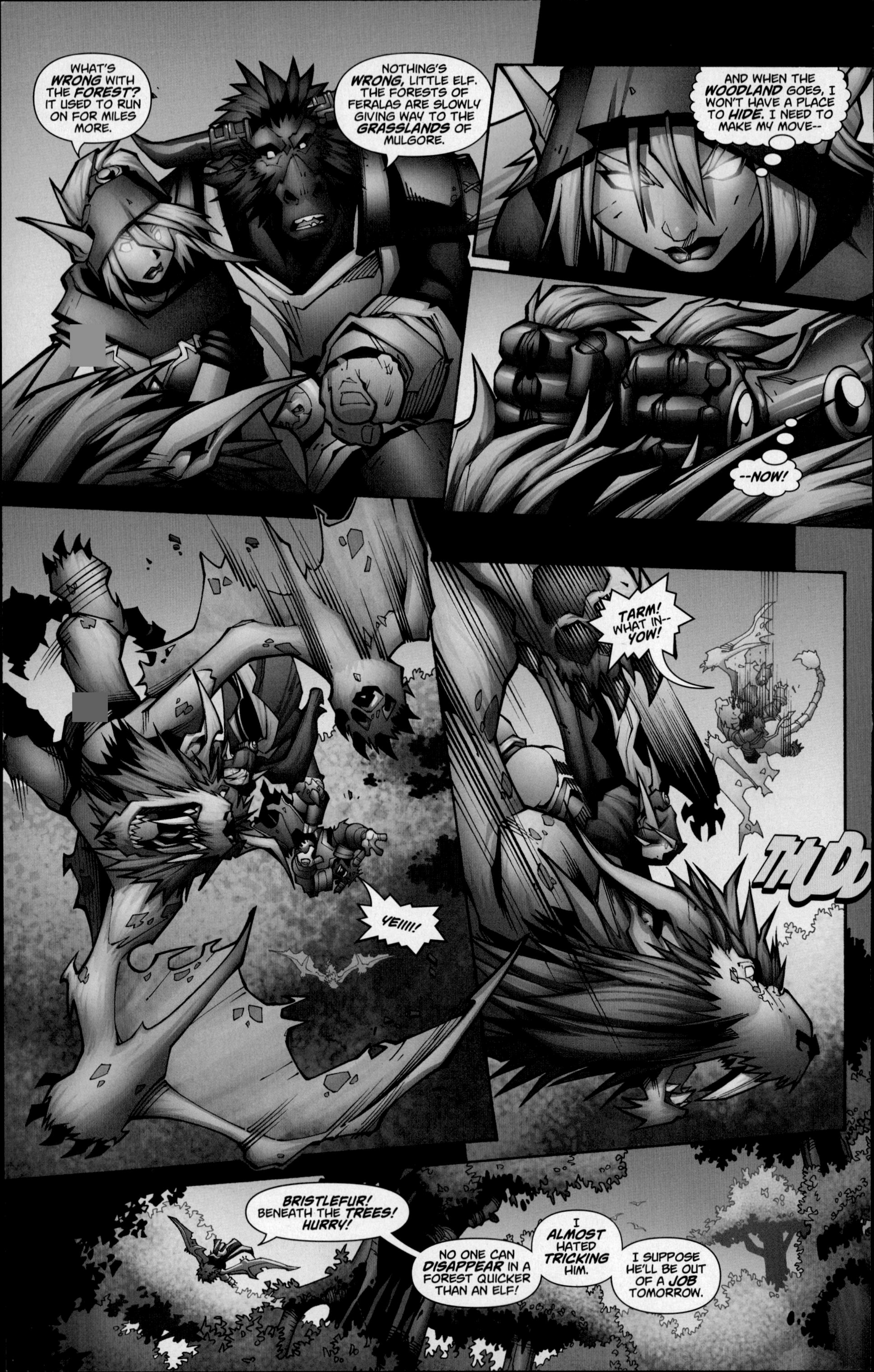
WHAT'S WRONG WITH THE FOREST? IT USED TO RUN ON FOR MILES MORE.
NOTHING'S WRONG, LITTLE ELF. THE FORESTS OF FERALAS ARE SLOWLY GIVING WAY TO THE GRASSLANDS OF MULGORE.
AND WHEN THE WOODLAND GOES, I WON'T HAVE A PLACE TO HIDE. I NEED TO MAKE MY MOVE--
--NOW!
YE!!!!!
TARM! WHAT IN-- YOW!
THUD
BRISTLEFUR! BENEATH THE TREES! HURRY!
NO ONE CAN DISAPPEAR IN A FOREST QUICKER THAN AN ELF!
I ALMOST HATED TRICKING HIM.
I SUPPOSE HE'LL BE OUT OF A JOB TOMORROW.

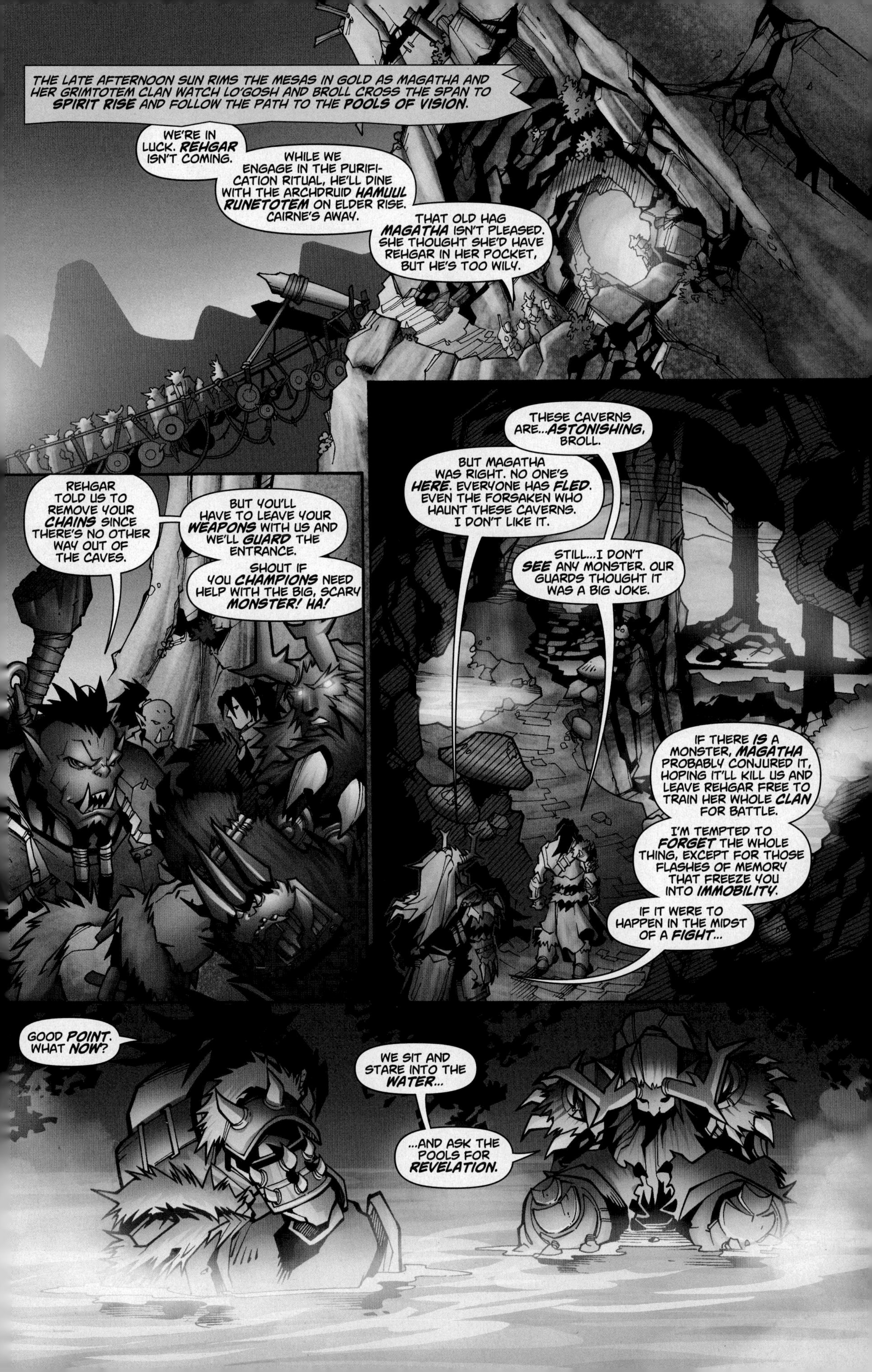
THE LATE AFTERNOON SUN RIMS THE MESAS IN GOLD AS MAGATHA AND HER GRIMTOTEM CLAN WATCH LO'GOSH AND BROLL CROSS THE SPAN TO SPIRIT RISE AND FOLLOW THE PATH TO THE POOLS OF VISION.
WE'RE IN LUCK. REHGAR ISN'T COMING.
WHILE WE ENGAGE IN THE PURIFICATION RITUAL, HE'LL DINE WITH THE ARCHDRUID HAMUUL RUNETOTEM ON ELDER RISE. CAIRNE'S AWAY.
THAT OLD HAG MAGATHA ISN'T PLEASED. SHE THOUGHT SHE'D HAVE REHGAR IN HER POCKET, BUT HE'S TOO WILY.
REHGAR TOLD US TO REMOVE YOUR CHAINS SINCE THERE'S NO OTHER WAY OUT OF THE CAVES.
BUT YOU'LL HAVE TO LEAVE YOUR WEAPONS WITH US AND WE'LL GUARD THE ENTRANCE.
SHOUT IF YOU CHAMPIONS NEED HELP WITH THE BIG, SCARY MONSTER! HA!
THESE CAVERNS ARE...ASTONISHING, BROLL.
BUT MAGATHA WAS RIGHT. NO ONE'S HERE. EVERYONE HAS FLED. EVEN THE FORSAKEN WHO HAUNT THESE CAVERNS. I DON'T LIKE IT.
STILL...I DON'T SEE ANY MONSTER. OUR GUARDS THOUGHT IT WAS A BIG JOKE.
IF THERE IS A MONSTER, MAGATHA PROBABLY CONJURED IT, HOPING IT'LL KILL US AND LEAVE REHGAR FREE TO TRAIN HER WHOLE CLAN FOR BATTLE.
I'M TEMPTED TO FORGET THE WHOLE THING, EXCEPT FOR THOSE FLASHES OF MEMORY THAT FREEZE YOU INTO IMMOBILITY.
IF IT WERE TO HAPPEN IN THE MIDST OF A FIGHT...
GOOD POINT. WHAT NOW?
WE SIT AND STARE INTO THE WATER...
...AND ASK THE POOLS FOR REVELATION.

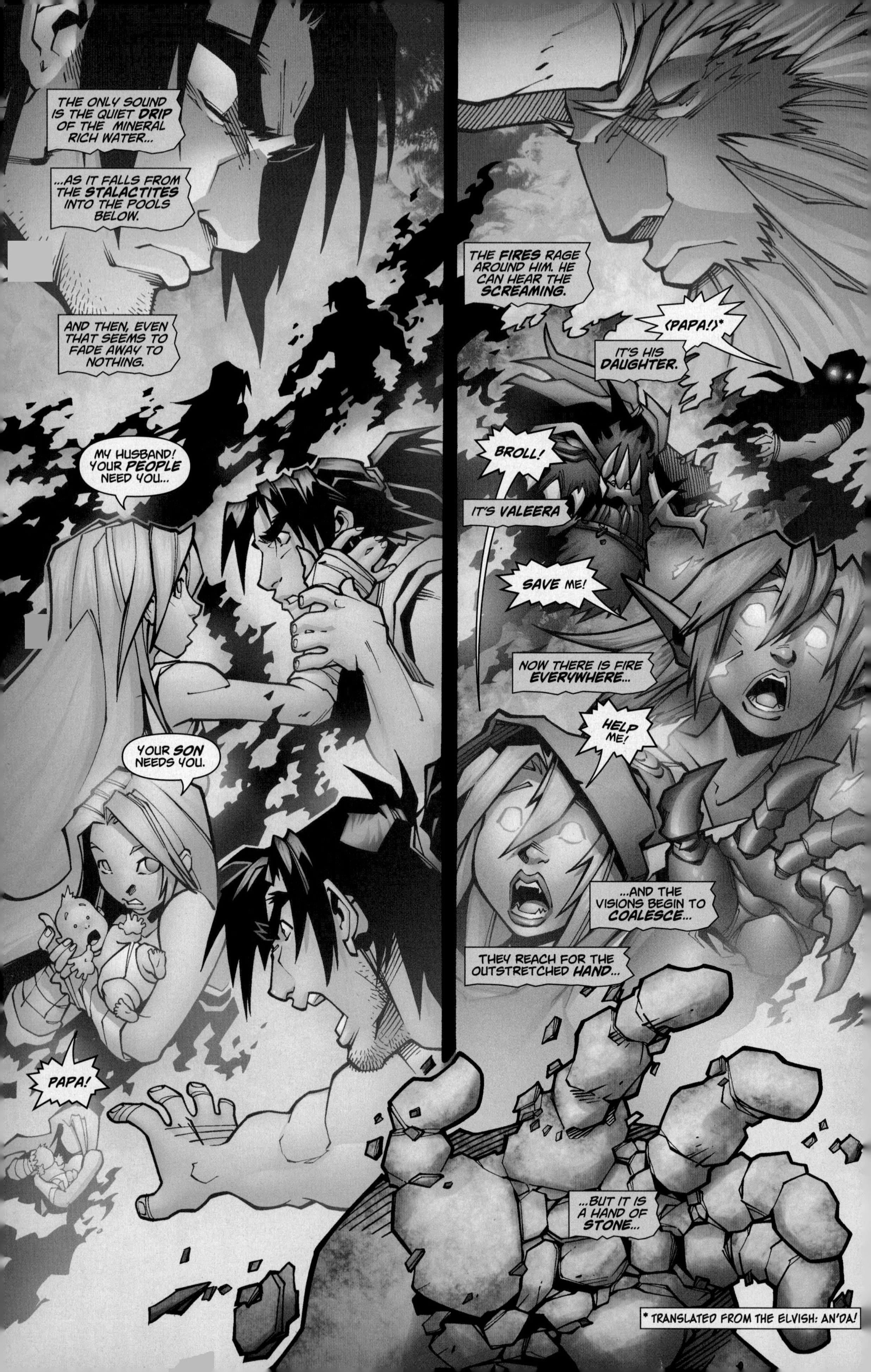
THE ONLY SOUND IS THE QUIET DRIP OF THE MINERAL RICH WATER...
...AS IT FALLS FROM THE STALACTITES INTO THE POOLS BELOW.
AND THEN, EVEN THAT SEEMS TO FADE AWAY TO NOTHING.
MY HUSBAND! YOUR PEOPLE NEED YOU...
YOUR SON NEEDS YOU.
PAPA!
THE FIRES RAGE AROUND HIM. HE CAN HEAR THE SCREAMING.
(PAPA!)*
IT'S HIS DAUGHTER.
BROLL!
IT'S VALEERA
SAVE ME!
NOW THERE IS FIRE EVERYWHERE...
HELP ME!
...AND THE VISIONS BEGIN TO COALESCE...
THEY REACH FOR THE OUTSTRETCHED HAND...
...BUT IT IS A HAND OF STONE...
* TRANSLATED FROM THE ELVISH: AN'DA!

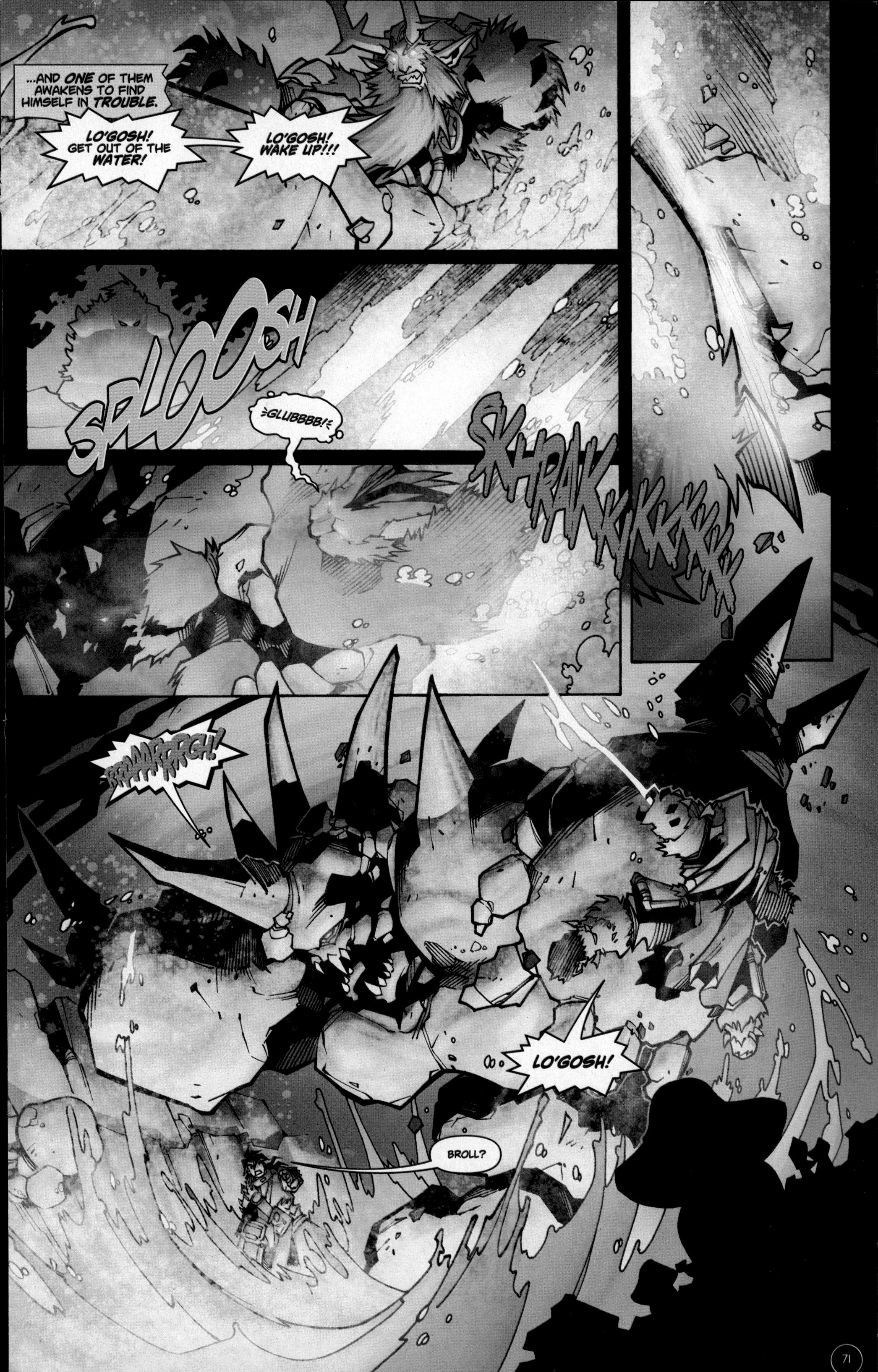
...AND ONE OF THEM AWAKENS TO FIND HIMSELF IN TROUBLE.
LO'GOSH! GET OUT OF THE WATER!
LO'GOSH! WAKE UP!!!
SPLOOOSH
GLUBBBB!
SKHRAKKKKKKK
BRAAARRRGH!
LO'GOSH!
BROLL?

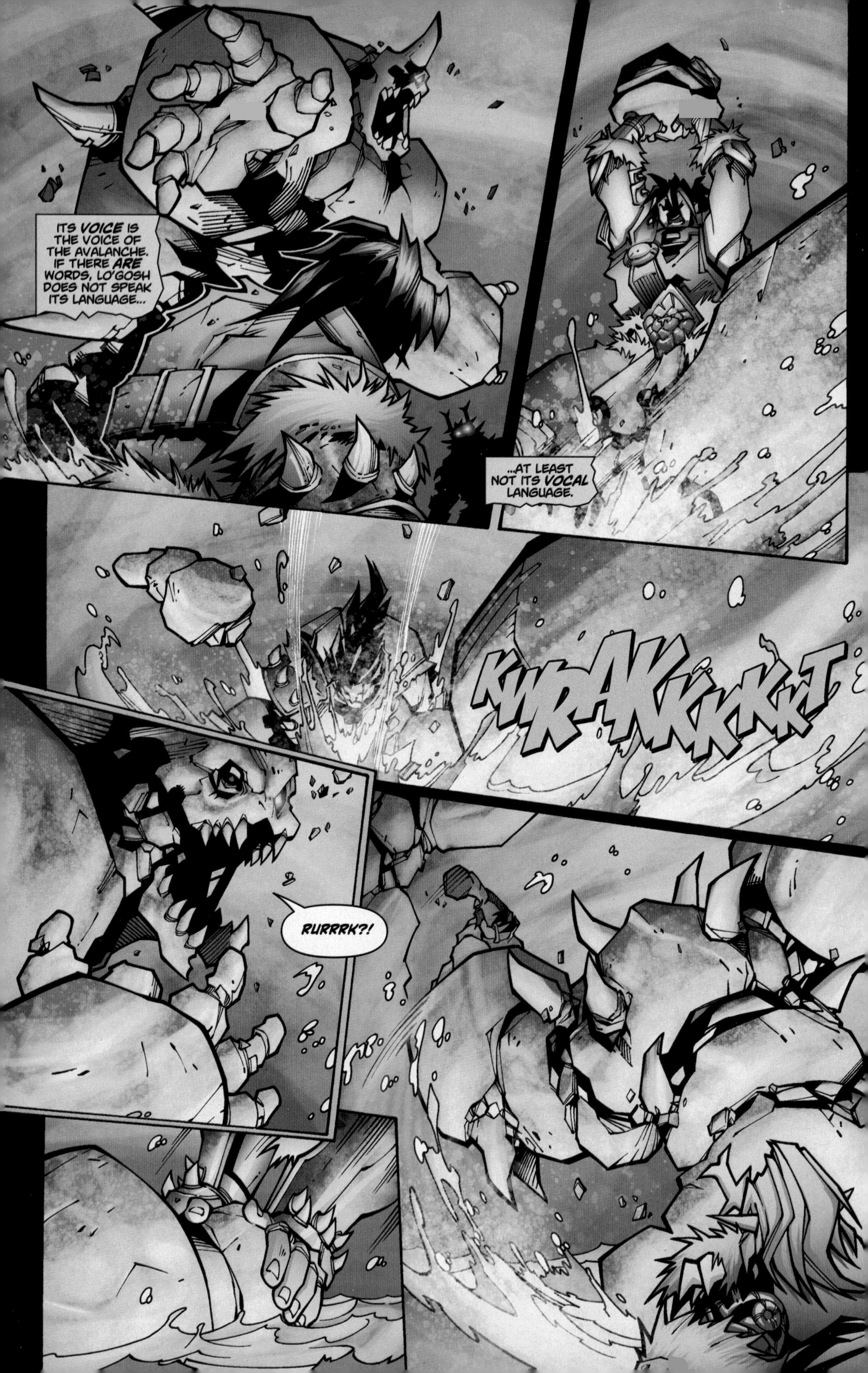
ITS VOICE IS THE VOICE OF THE AVALANCHE. IF THERE ARE WORDS, LO'GOSH DOES NOT SPEAK ITS LANGUAGE...
...AT LEAST NOT ITS VOCAL LANGUAGE.
KWRAKKKKKKT
RURRRK?!

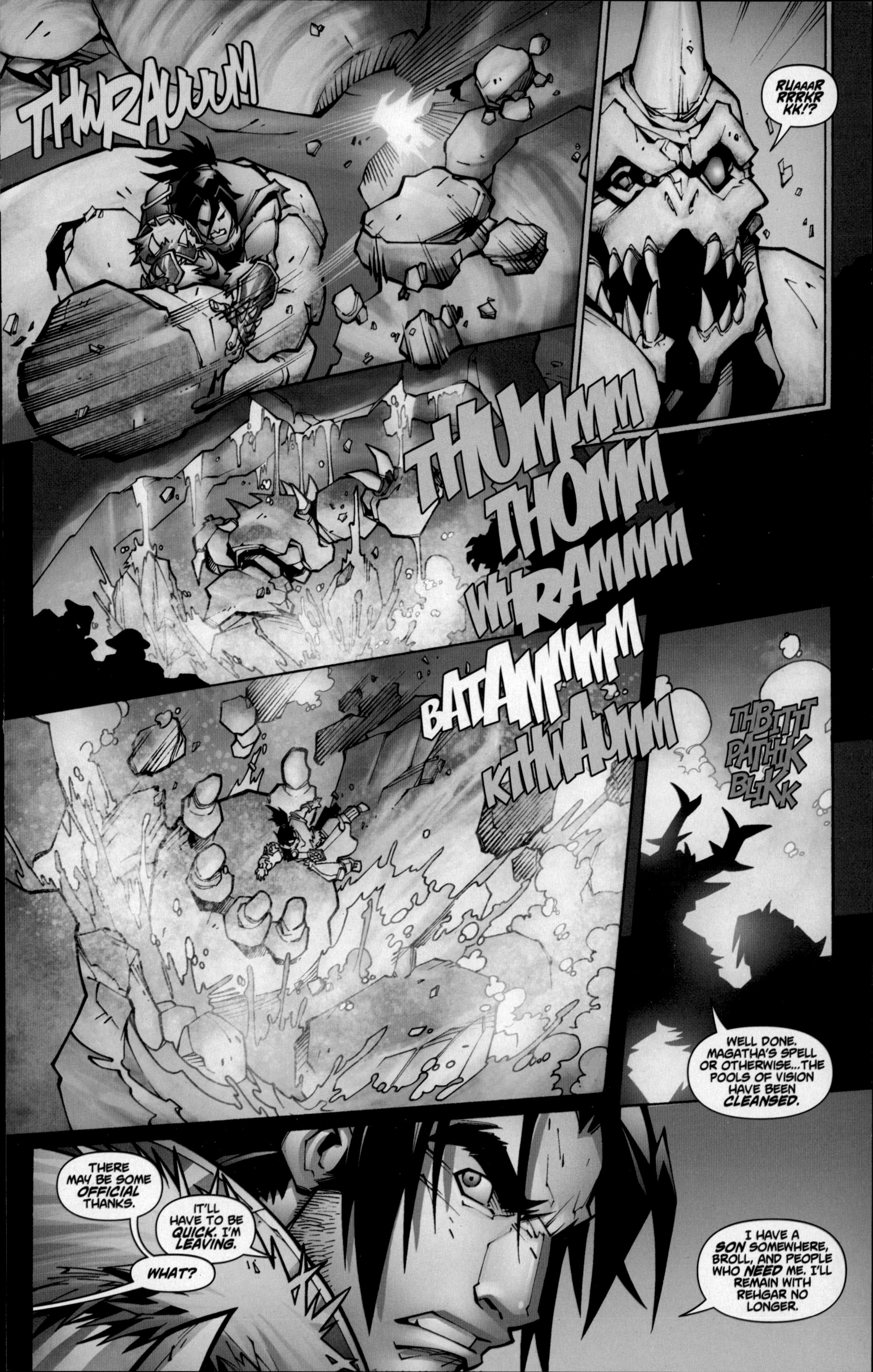
THWRAUUUM
RUAAAR RRRKR KK!?
THUMMM
THOMM
WHRAMMM
BATAMMM
KTHWAUMM
THBITT PATHIK BLIKK
WELL DONE. MAGATHA'S SPELL OR OTHERWISE... THE POOLS OF VISION HAVE BEEN CLEANSED.
THERE MAY BE SOME OFFICIAL THANKS.
IT'LL HAVE TO BE QUICK. I'M LEAVING.
WHAT?
I HAVE A SON SOMEWHERE, BROLL, AND PEOPLE WHO NEED ME. I'LL REMAIN WITH REHGAR NO LONGER.

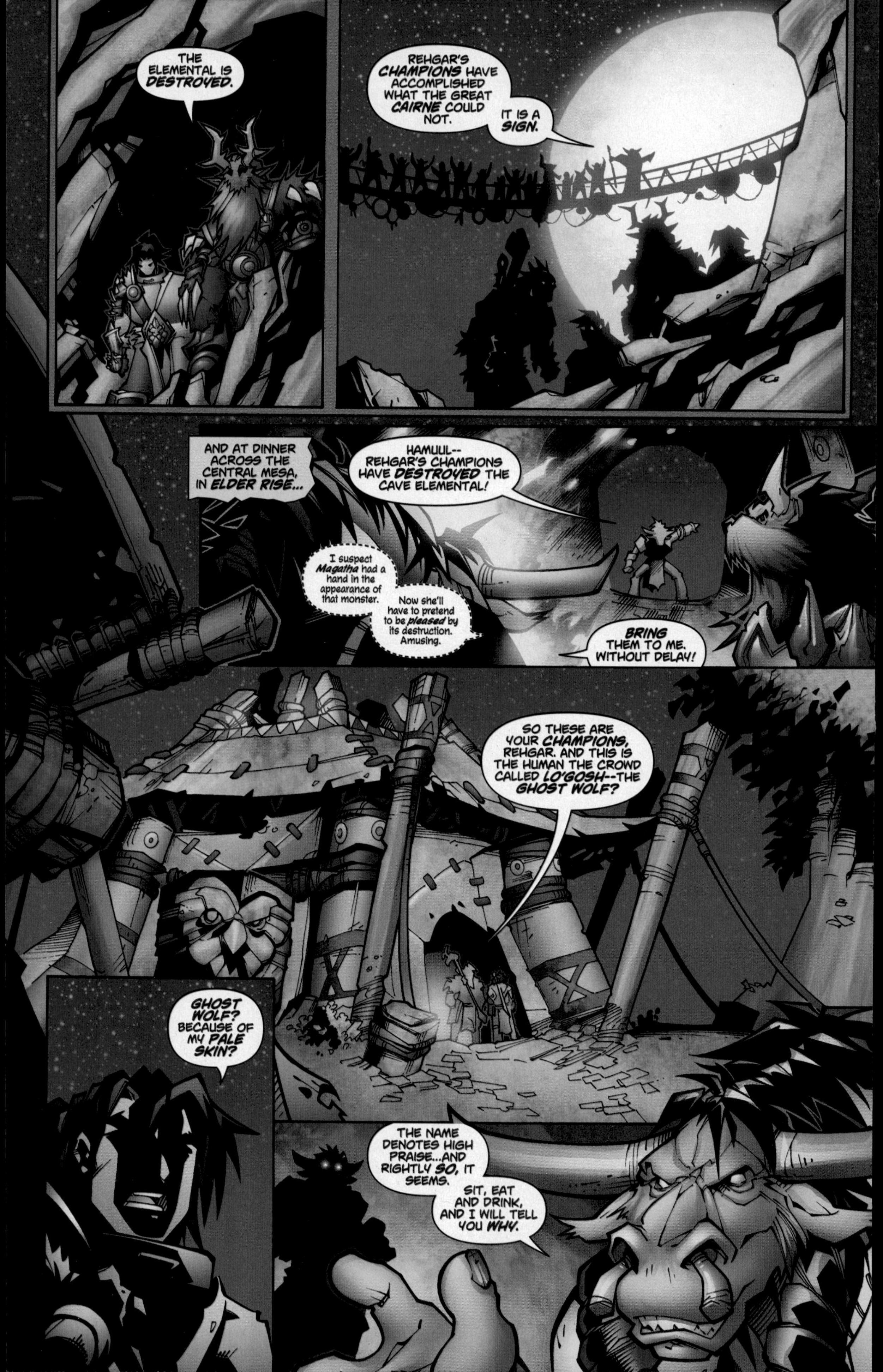
THE ELEMENTAL IS DESTROYED.
REHGAR'S CHAMPIONS HAVE ACCOMPLISHED WHAT THE GREAT CAIRNE COULD NOT.
IT IS A SIGN.
AND AT DINNER ACROSS THE CENTRAL MESA, IN ELDER RISE...
HAMUUL-- REHGAR'S CHAMPIONS HAVE DESTROYED THE CAVE ELEMENTAL!
I suspect Magatha had a hand in the appearance of that monster.
Now she'll have to pretend to be pleased by its destruction. Amusing.
BRING THEM TO ME. WITHOUT DELAY!
SO THESE ARE YOUR CHAMPIONS, REHGAR. AND THIS IS THE HUMAN THE CROWD CALLED LO'GOSH--THE GHOST WOLF?
GHOST WOLF? BECAUSE OF MY PALE SKIN?
THE NAME DENOTES HIGH PRAISE...AND RIGHTLY SO, IT SEEMS.
SIT, EAT AND DRINK, AND I WILL TELL YOU WHY.

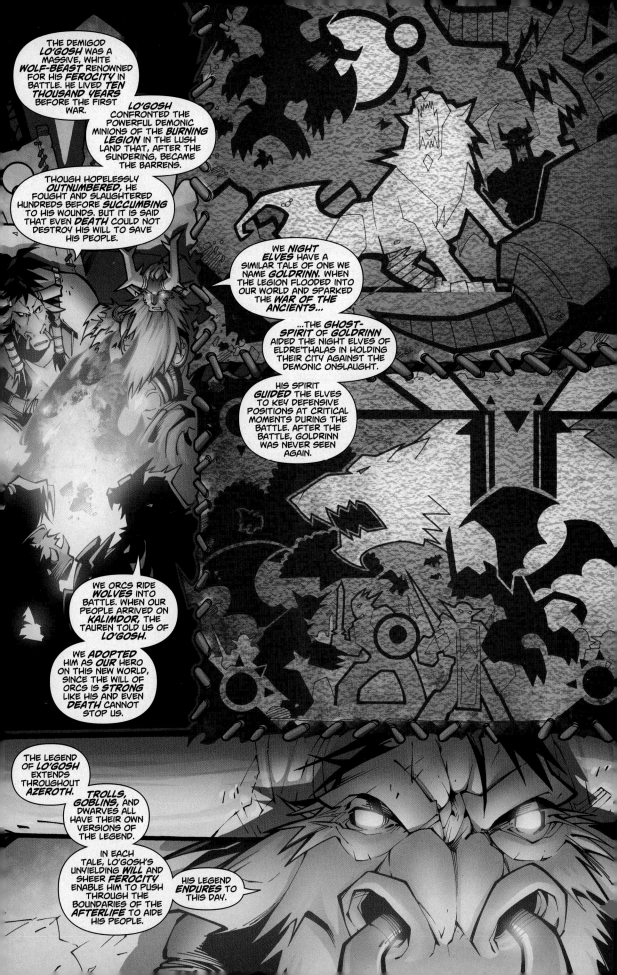

THE DEMIGOD *LO'GOSH* WAS A MASSIVE, WHITE *WOLF-BEAST* RENOWNED FOR HIS *FEROCITY* IN BATTLE. HE LIVED *TEN THOUSAND YEARS* BEFORE THE FIRST WAR.

LO'GOSH CONFRONTED THE POWERFUL DEMONIC MINIONS OF THE *BURNING LEGION* IN THE LUSH LAND THAT, AFTER THE SUNDERING, BECAME THE BARRENS.

THOUGH HOPELESSLY *OUTNUMBERED,* HE FOUGHT AND SLAUGHTERED HUNDREDS BEFORE *SUCCUMBING* TO HIS WOUNDS. BUT IT IS SAID THAT EVEN *DEATH* COULD NOT DESTROY HIS WILL TO SAVE HIS PEOPLE.

WE *NIGHT ELVES* HAVE A SIMILAR TALE OF ONE WE NAME *GOLDRINN.* WHEN THE LEGION FLOODED INTO OUR WORLD AND SPARKED THE *WAR OF THE ANCIENTS...*

...THE *GHOST-SPIRIT* OF GOLDRINN AIDED THE NIGHT ELVES OF ELDRE'THALAS IN HOLDING THEIR CITY AGAINST THE DEMONIC ONSLAUGHT.

HIS SPIRIT *GUIDED* THE ELVES TO KEY DEFENSIVE POSITIONS AT CRITICAL MOMENTS DURING THE BATTLE. AFTER THE BATTLE, GOLDRINN WAS NEVER SEEN AGAIN.

WE ORCS RIDE *WOLVES* INTO BATTLE. WHEN OUR PEOPLE ARRIVED ON *KALIMDOR,* THE TAUREN TOLD US OF *LO'GOSH.*

WE *ADOPTED* HIM AS *OUR* HERO ON THIS NEW WORLD, SINCE THE WILL OF ORCS IS *STRONG* LIKE HIS AND EVEN *DEATH* CANNOT STOP US.

THE LEGEND OF *LO'GOSH* EXTENDS THROUGHOUT *AZEROTH. TROLLS, GOBLINS,* AND *DWARVES* ALL HAVE THEIR OWN VERSIONS OF THE LEGEND.

IN EACH TALE, LO'GOSH'S UNYIELDING *WILL* AND SHEER *FEROCITY* ENABLE HIM TO PUSH THROUGH THE BOUNDARIES OF THE *AFTERLIFE* TO AIDE HIS PEOPLE.

HIS LEGEND *ENDURES* TO THIS DAY.

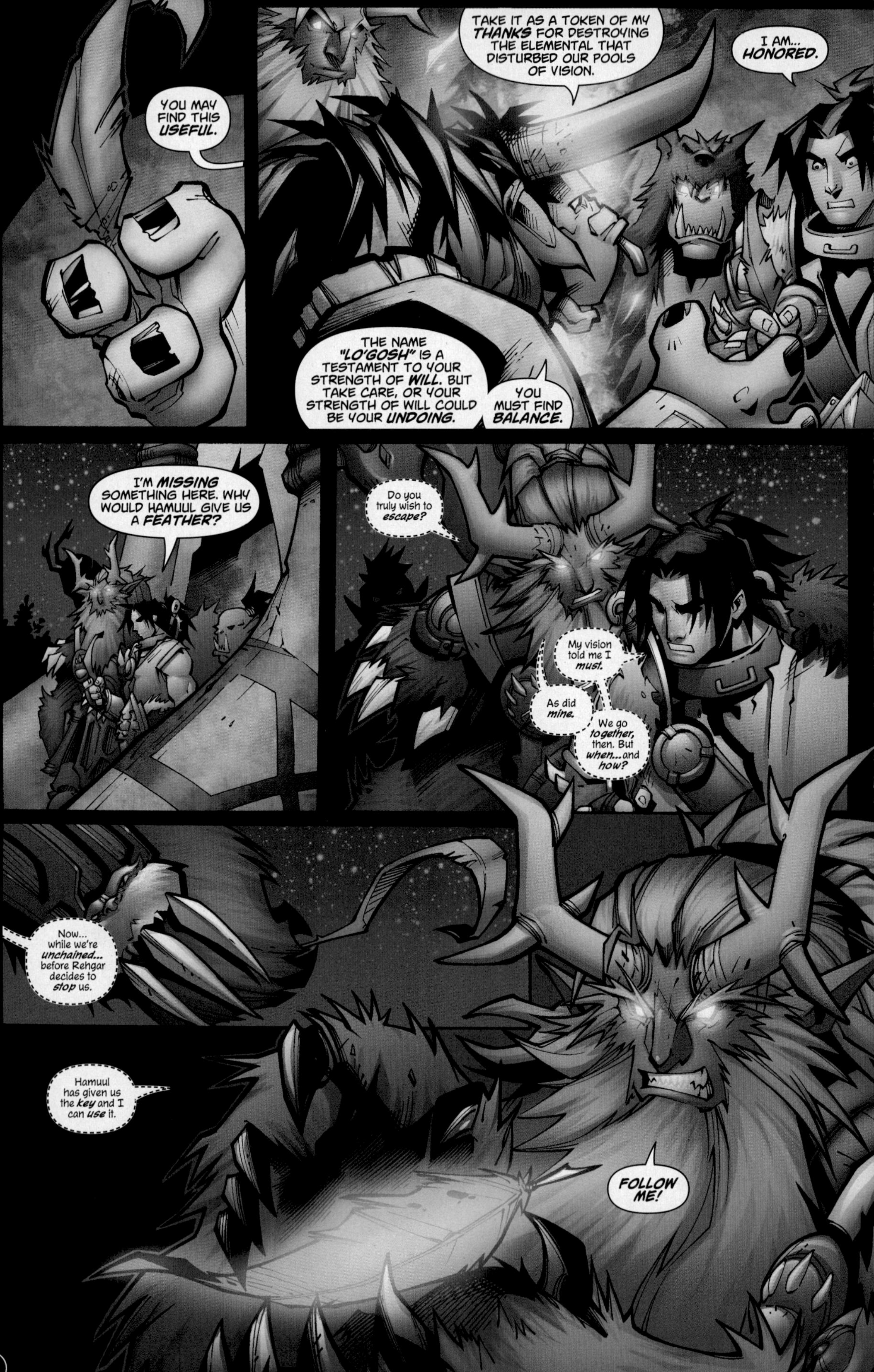
YOU MAY FIND THIS USEFUL.
TAKE IT AS A TOKEN OF MY THANKS FOR DESTROYING THE ELEMENTAL THAT DISTURBED OUR POOLS OF VISION.
I AM... HONORED.
THE NAME "LO'GOSH" IS A TESTAMENT TO YOUR STRENGTH OF WILL. BUT TAKE CARE, OR YOUR STRENGTH OF WILL COULD BE YOUR UNDOING.
YOU MUST FIND BALANCE.
I'M MISSING SOMETHING HERE. WHY WOULD HAMUUL GIVE US A FEATHER?
Do you truly wish to escape?
My vision told me I must.
As did mine.
We go together, then. But when...and how?
Now... while we're unchained... before Rehgar decides to stop us.
Hamuul has given us the key and I can use it.
FOLLOW ME!

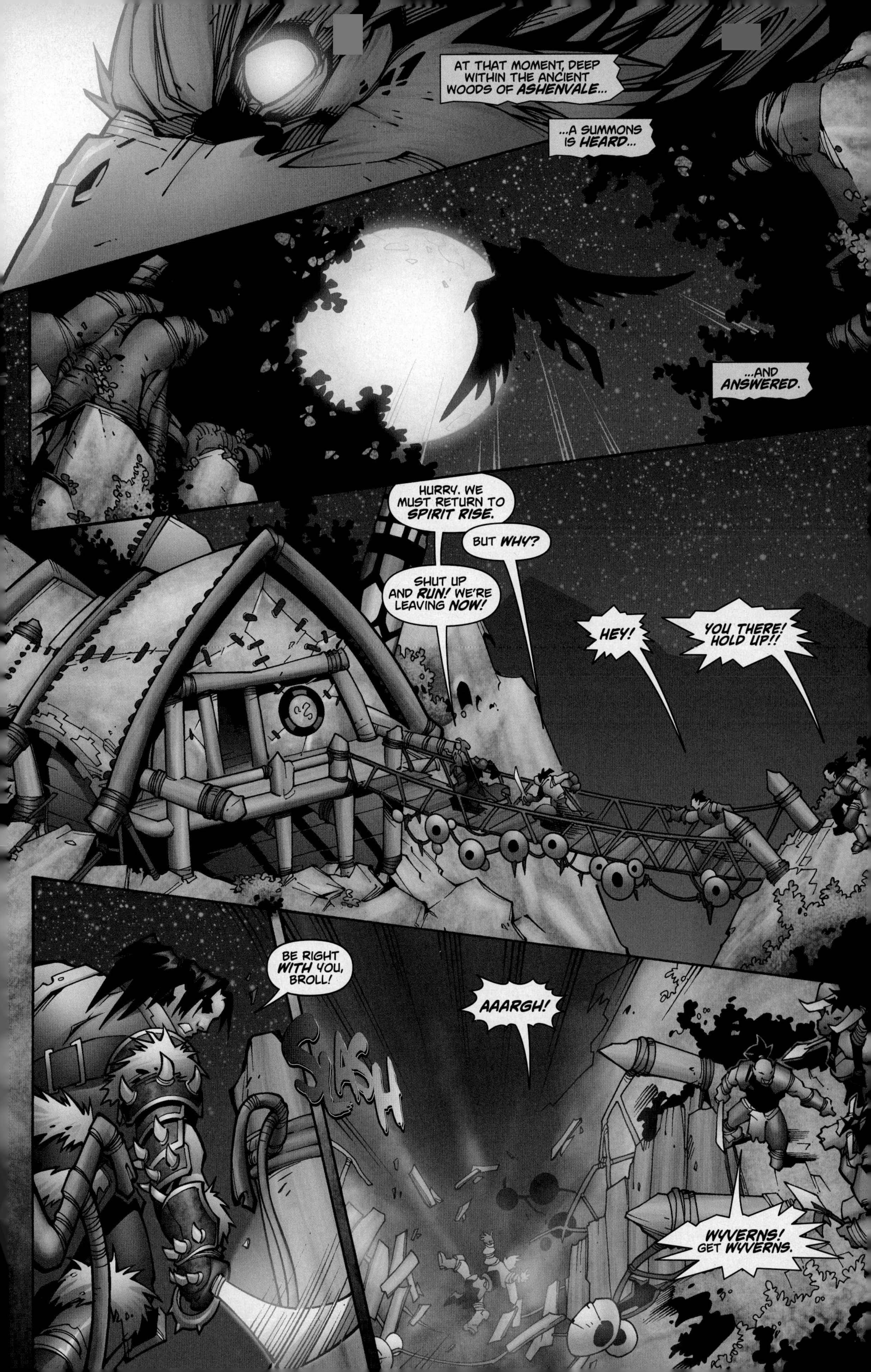

AT THAT MOMENT, DEEP WITHIN THE ANCIENT WOODS OF ASHENVALE...
...A SUMMONS IS HEARD...
...AND ANSWERED.
HURRY. WE MUST RETURN TO SPIRIT RISE.
BUT WHY?
SHUT UP AND RUN! WE'RE LEAVING NOW!
HEY!
YOU THERE! HOLD UP!!
BE RIGHT WITH YOU, BROLL!
AAARGH!
SLASH
WYVERNS! GET WYVERNS.

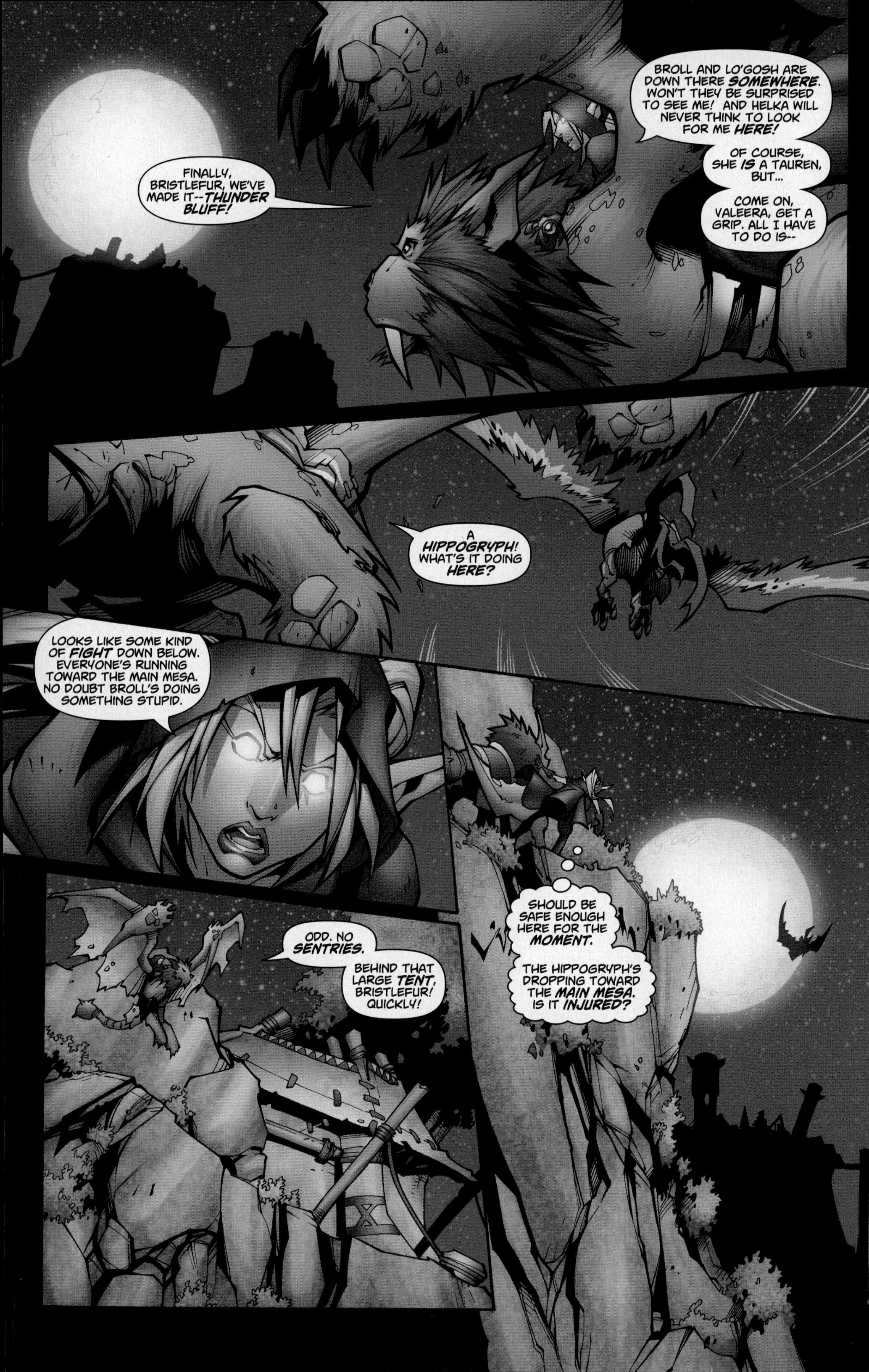
FINALLY, BRISTLEFUR, WE'VE MADE IT--THUNDER BLUFF!
BROLL AND LO'GOSH ARE DOWN THERE SOMEWHERE. WON'T THEY BE SURPRISED TO SEE ME! AND HELKA WILL NEVER THINK TO LOOK FOR ME HERE!
OF COURSE, SHE IS A TAUREN, BUT...
COME ON, VALEERA, GET A GRIP. ALL I HAVE TO DO IS--
A HIPPOGRYPH! WHAT'S IT DOING HERE?
LOOKS LIKE SOME KIND OF FIGHT DOWN BELOW. EVERYONE'S RUNNING TOWARD THE MAIN MESA. NO DOUBT BROLL'S DOING SOMETHING STUPID.
SHOULD BE SAFE ENOUGH HERE FOR THE MOMENT.
THE HIPPOGRYPH'S DROPPING TOWARD THE MAIN MESA. IS IT INJURED?
ODD. NO SENTRIES.
BEHIND THAT LARGE TENT, BRISTLEFUR! QUICKLY!

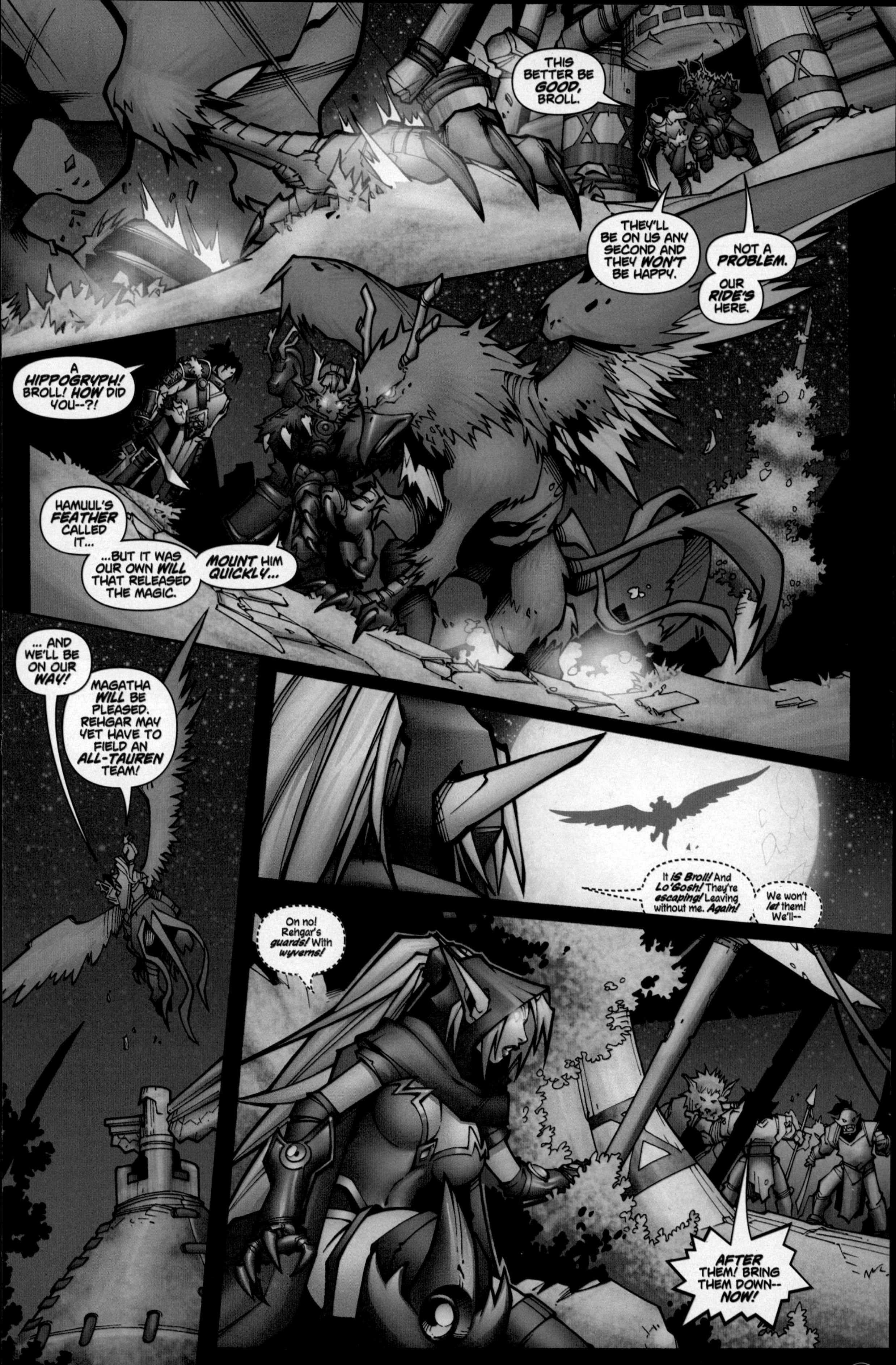
THIS BETTER BE GOOD, BROLL.
THEY'LL BE ON US ANY SECOND AND THEY WON'T BE HAPPY.
NOT A PROBLEM. OUR RIDE'S HERE.
A HIPPOGRYPH! BROLL! HOW DID YOU--?!
HAMUUL'S FEATHER CALLED IT...
...BUT IT WAS OUR OWN WILL THAT RELEASED THE MAGIC.
MOUNT HIM QUICKLY...
... AND WE'LL BE ON OUR WAY!
MAGATHA WILL BE PLEASED. REHGAR MAY YET HAVE TO FIELD AN ALL-TAUREN TEAM!
It IS Broll! And Lo'Gosh! They're escaping! Leaving without me. Again!
We won't let them! We'll--
On no! Rehgar's guards! With wyverns!
AFTER THEM! BRING THEM DOWN-- NOW!

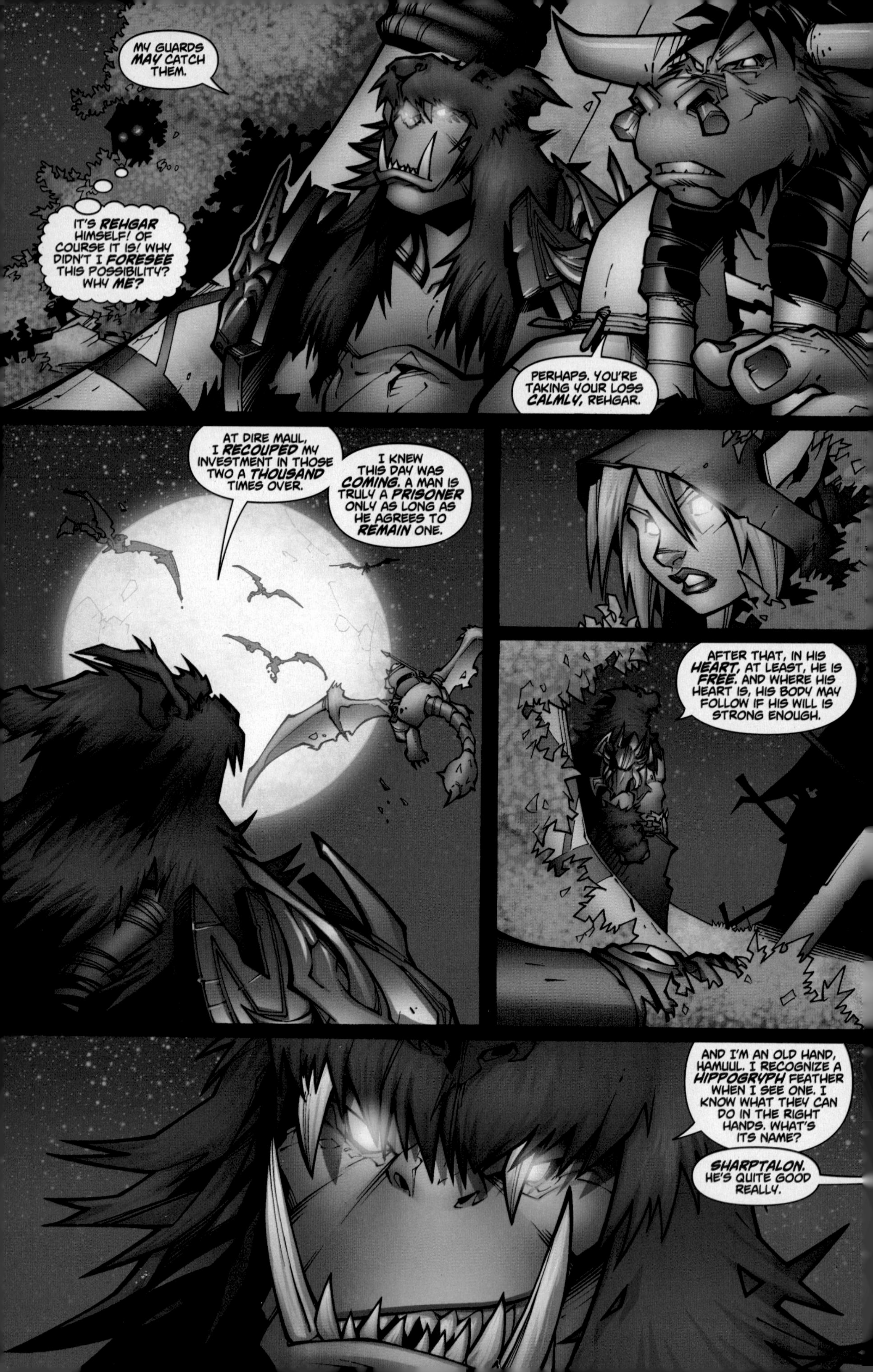
MY GUARDS MAY CATCH THEM.
IT'S REHGAR HIMSELF! OF COURSE IT IS! WHY DIDN'T I FORESEE THIS POSSIBILITY? WHY ME?
PERHAPS. YOU'RE TAKING YOUR LOSS CALMLY, REHGAR.
AT DIRE MAUL, I RECOUPED MY INVESTMENT IN THOSE TWO A THOUSAND TIMES OVER.
I KNEW THIS DAY WAS COMING. A MAN IS TRULY A PRISONER ONLY AS LONG AS HE AGREES TO REMAIN ONE.
AFTER THAT, IN HIS HEART, AT LEAST, HE IS FREE. AND WHERE HIS HEART IS, HIS BODY MAY FOLLOW IF HIS WILL IS STRONG ENOUGH.
AND I'M AN OLD HAND, HAMUUL. I RECOGNIZE A HIPPOGRYPH FEATHER WHEN I SEE ONE. I KNOW WHAT THEY CAN DO IN THE RIGHT HANDS. WHAT'S ITS NAME?
SHARPTALON. HE'S QUITE GOOD REALLY.

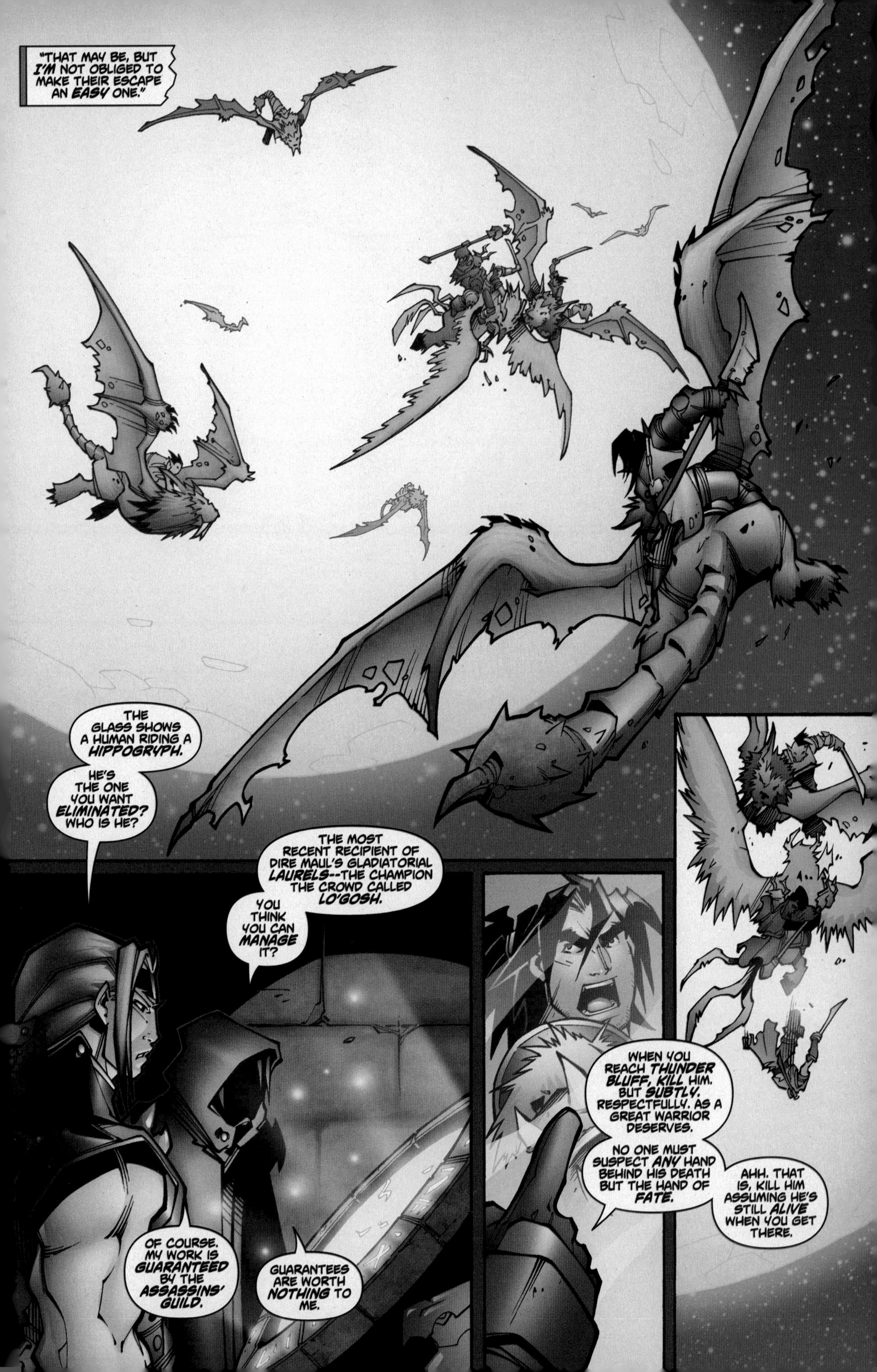
"THAT MAY BE, BUT I'M NOT OBLIGED TO MAKE THEIR ESCAPE AN EASY ONE."
THE GLASS SHOWS A HUMAN RIDING A HIPPOGRYPH.
HE'S THE ONE YOU WANT ELIMINATED? WHO IS HE?
THE MOST RECENT RECIPIENT OF DIRE MAUL'S GLADIATORIAL LAURELS--THE CHAMPION THE CROWD CALLED LO'GOSH.
YOU THINK YOU CAN MANAGE IT?
OF COURSE. MY WORK IS GUARANTEED BY THE ASSASSINS' GUILD.
GUARANTEES ARE WORTH NOTHING TO ME.
WHEN YOU REACH THUNDER BLUFF, KILL HIM. BUT SUBTLY. RESPECTFULLY. AS A GREAT WARRIOR DESERVES.
NO ONE MUST SUSPECT ANY HAND BEHIND HIS DEATH BUT THE HAND OF FATE.
AHH. THAT IS, KILL HIM ASSUMING HE'S STILL ALIVE WHEN YOU GET THERE.

CHAPTER 4

Issue #4 Cover
by Samwise Didier

Issue #4 Cover
by Jim Lee and Alex Sinclair

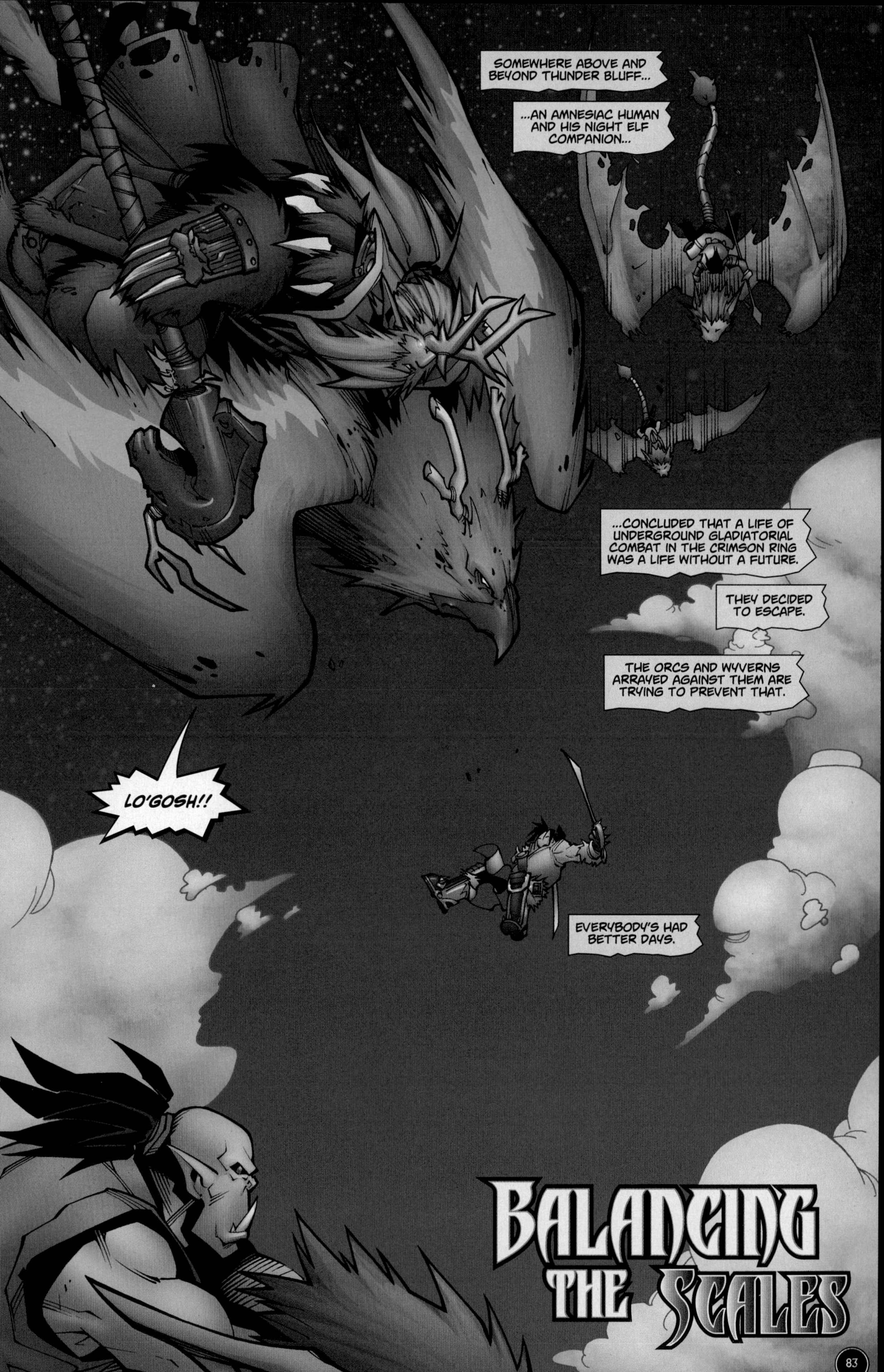
SOMEWHERE ABOVE AND BEYOND THUNDER BLUFF...
...AN AMNESIAC HUMAN AND HIS NIGHT ELF COMPANION...
...CONCLUDED THAT A LIFE OF UNDERGROUND GLADIATORIAL COMBAT IN THE CRIMSON RING WAS A LIFE WITHOUT A FUTURE.
THEY DECIDED TO ESCAPE.
THE ORCS AND WYVERNS ARRAYED AGAINST THEM ARE TRYING TO PREVENT THAT.
LO'GOSH!!
EVERYBODY'S HAD BETTER DAYS.
BALANCING THE SCALES

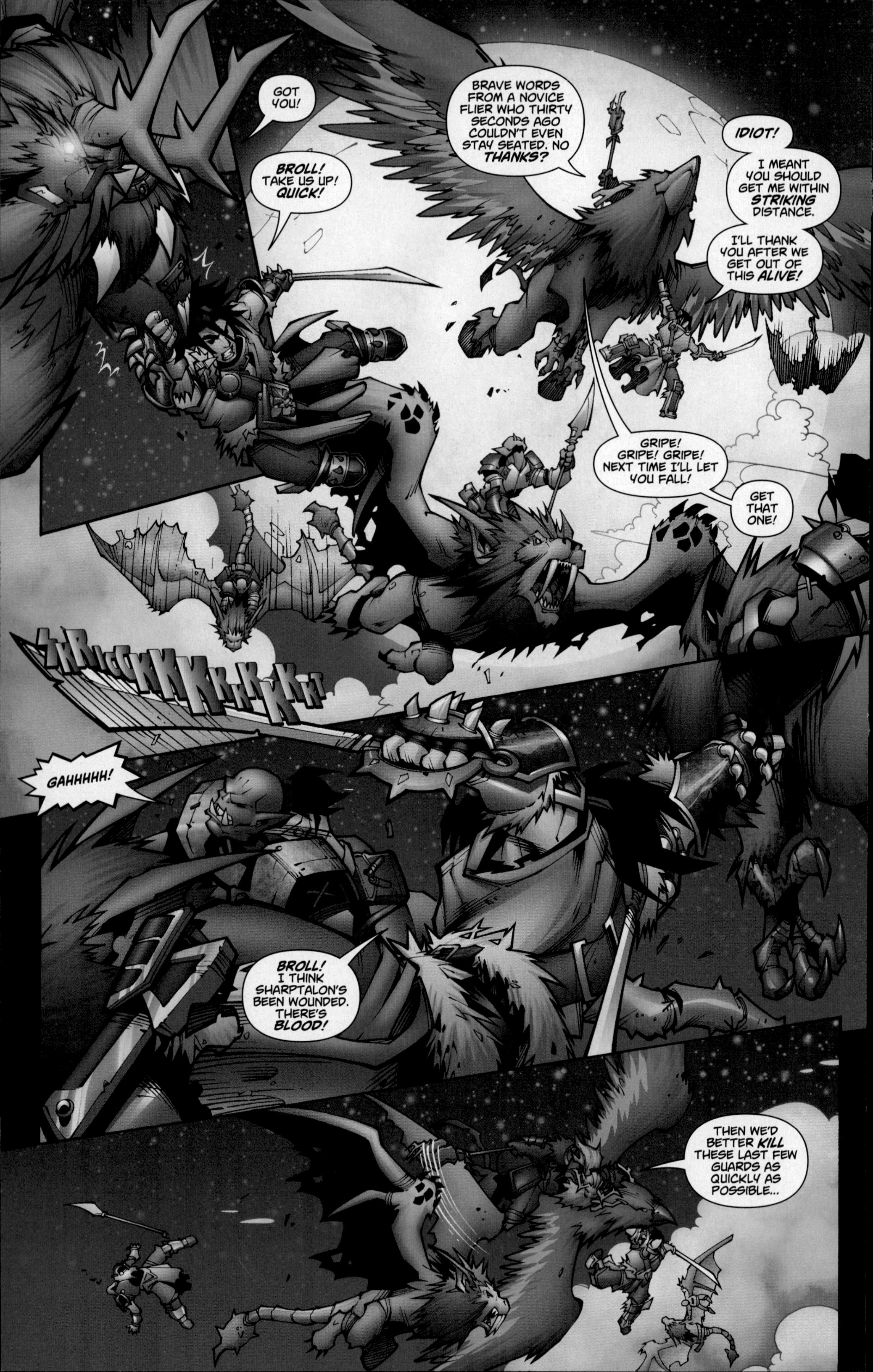
GOT YOU!
BROLL! TAKE US UP! QUICK!
BRAVE WORDS FROM A NOVICE FLIER WHO THIRTY SECONDS AGO COULDN'T EVEN STAY SEATED. NO THANKS?
IDIOT!
I MEANT YOU SHOULD GET ME WITHIN STRIKING DISTANCE.
I'LL THANK YOU AFTER WE GET OUT OF THIS ALIVE!
GRIPE! GRIPE! GRIPE! NEXT TIME I'LL LET YOU FALL!
GET THAT ONE!
SKRICCKKKKKKKKKRT
GAHHHHH!
BROLL! I THINK SHARPTALON'S BEEN WOUNDED. THERE'S BLOOD!
THEN WE'D BETTER KILL THESE LAST FEW GUARDS AS QUICKLY AS POSSIBLE...

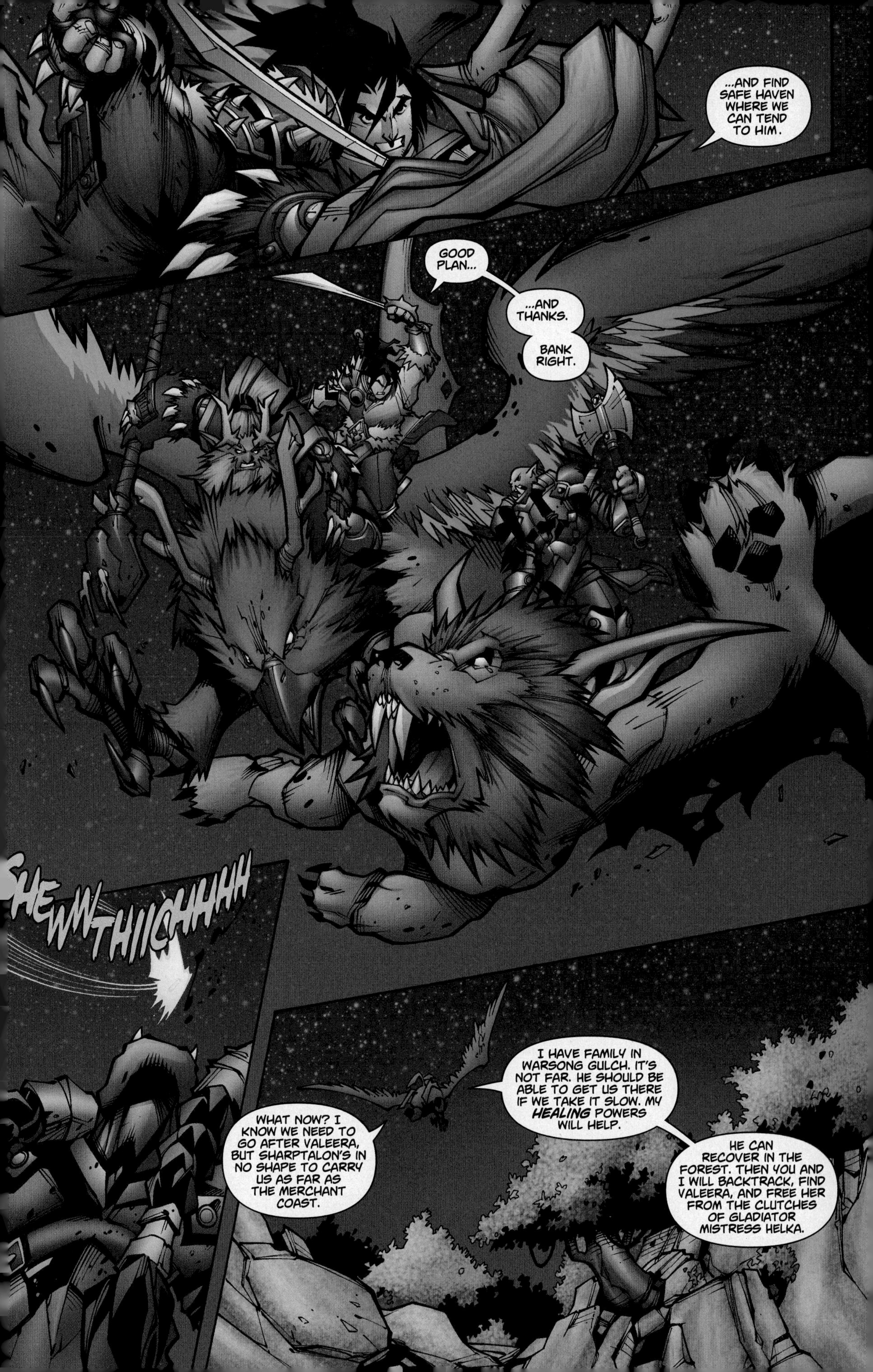
...AND FIND SAFE HAVEN WHERE WE CAN TEND TO HIM.
GOOD PLAN...
...AND THANKS.
BANK RIGHT.
SHEWWNTHIICHHHH
I HAVE FAMILY IN WARSONG GULCH. IT'S NOT FAR. HE SHOULD BE ABLE TO GET US THERE IF WE TAKE IT SLOW. MY *HEALING* POWERS WILL HELP.
WHAT NOW? I KNOW WE NEED TO GO AFTER VALEERA, BUT SHARPTALON'S IN NO SHAPE TO CARRY US AS FAR AS THE MERCHANT COAST.
HE CAN RECOVER IN THE FOREST. THEN YOU AND I WILL BACKTRACK, FIND VALEERA, AND FREE HER FROM THE CLUTCHES OF GLADIATOR MISTRESS HELKA.

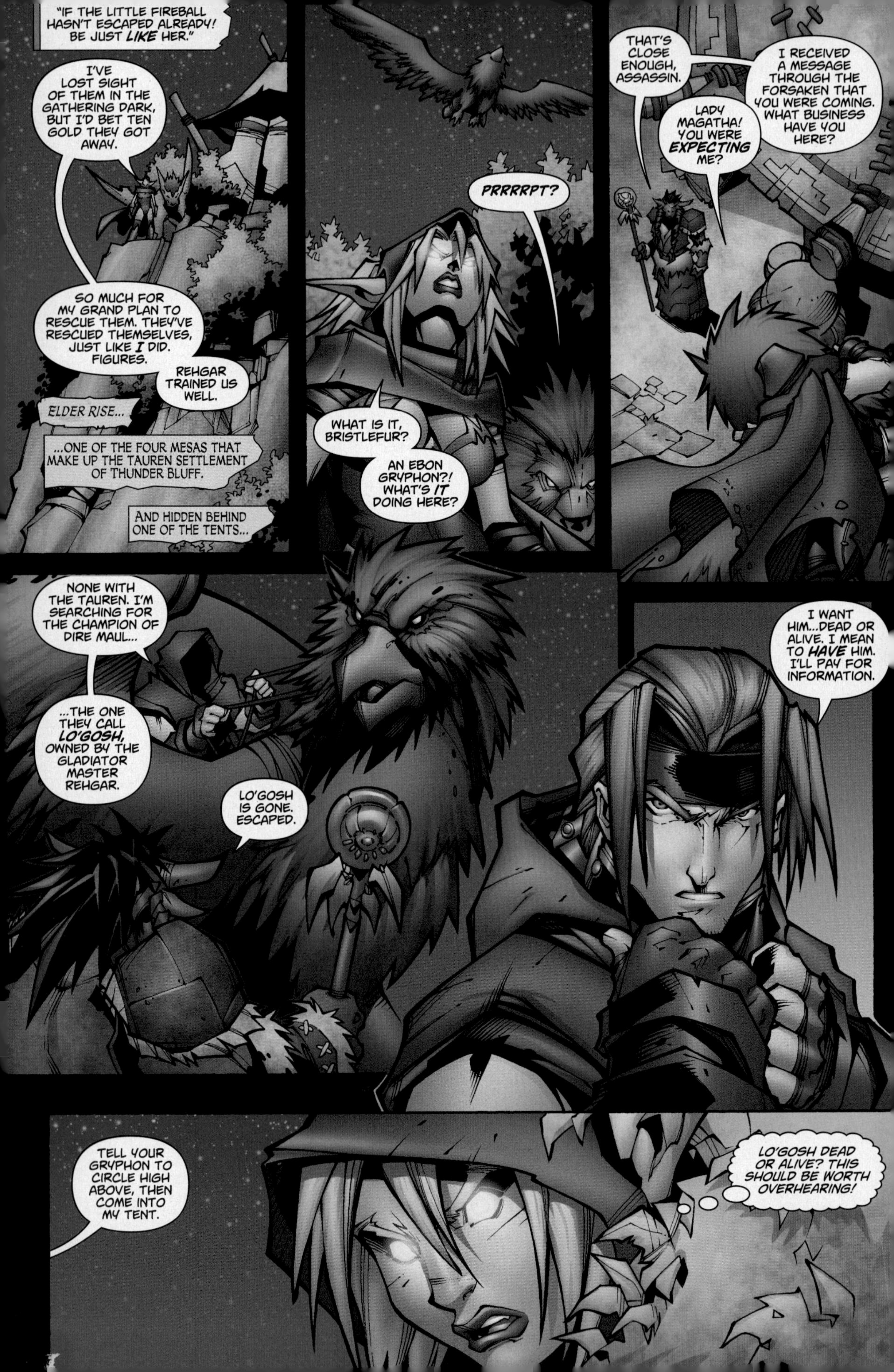
"IF THE LITTLE FIREBALL HASN'T ESCAPED ALREADY! BE JUST LIKE HER."
I'VE LOST SIGHT OF THEM IN THE GATHERING DARK, BUT I'D BET TEN GOLD THEY GOT AWAY.
SO MUCH FOR MY GRAND PLAN TO RESCUE THEM. THEY'VE RESCUED THEMSELVES, JUST LIKE I DID. FIGURES.
REHGAR TRAINED US WELL.
ELDER RISE...
...ONE OF THE FOUR MESAS THAT MAKE UP THE TAUREN SETTLEMENT OF THUNDER BLUFF.
AND HIDDEN BEHIND ONE OF THE TENTS...
PRRRRPT?
WHAT IS IT, BRISTLEFUR?
AN EBON GRYPHON?! WHAT'S IT DOING HERE?
THAT'S CLOSE ENOUGH, ASSASSIN.
LADY MAGATHA! YOU WERE EXPECTING ME?
I RECEIVED A MESSAGE THROUGH THE FORSAKEN THAT YOU WERE COMING. WHAT BUSINESS HAVE YOU HERE?
NONE WITH THE TAUREN. I'M SEARCHING FOR THE CHAMPION OF DIRE MAUL...
...THE ONE THEY CALL LO'GOSH, OWNED BY THE GLADIATOR MASTER REHGAR.
LO'GOSH IS GONE. ESCAPED.
I WANT HIM...DEAD OR ALIVE. I MEAN TO HAVE HIM. I'LL PAY FOR INFORMATION.
TELL YOUR GRYPHON TO CIRCLE HIGH ABOVE, THEN COME INTO MY TENT.
LO'GOSH DEAD OR ALIVE? THIS SHOULD BE WORTH OVERHEARING!

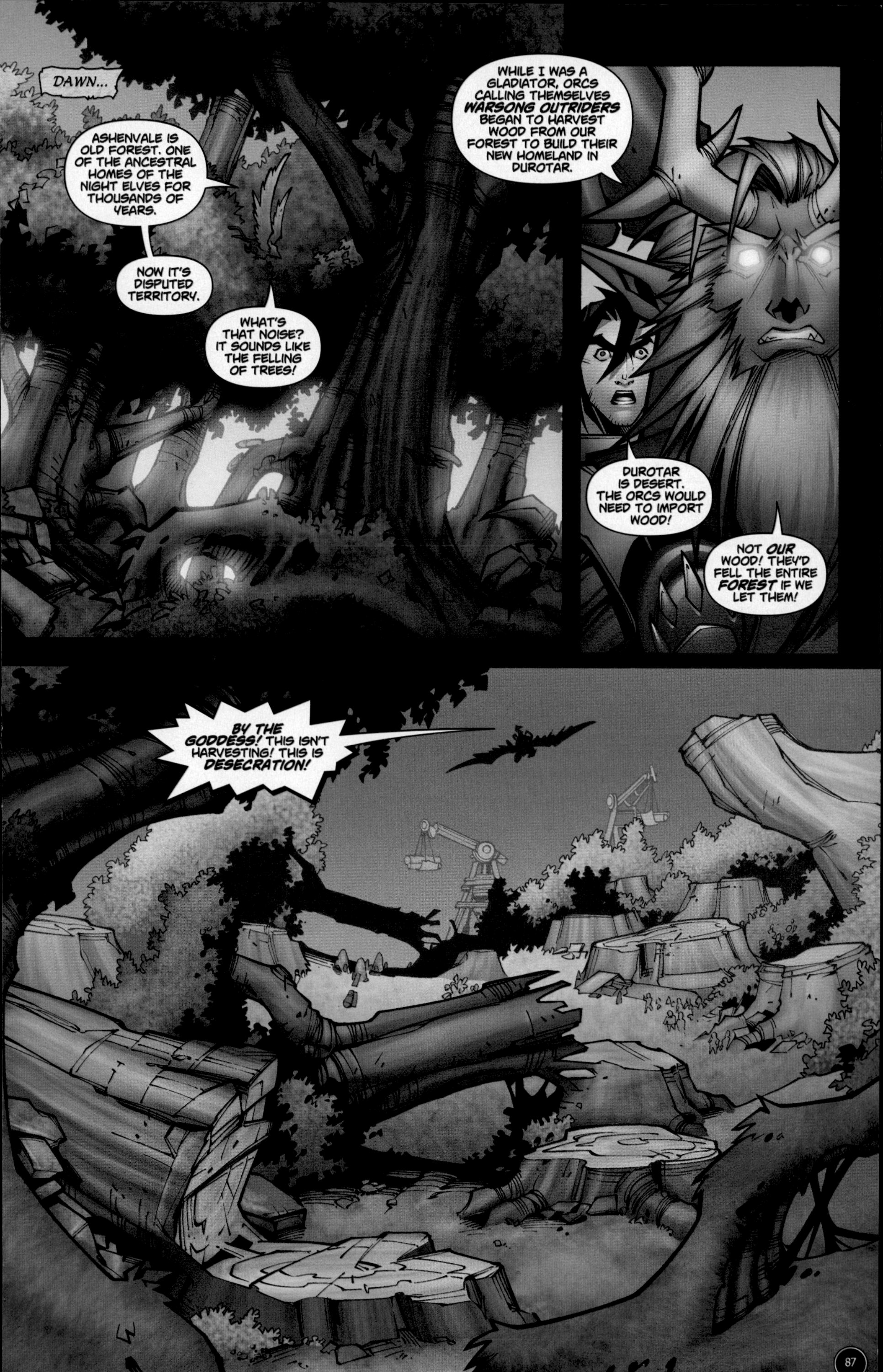
DAWN...
ASHENVALE IS OLD FOREST. ONE OF THE ANCESTRAL HOMES OF THE NIGHT ELVES FOR THOUSANDS OF YEARS.
NOW IT'S DISPUTED TERRITORY.
WHAT'S THAT NOISE? IT SOUNDS LIKE THE FELLING OF TREES!
WHILE I WAS A GLADIATOR, ORCS CALLING THEMSELVES WARSONG OUTRIDERS BEGAN TO HARVEST WOOD FROM OUR FOREST TO BUILD THEIR NEW HOMELAND IN DUROTAR.
DUROTAR IS DESERT. THE ORCS WOULD NEED TO IMPORT WOOD!
NOT OUR WOOD! THEY'D FELL THE ENTIRE FOREST IF WE LET THEM!
BY THE GODDESS! THIS ISN'T HARVESTING! THIS IS DESECRATION!

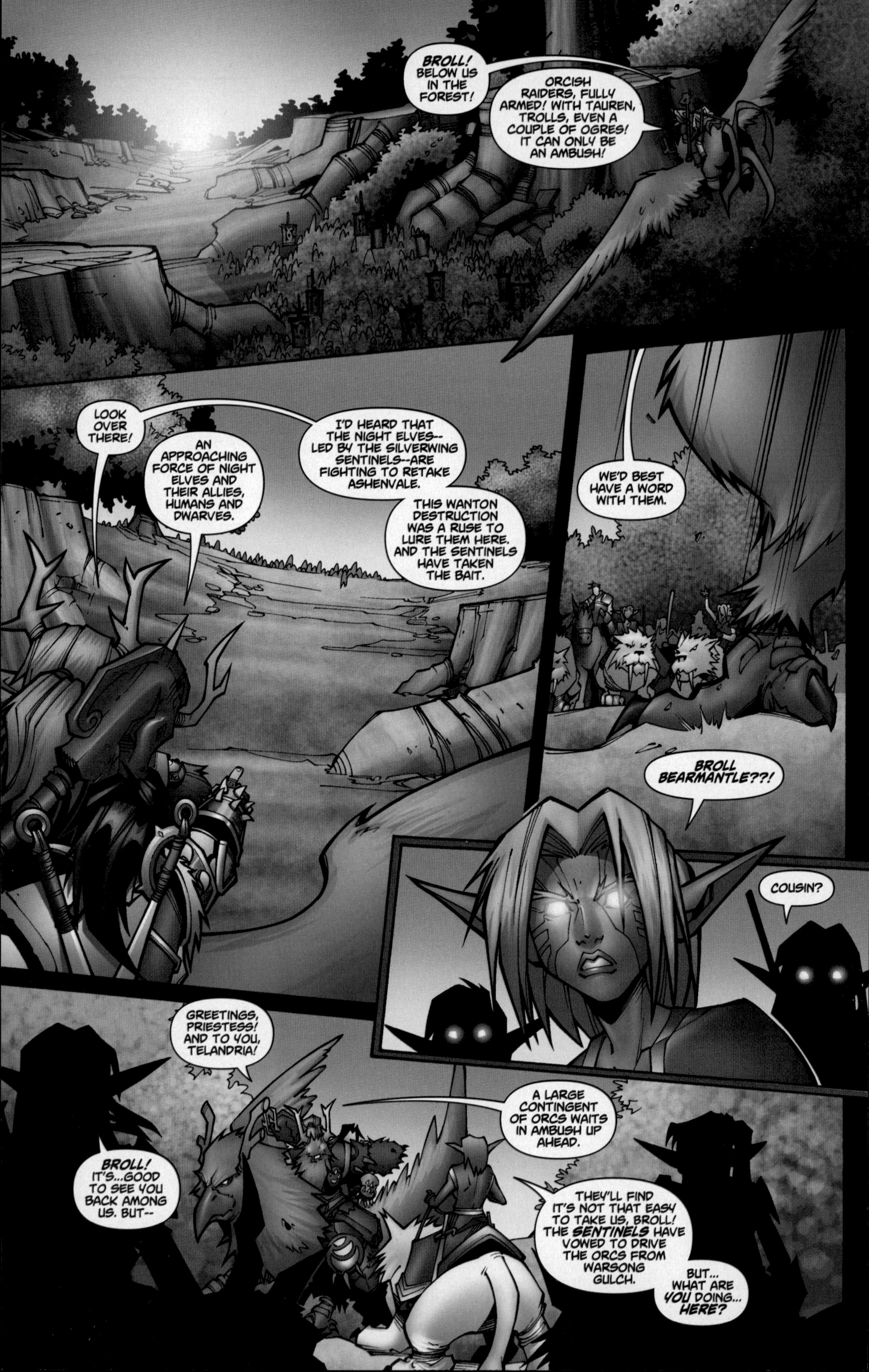
BROLL! BELOW US IN THE FOREST!
ORCISH RAIDERS, FULLY ARMED! WITH TAUREN, TROLLS, EVEN A COUPLE OF OGRES! IT CAN ONLY BE AN AMBUSH!
LOOK OVER THERE!
AN APPROACHING FORCE OF NIGHT ELVES AND THEIR ALLIES, HUMANS AND DWARVES.
I'D HEARD THAT THE NIGHT ELVES--LED BY THE SILVERWING SENTINELS--ARE FIGHTING TO RETAKE ASHENVALE.
THIS WANTON DESTRUCTION WAS A RUSE TO LURE THEM HERE. AND THE SENTINELS HAVE TAKEN THE BAIT.
WE'D BEST HAVE A WORD WITH THEM.
BROLL BEARMANTLE??!
COUSIN?
GREETINGS, PRIESTESS! AND TO YOU, TELANDRIA!
BROLL! IT'S...GOOD TO SEE YOU BACK AMONG US. BUT--
A LARGE CONTINGENT OF ORCS WAITS IN AMBUSH UP AHEAD.
THEY'LL FIND IT'S NOT THAT EASY TO TAKE US, BROLL! THE SENTINELS HAVE VOWED TO DRIVE THE ORCS FROM WARSONG GULCH.
BUT... WHAT ARE YOU DOING... HERE?

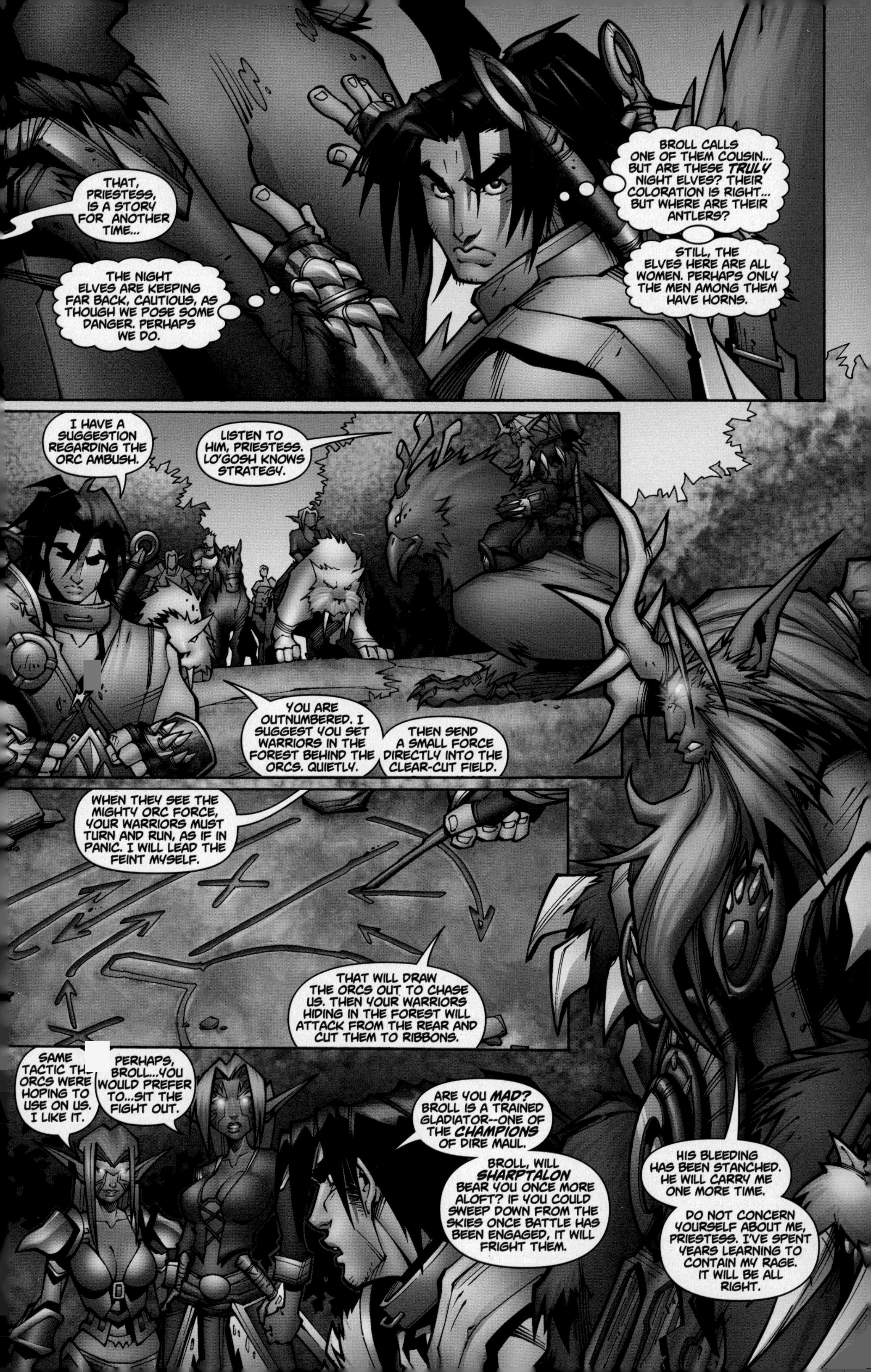
THAT, PRIESTESS, IS A STORY FOR ANOTHER TIME...
THE NIGHT ELVES ARE KEEPING FAR BACK, CAUTIOUS, AS THOUGH WE POSE SOME DANGER. PERHAPS WE DO.
BROLL CALLS ONE OF THEM COUSIN... BUT ARE THESE *TRULY* NIGHT ELVES? THEIR COLORATION IS RIGHT... BUT WHERE ARE THEIR ANTLERS?
STILL, THE ELVES HERE ARE ALL WOMEN. PERHAPS ONLY THE MEN AMONG THEM HAVE HORNS.
I HAVE A SUGGESTION REGARDING THE ORC AMBUSH.
LISTEN TO HIM, PRIESTESS. LO'GOSH KNOWS STRATEGY.
YOU ARE OUTNUMBERED. I SUGGEST YOU SET WARRIORS IN THE FOREST BEHIND THE ORCS. QUIETLY.
THEN SEND A SMALL FORCE DIRECTLY INTO THE CLEAR-CUT FIELD.
WHEN THEY SEE THE MIGHTY ORC FORCE, YOUR WARRIORS MUST TURN AND RUN, AS IF IN PANIC. I WILL LEAD THE FEINT MYSELF.
THAT WILL DRAW THE ORCS OUT TO CHASE US. THEN YOUR WARRIORS HIDING IN THE FOREST WILL ATTACK FROM THE REAR AND CUT THEM TO RIBBONS.
SAME TACTIC TH ORCS WERE HOPING TO USE ON US. I LIKE IT.
PERHAPS, BROLL...YOU WOULD PREFER TO...SIT THE FIGHT OUT.
ARE YOU *MAD?* BROLL IS A TRAINED GLADIATOR--ONE OF THE *CHAMPIONS* OF DIRE MAUL.
BROLL, WILL *SHARPTALON* BEAR YOU ONCE MORE ALOFT? IF YOU COULD SWEEP DOWN FROM THE SKIES ONCE BATTLE HAS BEEN ENGAGED, IT WILL FRIGHT THEM.
HIS BLEEDING HAS BEEN STANCHED. HE WILL CARRY ME ONE MORE TIME.
DO NOT CONCERN YOURSELF ABOUT ME, PRIESTESS. I'VE SPENT YEARS LEARNING TO CONTAIN MY RAGE. IT WILL BE ALL RIGHT.

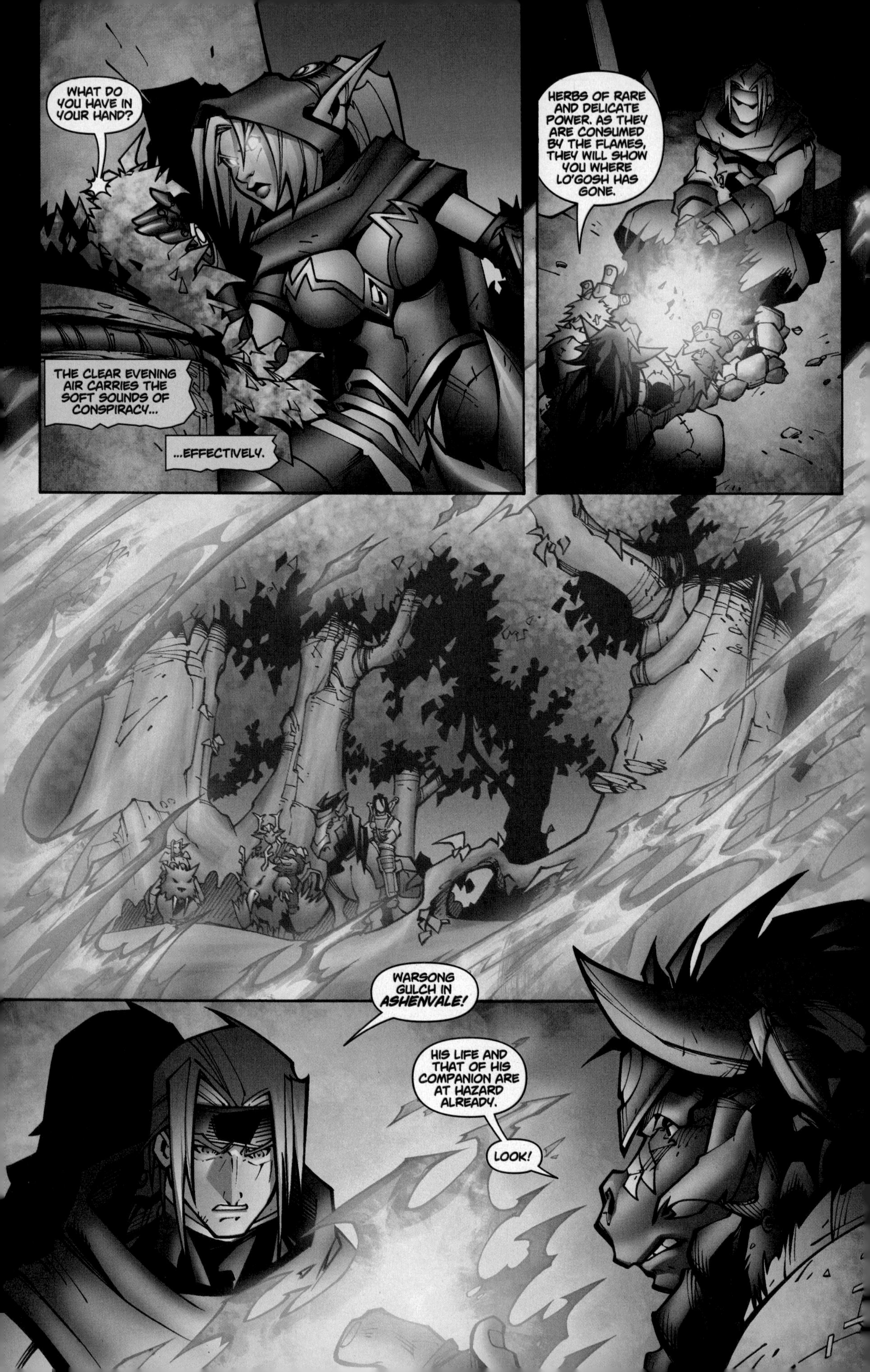

WHAT DO YOU HAVE IN YOUR HAND?
THE CLEAR EVENING AIR CARRIES THE SOFT SOUNDS OF CONSPIRACY...
...EFFECTIVELY.
HERBS OF RARE AND DELICATE POWER. AS THEY ARE CONSUMED BY THE FLAMES, THEY WILL SHOW YOU WHERE LO'GOSH HAS GONE.
WARSONG GULCH IN ASHENVALE!
HIS LIFE AND THAT OF HIS COMPANION ARE AT HAZARD ALREADY.
LOOK!

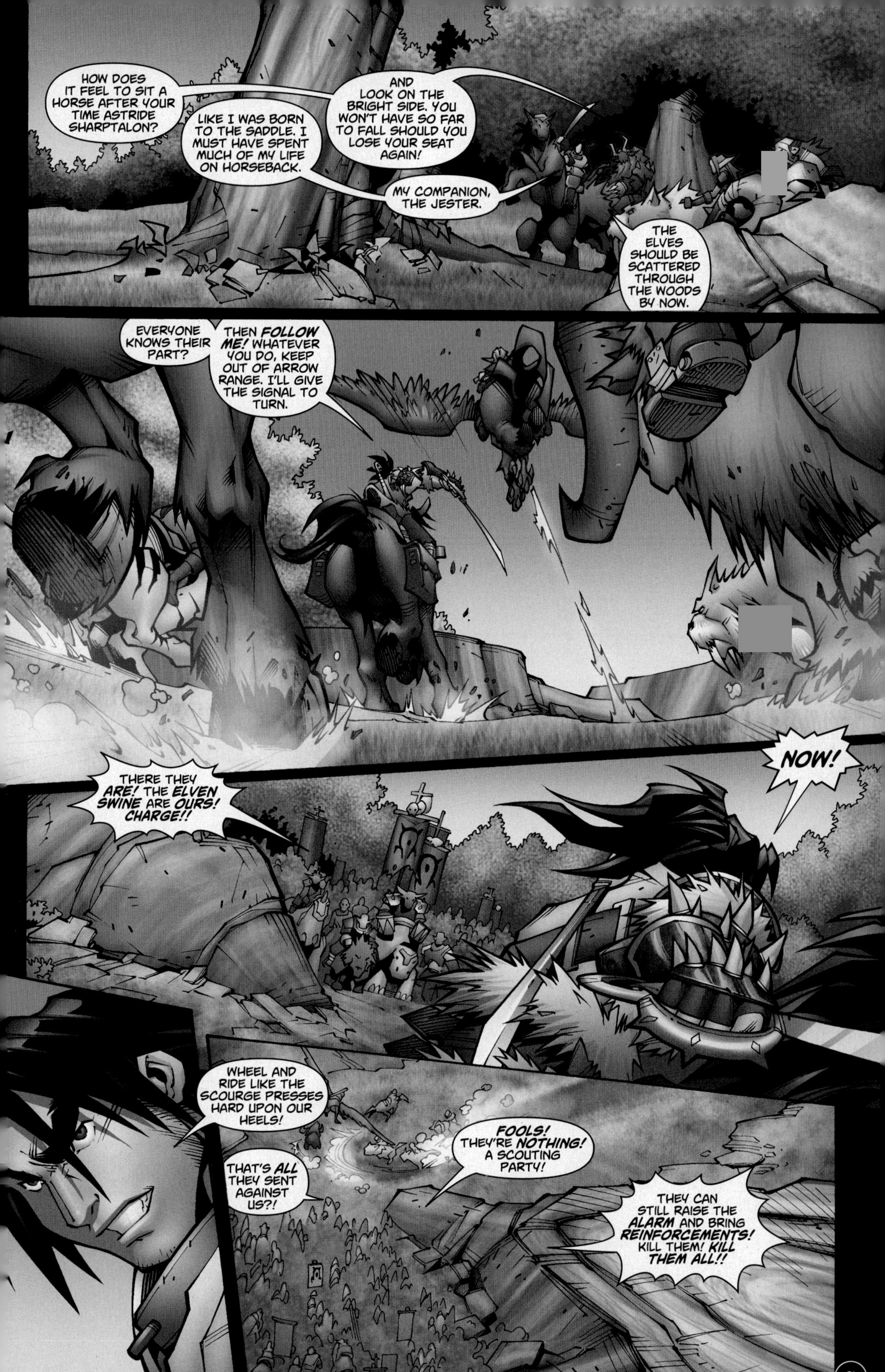
HOW DOES IT FEEL TO SIT A HORSE AFTER YOUR TIME ASTRIDE SHARPTALON?
LIKE I WAS BORN TO THE SADDLE. I MUST HAVE SPENT MUCH OF MY LIFE ON HORSEBACK.
AND LOOK ON THE BRIGHT SIDE. YOU WON'T HAVE SO FAR TO FALL SHOULD YOU LOSE YOUR SEAT AGAIN!
MY COMPANION, THE JESTER.
THE ELVES SHOULD BE SCATTERED THROUGH THE WOODS BY NOW.
EVERYONE KNOWS THEIR PART?
THEN FOLLOW ME! WHATEVER YOU DO, KEEP OUT OF ARROW RANGE. I'LL GIVE THE SIGNAL TO TURN.
THERE THEY ARE! THE ELVEN SWINE ARE OURS! CHARGE!!
NOW!
WHEEL AND RIDE LIKE THE SCOURGE PRESSES HARD UPON OUR HEELS!
THAT'S ALL THEY SENT AGAINST US?!
FOOLS! THEY'RE NOTHING! A SCOUTING PARTY!
THEY CAN STILL RAISE THE ALARM AND BRING REINFORCEMENTS! KILL THEM! KILL THEM ALL!!

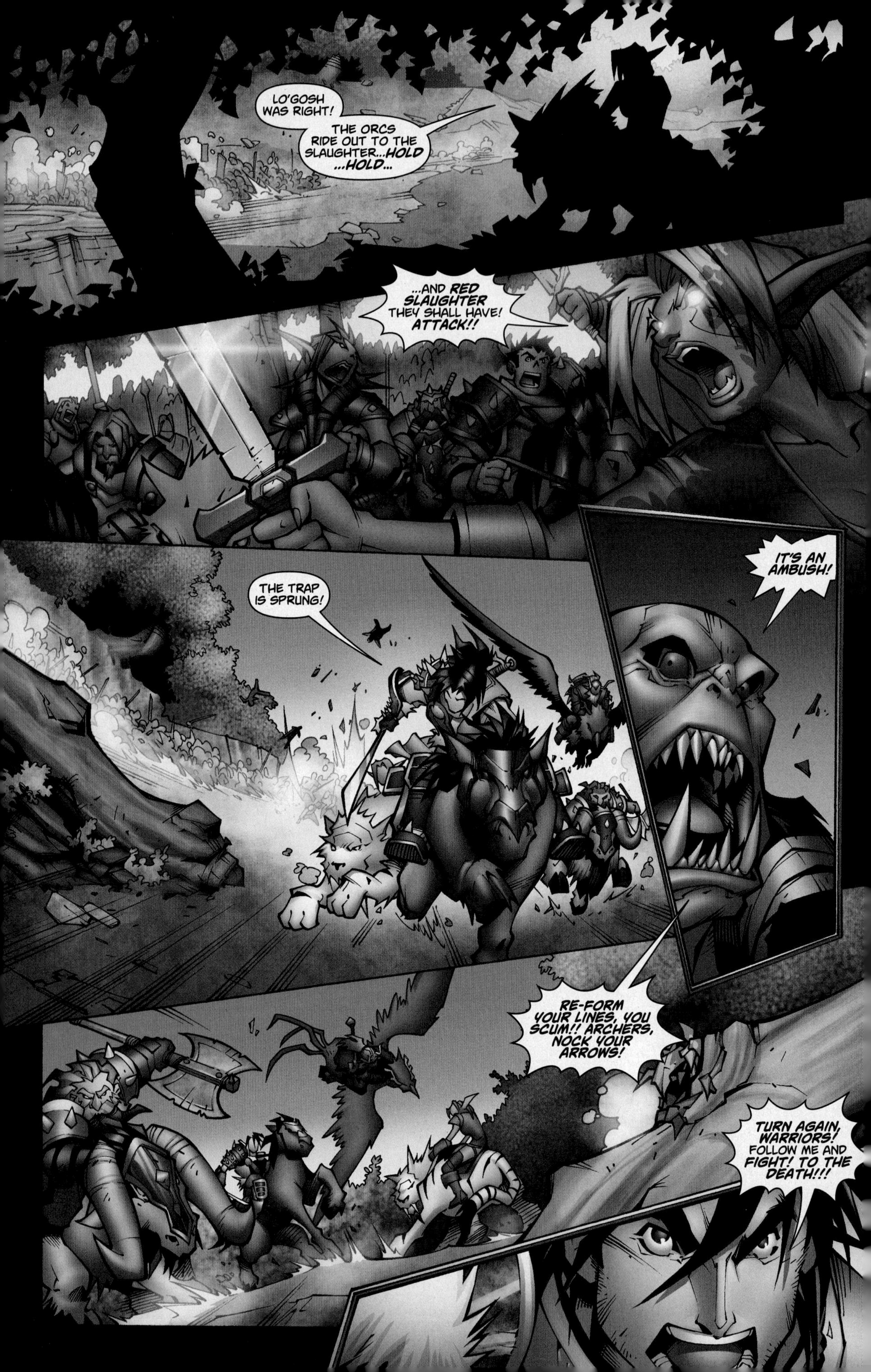
LO'GOSH WAS RIGHT!
THE ORCS RIDE OUT TO THE SLAUGHTER...HOLD ...HOLD...
...AND RED SLAUGHTER THEY SHALL HAVE! ATTACK!!
THE TRAP IS SPRUNG!
IT'S AN AMBUSH!
RE-FORM YOUR LINES, YOU SCUM!! ARCHERS, NOCK YOUR ARROWS!
TURN AGAIN, WARRIORS! FOLLOW ME AND FIGHT! TO THE DEATH!!!

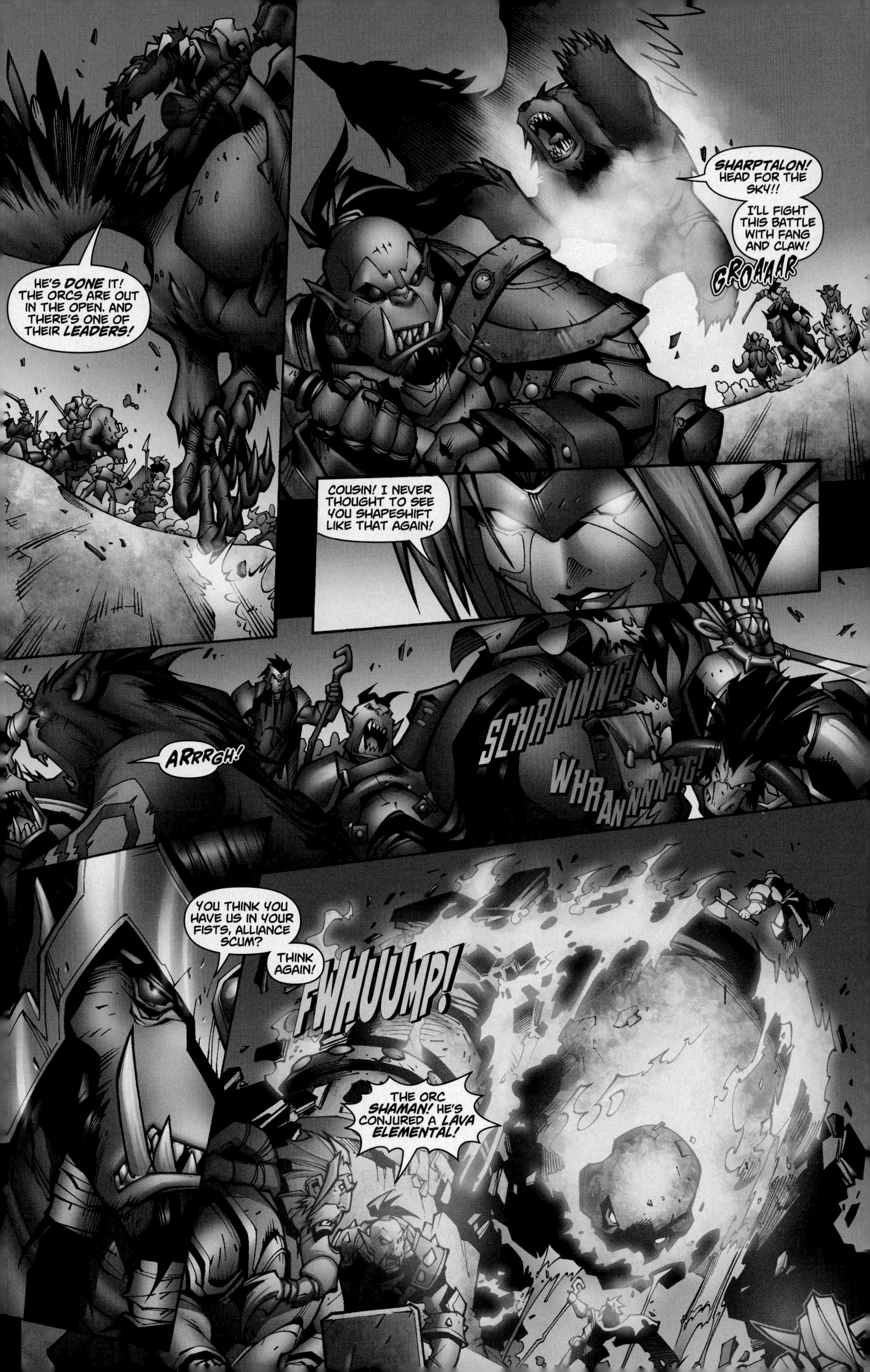
HE'S DONE IT! THE ORCS ARE OUT IN THE OPEN. AND THERE'S ONE OF THEIR LEADERS!
SHARPTALON! HEAD FOR THE SKY!!
I'LL FIGHT THIS BATTLE WITH FANG AND CLAW!
GROAAAR
COUSIN! I NEVER THOUGHT TO SEE YOU SHAPESHIFT LIKE THAT AGAIN!
ARRRGH!
SCHRINNNG!
WHRANNNNHG!
YOU THINK YOU HAVE US IN YOUR FISTS, ALLIANCE SCUM?
THINK AGAIN!
FWHOOMP!
THE ORC SHAMAN! HE'S CONJURED A LAVA ELEMENTAL!

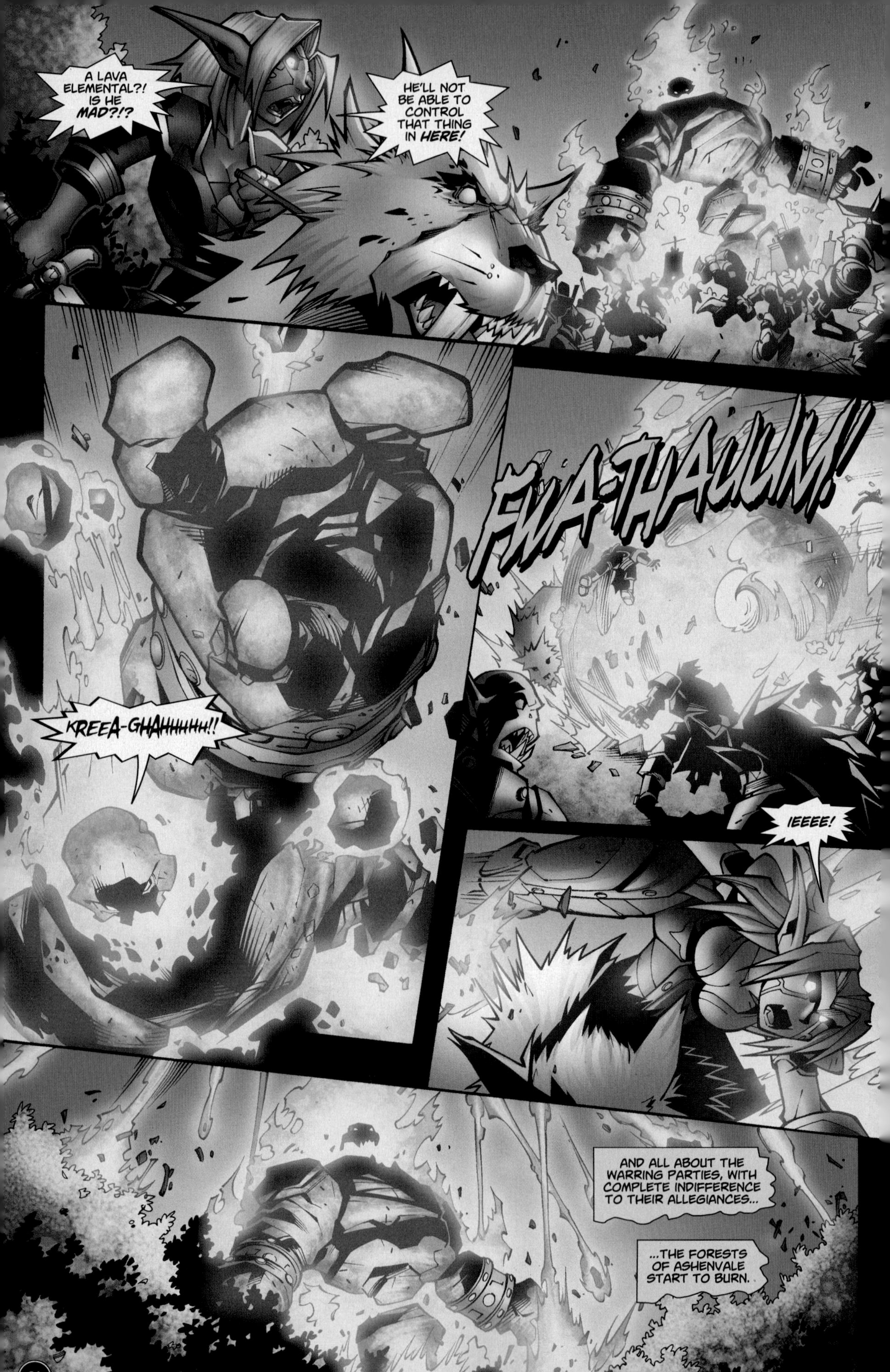
A LAVA ELEMENTAL?! IS HE MAD?!?
HE'LL NOT BE ABLE TO CONTROL THAT THING IN HERE!
FWA-THAUUM!
KREEA-GHAHHHHH!!
IEEEE!
AND ALL ABOUT THE WARRING PARTIES, WITH COMPLETE INDIFFERENCE TO THEIR ALLEGIANCES...
...THE FORESTS OF ASHENVALE START TO BURN.

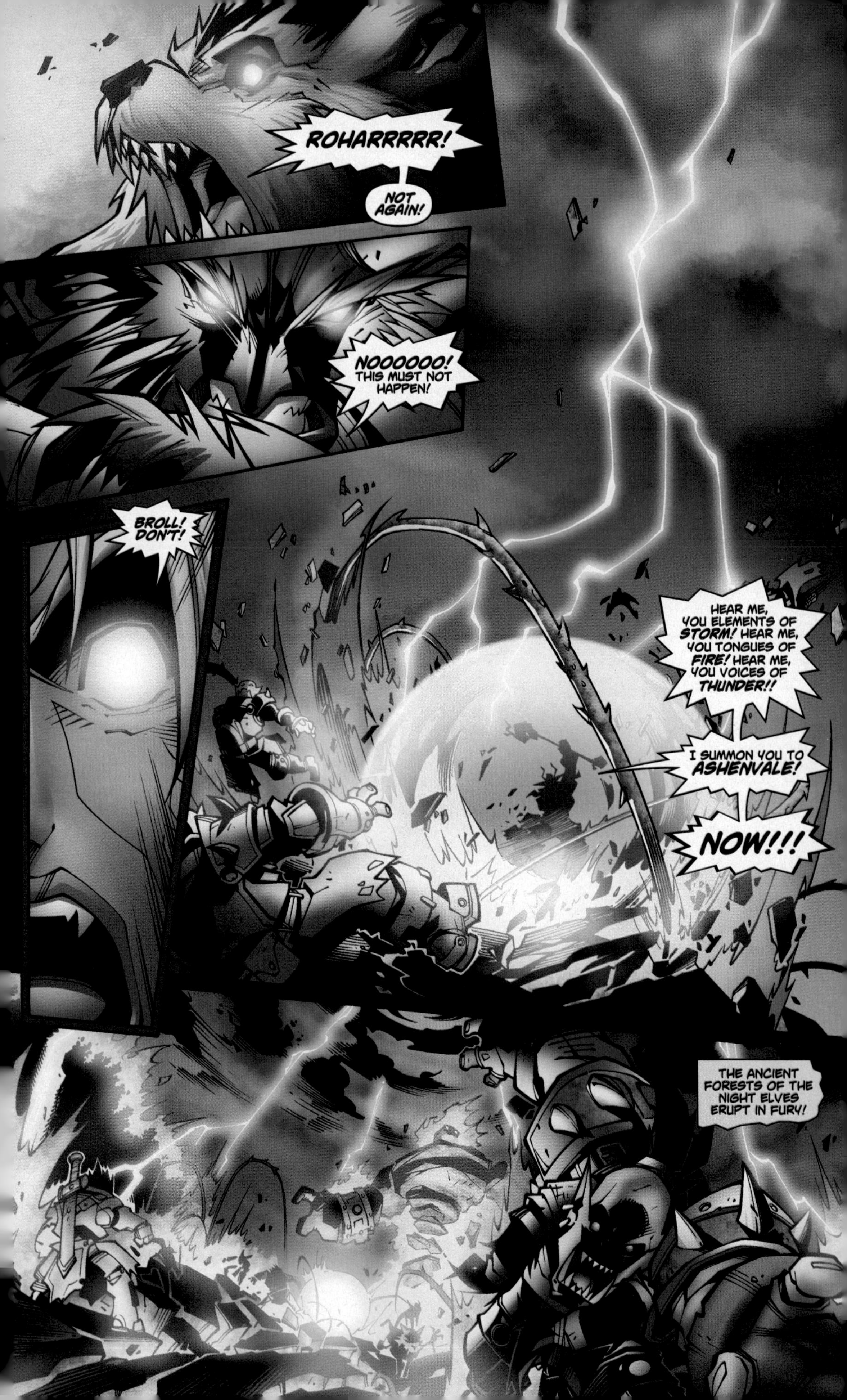
ROHARRRRR!
NOT AGAIN!
NOOOOOO! THIS MUST NOT HAPPEN!
BROLL! DON'T!
HEAR ME, YOU ELEMENTS OF STORM! HEAR ME, YOU TONGUES OF FIRE! HEAR ME, YOU VOICES OF THUNDER!!
I SUMMON YOU TO ASHENVALE!
NOW!!!
THE ANCIENT FORESTS OF THE NIGHT ELVES ERUPT IN FURY!

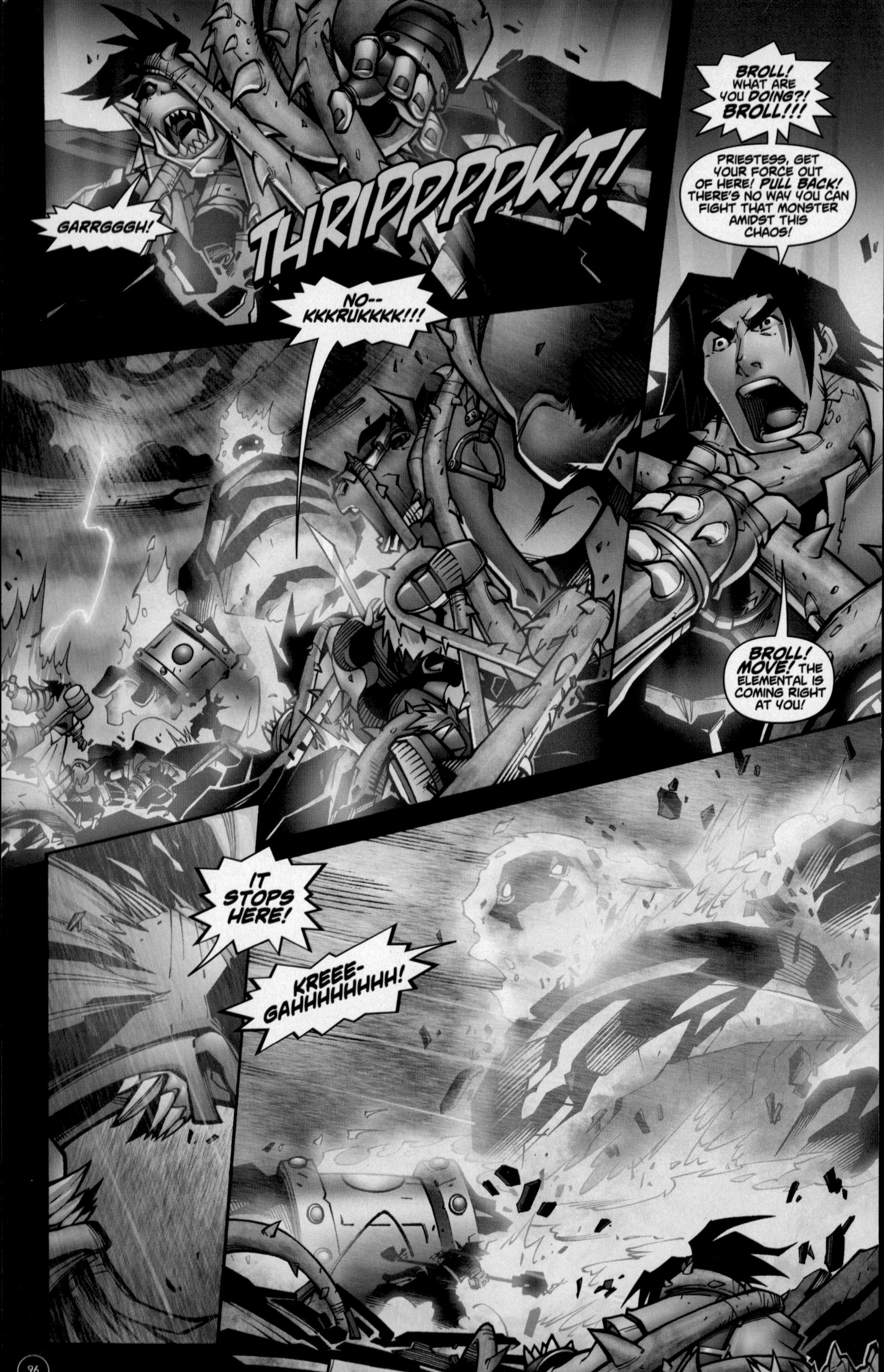
GARRGGGH!
THRIPPPPPKT!
BROLL! WHAT ARE YOU DOING?! BROLL!!!
PRIESTESS, GET YOUR FORCE OUT OF HERE! PULL BACK! THERE'S NO WAY YOU CAN FIGHT THAT MONSTER AMIDST THIS CHAOS!
NO-- KKKRUKKKK!!!
BROLL! MOVE! THE ELEMENTAL IS COMING RIGHT AT YOU!
IT STOPS HERE!
KREEE-GAHHHHHHHH!

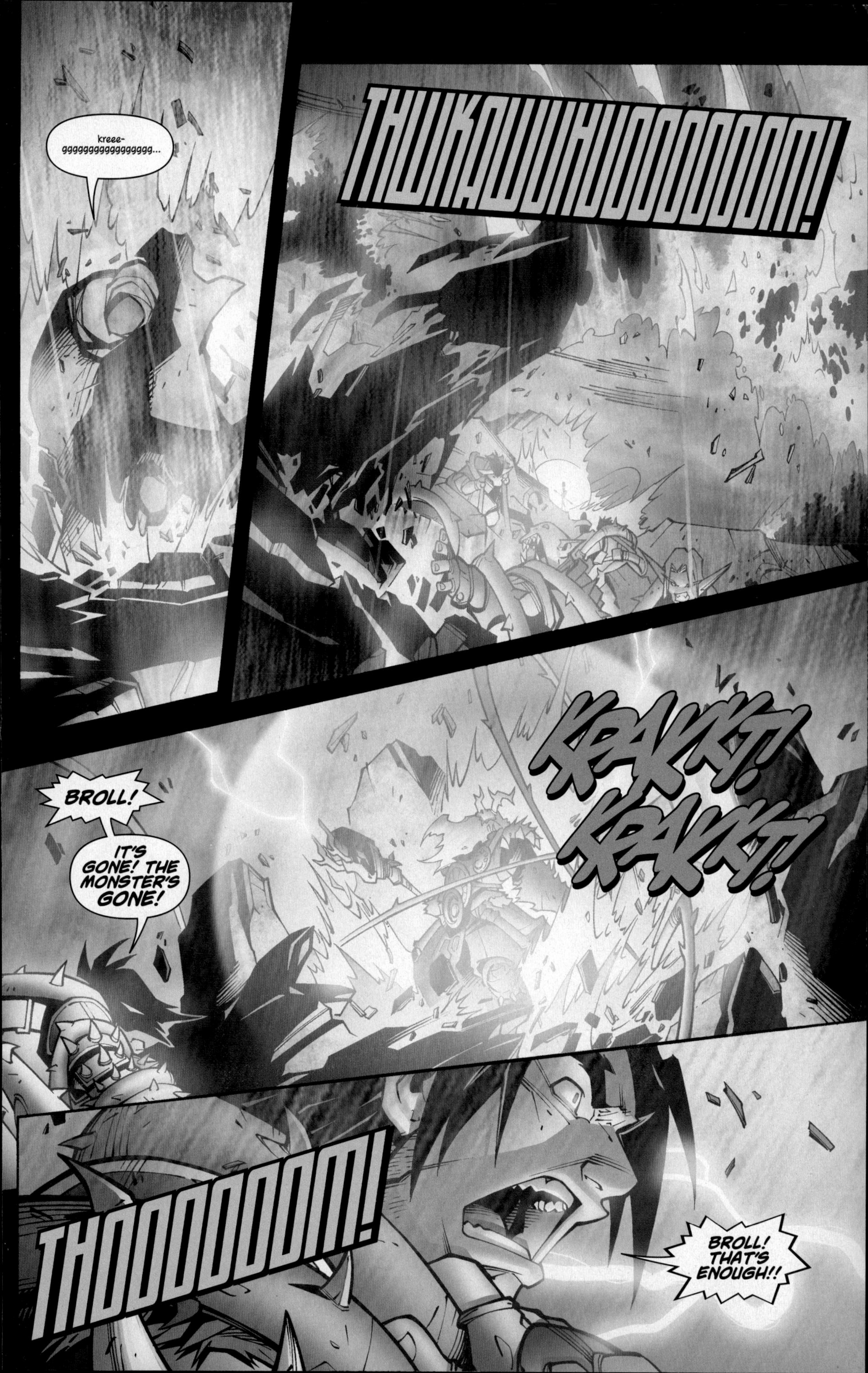
kreee-
gggggggggggggggg...
THWAKOWWHOOOOOOOM!
BROLL!
IT'S GONE! THE MONSTER'S GONE!
KRAKKT! KRAKKT!
THOOOOOOOM!
BROLL! THAT'S ENOUGH!!

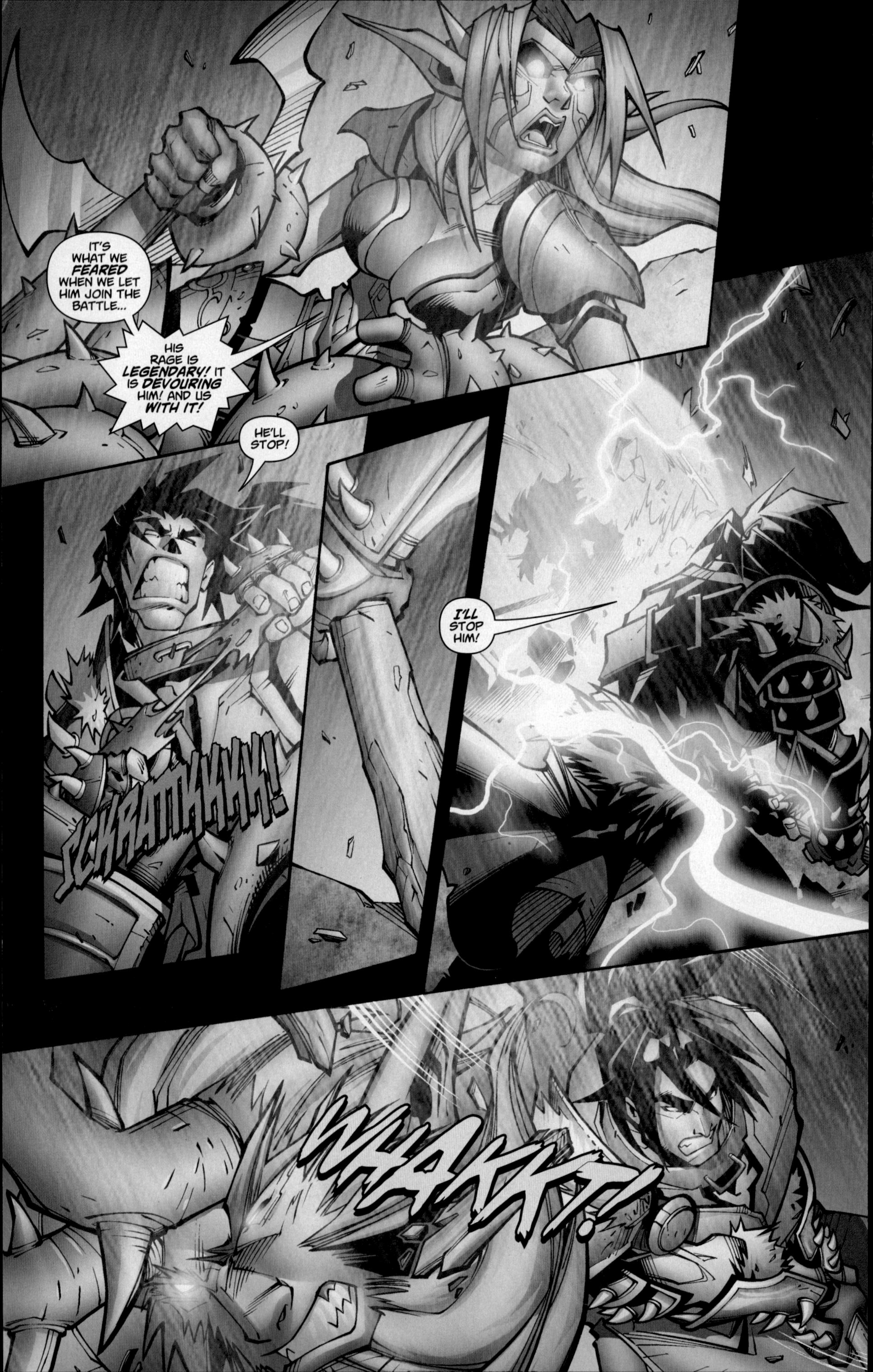
IT'S WHAT WE *FEARED* WHEN WE LET HIM JOIN THE BATTLE...
HIS RAGE IS *LEGENDARY!* IT IS *DEVOURING* HIM! AND US *WITH IT!*
HE'LL STOP!
SCHRAKKKKK!
I'LL STOP HIM!
WHAKK!

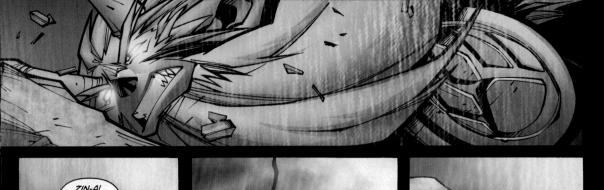

ZIN-AL ELUNE! THE NATURE MADNESS IS FADING!

IT'S OVER.

ON YOUR FEET, ORC. YOU'VE A LONG MARCH AHEAD OF YOU.

FASCINATING.

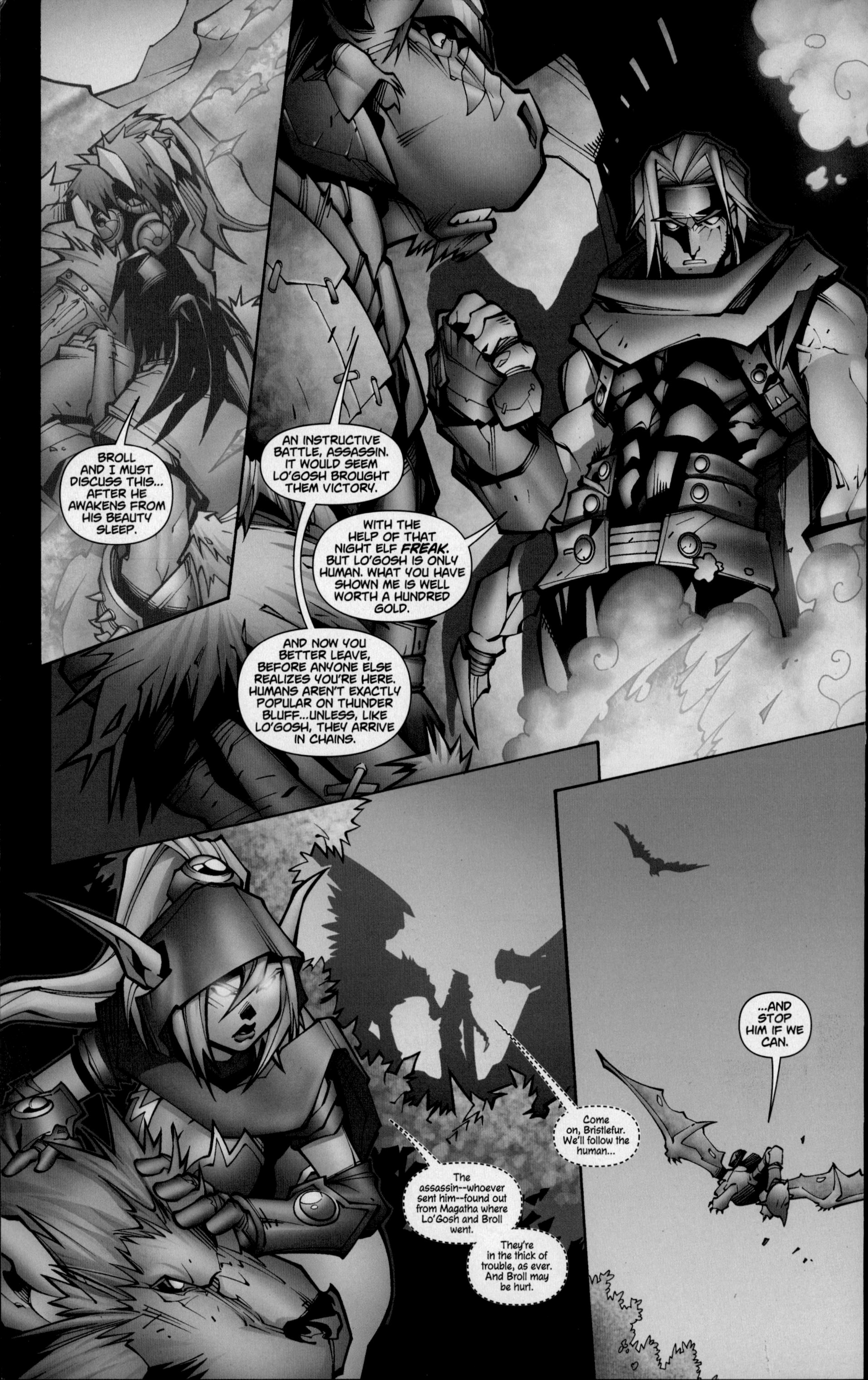
BROLL AND I MUST DISCUSS THIS... AFTER HE AWAKENS FROM HIS BEAUTY SLEEP.
AN INSTRUCTIVE BATTLE, ASSASSIN. IT WOULD SEEM LO'GOSH BROUGHT THEM VICTORY.
WITH THE HELP OF THAT NIGHT ELF FREAK. BUT LO'GOSH IS ONLY HUMAN. WHAT YOU HAVE SHOWN ME IS WELL WORTH A HUNDRED GOLD.
AND NOW YOU BETTER LEAVE, BEFORE ANYONE ELSE REALIZES YOU'RE HERE. HUMANS AREN'T EXACTLY POPULAR ON THUNDER BLUFF...UNLESS, LIKE LO'GOSH, THEY ARRIVE IN CHAINS.
The assassin--whoever sent him--found out from Magatha where Lo'Gosh and Broll went.
They're in the thick of trouble, as ever. And Broll may be hurt.
Come on, Bristlefur. We'll follow the human...
...AND STOP HIM IF WE CAN.

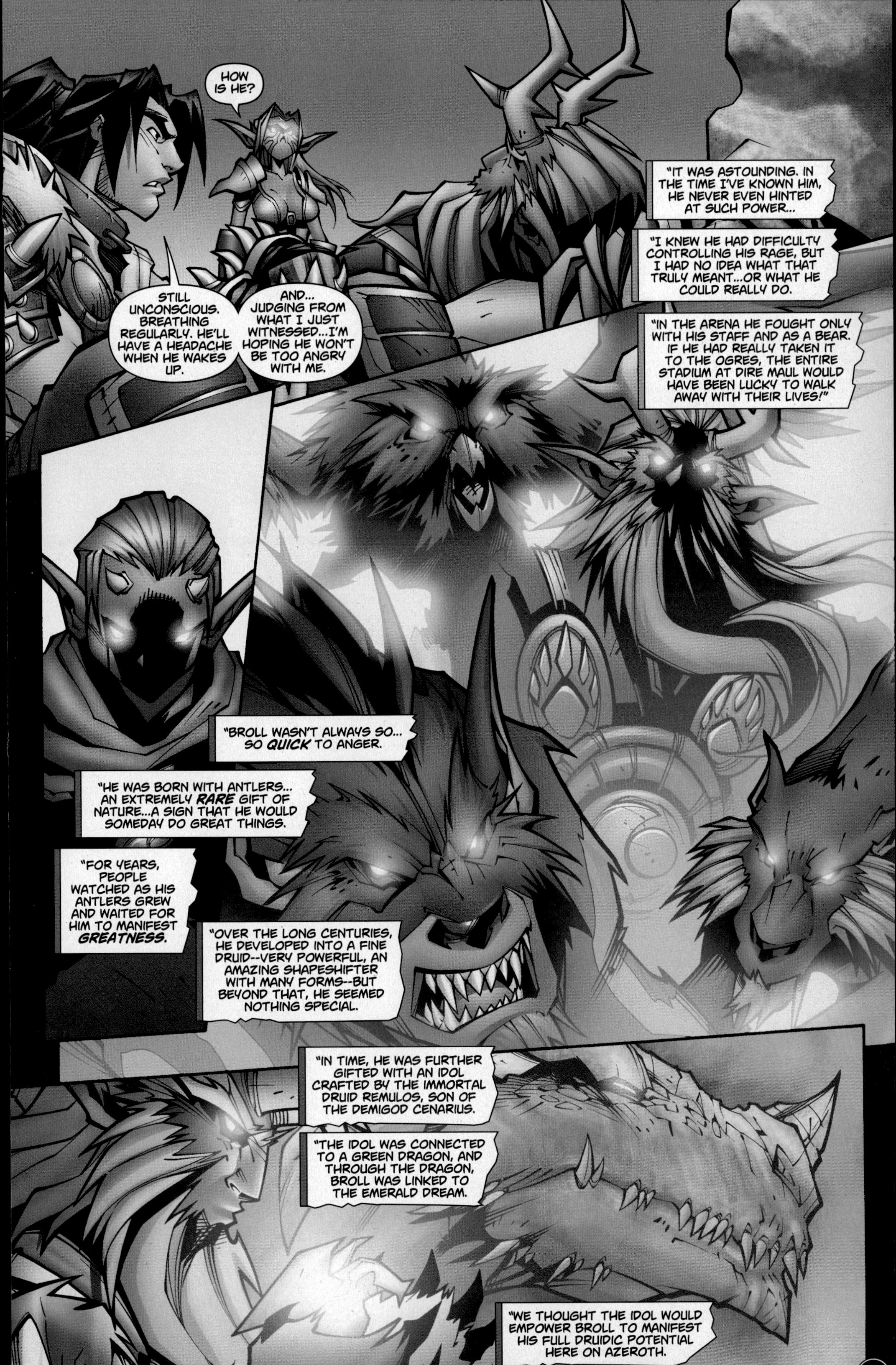
HOW IS HE?
"IT WAS ASTOUNDING. IN THE TIME I'VE KNOWN HIM, HE NEVER EVEN HINTED AT SUCH POWER...
"I KNEW HE HAD DIFFICULTY CONTROLLING HIS RAGE, BUT I HAD NO IDEA WHAT THAT TRULY MEANT...OR WHAT HE COULD REALLY DO.
STILL UNCONSCIOUS. BREATHING REGULARLY. HE'LL HAVE A HEADACHE WHEN HE WAKES UP.
AND... JUDGING FROM WHAT I JUST WITNESSED...I'M HOPING HE WON'T BE TOO ANGRY WITH ME.
"IN THE ARENA HE FOUGHT ONLY WITH HIS STAFF AND AS A BEAR. IF HE HAD REALLY TAKEN IT TO THE OGRES, THE ENTIRE STADIUM AT DIRE MAUL WOULD HAVE BEEN LUCKY TO WALK AWAY WITH THEIR LIVES!"
"BROLL WASN'T ALWAYS SO... SO QUICK TO ANGER.
"HE WAS BORN WITH ANTLERS... AN EXTREMELY RARE GIFT OF NATURE...A SIGN THAT HE WOULD SOMEDAY DO GREAT THINGS.
"FOR YEARS, PEOPLE WATCHED AS HIS ANTLERS GREW AND WAITED FOR HIM TO MANIFEST GREATNESS.
"OVER THE LONG CENTURIES, HE DEVELOPED INTO A FINE DRUID--VERY POWERFUL, AN AMAZING SHAPESHIFTER WITH MANY FORMS--BUT BEYOND THAT, HE SEEMED NOTHING SPECIAL.
"IN TIME, HE WAS FURTHER GIFTED WITH AN IDOL CRAFTED BY THE IMMORTAL DRUID REMULOS, SON OF THE DEMIGOD CENARIUS.
"THE IDOL WAS CONNECTED TO A GREEN DRAGON, AND THROUGH THE DRAGON, BROLL WAS LINKED TO THE EMERALD DREAM.
"WE THOUGHT THE IDOL WOULD EMPOWER BROLL TO MANIFEST HIS FULL DRUIDIC POTENTIAL HERE ON AZEROTH.

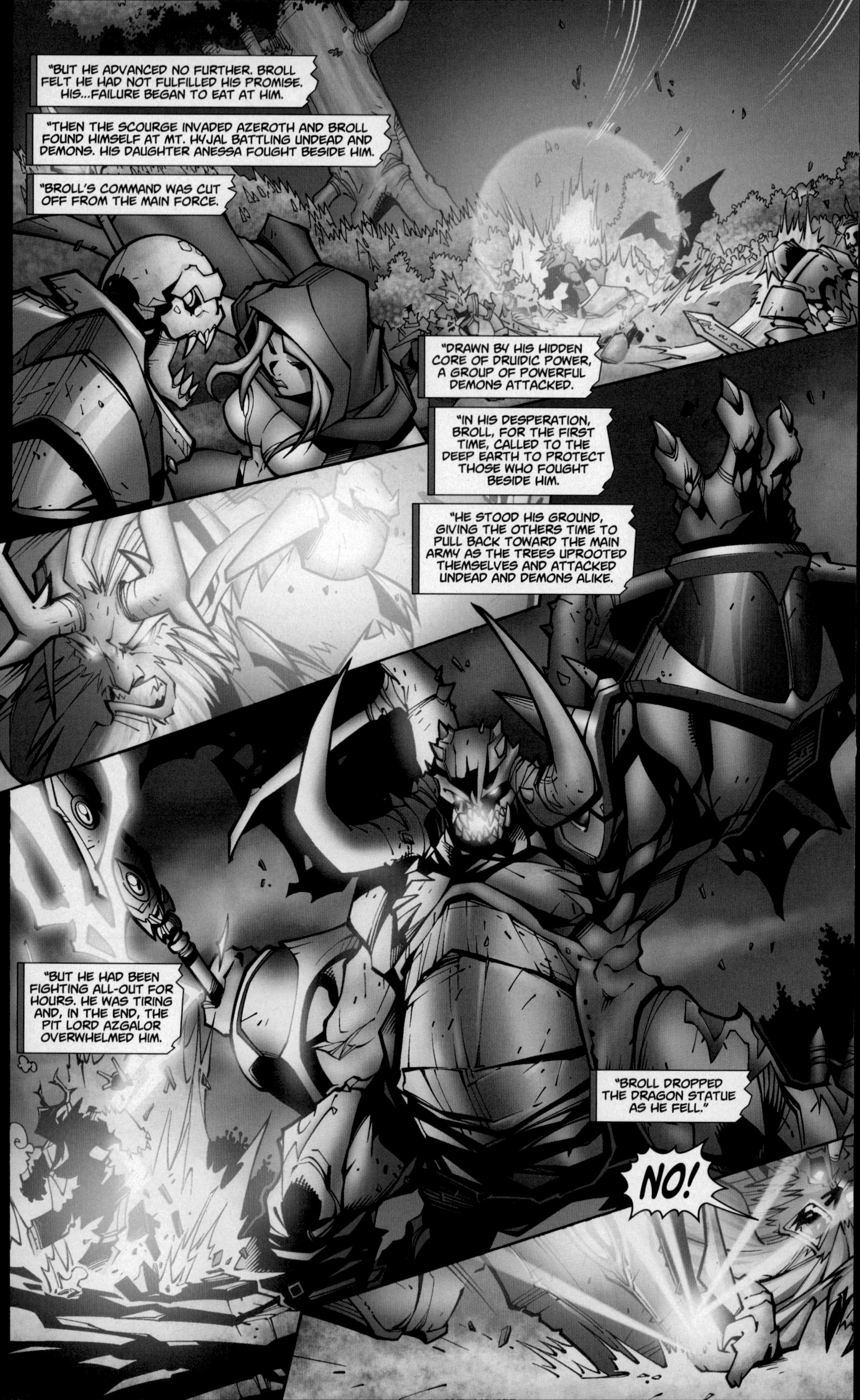
"BUT HE ADVANCED NO FURTHER. BROLL FELT HE HAD NOT FULFILLED HIS PROMISE. HIS...FAILURE BEGAN TO EAT AT HIM.
"THEN THE SCOURGE INVADED AZEROTH AND BROLL FOUND HIMSELF AT MT. HYJAL BATTLING UNDEAD AND DEMONS. HIS DAUGHTER ANESSA FOUGHT BESIDE HIM.
"BROLL'S COMMAND WAS CUT OFF FROM THE MAIN FORCE.
"DRAWN BY HIS HIDDEN CORE OF DRUIDIC POWER, A GROUP OF POWERFUL DEMONS ATTACKED.
"IN HIS DESPERATION, BROLL, FOR THE FIRST TIME, CALLED TO THE DEEP EARTH TO PROTECT THOSE WHO FOUGHT BESIDE HIM.
"HE STOOD HIS GROUND, GIVING THE OTHERS TIME TO PULL BACK TOWARD THE MAIN ARMY AS THE TREES UPROOTED THEMSELVES AND ATTACKED UNDEAD AND DEMONS ALIKE.
"BUT HE HAD BEEN FIGHTING ALL-OUT FOR HOURS. HE WAS TIRING AND, IN THE END, THE PIT LORD AZGALOR OVERWHELMED HIM.
"BROLL DROPPED THE DRAGON STATUE AS HE FELL."
NO!

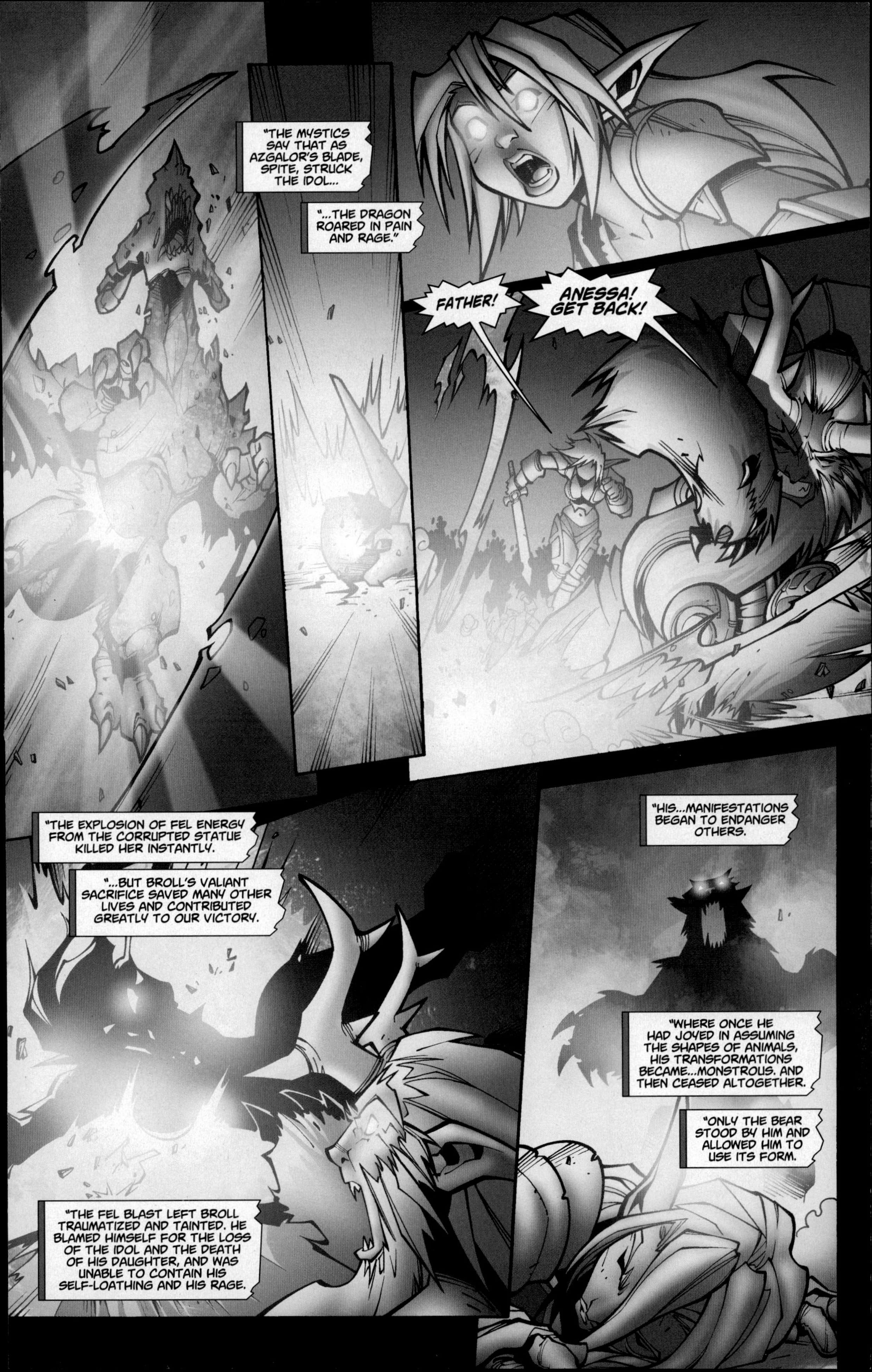
"THE MYSTICS SAY THAT AS AZGALOR'S BLADE, SPITE, STRUCK THE IDOL...
"...THE DRAGON ROARED IN PAIN AND RAGE."
FATHER!
ANESSA! GET BACK!
"THE EXPLOSION OF FEL ENERGY FROM THE CORRUPTED STATUE KILLED HER INSTANTLY.
"...BUT BROLL'S VALIANT SACRIFICE SAVED MANY OTHER LIVES AND CONTRIBUTED GREATLY TO OUR VICTORY.
"THE FEL BLAST LEFT BROLL TRAUMATIZED AND TAINTED. HE BLAMED HIMSELF FOR THE LOSS OF THE IDOL AND THE DEATH OF HIS DAUGHTER, AND WAS UNABLE TO CONTAIN HIS SELF-LOATHING AND HIS RAGE.
"HIS...MANIFESTATIONS BEGAN TO ENDANGER OTHERS.
"WHERE ONCE HE HAD JOYED IN ASSUMING THE SHAPES OF ANIMALS, HIS TRANSFORMATIONS BECAME...MONSTROUS. AND THEN CEASED ALTOGETHER.
"ONLY THE BEAR STOOD BY HIM AND ALLOWED HIM TO USE ITS FORM.

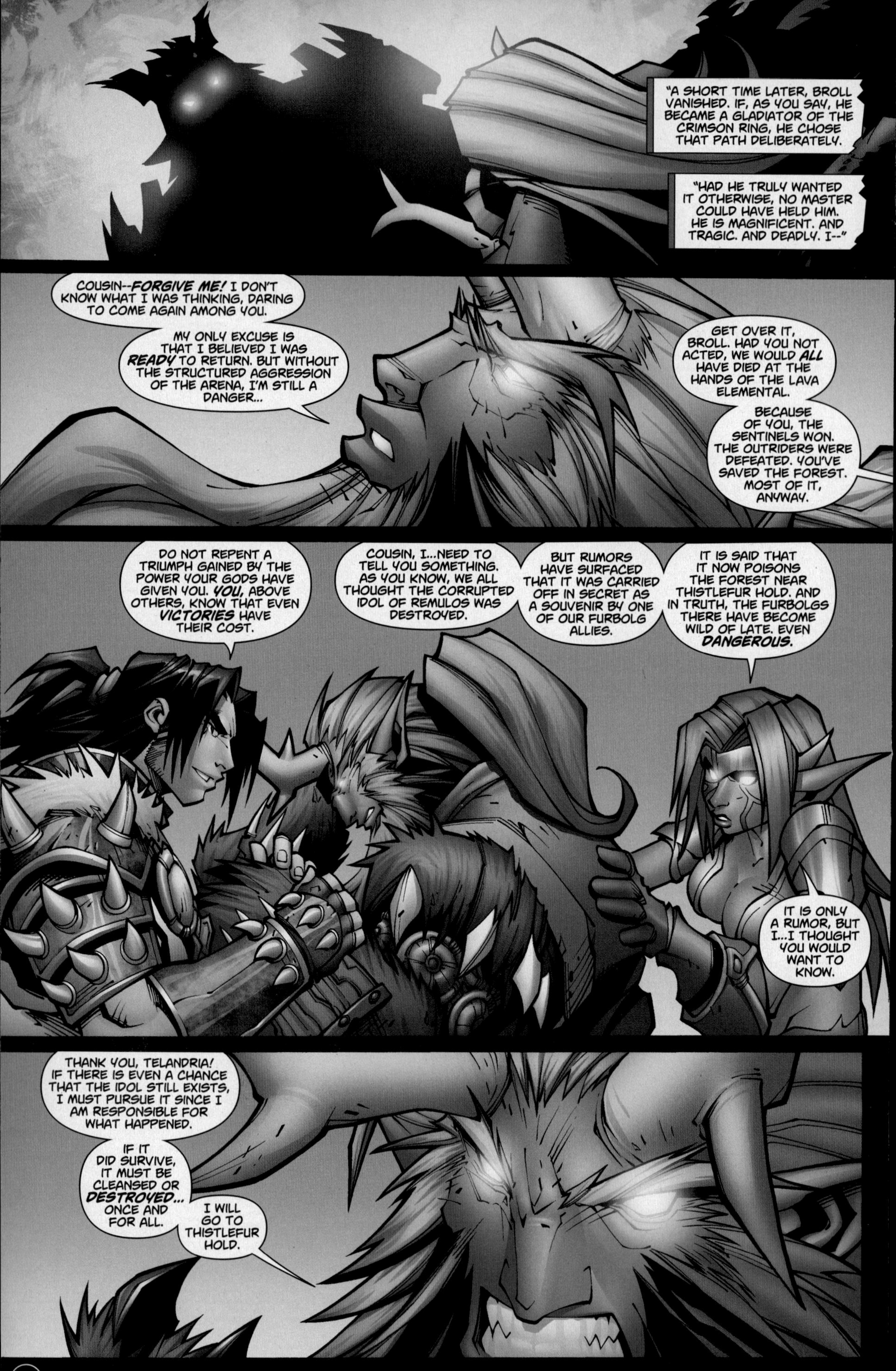
"A SHORT TIME LATER, BROLL VANISHED. IF, AS YOU SAY, HE BECAME A GLADIATOR OF THE CRIMSON RING, HE CHOSE THAT PATH DELIBERATELY.
"HAD HE TRULY WANTED IT OTHERWISE, NO MASTER COULD HAVE HELD HIM. HE IS MAGNIFICENT. AND TRAGIC. AND DEADLY. I--"
COUSIN--FORGIVE ME! I DON'T KNOW WHAT I WAS THINKING, DARING TO COME AGAIN AMONG YOU.
MY ONLY EXCUSE IS THAT I BELIEVED I WAS READY TO RETURN. BUT WITHOUT THE STRUCTURED AGGRESSION OF THE ARENA, I'M STILL A DANGER...
GET OVER IT, BROLL. HAD YOU NOT ACTED, WE WOULD ALL HAVE DIED AT THE HANDS OF THE LAVA ELEMENTAL.
BECAUSE OF YOU, THE SENTINELS WON. THE OUTRIDERS WERE DEFEATED. YOU'VE SAVED THE FOREST. MOST OF IT, ANYWAY.
DO NOT REPENT A TRIUMPH GAINED BY THE POWER YOUR GODS HAVE GIVEN YOU. YOU, ABOVE OTHERS, KNOW THAT EVEN VICTORIES HAVE THEIR COST.
COUSIN, I...NEED TO TELL YOU SOMETHING. AS YOU KNOW, WE ALL THOUGHT THE CORRUPTED IDOL OF REMULOS WAS DESTROYED.
BUT RUMORS HAVE SURFACED THAT IT WAS CARRIED OFF IN SECRET AS A SOUVENIR BY ONE OF OUR FURBOLG ALLIES.
IT IS SAID THAT IT NOW POISONS THE FOREST NEAR THISTLEFUR HOLD. AND IN TRUTH, THE FURBOLGS THERE HAVE BECOME WILD OF LATE. EVEN DANGEROUS.
IT IS ONLY A RUMOR, BUT I...I THOUGHT YOU WOULD WANT TO KNOW.
THANK YOU, TELANDRIA! IF THERE IS EVEN A CHANCE THAT THE IDOL STILL EXISTS, I MUST PURSUE IT SINCE I AM RESPONSIBLE FOR WHAT HAPPENED.
IF IT DID SURVIVE, IT MUST BE CLEANSED OR DESTROYED... ONCE AND FOR ALL.
I WILL GO TO THISTLEFUR HOLD.

CHAPTER 5

Issue #5 Cover
by Samwise Didier

Issue #5 Cover
by Jim Lee and Alex Sinclair

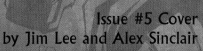

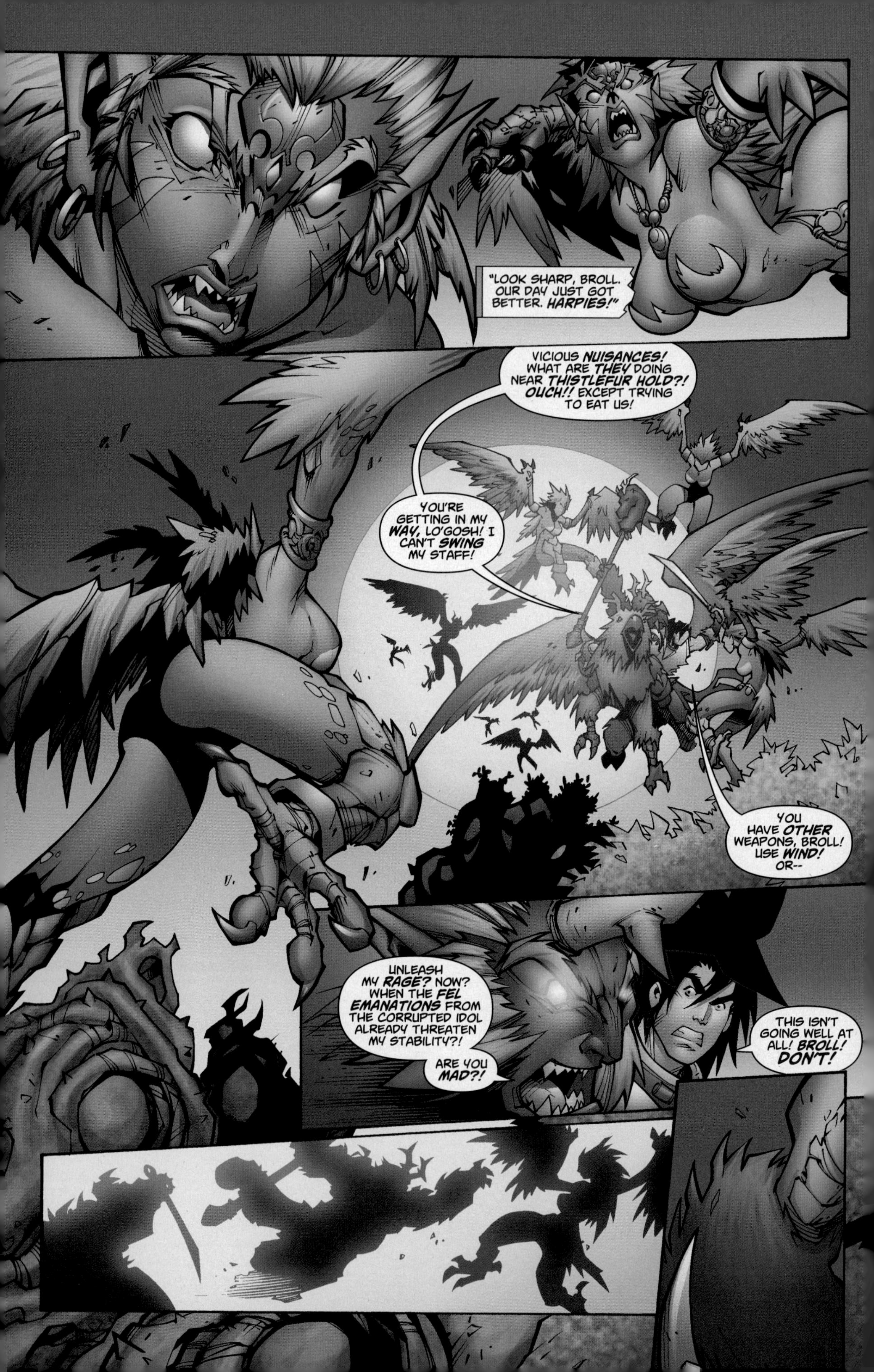
"LOOK SHARP, BROLL. OUR DAY JUST GOT BETTER. HARPIES!"
VICIOUS NUISANCES! WHAT ARE THEY DOING NEAR THISTLEFUR HOLD?! OUCH!! EXCEPT TRYING TO EAT US!
YOU'RE GETTING IN MY WAY, LO'GOSH! I CAN'T SWING MY STAFF!
YOU HAVE OTHER WEAPONS, BROLL! USE WIND! OR--
UNLEASH MY RAGE? NOW? WHEN THE FEL EMANATIONS FROM THE CORRUPTED IDOL ALREADY THREATEN MY STABILITY?!
ARE YOU MAD?!
THIS ISN'T GOING WELL AT ALL! BROLL! DON'T!

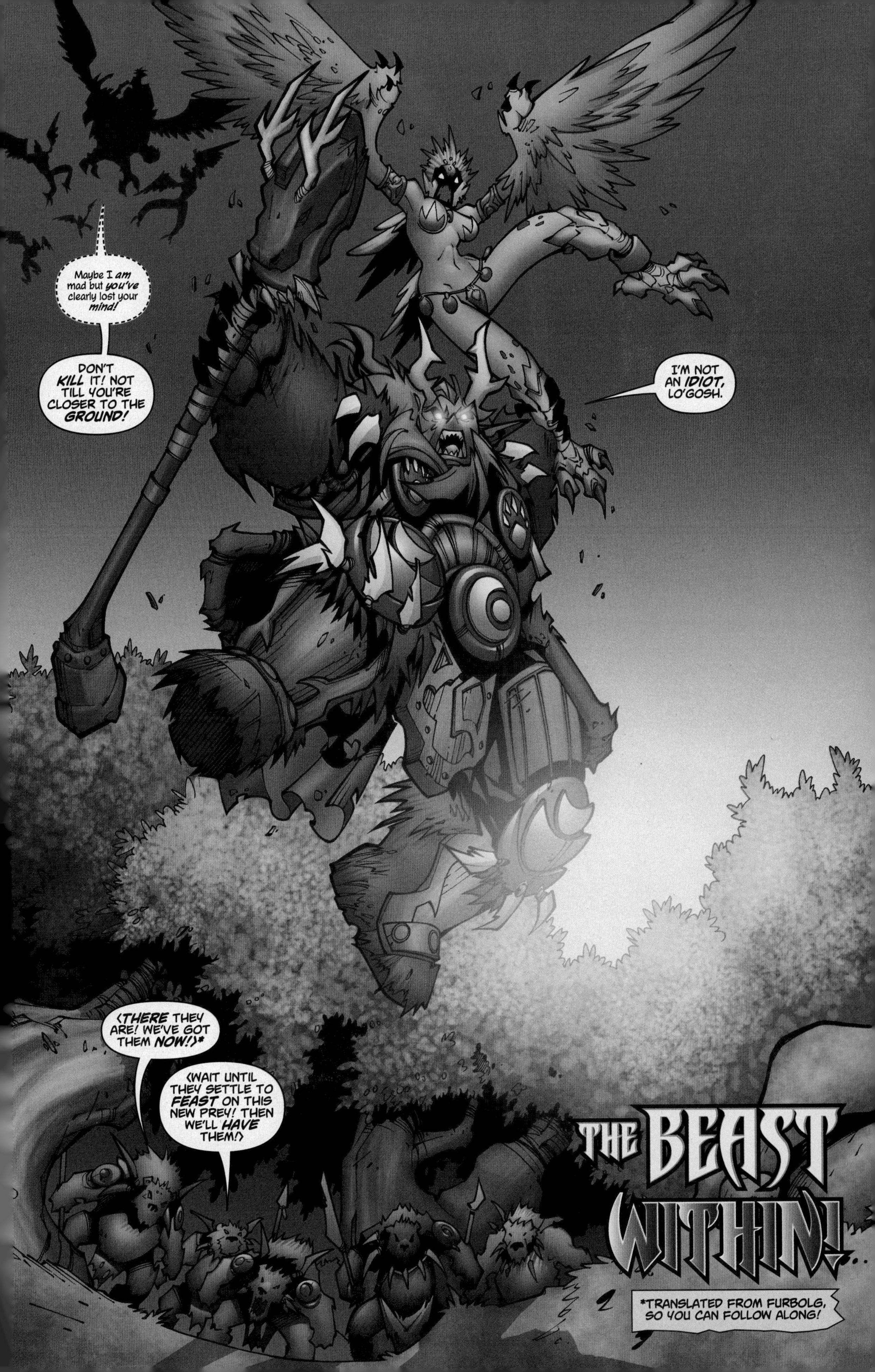

Maybe I *am* mad but *you've* clearly lost your *mind!*
DON'T **KILL** IT! NOT TILL YOU'RE CLOSER TO THE **GROUND!**
I'M NOT AN *IDIOT,* LO'GOSH.
‹*THERE* THEY ARE! WE'VE GOT THEM *NOW!*›*
‹WAIT UNTIL THEY SETTLE TO **FEAST** ON THIS NEW PREY! THEN WE'LL *HAVE* THEM!›
THE BEAST WITHIN!
*TRANSLATED FROM FURBOLG, SO YOU CAN FOLLOW ALONG!

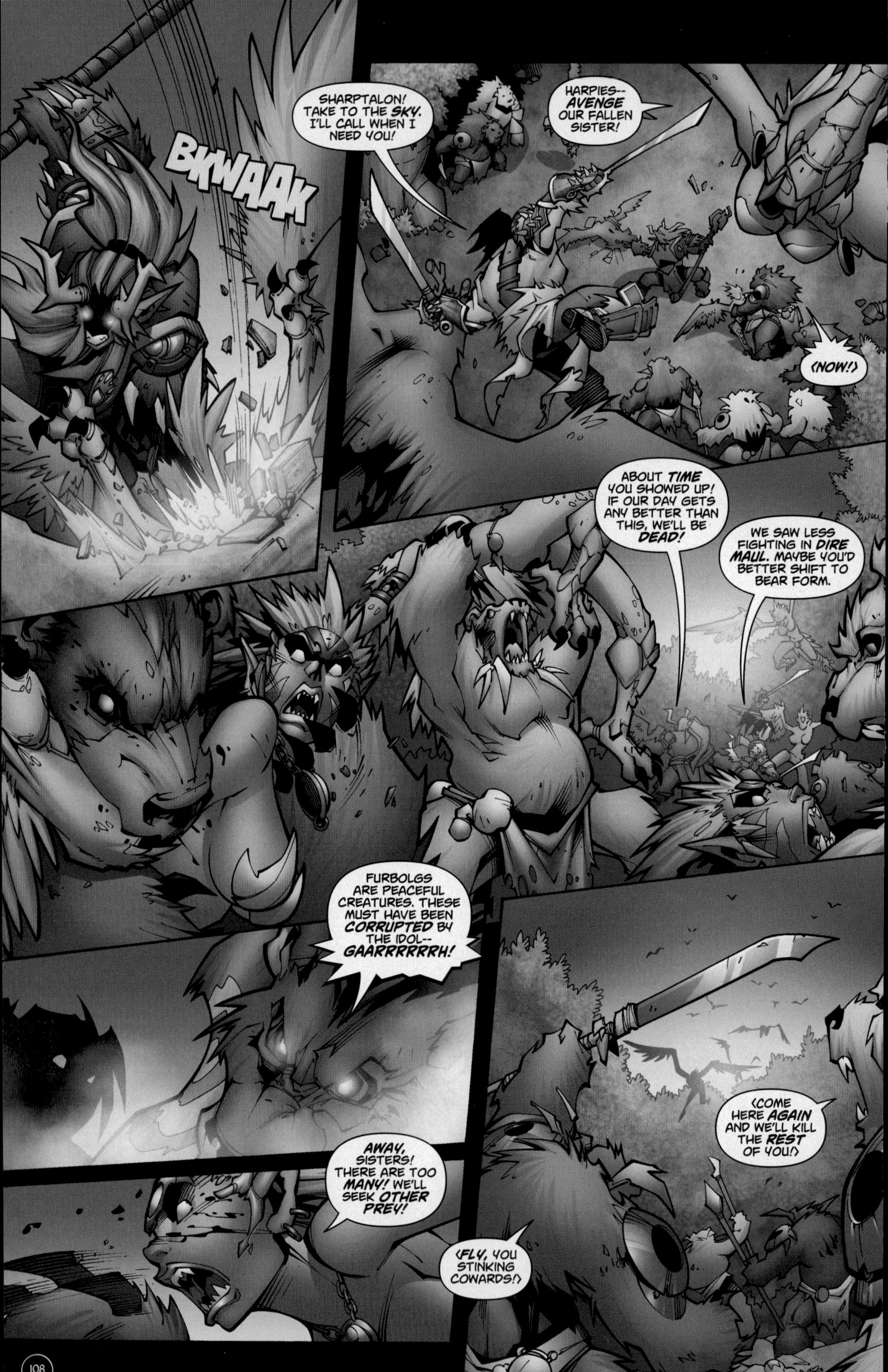
BKWAAK
SHARPTALON! TAKE TO THE SKY. I'LL CALL WHEN I NEED YOU!
HARPIES-- AVENGE OUR FALLEN SISTER!
<NOW!>
ABOUT TIME YOU SHOWED UP! IF OUR DAY GETS ANY BETTER THAN THIS, WE'LL BE DEAD!
WE SAW LESS FIGHTING IN DIRE MAUL. MAYBE YOU'D BETTER SHIFT TO BEAR FORM.
FURBOLGS ARE PEACEFUL CREATURES. THESE MUST HAVE BEEN CORRUPTED BY THE IDOL-- GAARRRRRRH!
AWAY, SISTERS! THERE ARE TOO MANY! WE'LL SEEK OTHER PREY!
<FLY, YOU STINKING COWARDS!>
<COME HERE AGAIN AND WE'LL KILL THE REST OF YOU!>

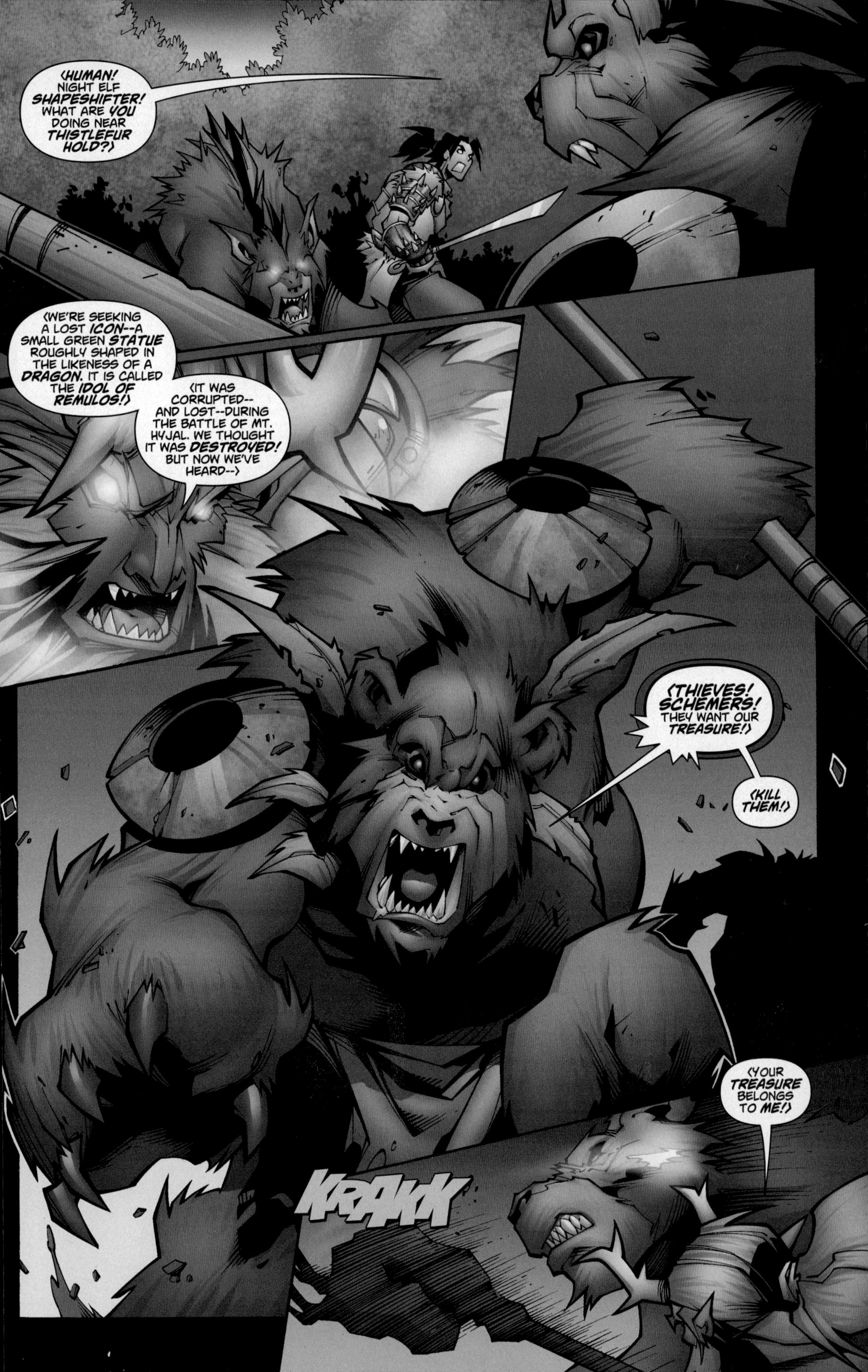

‹HUMAN! NIGHT ELF SHAPESHIFTER! WHAT ARE YOU DOING NEAR THISTLEFUR HOLD?›
‹WE'RE SEEKING A LOST ICON--A SMALL GREEN STATUE ROUGHLY SHAPED IN THE LIKENESS OF A DRAGON. IT IS CALLED THE IDOL OF REMULOS!›
‹IT WAS CORRUPTED--AND LOST--DURING THE BATTLE OF MT. HYJAL. WE THOUGHT IT WAS DESTROYED! BUT NOW WE'VE HEARD--›
‹THIEVES! SCHEMERS! THEY WANT OUR TREASURE!›
‹KILL THEM!›
‹YOUR TREASURE BELONGS TO ME!›
KRAKK

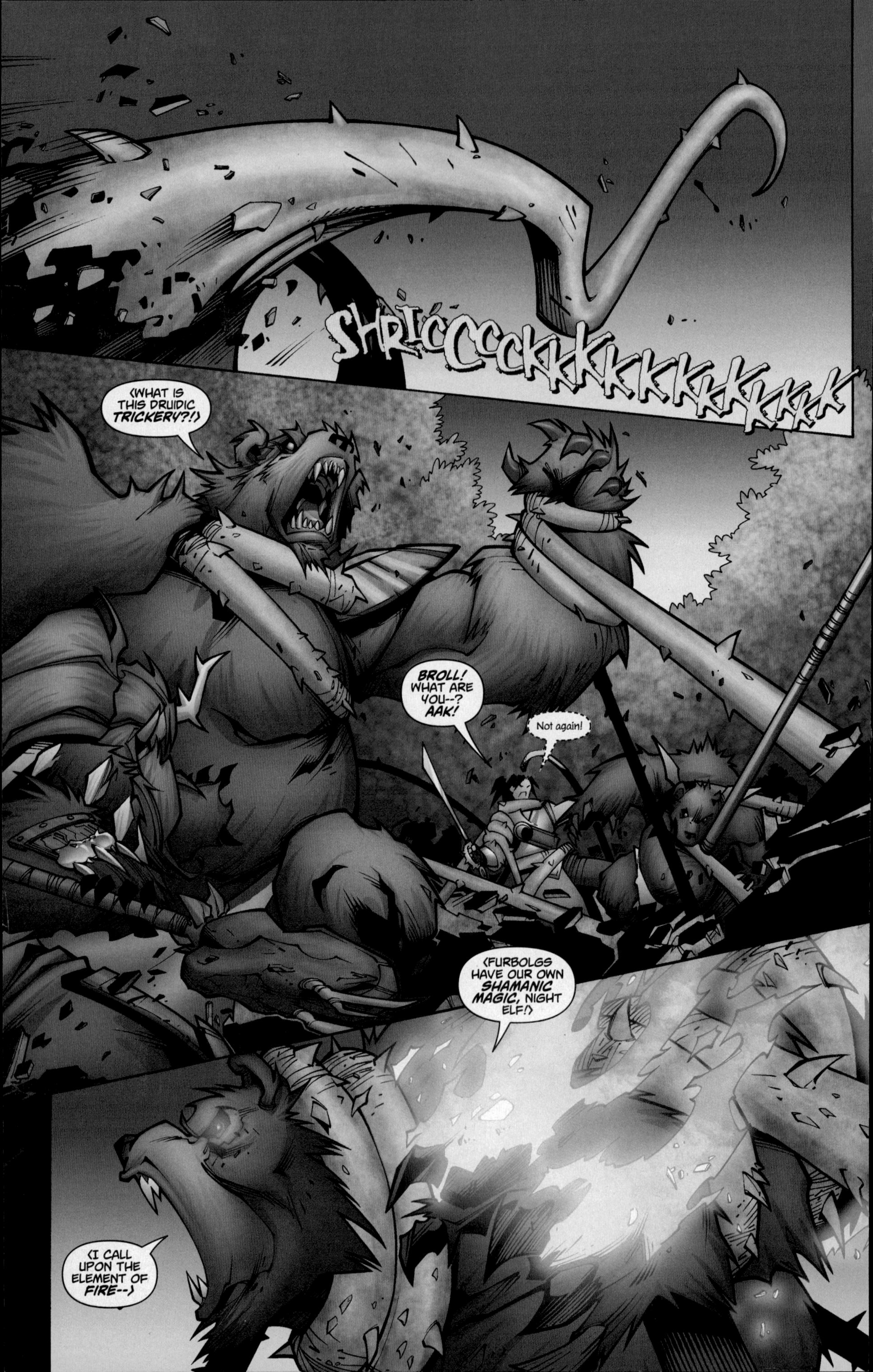
SHRICCCCKKKKKKKKKKK
‹WHAT IS THIS DRUIDIC TRICKERY?!›
BROLL! WHAT ARE YOU--? AAK!
Not again!
‹FURBOLGS HAVE OUR OWN SHAMANIC MAGIC, NIGHT ELF!›
‹I CALL UPON THE ELEMENT OF FIRE--›

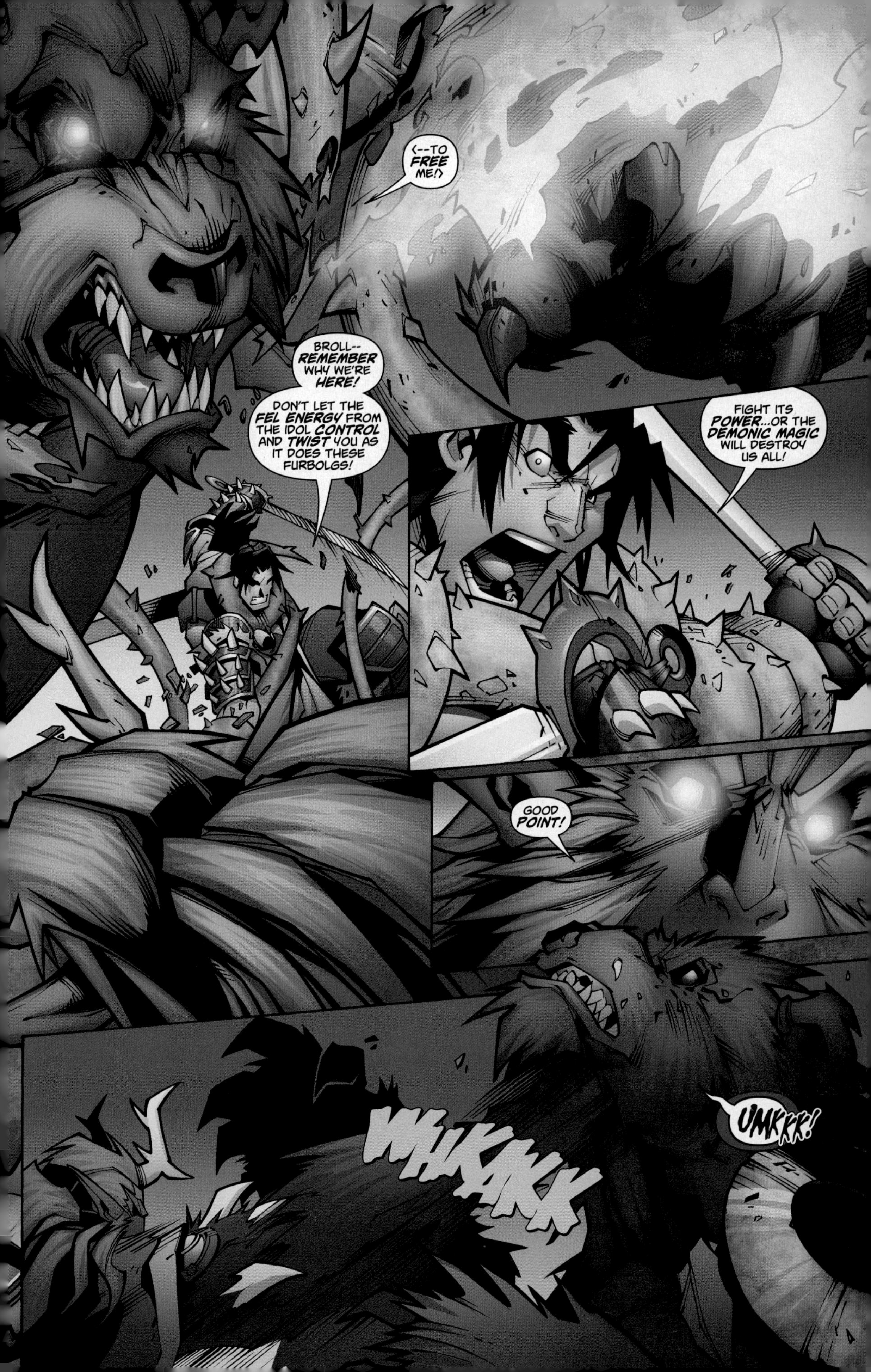

<--TO FREE ME!>
BROLL-- REMEMBER WHY WE'RE HERE!
DON'T LET THE FEL ENERGY FROM THE IDOL CONTROL AND TWIST YOU AS IT DOES THESE FURBOLGS!
FIGHT ITS POWER...OR THE DEMONIC MAGIC WILL DESTROY US ALL!
GOOD POINT!
WHKAKK
UMKKK!

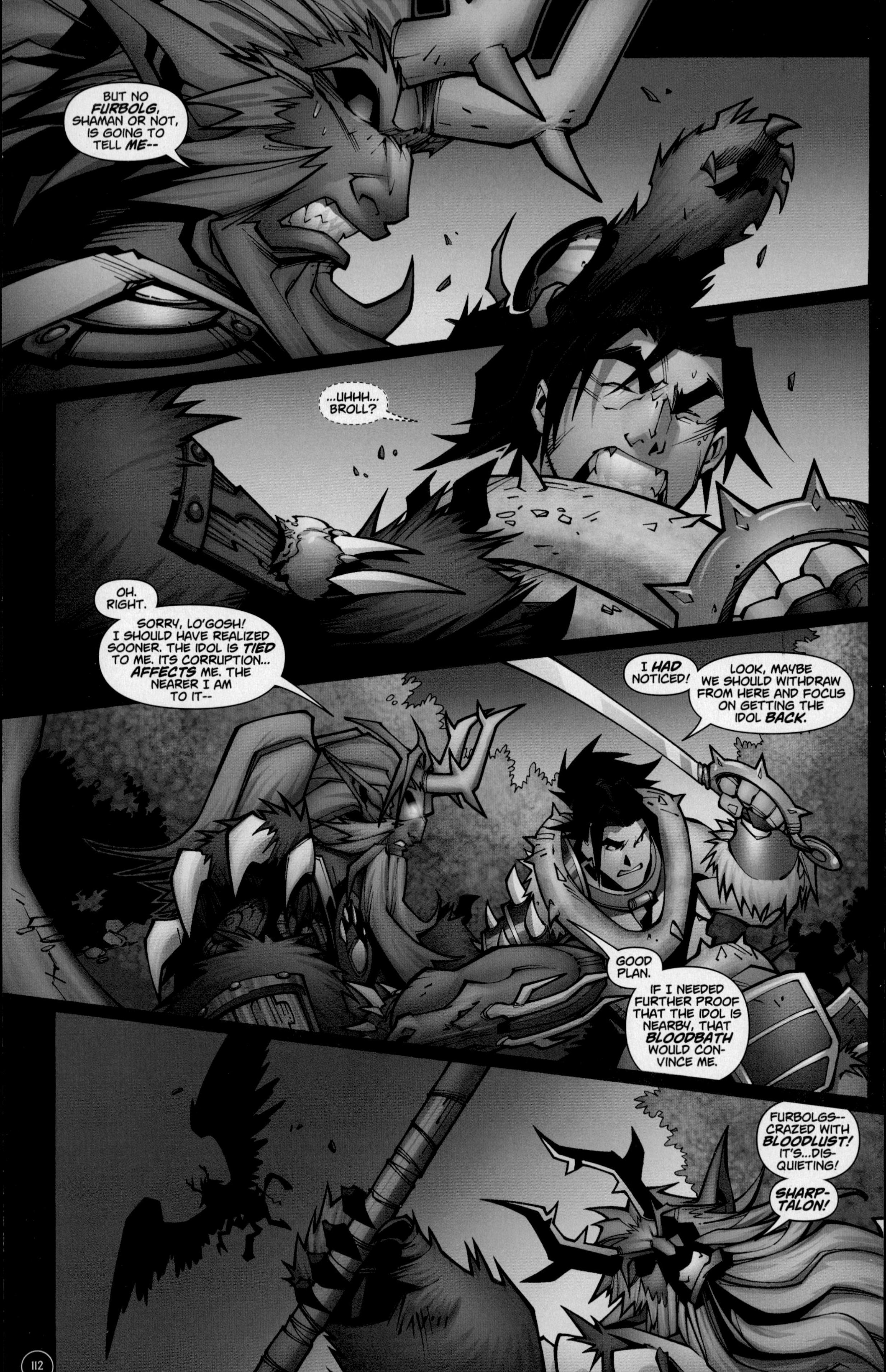
BUT NO FURBOLG, SHAMAN OR NOT, IS GOING TO TELL ME--
...UHHH... BROLL?
OH. RIGHT.
SORRY, LO'GOSH! I SHOULD HAVE REALIZED SOONER. THE IDOL IS TIED TO ME. ITS CORRUPTION... AFFECTS ME. THE NEARER I AM TO IT--
I HAD NOTICED!
LOOK, MAYBE WE SHOULD WITHDRAW FROM HERE AND FOCUS ON GETTING THE IDOL BACK.
GOOD PLAN.
IF I NEEDED FURTHER PROOF THAT THE IDOL IS NEARBY, THAT BLOODBATH WOULD CONVINCE ME.
FURBOLGS--CRAZED WITH BLOODLUST! IT'S...DISQUIETING!
SHARP-TALON!

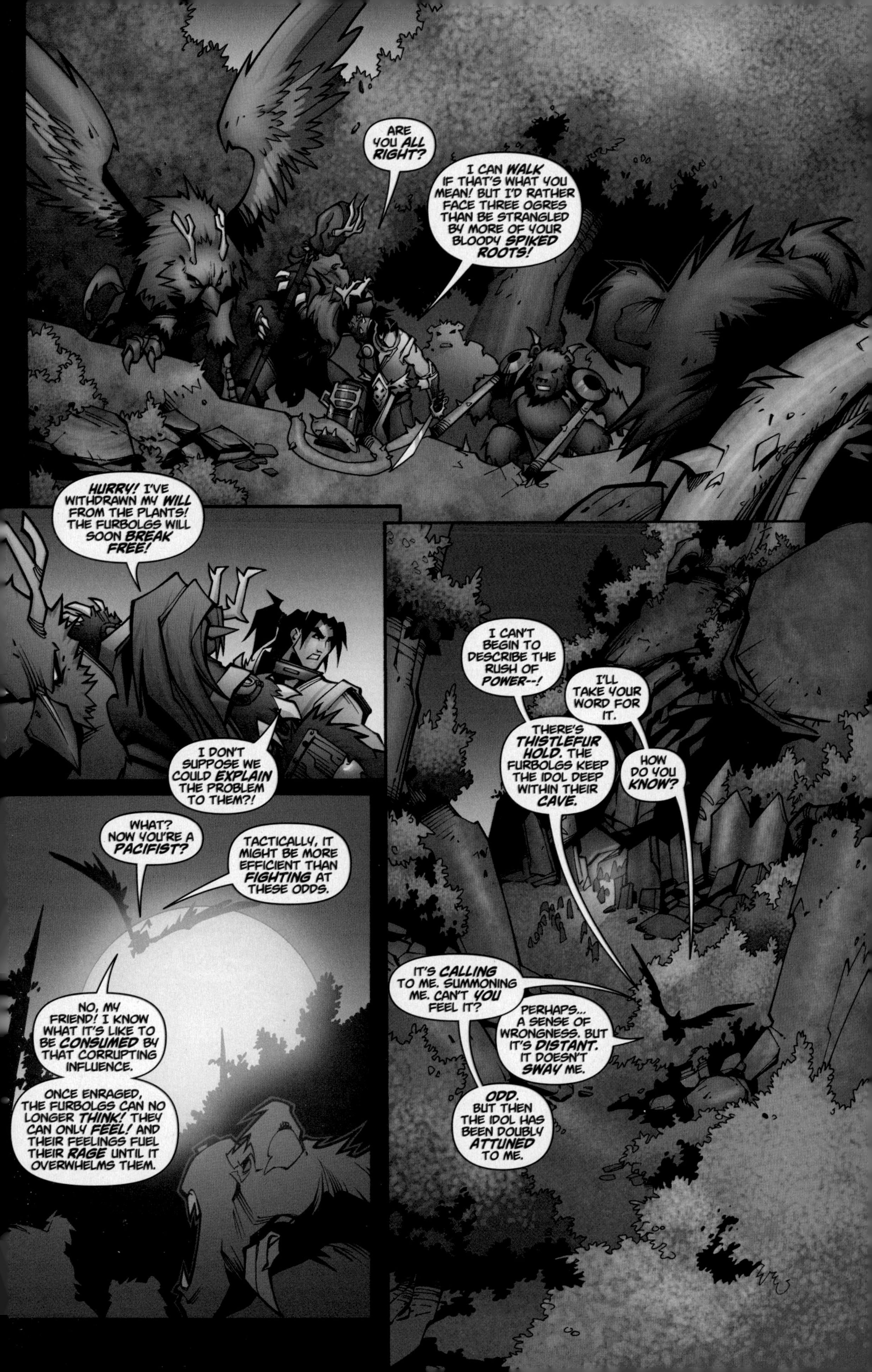
ARE YOU ALL RIGHT?
I CAN WALK IF THAT'S WHAT YOU MEAN! BUT I'D RATHER FACE THREE OGRES THAN BE STRANGLED BY MORE OF YOUR BLOODY SPIKED ROOTS!
HURRY! I'VE WITHDRAWN MY WILL FROM THE PLANTS! THE FURBOLGS WILL SOON BREAK FREE!
I DON'T SUPPOSE WE COULD EXPLAIN THE PROBLEM TO THEM?!
WHAT? NOW YOU'RE A PACIFIST?
TACTICALLY, IT MIGHT BE MORE EFFICIENT THAN FIGHTING AT THESE ODDS.
NO, MY FRIEND! I KNOW WHAT IT'S LIKE TO BE CONSUMED BY THAT CORRUPTING INFLUENCE.
ONCE ENRAGED, THE FURBOLGS CAN NO LONGER THINK! THEY CAN ONLY FEEL! AND THEIR FEELINGS FUEL THEIR RAGE UNTIL IT OVERWHELMS THEM.
I CAN'T BEGIN TO DESCRIBE THE RUSH OF POWER--!
I'LL TAKE YOUR WORD FOR IT.
THERE'S THISTLEFUR HOLD. THE FURBOLGS KEEP THE IDOL DEEP WITHIN THEIR CAVE.
HOW DO YOU KNOW?
IT'S CALLING TO ME. SUMMONING ME. CAN'T YOU FEEL IT?
PERHAPS... A SENSE OF WRONGNESS. BUT IT'S DISTANT. IT DOESN'T SWAY ME.
ODD. BUT THEN THE IDOL HAS BEEN DOUBLY ATTUNED TO ME.

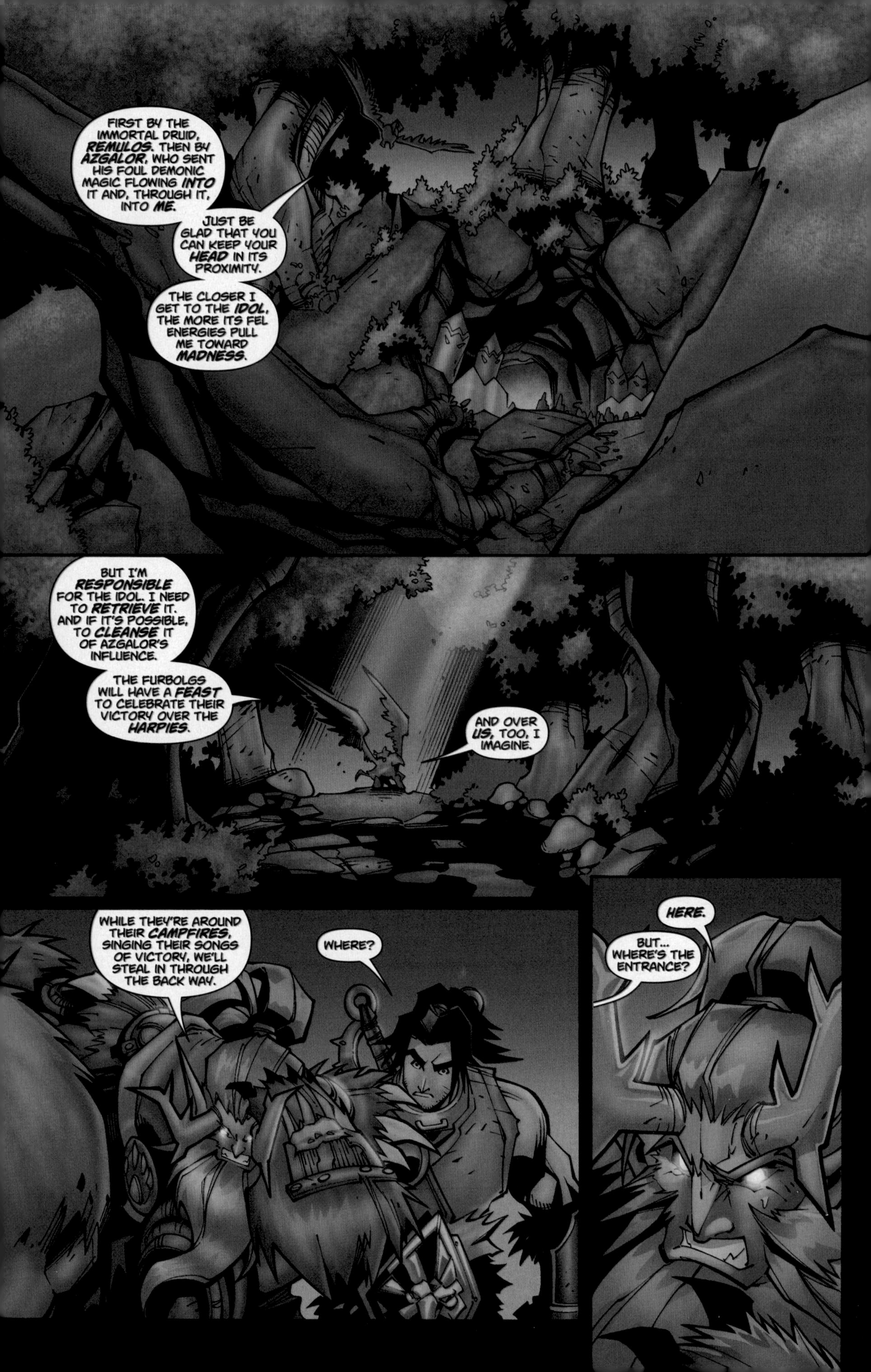
FIRST BY THE IMMORTAL DRUID, REMULOS. THEN BY AZGALOR, WHO SENT HIS FOUL DEMONIC MAGIC FLOWING INTO IT AND, THROUGH IT, INTO ME.
JUST BE GLAD THAT YOU CAN KEEP YOUR HEAD IN ITS PROXIMITY.
THE CLOSER I GET TO THE IDOL, THE MORE ITS FEL ENERGIES PULL ME TOWARD MADNESS.
BUT I'M RESPONSIBLE FOR THE IDOL. I NEED TO RETRIEVE IT. AND IF IT'S POSSIBLE, TO CLEANSE IT OF AZGALOR'S INFLUENCE.
THE FURBOLGS WILL HAVE A FEAST TO CELEBRATE THEIR VICTORY OVER THE HARPIES.
AND OVER US, TOO, I IMAGINE.
WHILE THEY'RE AROUND THEIR CAMPFIRES, SINGING THEIR SONGS OF VICTORY, WE'LL STEAL IN THROUGH THE BACK WAY.
WHERE?
HERE.
BUT... WHERE'S THE ENTRANCE?

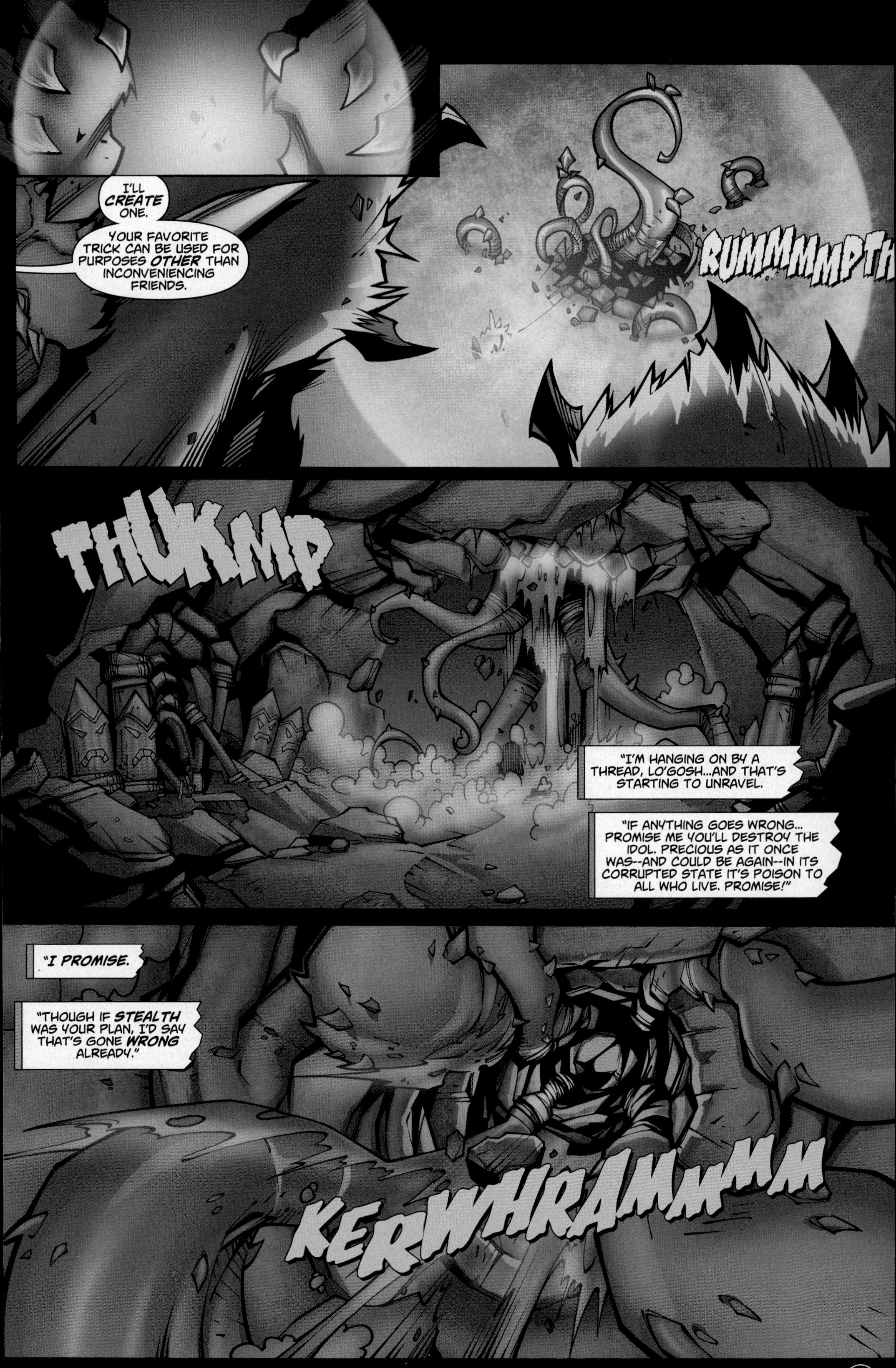
I'LL CREATE ONE.
YOUR FAVORITE TRICK CAN BE USED FOR PURPOSES OTHER THAN INCONVENIENCING FRIENDS.
RUMMMMMPTH
THUKMP
"I'M HANGING ON BY A THREAD, LO'GOSH...AND THAT'S STARTING TO UNRAVEL.
"IF ANYTHING GOES WRONG... PROMISE ME YOU'LL DESTROY THE IDOL. PRECIOUS AS IT ONCE WAS--AND COULD BE AGAIN--IN ITS CORRUPTED STATE IT'S POISON TO ALL WHO LIVE. PROMISE!"
"I PROMISE.
"THOUGH IF STEALTH WAS YOUR PLAN, I'D SAY THAT'S GONE WRONG ALREADY."
KERWHRAMMMMM

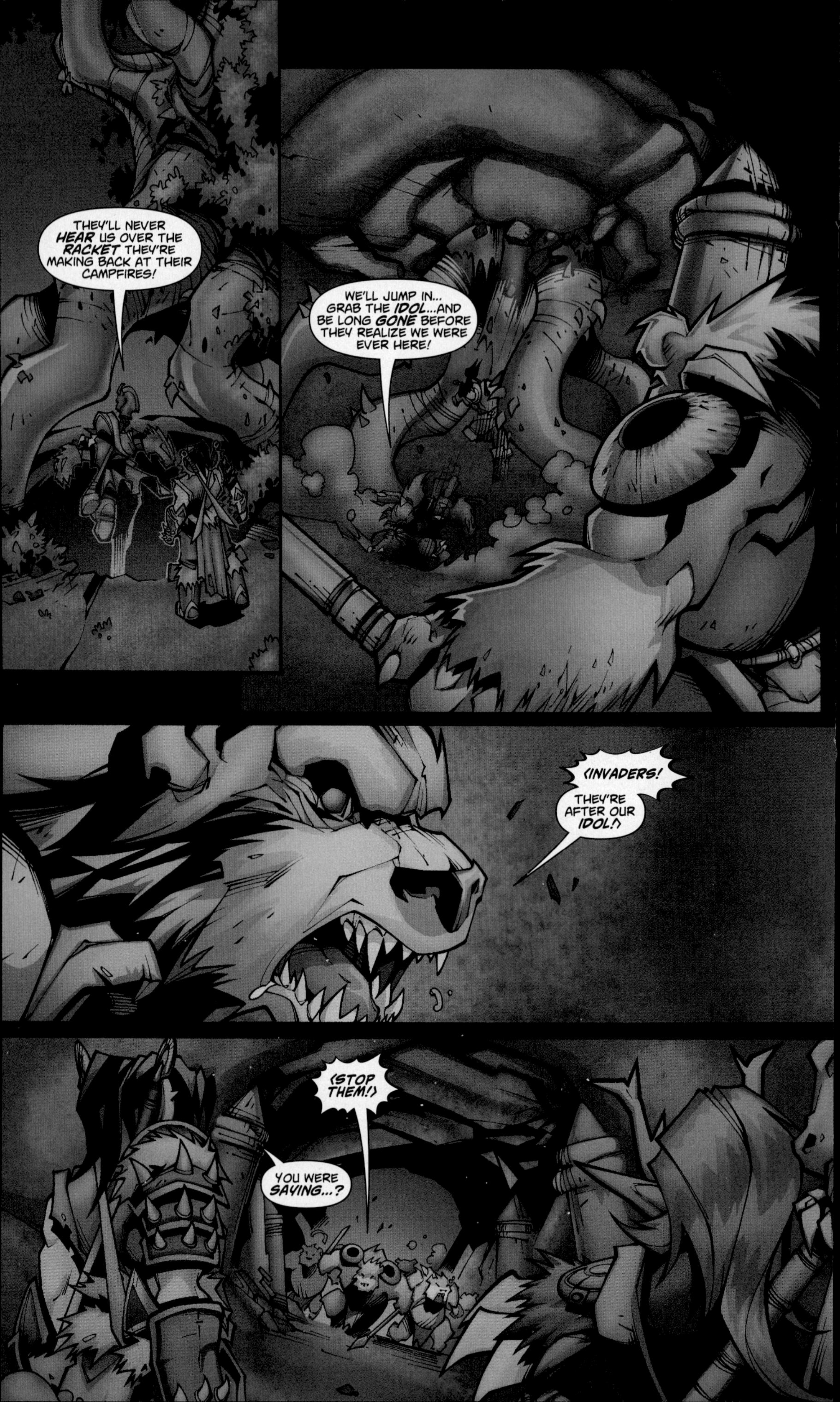
THEY'LL NEVER HEAR US OVER THE RACKET THEY'RE MAKING BACK AT THEIR CAMPFIRES!
WE'LL JUMP IN... GRAB THE IDOL...AND BE LONG GONE BEFORE THEY REALIZE WE WERE EVER HERE!
‹INVADERS!
THEY'RE AFTER OUR IDOL!›
‹STOP THEM!›
YOU WERE SAYING...?

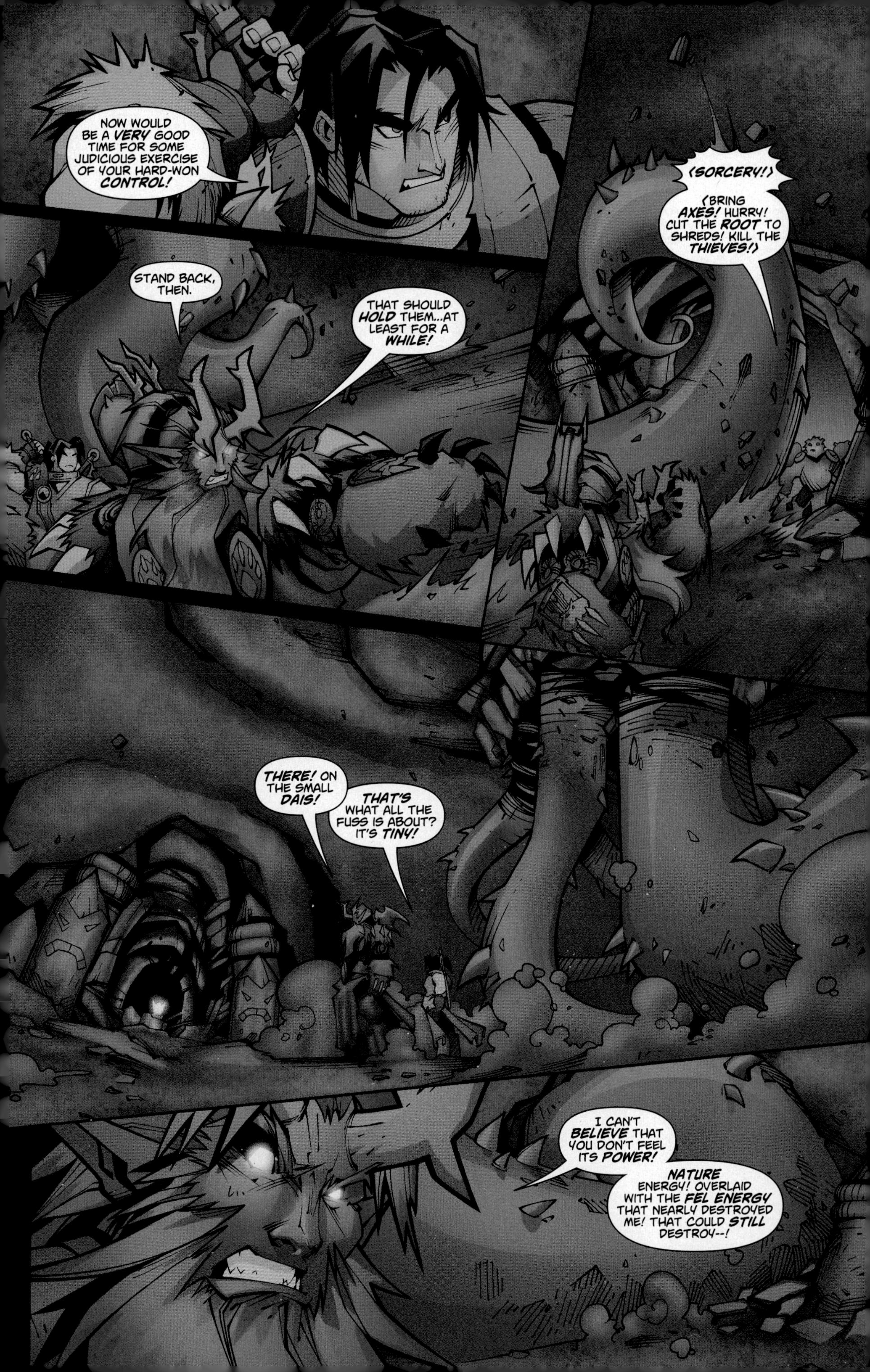
NOW WOULD BE A VERY GOOD TIME FOR SOME JUDICIOUS EXERCISE OF YOUR HARD-WON CONTROL!
STAND BACK, THEN.
THAT SHOULD HOLD THEM...AT LEAST FOR A WHILE!
⟨SORCERY!⟩
⟨BRING AXES! HURRY! CUT THE ROOT TO SHREDS! KILL THE THIEVES!⟩
THERE! ON THE SMALL DAIS!
THAT'S WHAT ALL THE FUSS IS ABOUT? IT'S TINY!
I CAN'T BELIEVE THAT YOU DON'T FEEL ITS POWER!
NATURE ENERGY! OVERLAID WITH THE FEL ENERGY THAT NEARLY DESTROYED ME! THAT COULD STILL DESTROY--!

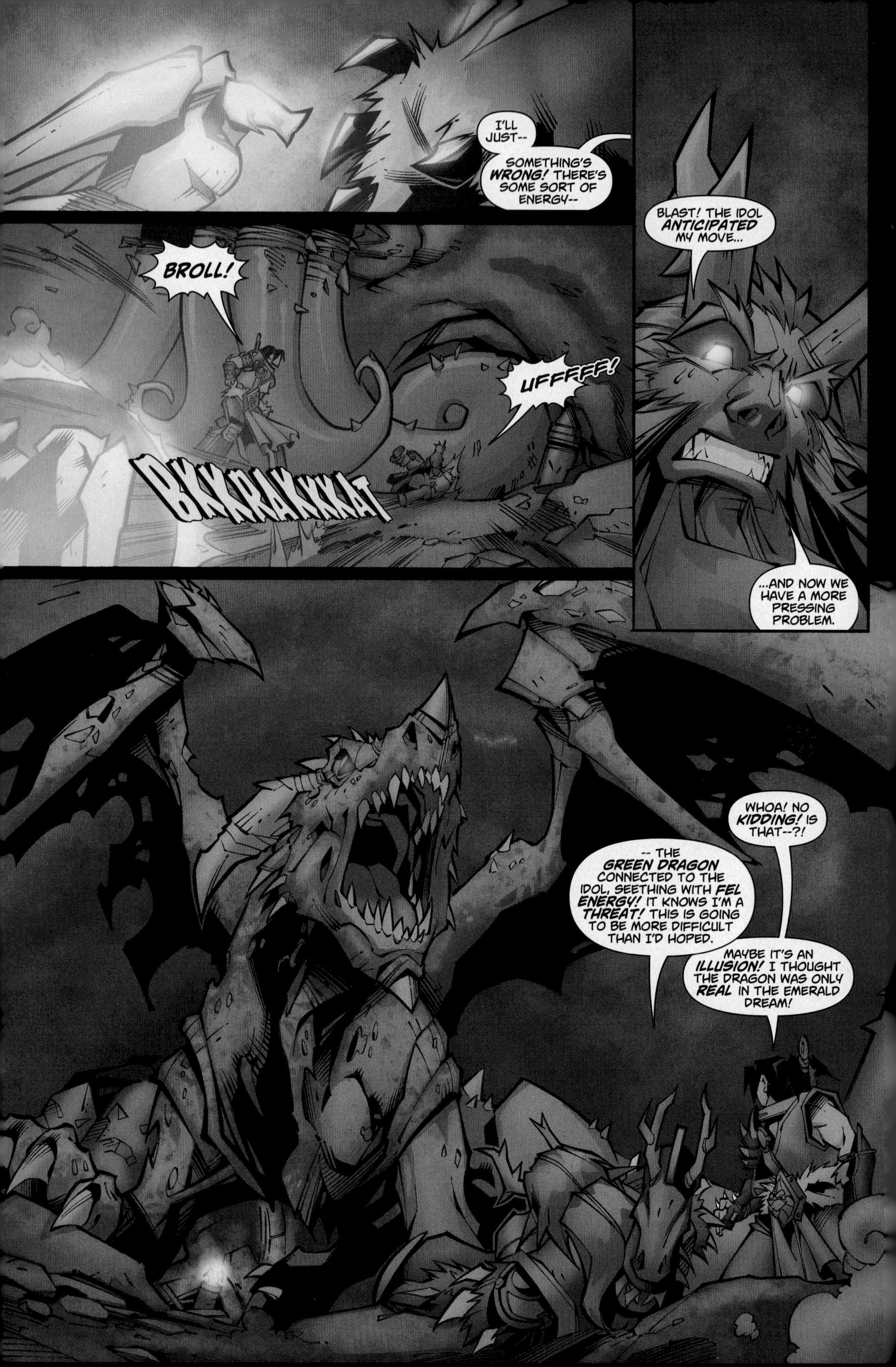
I'LL JUST--
SOMETHING'S WRONG! THERE'S SOME SORT OF ENERGY--
BLAST! THE IDOL ANTICIPATED MY MOVE...
BROLL!
UFFFFF!
BKKRAKKKAT
...AND NOW WE HAVE A MORE PRESSING PROBLEM.
WHOA! NO KIDDING! IS THAT--?!
-- THE GREEN DRAGON CONNECTED TO THE IDOL, SEETHING WITH FEL ENERGY! IT KNOWS I'M A THREAT! THIS IS GOING TO BE MORE DIFFICULT THAN I'D HOPED.
MAYBE IT'S AN ILLUSION! I THOUGHT THE DRAGON WAS ONLY REAL IN THE EMERALD DREAM!

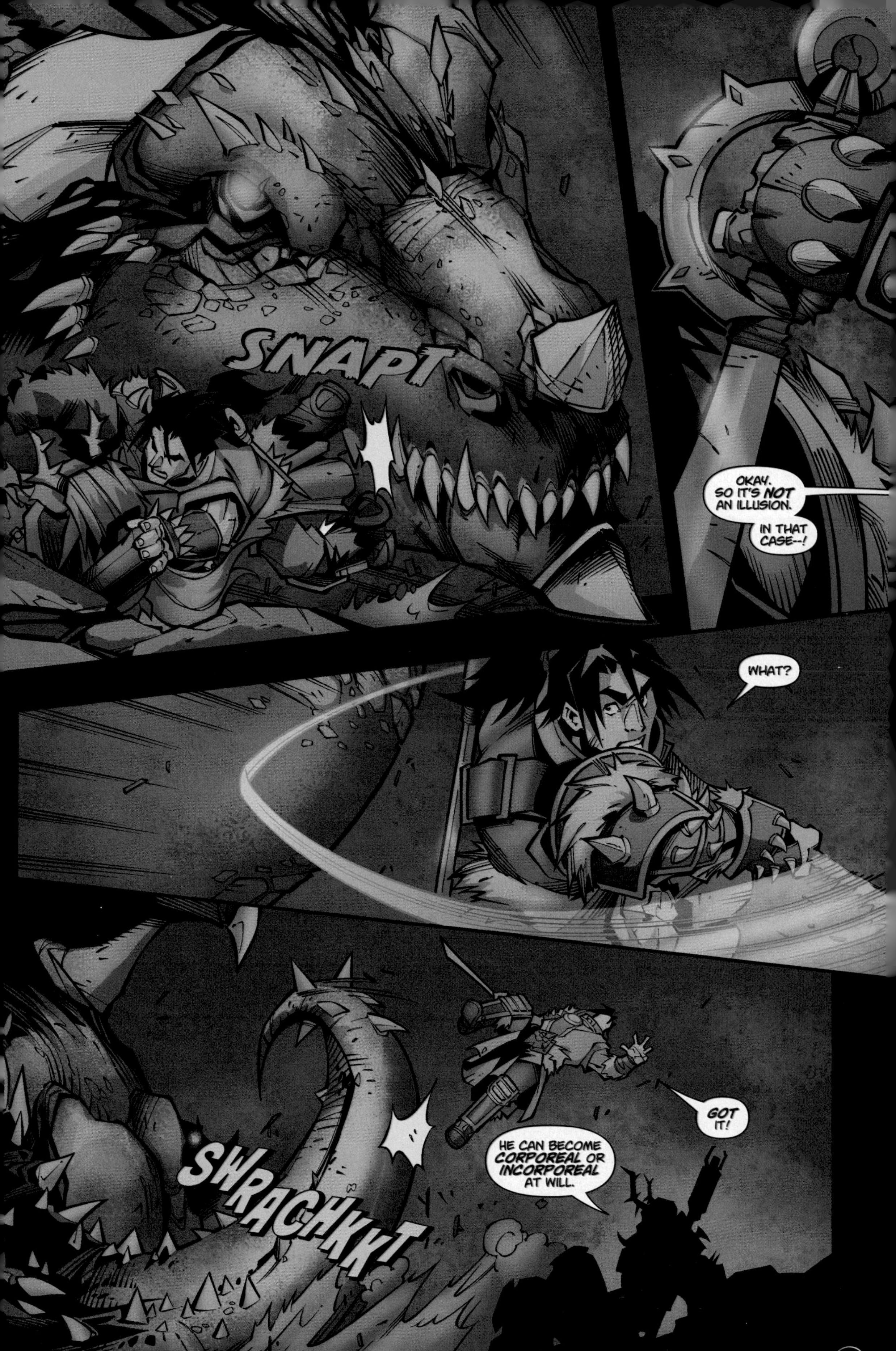
SNAPT
OKAY. SO IT'S NOT AN ILLUSION.
IN THAT CASE--!
WHAT?
GOT IT!
HE CAN BECOME CORPOREAL OR INCORPOREAL AT WILL.
SWRACHKKKT

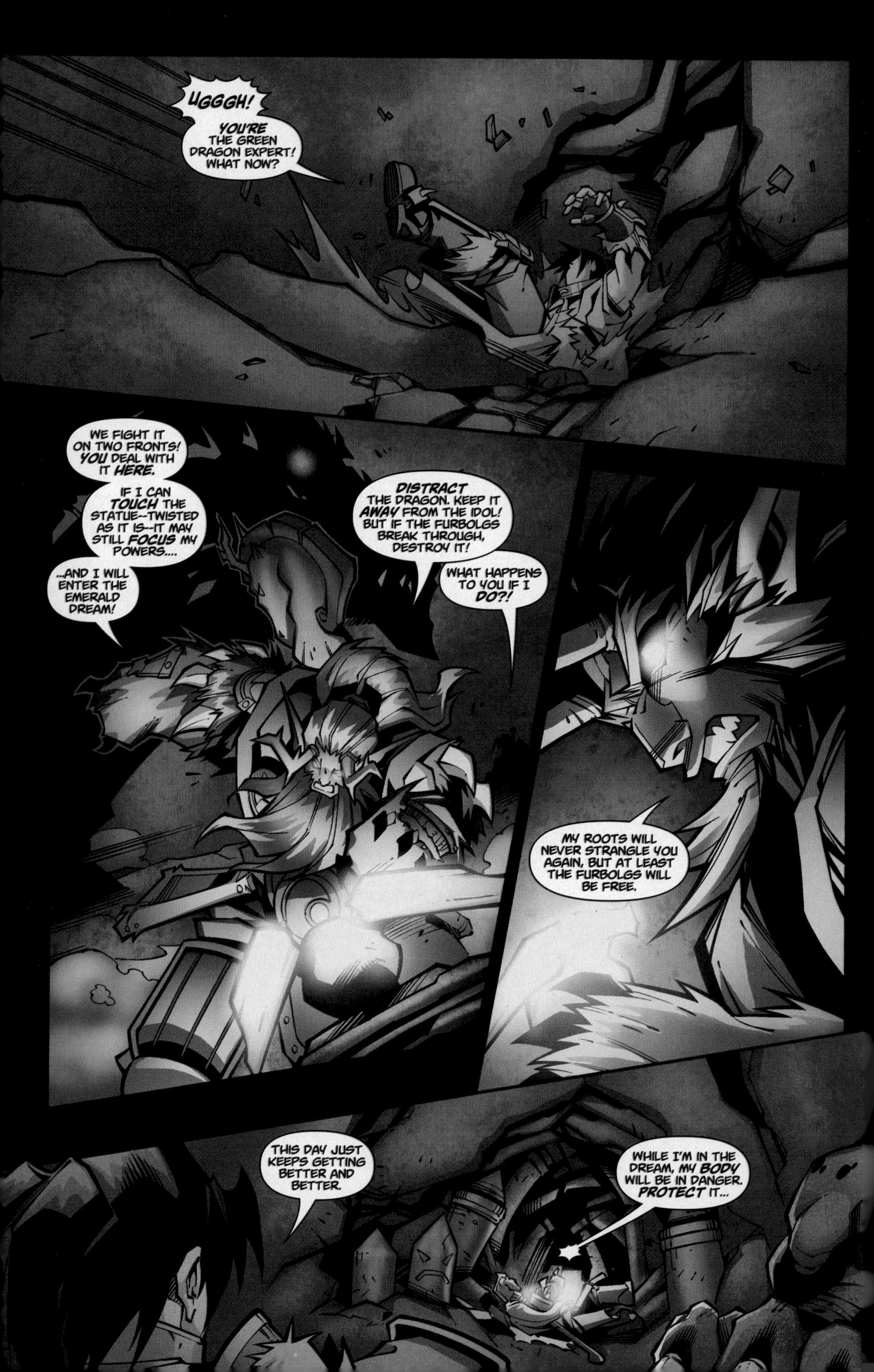
UGGGH!
YOU'RE THE GREEN DRAGON EXPERT! WHAT NOW?
WE FIGHT IT ON TWO FRONTS! YOU DEAL WITH IT HERE.
IF I CAN TOUCH THE STATUE--TWISTED AS IT IS--IT MAY STILL FOCUS MY POWERS....
...AND I WILL ENTER THE EMERALD DREAM!
DISTRACT THE DRAGON. KEEP IT AWAY FROM THE IDOL! BUT IF THE FURBOLGS BREAK THROUGH, DESTROY IT!
WHAT HAPPENS TO YOU IF I DO?!
MY ROOTS WILL NEVER STRANGLE YOU AGAIN, BUT AT LEAST THE FURBOLGS WILL BE FREE.
THIS DAY JUST KEEPS GETTING BETTER AND BETTER.
WHILE I'M IN THE DREAM, MY BODY WILL BE IN DANGER. PROTECT IT...

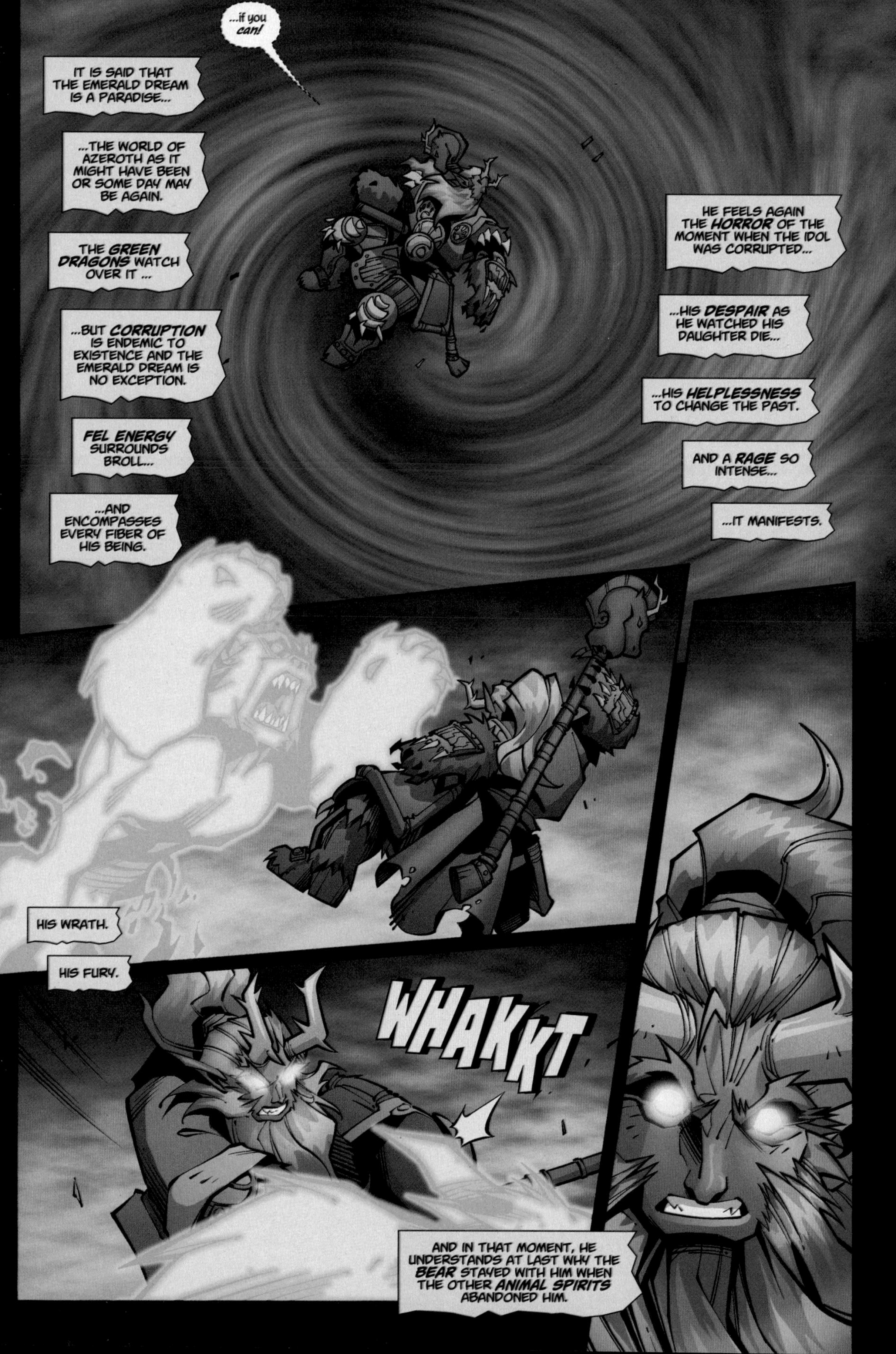
...if you can!
IT IS SAID THAT THE EMERALD DREAM IS A PARADISE...
...THE WORLD OF AZEROTH AS IT MIGHT HAVE BEEN OR SOME DAY MAY BE AGAIN.
THE GREEN DRAGONS WATCH OVER IT ...
...BUT CORRUPTION IS ENDEMIC TO EXISTENCE AND THE EMERALD DREAM IS NO EXCEPTION.
FEL ENERGY SURROUNDS BROLL...
...AND ENCOMPASSES EVERY FIBER OF HIS BEING.
HE FEELS AGAIN THE HORROR OF THE MOMENT WHEN THE IDOL WAS CORRUPTED...
...HIS DESPAIR AS HE WATCHED HIS DAUGHTER DIE...
...HIS HELPLESSNESS TO CHANGE THE PAST.
AND A RAGE SO INTENSE...
...IT MANIFESTS.
HIS WRATH.
HIS FURY.
WHAKKT
AND IN THAT MOMENT, HE UNDERSTANDS AT LAST WHY THE BEAR STAYED WITH HIM WHEN THE OTHER ANIMAL SPIRITS ABANDONED HIM.

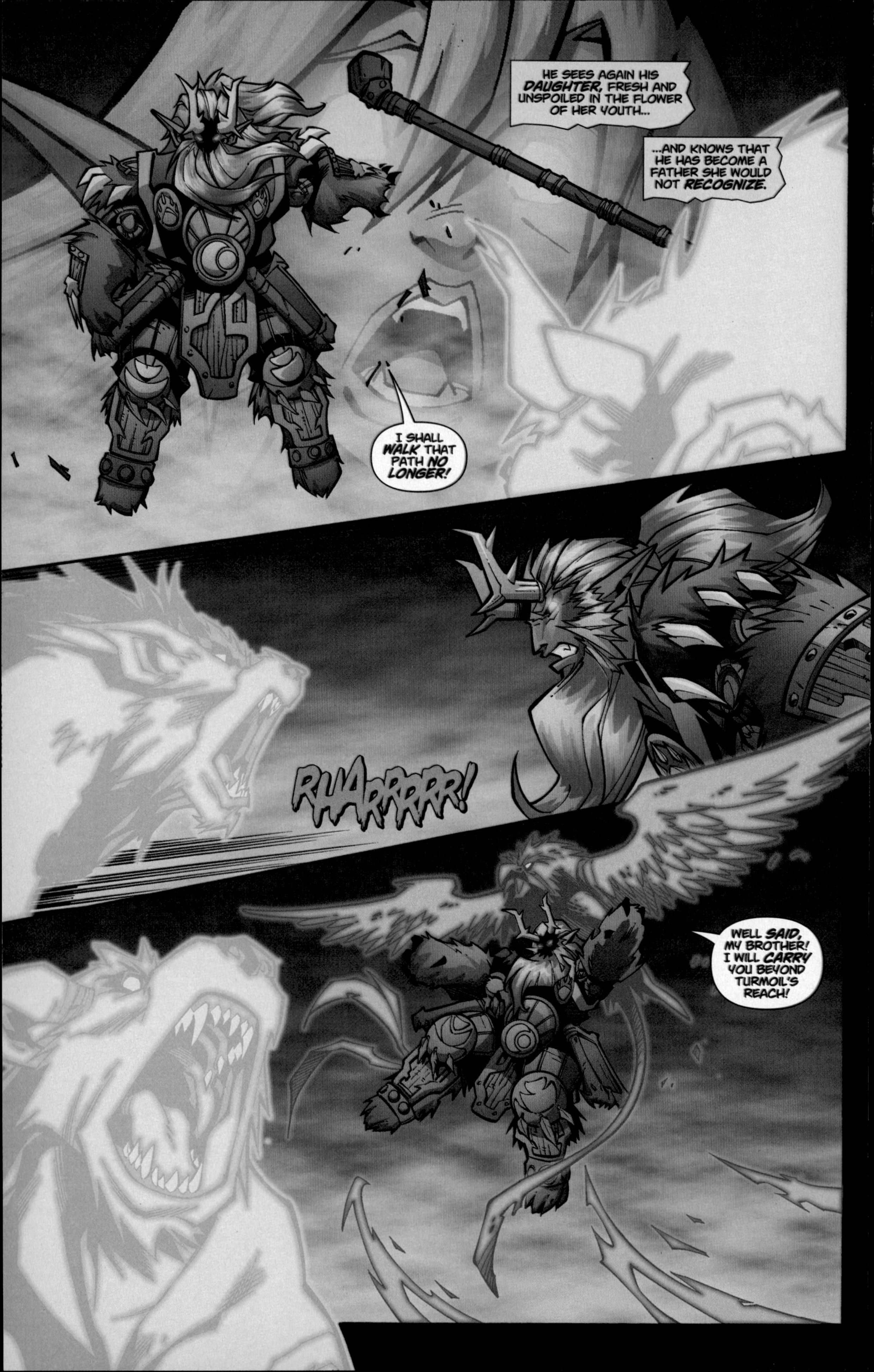
HE SEES AGAIN HIS DAUGHTER, FRESH AND UNSPOILED IN THE FLOWER OF HER YOUTH...
...AND KNOWS THAT HE HAS BECOME A FATHER SHE WOULD NOT RECOGNIZE.
I SHALL WALK THAT PATH NO LONGER!
RHARRRR!
WELL SAID, MY BROTHER! I WILL CARRY YOU BEYOND TURMOIL'S REACH!

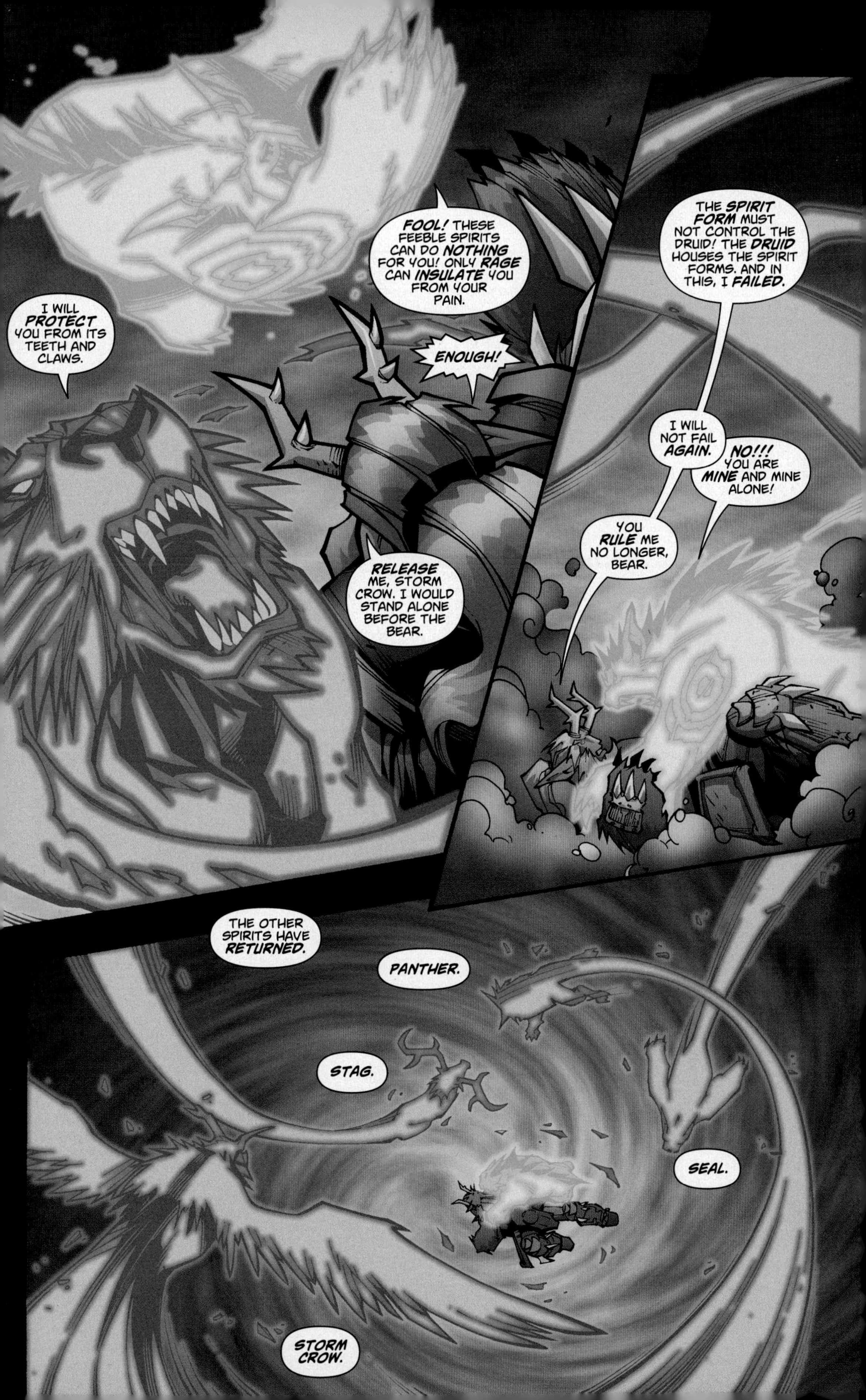

I WILL PROTECT YOU FROM ITS TEETH AND CLAWS.
FOOL! THESE FEEBLE SPIRITS CAN DO NOTHING FOR YOU! ONLY RAGE CAN INSULATE YOU FROM YOUR PAIN.
ENOUGH!
RELEASE ME, STORM CROW. I WOULD STAND ALONE BEFORE THE BEAR.
THE SPIRIT FORM MUST NOT CONTROL THE DRUID! THE DRUID HOUSES THE SPIRIT FORMS. AND IN THIS, I FAILED.
I WILL NOT FAIL AGAIN.
NO!!! YOU ARE MINE AND MINE ALONE!
YOU RULE ME NO LONGER, BEAR.
THE OTHER SPIRITS HAVE RETURNED.
PANTHER.
STAG.
SEAL.
STORM CROW.

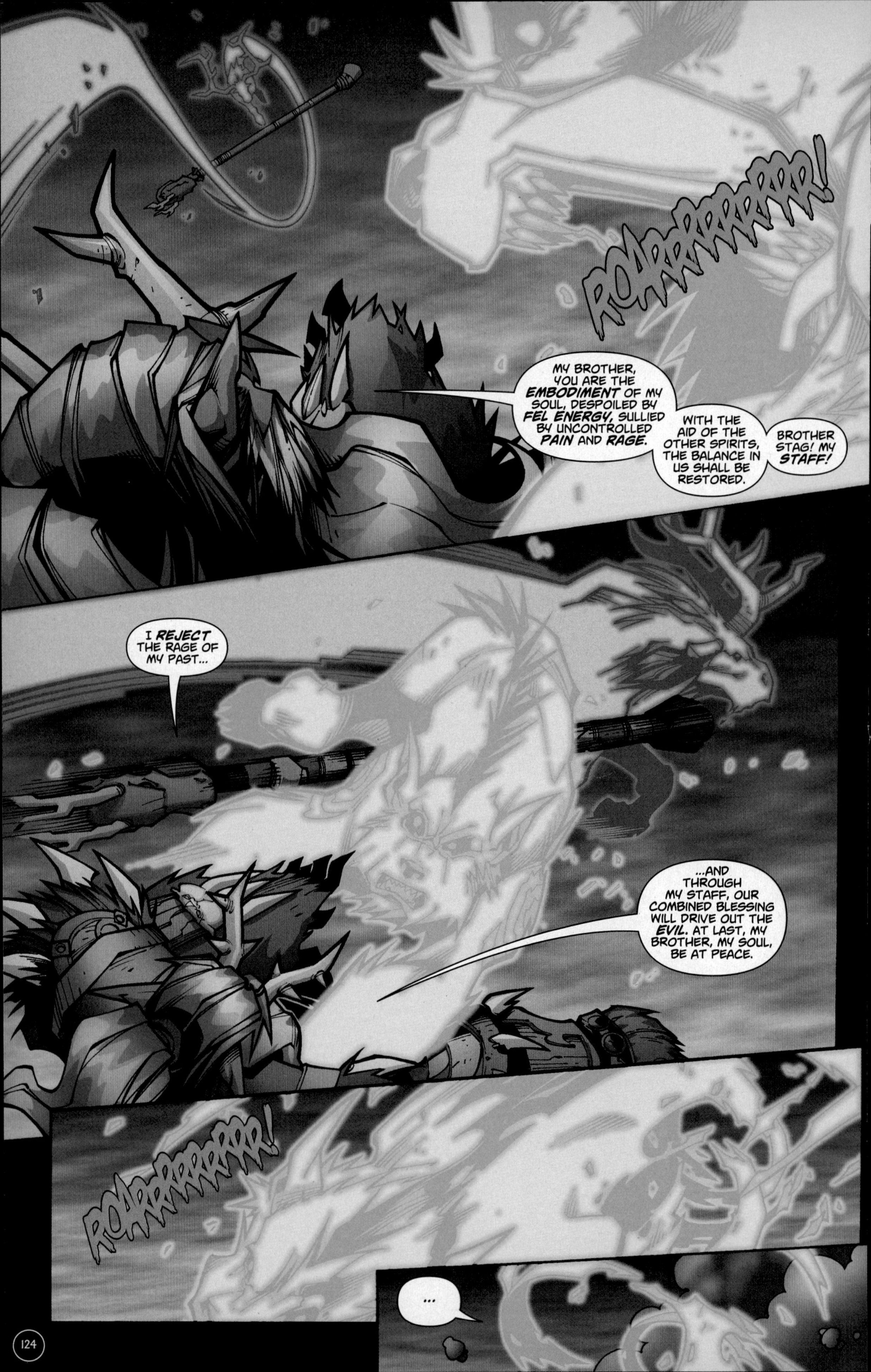
ROARRRRRRRRR!
MY BROTHER, YOU ARE THE EMBODIMENT OF MY SOUL, DESPOILED BY FEL ENERGY, SULLIED BY UNCONTROLLED PAIN AND RAGE.
WITH THE AID OF THE OTHER SPIRITS, THE BALANCE IN US SHALL BE RESTORED.
BROTHER STAG! MY STAFF!
I REJECT THE RAGE OF MY PAST...
...AND THROUGH MY STAFF, OUR COMBINED BLESSING WILL DRIVE OUT THE EVIL. AT LAST, MY BROTHER, MY SOUL, BE AT PEACE.
ROARRRRRRRRR!
...

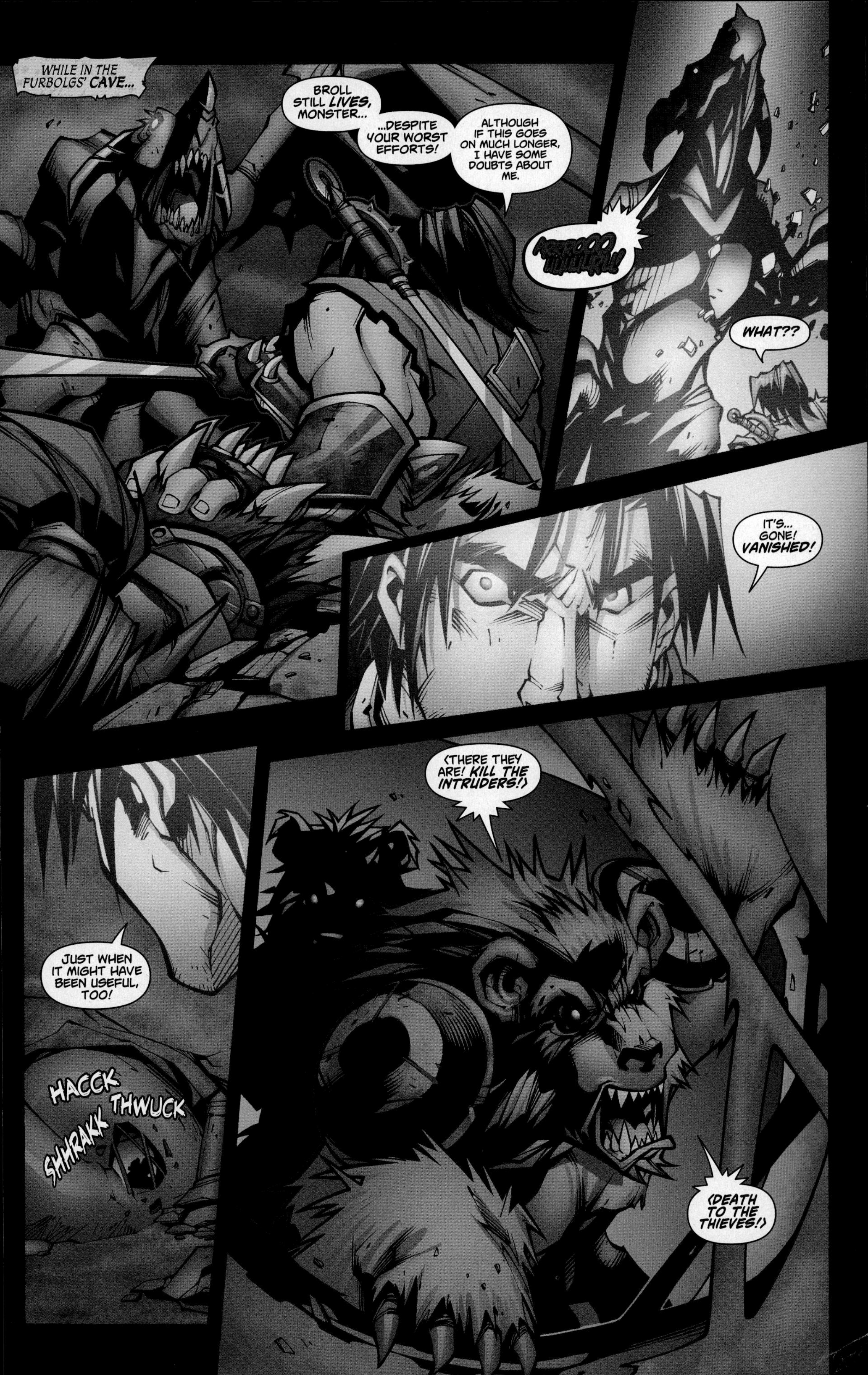

WHILE IN THE FURBOLGS' CAVE...
BROLL STILL LIVES, MONSTER...
...DESPITE YOUR WORST EFFORTS!
ALTHOUGH IF THIS GOES ON MUCH LONGER, I HAVE SOME DOUBTS ABOUT ME.
WHAT??
IT'S... GONE! VANISHED!
JUST WHEN IT MIGHT HAVE BEEN USEFUL, TOO!
HACCK
SHHRAKK
THWUCK
(THERE THEY ARE! KILL THE INTRUDERS!)
(DEATH TO THE THIEVES!)

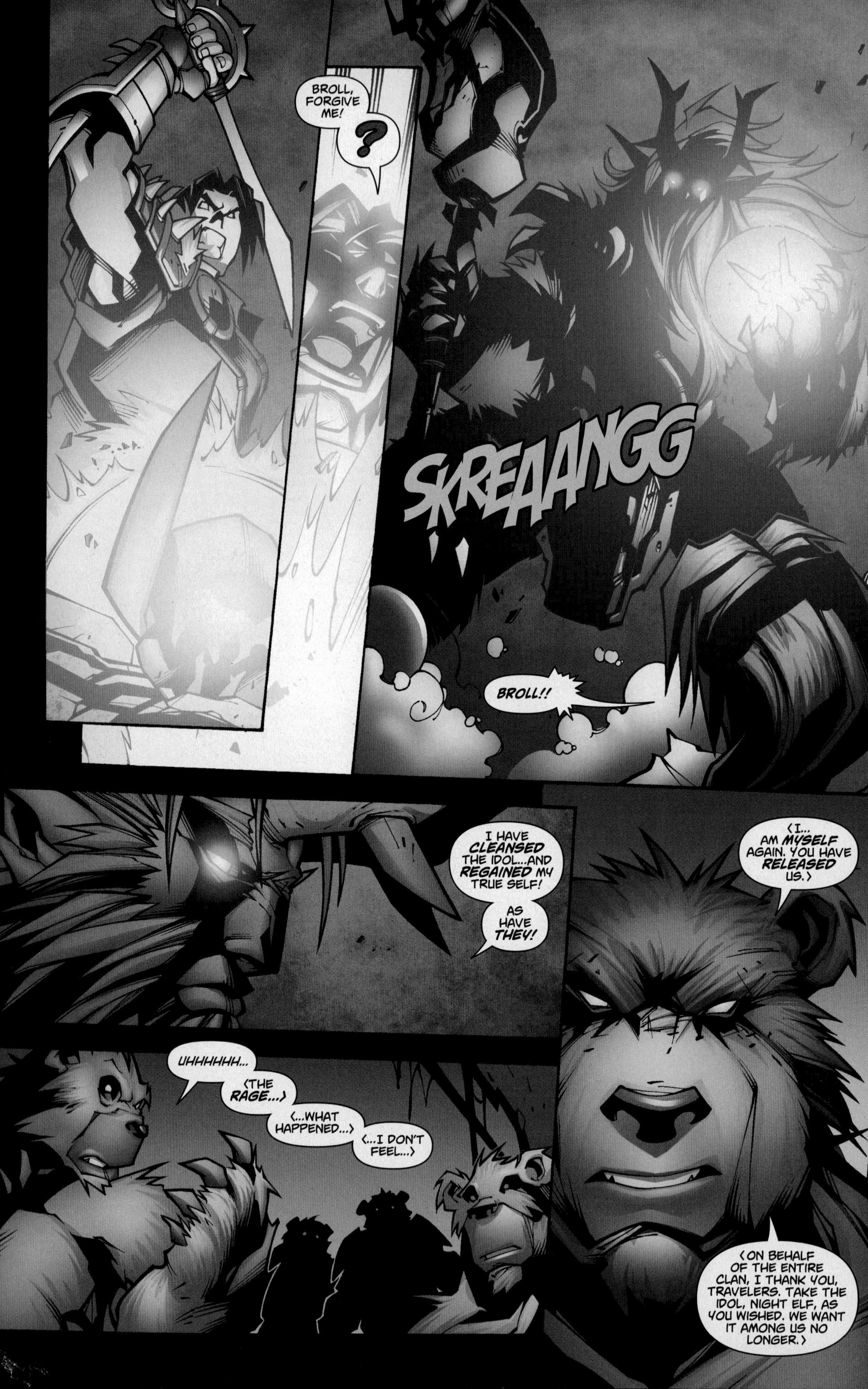

BROLL, FORGIVE ME!
?
SKREAANGG
BROLL!!
I HAVE CLEANSED THE IDOL...AND REGAINED MY TRUE SELF!
AS HAVE THEY!
‹I... AM MYSELF AGAIN. YOU HAVE RELEASED US.›
UHHHHHH...
‹THE RAGE...›
‹...WHAT HAPPENED...›
‹...I DON'T FEEL...›
‹ON BEHALF OF THE ENTIRE CLAN, I THANK YOU, TRAVELERS. TAKE THE IDOL, NIGHT ELF, AS YOU WISHED. WE WANT IT AMONG US NO LONGER.›

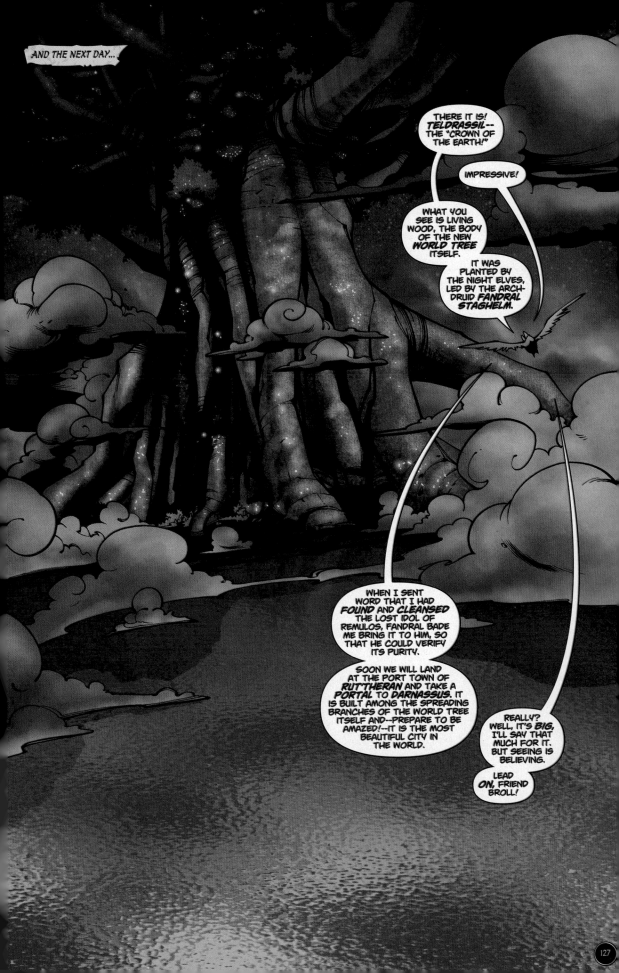

THERE IT IS! *TELDRASSIL*-- THE "CROWN OF THE EARTH!"

IMPRESSIVE!

WHAT YOU SEE IS LIVING WOOD, THE BODY OF THE NEW *WORLD TREE* ITSELF.

IT WAS PLANTED BY THE NIGHT ELVES, LED BY THE ARCH-DRUID *FANDRAL STAGHELM.*

WHEN I SENT WORD THAT I HAD *FOUND* AND *CLEANSED* THE LOST IDOL OF REMULOS, FANDRAL BADE ME BRING IT TO HIM, SO THAT HE COULD VERIFY ITS PURITY.

SOON WE WILL LAND AT THE PORT TOWN OF *RUT'THERAN* AND TAKE A *PORTAL* TO *DARNASSUS.* IT IS BUILT AMONG THE SPREADING BRANCHES OF THE WORLD TREE ITSELF AND--PREPARE TO BE AMAZED!--IT IS THE MOST BEAUTIFUL CITY IN THE WORLD.

REALLY? WELL, IT'S *BIG,* I'LL SAY THAT MUCH FOR IT. BUT SEEING IS BELIEVING.

LEAD *ON,* FRIEND BROLL!

127

CHAPTER 6

Issue #6 Cover
by Samwise Didier

Issue #6 Cover
by Jim Lee and Alex Sinclair

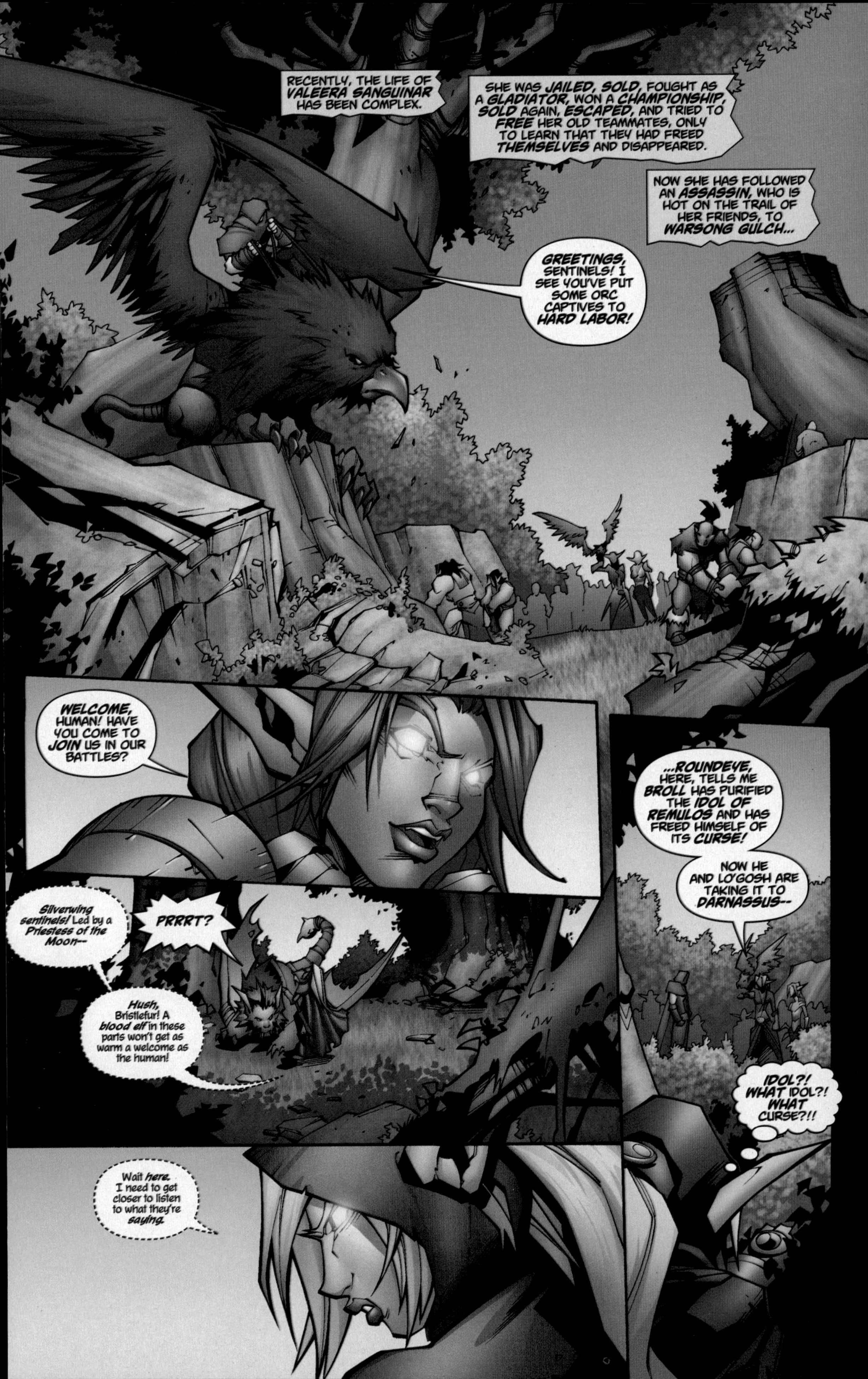
RECENTLY, THE LIFE OF VALEERA SANGUINAR HAS BEEN COMPLEX.
SHE WAS JAILED, SOLD, FOUGHT AS A GLADIATOR, WON A CHAMPIONSHIP, SOLD AGAIN, ESCAPED, AND TRIED TO FREE HER OLD TEAMMATES, ONLY TO LEARN THAT THEY HAD FREED THEMSELVES AND DISAPPEARED.
NOW SHE HAS FOLLOWED AN ASSASSIN, WHO IS HOT ON THE TRAIL OF HER FRIENDS, TO WARSONG GULCH...
GREETINGS, SENTINELS! I SEE YOU'VE PUT SOME ORC CAPTIVES TO HARD LABOR!
WELCOME, HUMAN! HAVE YOU COME TO JOIN US IN OUR BATTLES?
Silverwing sentinels! Led by a Priestess of the Moon--
PRRRT?
Hush, Bristlefur! A blood elf in these parts won't get as warm a welcome as the human!
...ROUNDEYE, HERE, TELLS ME BROLL HAS PURIFIED THE IDOL OF REMULOS AND HAS FREED HIMSELF OF ITS CURSE!
NOW HE AND LO'GOSH ARE TAKING IT TO DARNASSUS--
IDOL?! WHAT IDOL?! WHAT CURSE?!!
Wait here. I need to get closer to listen to what they're saying.

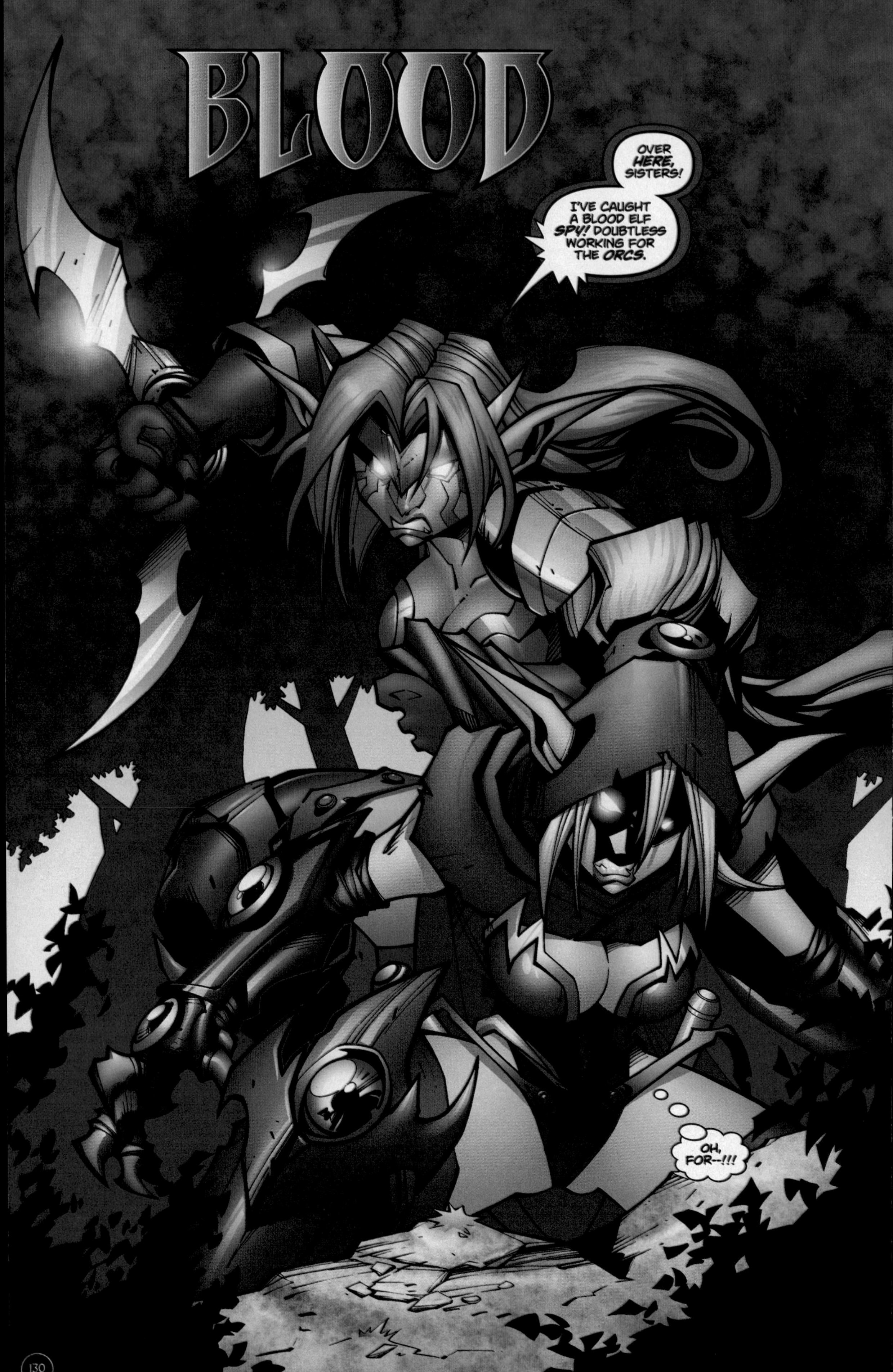
BLOOD
OVER HERE, SISTERS!
I'VE CAUGHT A BLOOD ELF SPY! DOUBTLESS WORKING FOR THE ORCS.
OH, FOR--!!!

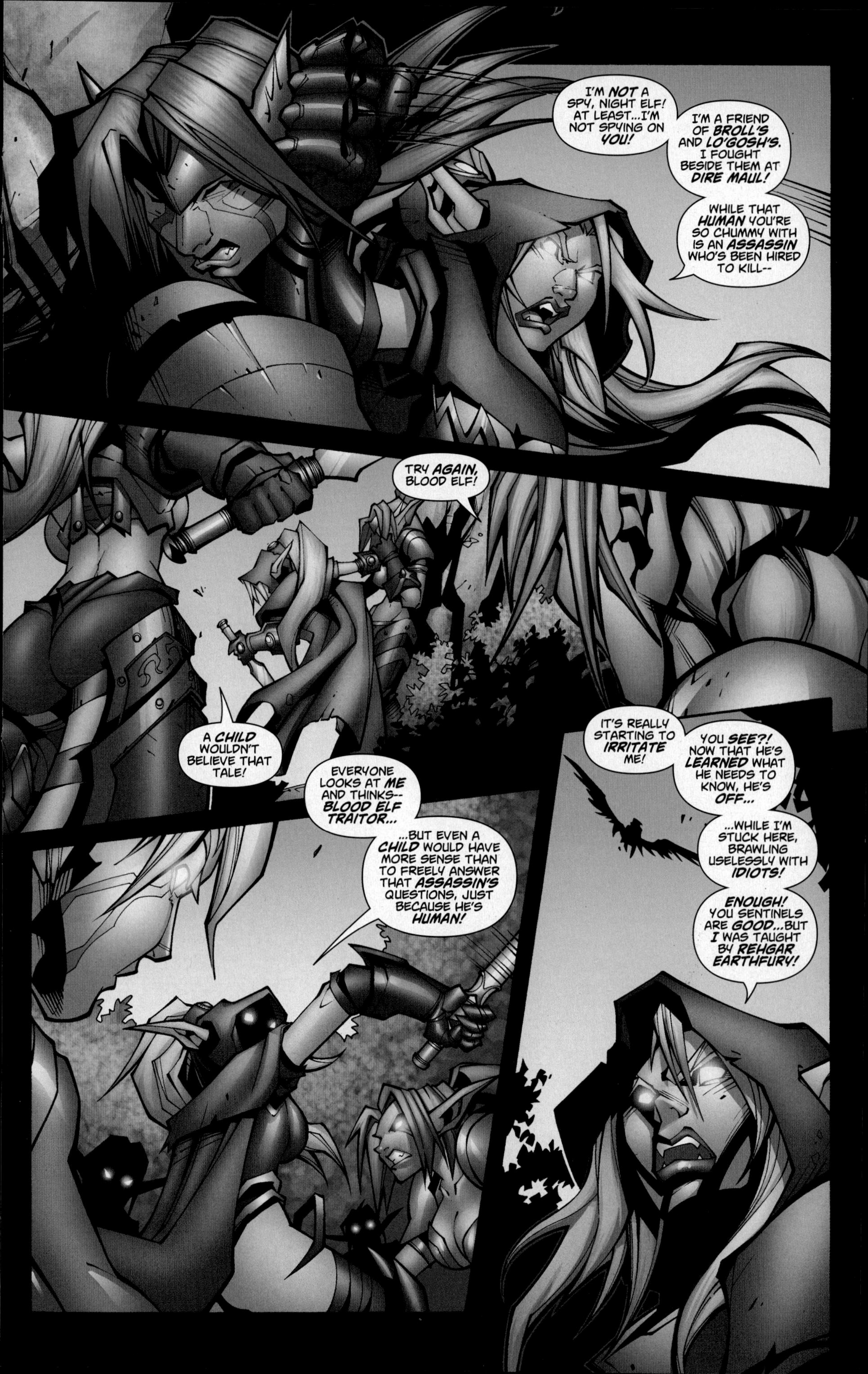
I'M NOT A SPY, NIGHT ELF! AT LEAST...I'M NOT SPYING ON YOU!
I'M A FRIEND OF BROLL'S AND LO'GOSH'S. I FOUGHT BESIDE THEM AT DIRE MAUL!
WHILE THAT HUMAN YOU'RE SO CHUMMY WITH IS AN ASSASSIN WHO'S BEEN HIRED TO KILL--
TRY AGAIN, BLOOD ELF!
A CHILD WOULDN'T BELIEVE THAT TALE!
EVERYONE LOOKS AT ME AND THINKS-- BLOOD ELF TRAITOR...
...BUT EVEN A CHILD WOULD HAVE MORE SENSE THAN TO FREELY ANSWER THAT ASSASSIN'S QUESTIONS, JUST BECAUSE HE'S HUMAN!
IT'S REALLY STARTING TO IRRITATE ME!
YOU SEE?! NOW THAT HE'S LEARNED WHAT HE NEEDS TO KNOW, HE'S OFF...
...WHILE I'M STUCK HERE, BRAWLING USELESSLY WITH IDIOTS!
ENOUGH! YOU SENTINELS ARE GOOD...BUT I WAS TAUGHT BY REHGAR EARTHFURY!

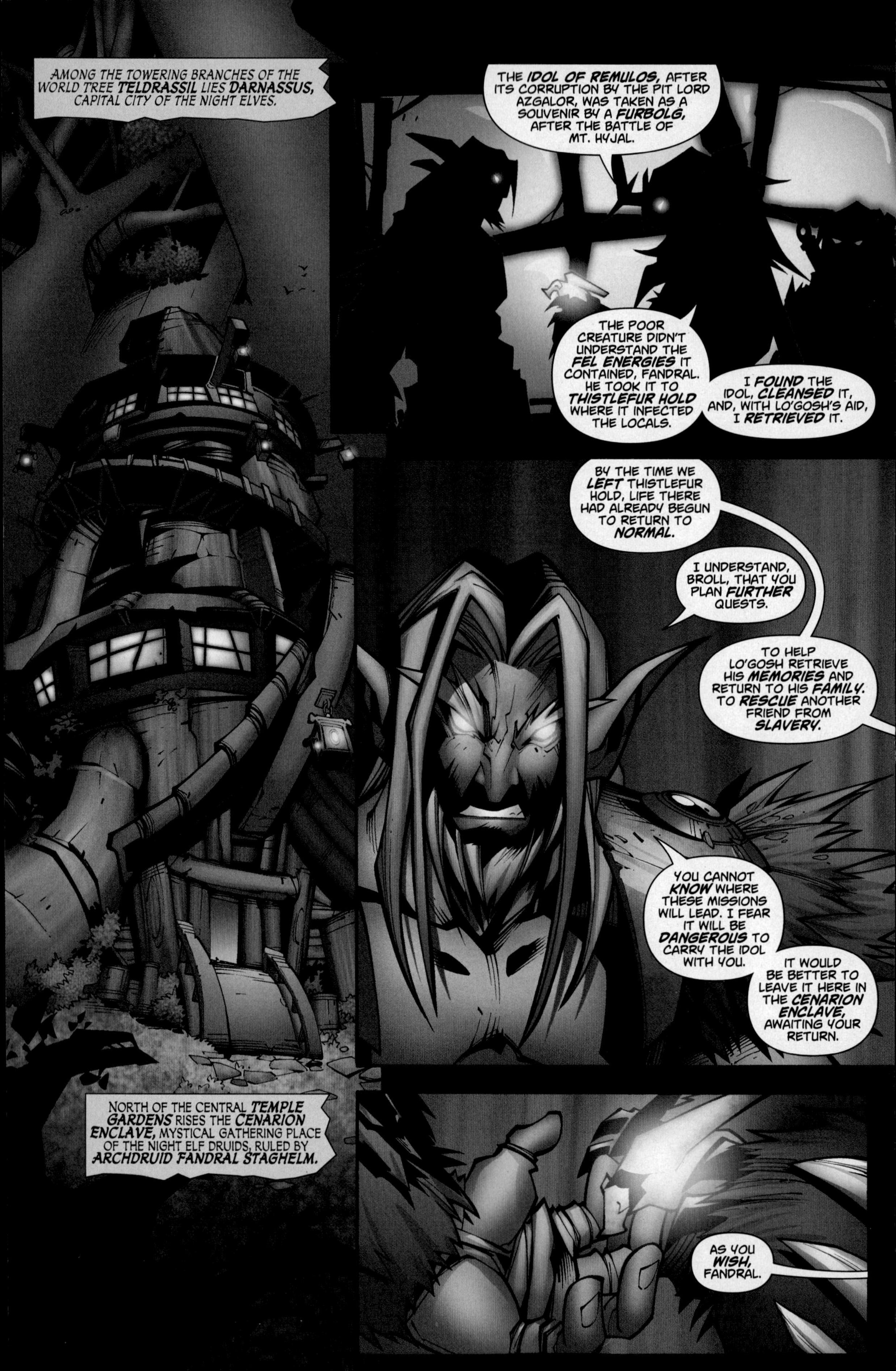
AMONG THE TOWERING BRANCHES OF THE WORLD TREE TELDRASSIL LIES DARNASSUS, CAPITAL CITY OF THE NIGHT ELVES.
THE IDOL OF REMULOS, AFTER ITS CORRUPTION BY THE PIT LORD AZGALOR, WAS TAKEN AS A SOUVENIR BY A FURBOLG, AFTER THE BATTLE OF MT. HYJAL.
THE POOR CREATURE DIDN'T UNDERSTAND THE FEL ENERGIES IT CONTAINED, FANDRAL. HE TOOK IT TO THISTLEFUR HOLD WHERE IT INFECTED THE LOCALS.
I FOUND THE IDOL, CLEANSED IT, AND, WITH LO'GOSH'S AID, I RETRIEVED IT.
BY THE TIME WE LEFT THISTLEFUR HOLD, LIFE THERE HAD ALREADY BEGUN TO RETURN TO NORMAL.
I UNDERSTAND, BROLL, THAT YOU PLAN FURTHER QUESTS.
TO HELP LO'GOSH RETRIEVE HIS MEMORIES AND RETURN TO HIS FAMILY. TO RESCUE ANOTHER FRIEND FROM SLAVERY.
YOU CANNOT KNOW WHERE THESE MISSIONS WILL LEAD. I FEAR IT WILL BE DANGEROUS TO CARRY THE IDOL WITH YOU.
IT WOULD BE BETTER TO LEAVE IT HERE IN THE CENARION ENCLAVE, AWAITING YOUR RETURN.
NORTH OF THE CENTRAL TEMPLE GARDENS RISES THE CENARION ENCLAVE, MYSTICAL GATHERING PLACE OF THE NIGHT ELF DRUIDS, RULED BY ARCHDRUID FANDRAL STAGHELM.
AS YOU WISH, FANDRAL.

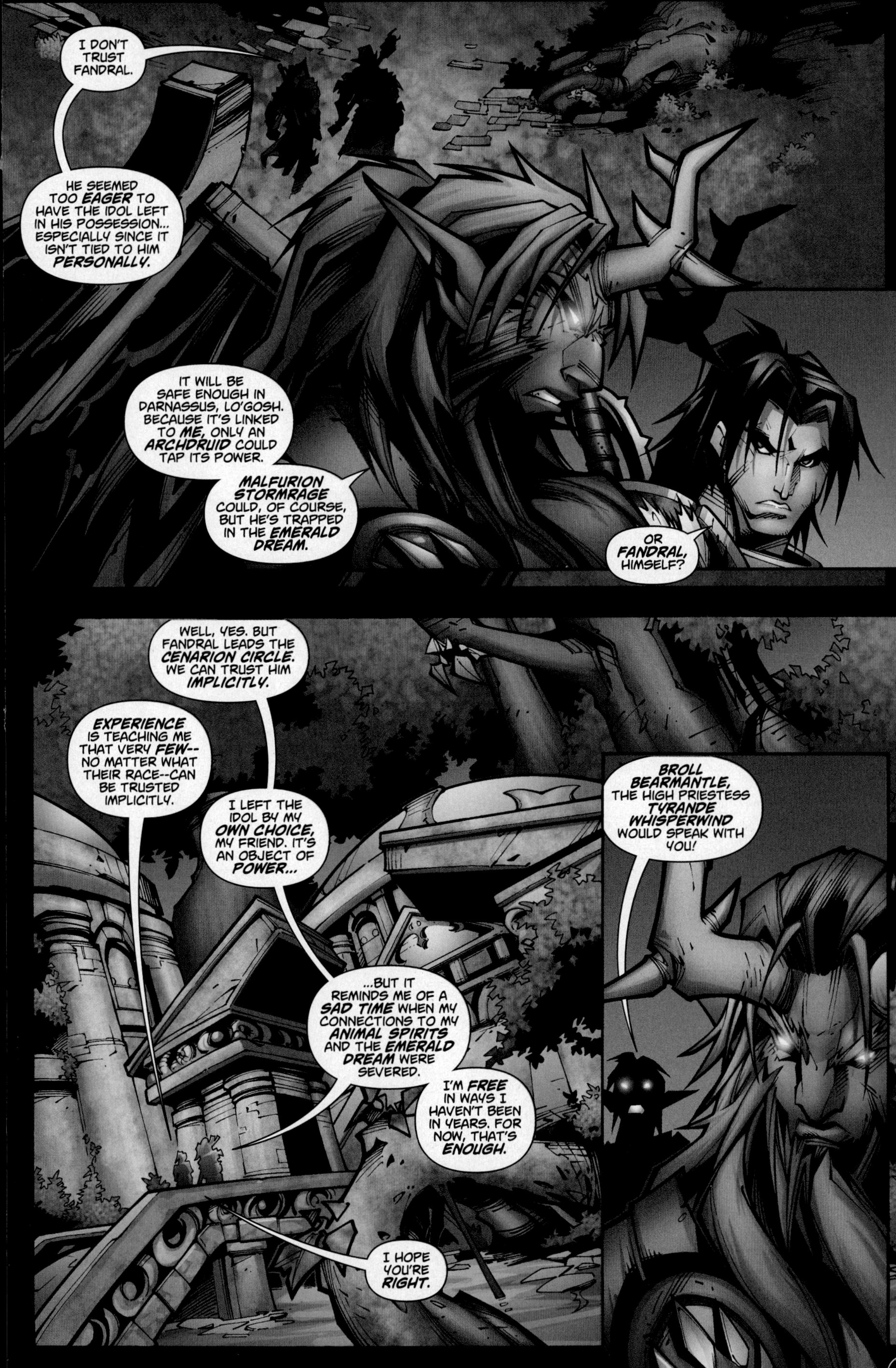
I DON'T TRUST FANDRAL.
HE SEEMED TOO EAGER TO HAVE THE IDOL LEFT IN HIS POSSESSION... ESPECIALLY SINCE IT ISN'T TIED TO HIM PERSONALLY.
IT WILL BE SAFE ENOUGH IN DARNASSUS, LO'GOSH. BECAUSE IT'S LINKED TO ME, ONLY AN ARCHDRUID COULD TAP ITS POWER.
MALFURION STORMRAGE COULD, OF COURSE, BUT HE'S TRAPPED IN THE EMERALD DREAM.
OR FANDRAL, HIMSELF?
WELL, YES. BUT FANDRAL LEADS THE CENARION CIRCLE. WE CAN TRUST HIM IMPLICITLY.
EXPERIENCE IS TEACHING ME THAT VERY FEW-- NO MATTER WHAT THEIR RACE--CAN BE TRUSTED IMPLICITLY.
I LEFT THE IDOL BY MY OWN CHOICE, MY FRIEND. IT'S AN OBJECT OF POWER...
...BUT IT REMINDS ME OF A SAD TIME WHEN MY CONNECTIONS TO MY ANIMAL SPIRITS AND THE EMERALD DREAM WERE SEVERED.
I'M FREE IN WAYS I HAVEN'T BEEN IN YEARS. FOR NOW, THAT'S ENOUGH.
I HOPE YOU'RE RIGHT.
BROLL BEARMANTLE, THE HIGH PRIESTESS TYRANDE WHISPERWIND WOULD SPEAK WITH YOU!

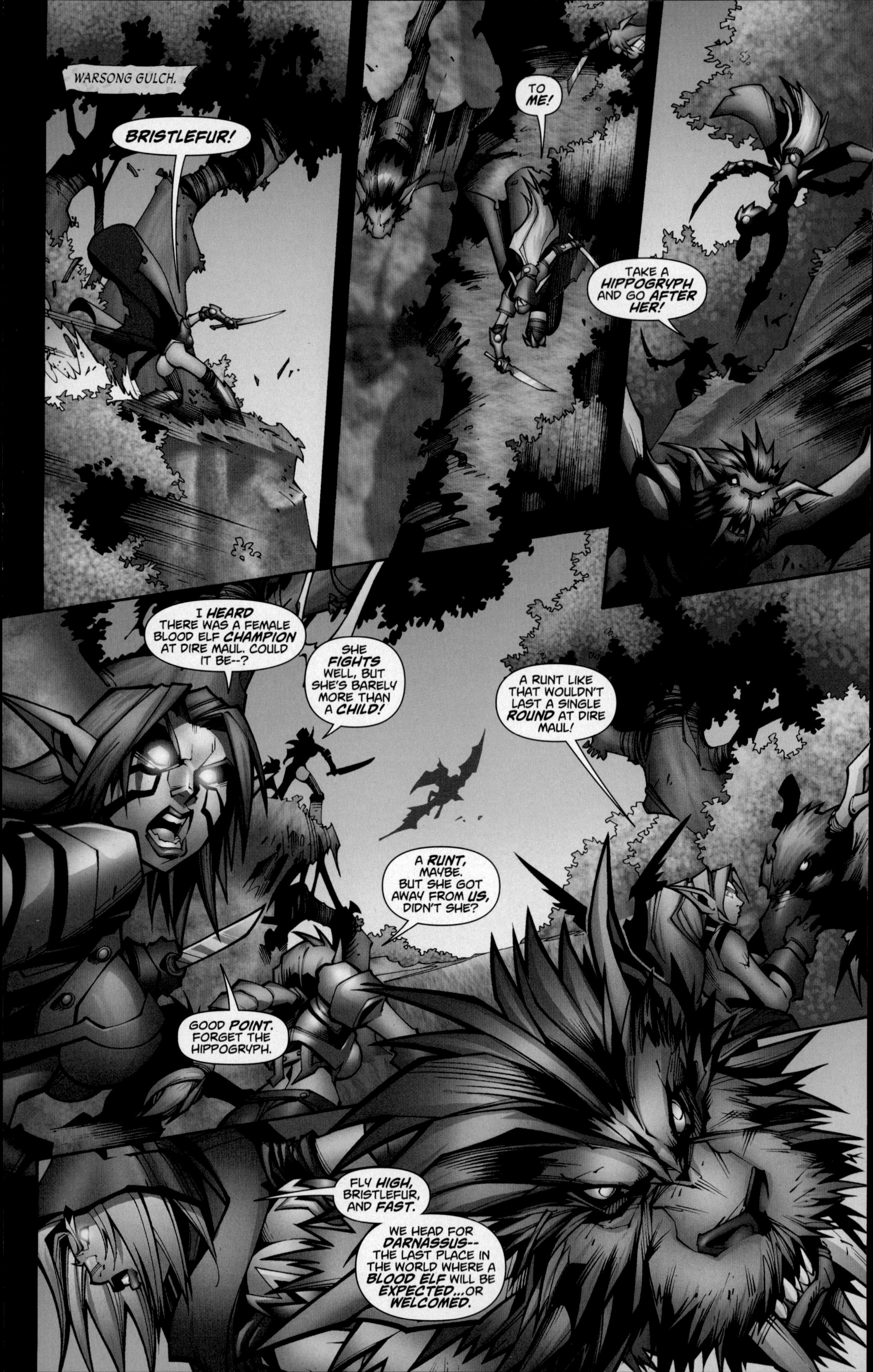
WARSONG GULCH.
BRISTLEFUR!
TO ME!
TAKE A HIPPOGRYPH AND GO AFTER HER!
I HEARD THERE WAS A FEMALE BLOOD ELF CHAMPION AT DIRE MAUL. COULD IT BE--?
SHE FIGHTS WELL, BUT SHE'S BARELY MORE THAN A CHILD!
A RUNT LIKE THAT WOULDN'T LAST A SINGLE ROUND AT DIRE MAUL!
A RUNT, MAYBE. BUT SHE GOT AWAY FROM US, DIDN'T SHE?
GOOD POINT. FORGET THE HIPPOGRYPH.
FLY HIGH, BRISTLEFUR, AND FAST.
WE HEAD FOR DARNASSUS-- THE LAST PLACE IN THE WORLD WHERE A BLOOD ELF WILL BE EXPECTED...OR WELCOMED.

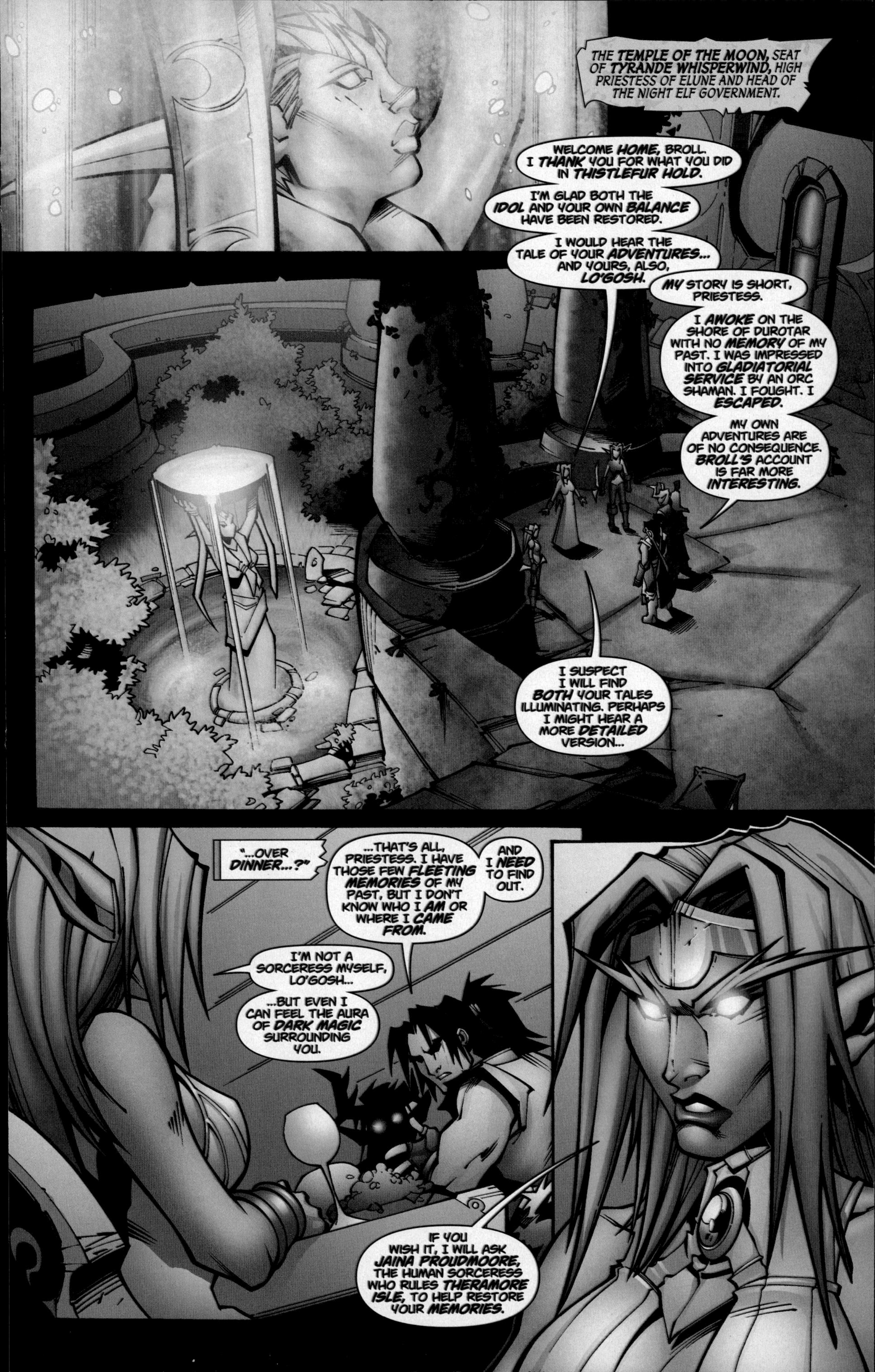
THE TEMPLE OF THE MOON, SEAT OF TYRANDE WHISPERWIND, HIGH PRIESTESS OF ELUNE AND HEAD OF THE NIGHT ELF GOVERNMENT.
WELCOME HOME, BROLL. I THANK YOU FOR WHAT YOU DID IN THISTLEFUR HOLD.
I'M GLAD BOTH THE IDOL AND YOUR OWN BALANCE HAVE BEEN RESTORED.
I WOULD HEAR THE TALE OF YOUR ADVENTURES... AND YOURS, ALSO, LO'GOSH.
MY STORY IS SHORT, PRIESTESS.
I AWOKE ON THE SHORE OF DUROTAR WITH NO MEMORY OF MY PAST. I WAS IMPRESSED INTO GLADIATORIAL SERVICE BY AN ORC SHAMAN. I FOUGHT. I ESCAPED.
MY OWN ADVENTURES ARE OF NO CONSEQUENCE. BROLL'S ACCOUNT IS FAR MORE INTERESTING.
I SUSPECT I WILL FIND BOTH YOUR TALES ILLUMINATING. PERHAPS I MIGHT HEAR A MORE DETAILED VERSION...
"...OVER DINNER...?"
...THAT'S ALL, PRIESTESS. I HAVE THOSE FEW FLEETING MEMORIES OF MY PAST, BUT I DON'T KNOW WHO I AM OR WHERE I CAME FROM.
AND I NEED TO FIND OUT.
I'M NOT A SORCERESS MYSELF, LO'GOSH...
...BUT EVEN I CAN FEEL THE AURA OF DARK MAGIC SURROUNDING YOU.
IF YOU WISH IT, I WILL ASK JAINA PROUDMOORE, THE HUMAN SORCERESS WHO RULES THERAMORE ISLE, TO HELP RESTORE YOUR MEMORIES.

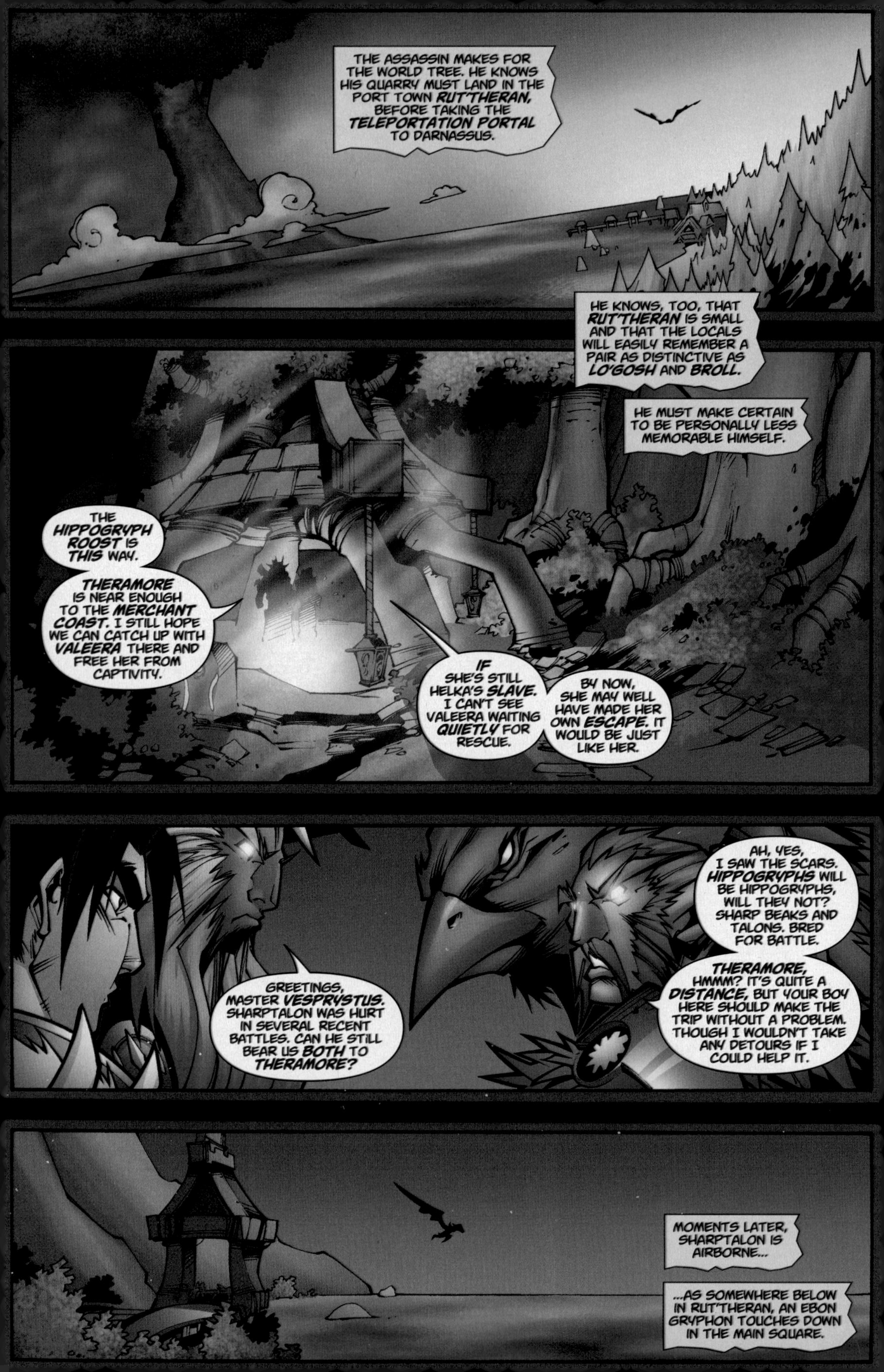
THE ASSASSIN MAKES FOR THE WORLD TREE. HE KNOWS HIS QUARRY MUST LAND IN THE PORT TOWN RUT'THERAN, BEFORE TAKING THE TELEPORTATION PORTAL TO DARNASSUS.
HE KNOWS, TOO, THAT RUT'THERAN IS SMALL AND THAT THE LOCALS WILL EASILY REMEMBER A PAIR AS DISTINCTIVE AS LO'GOSH AND BROLL.
HE MUST MAKE CERTAIN TO BE PERSONALLY LESS MEMORABLE HIMSELF.
THE HIPPOGRYPH ROOST IS THIS WAY.
THERAMORE IS NEAR ENOUGH TO THE MERCHANT COAST. I STILL HOPE WE CAN CATCH UP WITH VALEERA THERE AND FREE HER FROM CAPTIVITY.
IF SHE'S STILL HELKA'S SLAVE. I CAN'T SEE VALEERA WAITING QUIETLY FOR RESCUE.
BY NOW, SHE MAY WELL HAVE MADE HER OWN ESCAPE. IT WOULD BE JUST LIKE HER.
GREETINGS, MASTER VESPRYSTUS. SHARPTALON WAS HURT IN SEVERAL RECENT BATTLES. CAN HE STILL BEAR US BOTH TO THERAMORE?
AH, YES, I SAW THE SCARS. HIPPOGRYPHS WILL BE HIPPOGRYPHS, WILL THEY NOT? SHARP BEAKS AND TALONS. BRED FOR BATTLE.
THERAMORE, HMMM? IT'S QUITE A DISTANCE, BUT YOUR BOY HERE SHOULD MAKE THE TRIP WITHOUT A PROBLEM. THOUGH I WOULDN'T TAKE ANY DETOURS IF I COULD HELP IT.
MOMENTS LATER, SHARPTALON IS AIRBORNE...
...AS SOMEWHERE BELOW IN RUT'THERAN, AN EBON GRYPHON TOUCHES DOWN IN THE MAIN SQUARE.

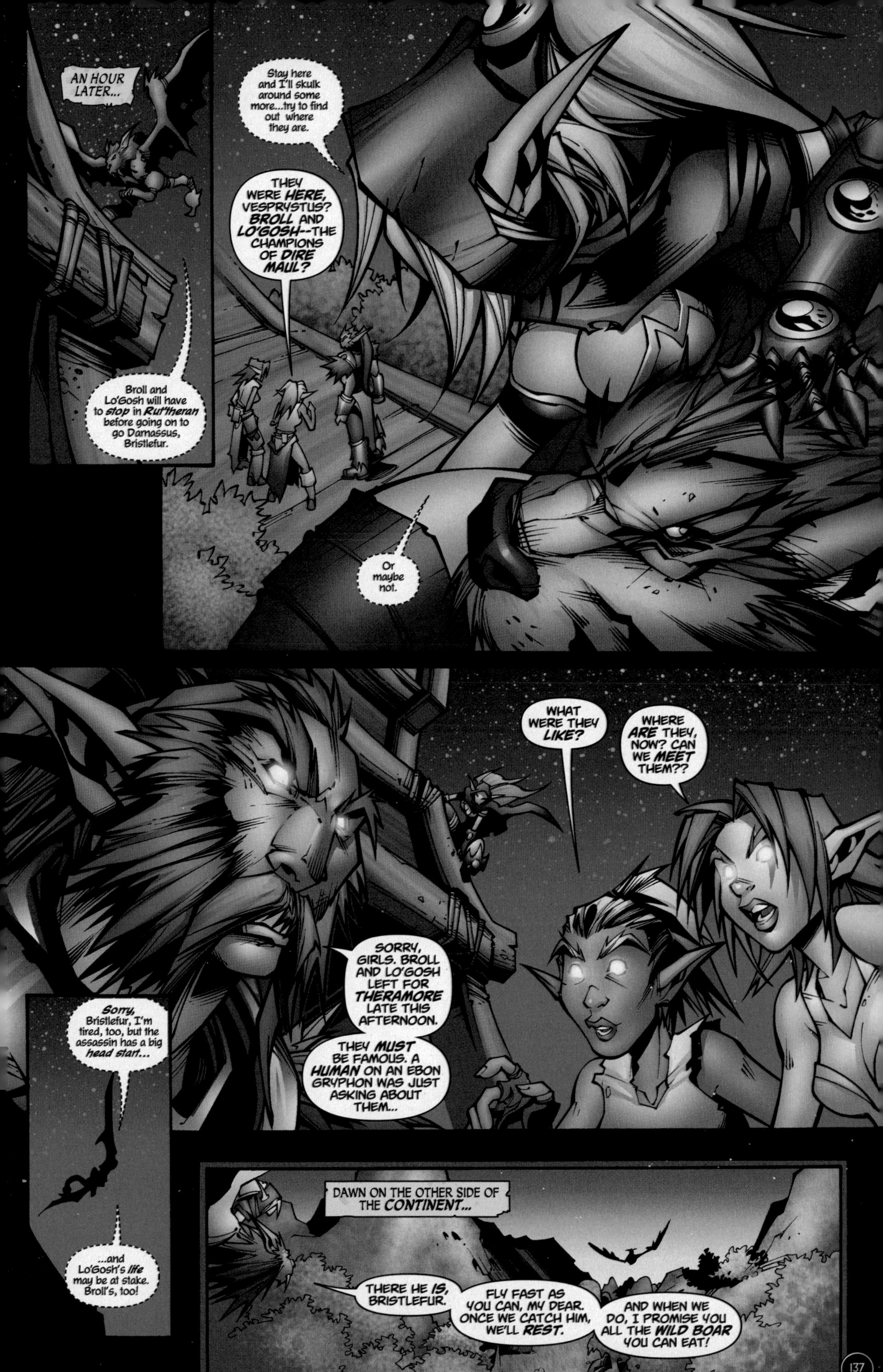

AN HOUR LATER...
Stay here and I'll skulk around some more...try to find out where they are.
THEY WERE HERE, VESPRYSTUS? BROLL AND LO'GOSH--THE CHAMPIONS OF DIRE MAUL?
Broll and Lo'Gosh will have to stop in Rut'theran before going on to go Darnassus, Bristlefur.
Or maybe not.
WHAT WERE THEY LIKE?
WHERE ARE THEY, NOW? CAN WE MEET THEM??
SORRY, GIRLS. BROLL AND LO'GOSH LEFT FOR THERAMORE LATE THIS AFTERNOON.
THEY MUST BE FAMOUS. A HUMAN ON AN EBON GRYPHON WAS JUST ASKING ABOUT THEM...
Sorry, Bristlefur, I'm tired, too, but the assassin has a big head start...
...and Lo'Gosh's life may be at stake. Broll's, too!
DAWN ON THE OTHER SIDE OF THE CONTINENT...
THERE HE IS, BRISTLEFUR.
FLY FAST AS YOU CAN, MY DEAR. ONCE WE CATCH HIM, WE'LL REST.
AND WHEN WE DO, I PROMISE YOU ALL THE WILD BOAR YOU CAN EAT!

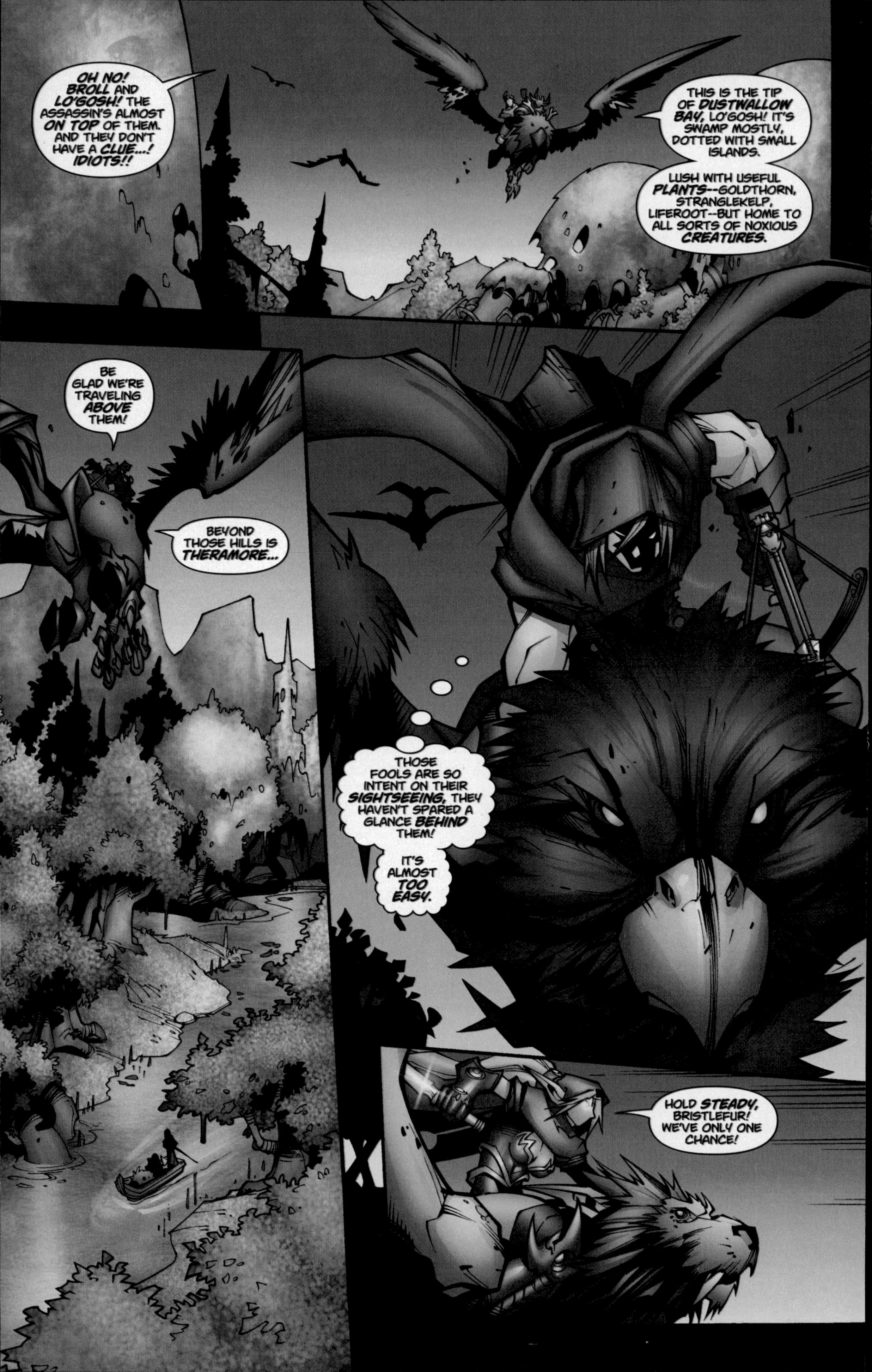
OH NO! BROLL AND LO'GOSH! THE ASSASSIN'S ALMOST ON TOP OF THEM. AND THEY DON'T HAVE A CLUE...! IDIOTS!!
THIS IS THE TIP OF DUSTWALLOW BAY, LO'GOSH! IT'S SWAMP MOSTLY, DOTTED WITH SMALL ISLANDS.
LUSH WITH USEFUL PLANTS--GOLDTHORN, STRANGLEKELP, LIFEROOT--BUT HOME TO ALL SORTS OF NOXIOUS CREATURES.
BE GLAD WE'RE TRAVELING ABOVE THEM!
BEYOND THOSE HILLS IS THERAMORE...
THOSE FOOLS ARE SO INTENT ON THEIR SIGHTSEEING, THEY HAVEN'T SPARED A GLANCE BEHIND THEM!
IT'S ALMOST TOO EASY.
HOLD STEADY, BRISTLEFUR! WE'VE ONLY ONE CHANCE!

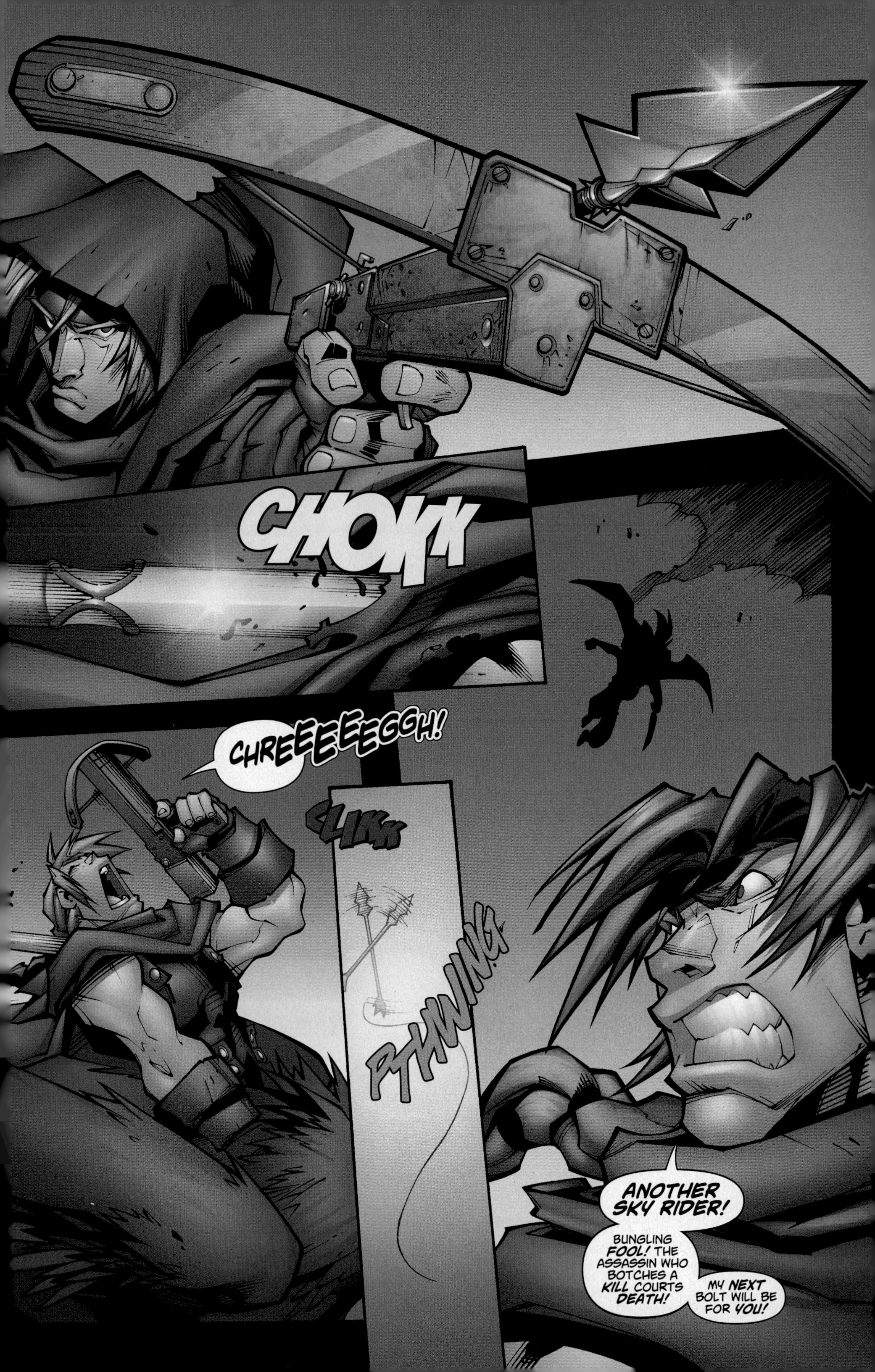
CHOKK
CHREEEEEEGGH!
CLIKK
PTWING!
ANOTHER SKY RIDER!
BUNGLING FOOL! THE ASSASSIN WHO BOTCHES A KILL COURTS DEATH!
MY NEXT BOLT WILL BE FOR YOU!

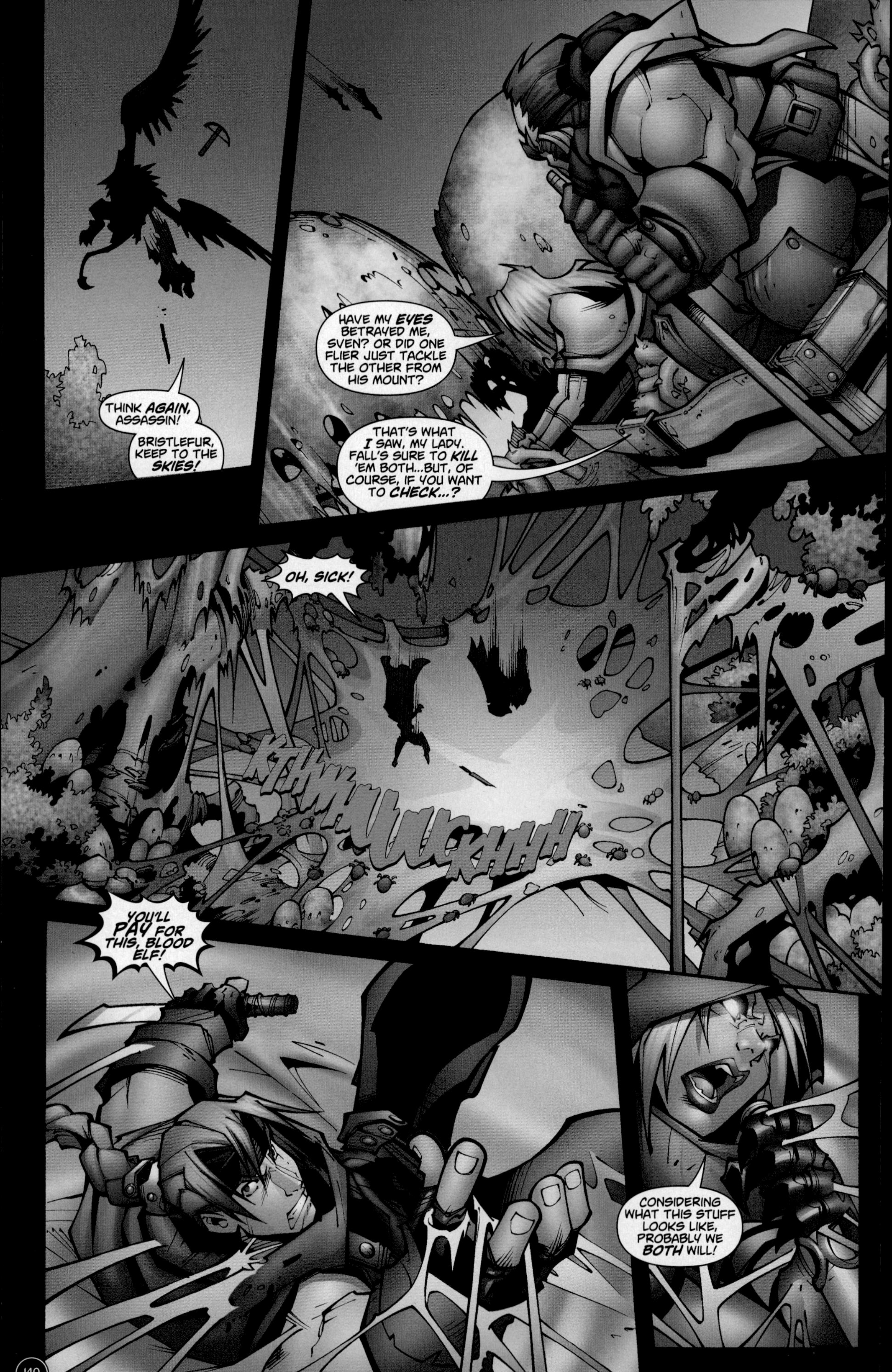
THINK AGAIN, ASSASSIN!
BRISTLEFUR, KEEP TO THE SKIES!
HAVE MY EYES BETRAYED ME, SVEN? OR DID ONE FLIER JUST TACKLE THE OTHER FROM HIS MOUNT?
THAT'S WHAT I SAW, MY LADY. FALL'S SURE TO KILL 'EM BOTH...BUT, OF COURSE, IF YOU WANT TO CHECK...?
OH, SICK!
KTHWHUUUCKHHH
YOU'LL PAY FOR THIS, BLOOD ELF!
CONSIDERING WHAT THIS STUFF LOOKS LIKE, PROBABLY WE BOTH WILL!

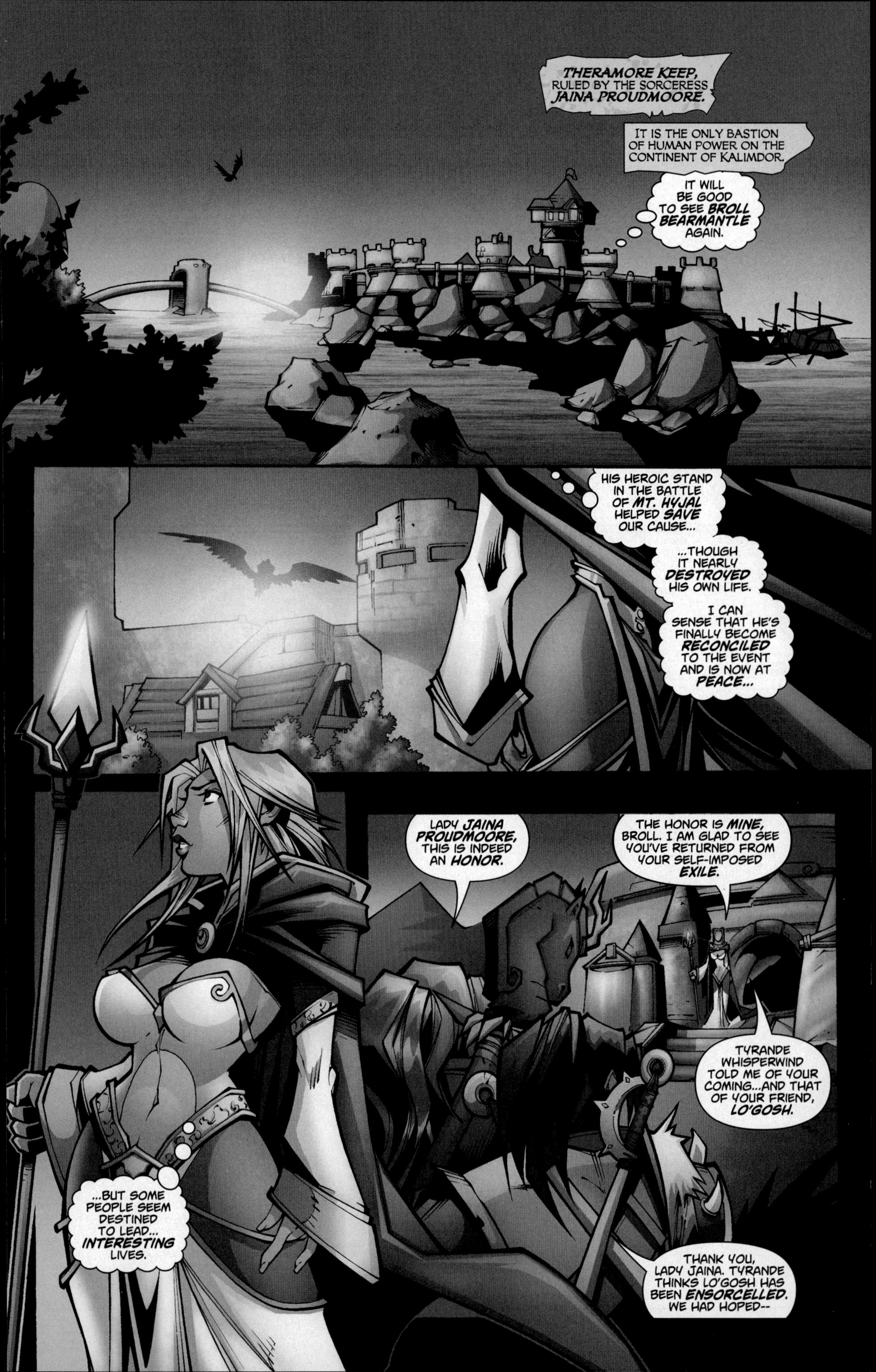
THERAMORE KEEP, RULED BY THE SORCERESS JAINA PROUDMOORE.
IT IS THE ONLY BASTION OF HUMAN POWER ON THE CONTINENT OF KALIMDOR.
IT WILL BE GOOD TO SEE BROLL BEARMANTLE AGAIN.
HIS HEROIC STAND IN THE BATTLE OF MT. HYJAL HELPED SAVE OUR CAUSE...
...THOUGH IT NEARLY DESTROYED HIS OWN LIFE.
I CAN SENSE THAT HE'S FINALLY BECOME RECONCILED TO THE EVENT AND IS NOW AT PEACE...
LADY JAINA PROUDMOORE, THIS IS INDEED AN HONOR.
THE HONOR IS MINE, BROLL. I AM GLAD TO SEE YOU'VE RETURNED FROM YOUR SELF-IMPOSED EXILE.
TYRANDE WHISPERWIND TOLD ME OF YOUR COMING...AND THAT OF YOUR FRIEND, LO'GOSH.
...BUT SOME PEOPLE SEEM DESTINED TO LEAD... INTERESTING LIVES.
THANK YOU, LADY JAINA. TYRANDE THINKS LO'GOSH HAS BEEN ENSORCELLED. WE HAD HOPED--

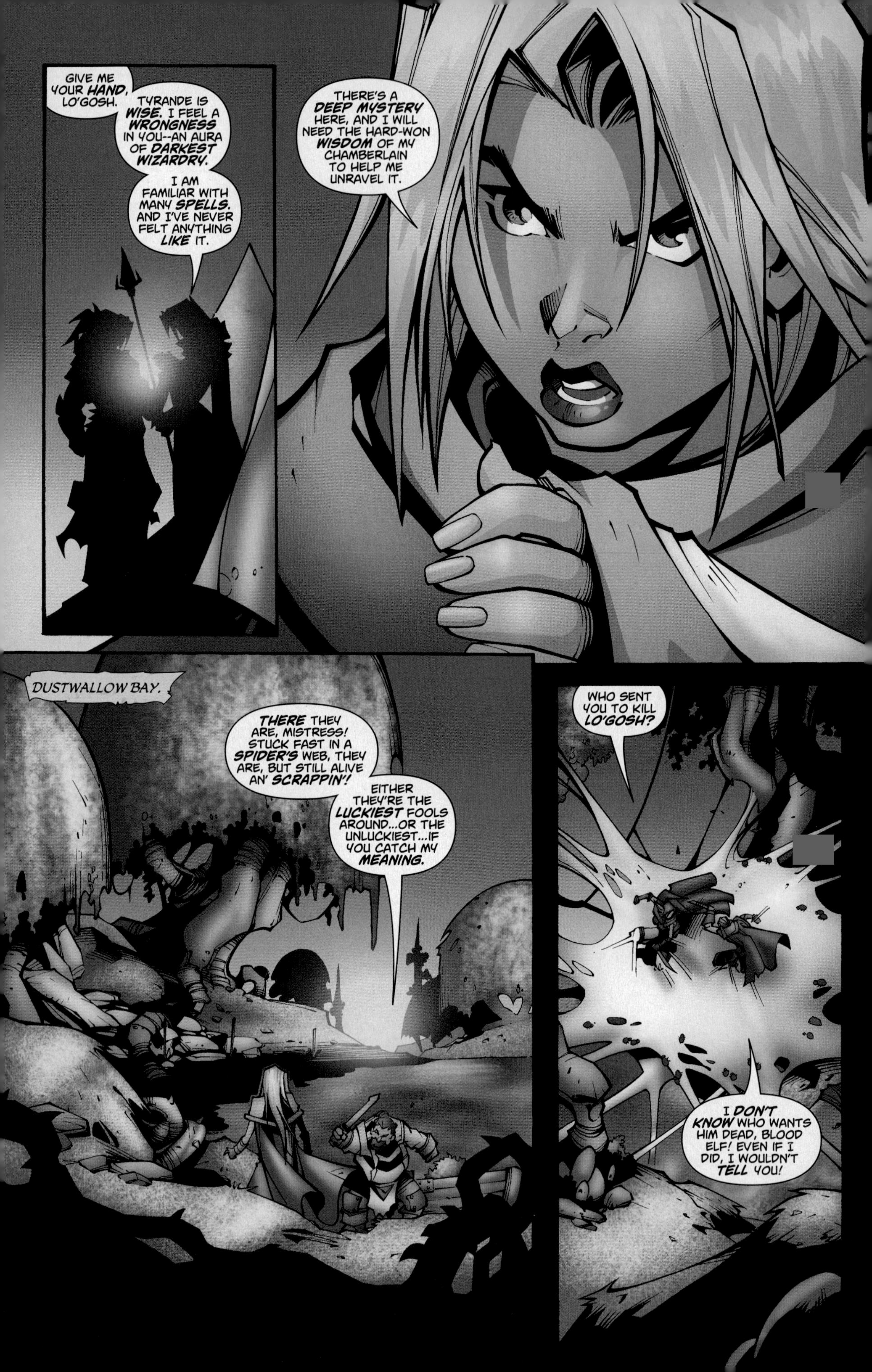
GIVE ME YOUR HAND, LO'GOSH.
TYRANDE IS WISE. I FEEL A WRONGNESS IN YOU--AN AURA OF DARKEST WIZARDRY.
I AM FAMILIAR WITH MANY SPELLS. AND I'VE NEVER FELT ANYTHING LIKE IT.
THERE'S A DEEP MYSTERY HERE, AND I WILL NEED THE HARD-WON WISDOM OF MY CHAMBERLAIN TO HELP ME UNRAVEL IT.
DUSTWALLOW BAY.
THERE THEY ARE, MISTRESS! STUCK FAST IN A SPIDER'S WEB, THEY ARE, BUT STILL ALIVE AN' SCRAPPIN'!
EITHER THEY'RE THE LUCKIEST FOOLS AROUND...OR THE UNLUCKIEST...IF YOU CATCH MY MEANING.
WHO SENT YOU TO KILL LO'GOSH?
I DON'T KNOW WHO WANTS HIM DEAD, BLOOD ELF! EVEN IF I DID, I WOULDN'T TELL YOU!

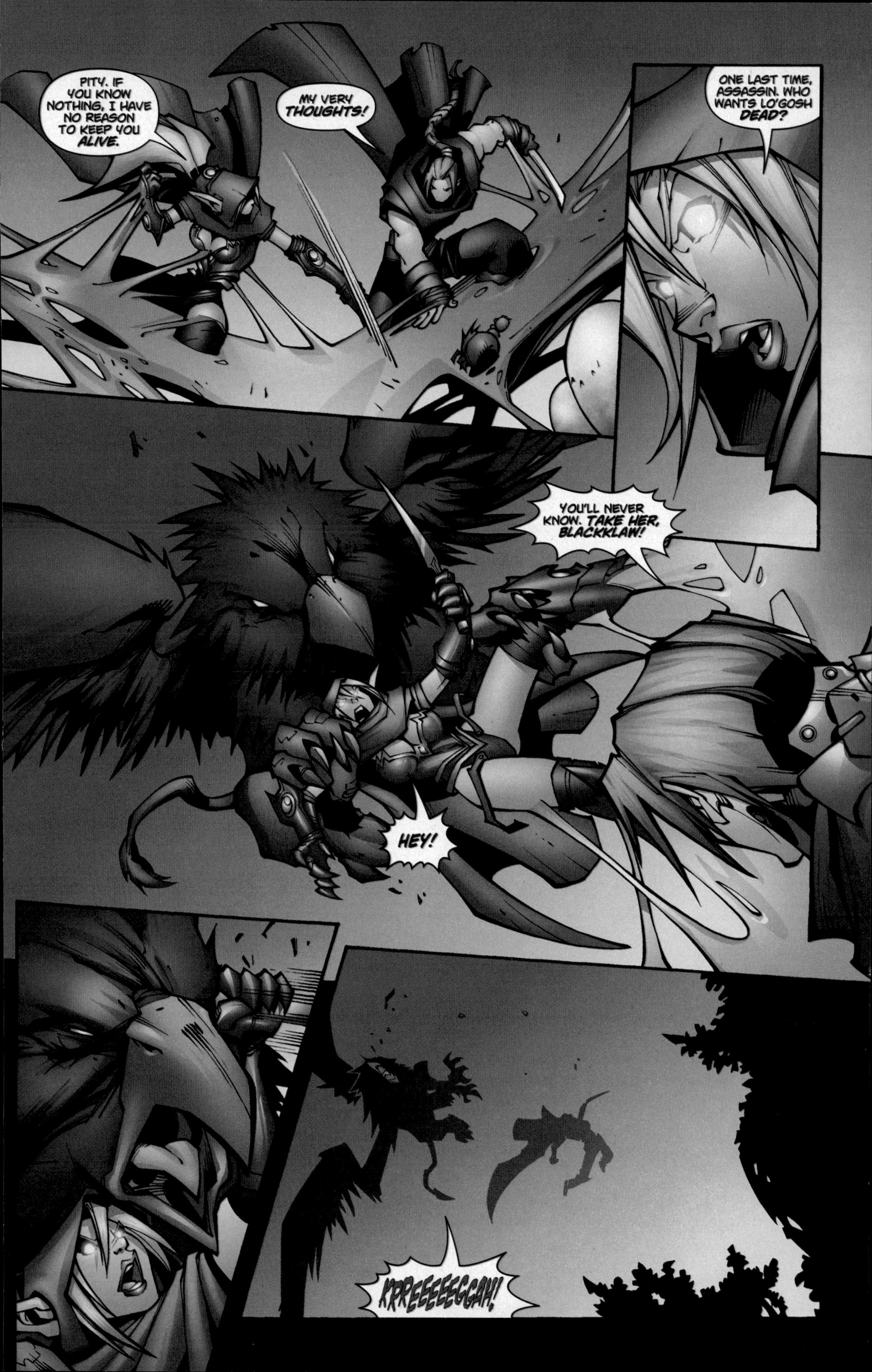
PITY. IF YOU KNOW NOTHING, I HAVE NO REASON TO KEEP YOU ALIVE.
MY VERY THOUGHTS!
ONE LAST TIME, ASSASSIN. WHO WANTS LO'GOSH DEAD?
YOU'LL NEVER KNOW. TAKE HER, BLACKKLAW!
HEY!
KRREEEEEEGGAH!

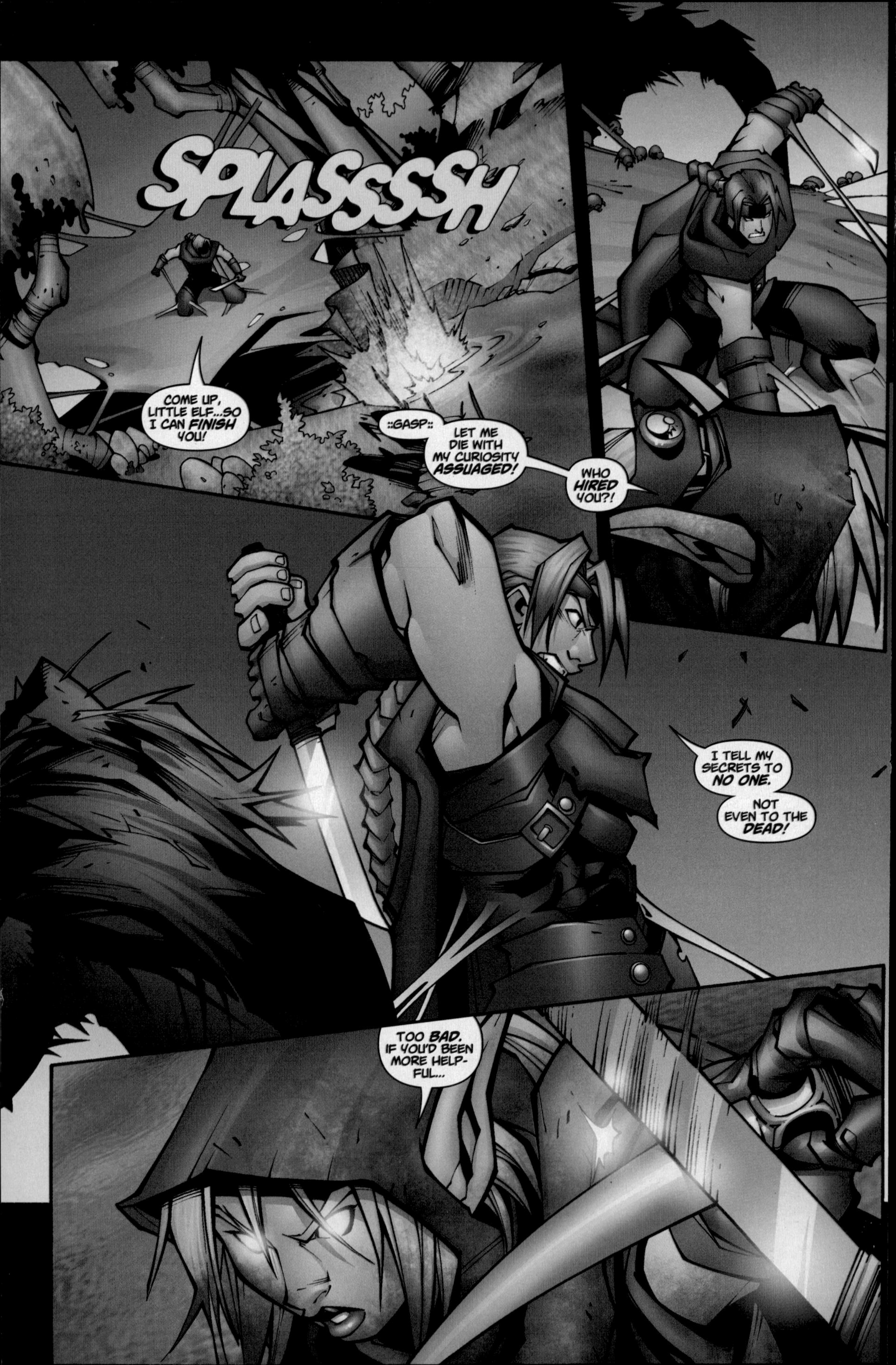
SPLASSSSH
COME UP, LITTLE ELF...SO I CAN FINISH YOU!
::GASP::
LET ME DIE WITH MY CURIOSITY ASSUAGED!
WHO HIRED YOU?!
I TELL MY SECRETS TO NO ONE.
NOT EVEN TO THE DEAD!
TOO BAD. IF YOU'D BEEN MORE HELP-FUL...

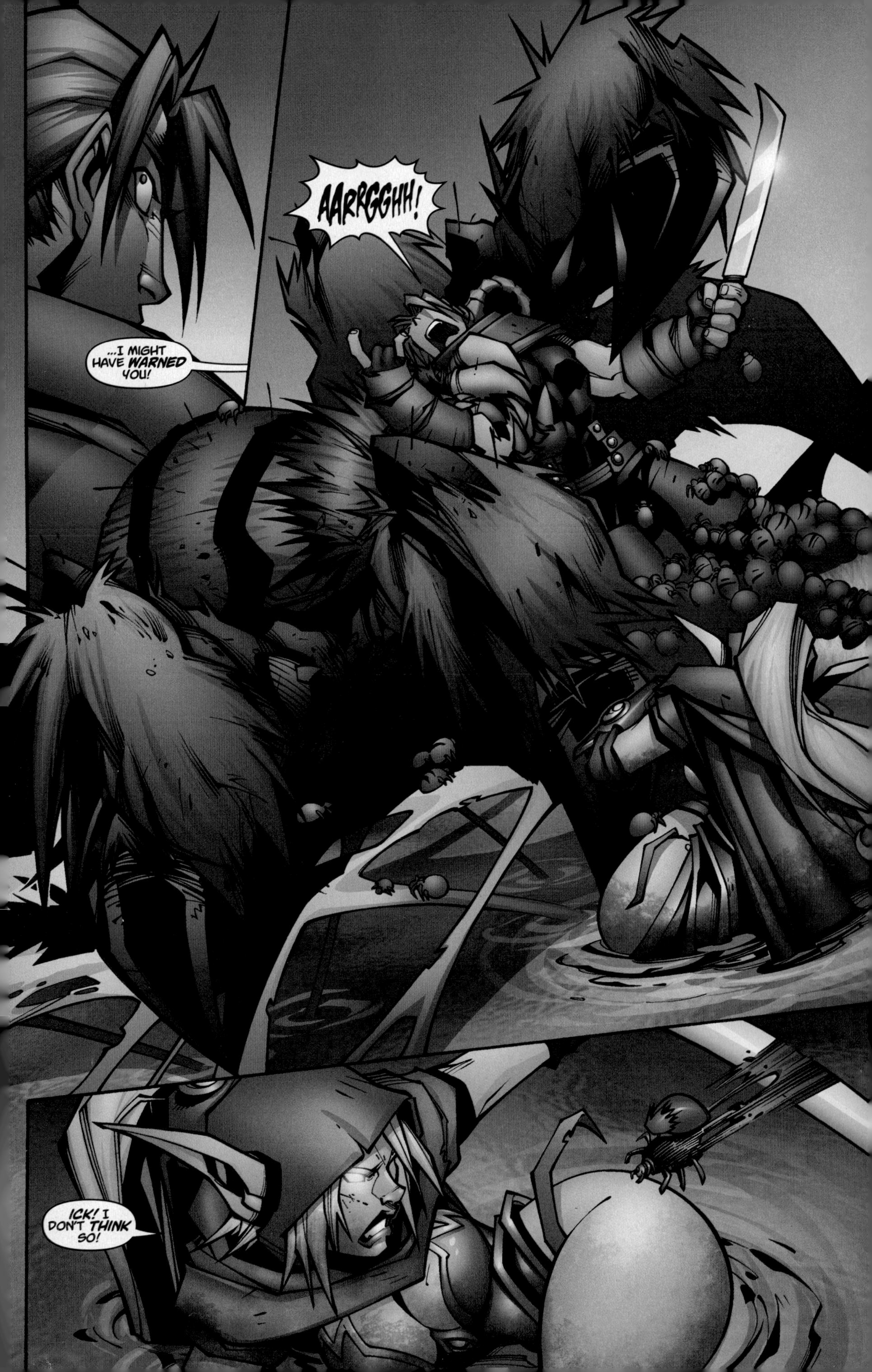
...I MIGHT HAVE WARNED YOU!
AARRGGHH!
ICK! I DON'T THINK SO!

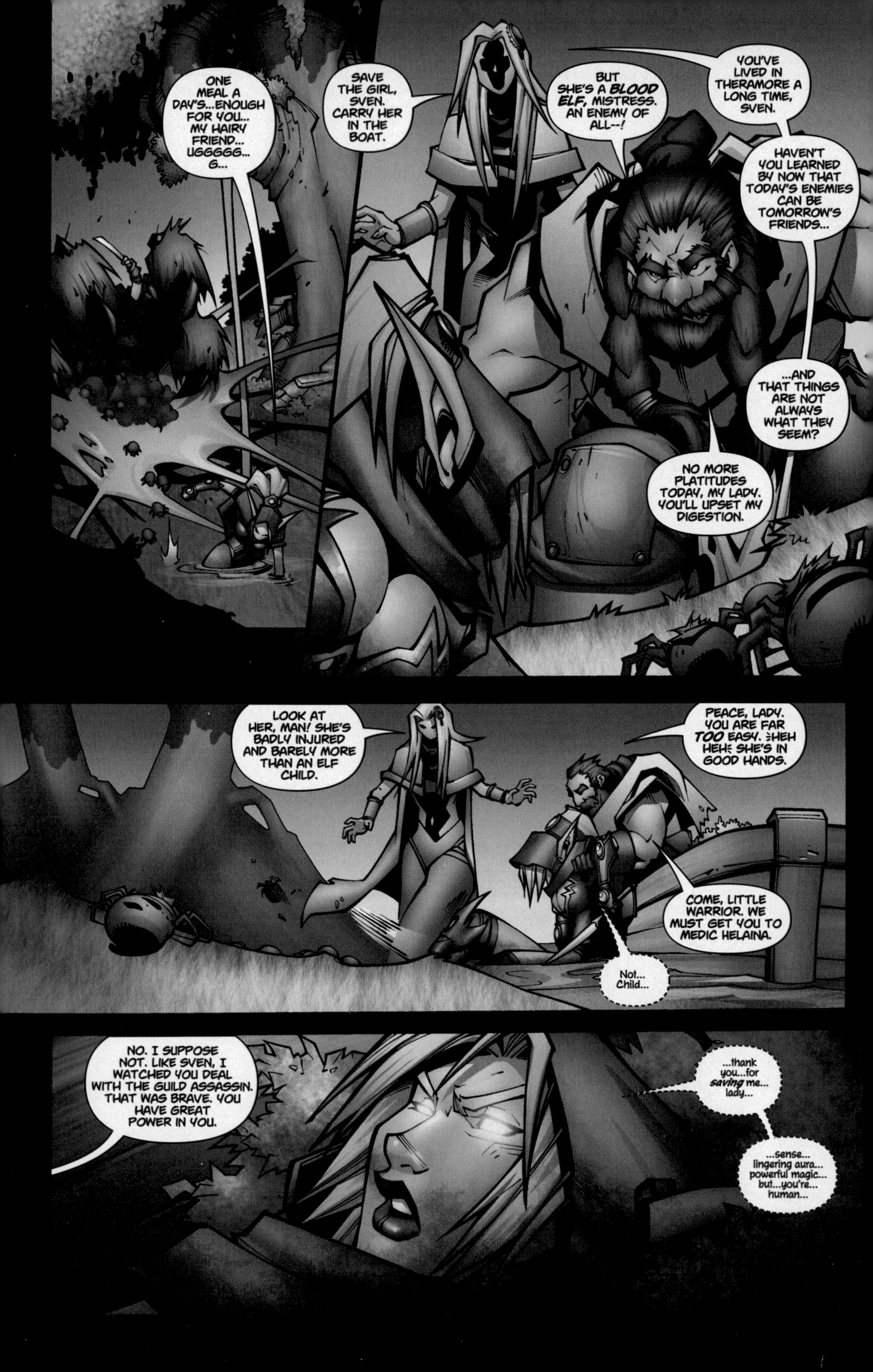
ONE MEAL A DAY'S...ENOUGH FOR YOU... MY HAIRY FRIEND... UGGGGG... G...
SAVE THE GIRL, SVEN. CARRY HER IN THE BOAT.
BUT SHE'S A BLOOD ELF, MISTRESS. AN ENEMY OF ALL--!
YOU'VE LIVED IN THERAMORE A LONG TIME, SVEN.
HAVEN'T YOU LEARNED BY NOW THAT TODAY'S ENEMIES CAN BE TOMORROW'S FRIENDS...
...AND THAT THINGS ARE NOT ALWAYS WHAT THEY SEEM?
NO MORE PLATITUDES TODAY, MY LADY. YOU'LL UPSET MY DIGESTION.
LOOK AT HER, MAN! SHE'S BADLY INJURED AND BARELY MORE THAN AN ELF CHILD.
PEACE, LADY. YOU ARE FAR TOO EASY. HEH HEH SHE'S IN GOOD HANDS.
COME, LITTLE WARRIOR. WE MUST GET YOU TO MEDIC HELAINA.
Not... Child...
NO. I SUPPOSE NOT. LIKE SVEN, I WATCHED YOU DEAL WITH THE GUILD ASSASSIN. THAT WAS BRAVE. YOU HAVE GREAT POWER IN YOU.
...thank you...for saving me... lady...
...sense... lingering aura... powerful magic... but...you're... human...

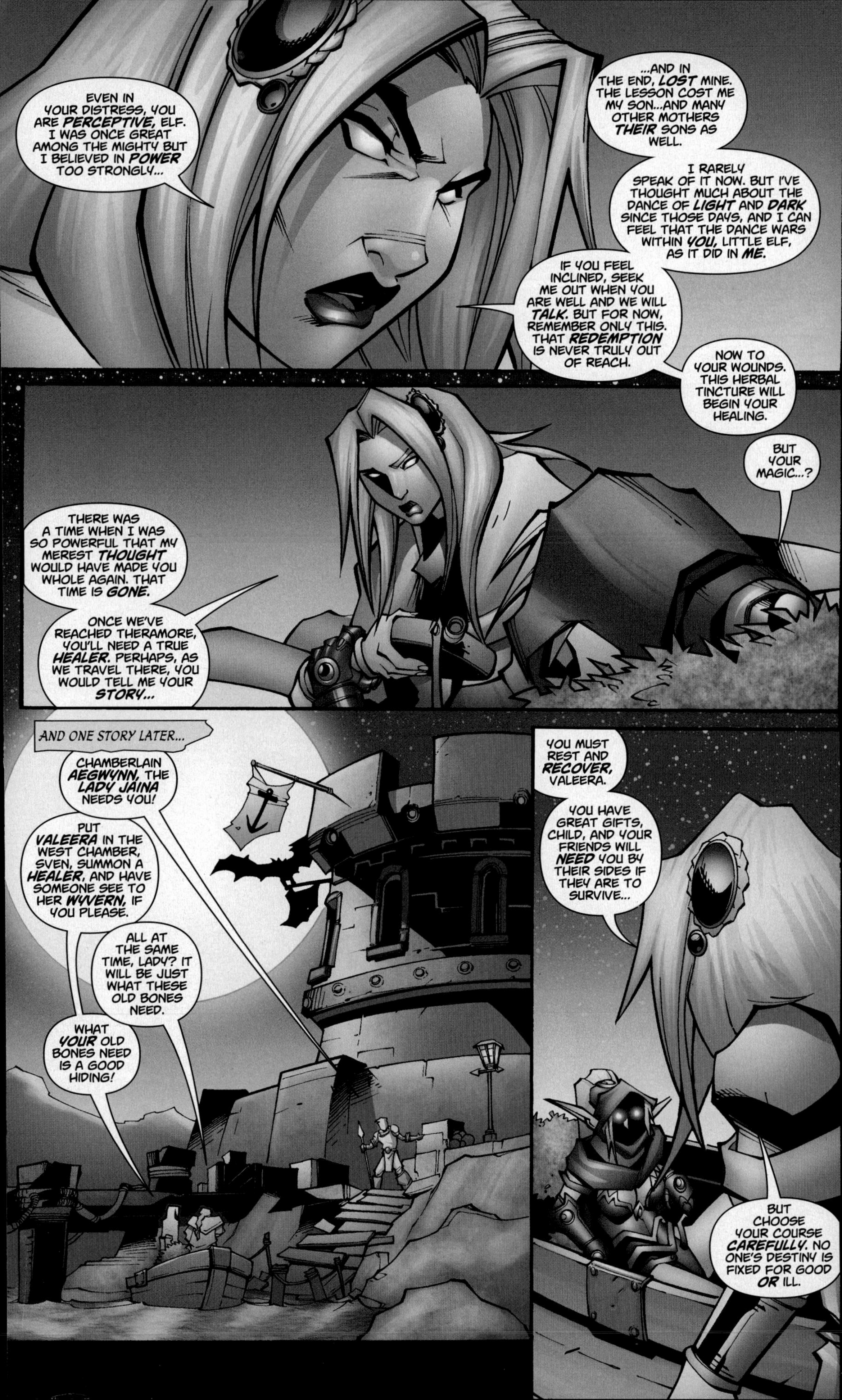
EVEN IN YOUR DISTRESS, YOU ARE PERCEPTIVE, ELF. I WAS ONCE GREAT AMONG THE MIGHTY BUT I BELIEVED IN POWER TOO STRONGLY...
...AND IN THE END, LOST MINE. THE LESSON COST ME MY SON...AND MANY OTHER MOTHERS THEIR SONS AS WELL.
I RARELY SPEAK OF IT NOW. BUT I'VE THOUGHT MUCH ABOUT THE DANCE OF LIGHT AND DARK SINCE THOSE DAYS, AND I CAN FEEL THAT THE DANCE WARS WITHIN YOU, LITTLE ELF, AS IT DID IN ME.
IF YOU FEEL INCLINED, SEEK ME OUT WHEN YOU ARE WELL AND WE WILL TALK. BUT FOR NOW, REMEMBER ONLY THIS. THAT REDEMPTION IS NEVER TRULY OUT OF REACH.
NOW TO YOUR WOUNDS. THIS HERBAL TINCTURE WILL BEGIN YOUR HEALING.
BUT YOUR MAGIC...?
THERE WAS A TIME WHEN I WAS SO POWERFUL THAT MY MEREST THOUGHT WOULD HAVE MADE YOU WHOLE AGAIN. THAT TIME IS GONE.
ONCE WE'VE REACHED THERAMORE, YOU'LL NEED A TRUE HEALER. PERHAPS, AS WE TRAVEL THERE, YOU WOULD TELL ME YOUR STORY...
AND ONE STORY LATER...
CHAMBERLAIN AEGWYNN, THE LADY JAINA NEEDS YOU!
PUT VALEERA IN THE WEST CHAMBER, SVEN, SUMMON A HEALER, AND HAVE SOMEONE SEE TO HER WYVERN, IF YOU PLEASE.
ALL AT THE SAME TIME, LADY? IT WILL BE JUST WHAT THESE OLD BONES NEED.
WHAT YOUR OLD BONES NEED IS A GOOD HIDING!
YOU MUST REST AND RECOVER, VALEERA.
YOU HAVE GREAT GIFTS, CHILD, AND YOUR FRIENDS WILL NEED YOU BY THEIR SIDES IF THEY ARE TO SURVIVE...
BUT CHOOSE YOUR COURSE CAREFULLY. NO ONE'S DESTINY IS FIXED FOR GOOD OR ILL.

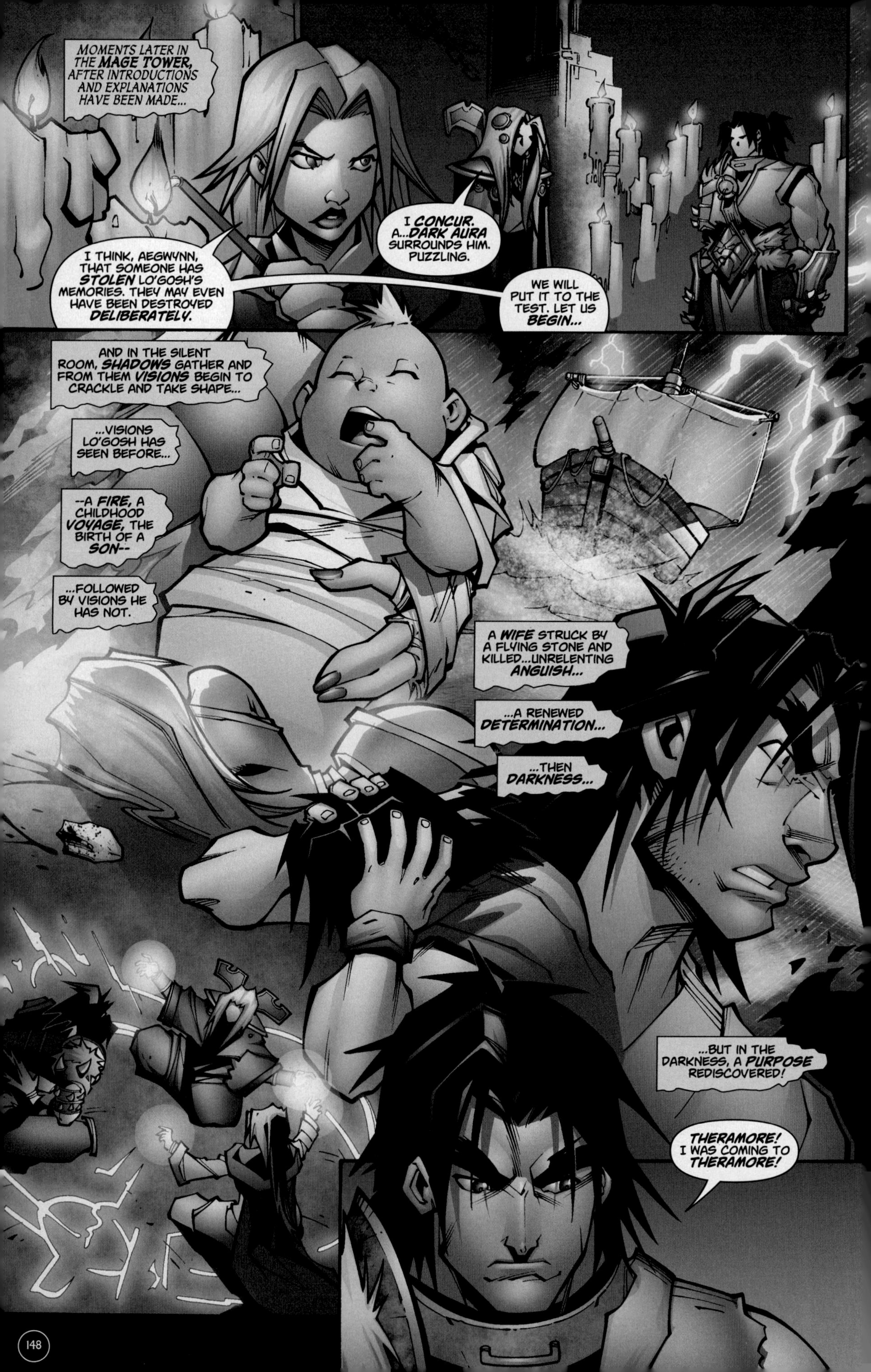
MOMENTS LATER IN THE MAGE TOWER, AFTER INTRODUCTIONS AND EXPLANATIONS HAVE BEEN MADE...
I THINK, AEGWYNN, THAT SOMEONE HAS STOLEN LO'GOSH'S MEMORIES. THEY MAY EVEN HAVE BEEN DESTROYED DELIBERATELY.
I CONCUR. A...DARK AURA SURROUNDS HIM. PUZZLING.
WE WILL PUT IT TO THE TEST. LET US BEGIN...
AND IN THE SILENT ROOM, SHADOWS GATHER AND FROM THEM VISIONS BEGIN TO CRACKLE AND TAKE SHAPE...
...VISIONS LO'GOSH HAS SEEN BEFORE...
--A FIRE, A CHILDHOOD VOYAGE, THE BIRTH OF A SON--
...FOLLOWED BY VISIONS HE HAS NOT.
A WIFE STRUCK BY A FLYING STONE AND KILLED...UNRELENTING ANGUISH...
...A RENEWED DETERMINATION...
...THEN DARKNESS...
...BUT IN THE DARKNESS, A PURPOSE REDISCOVERED!
THERAMORE! I WAS COMING TO THERAMORE!

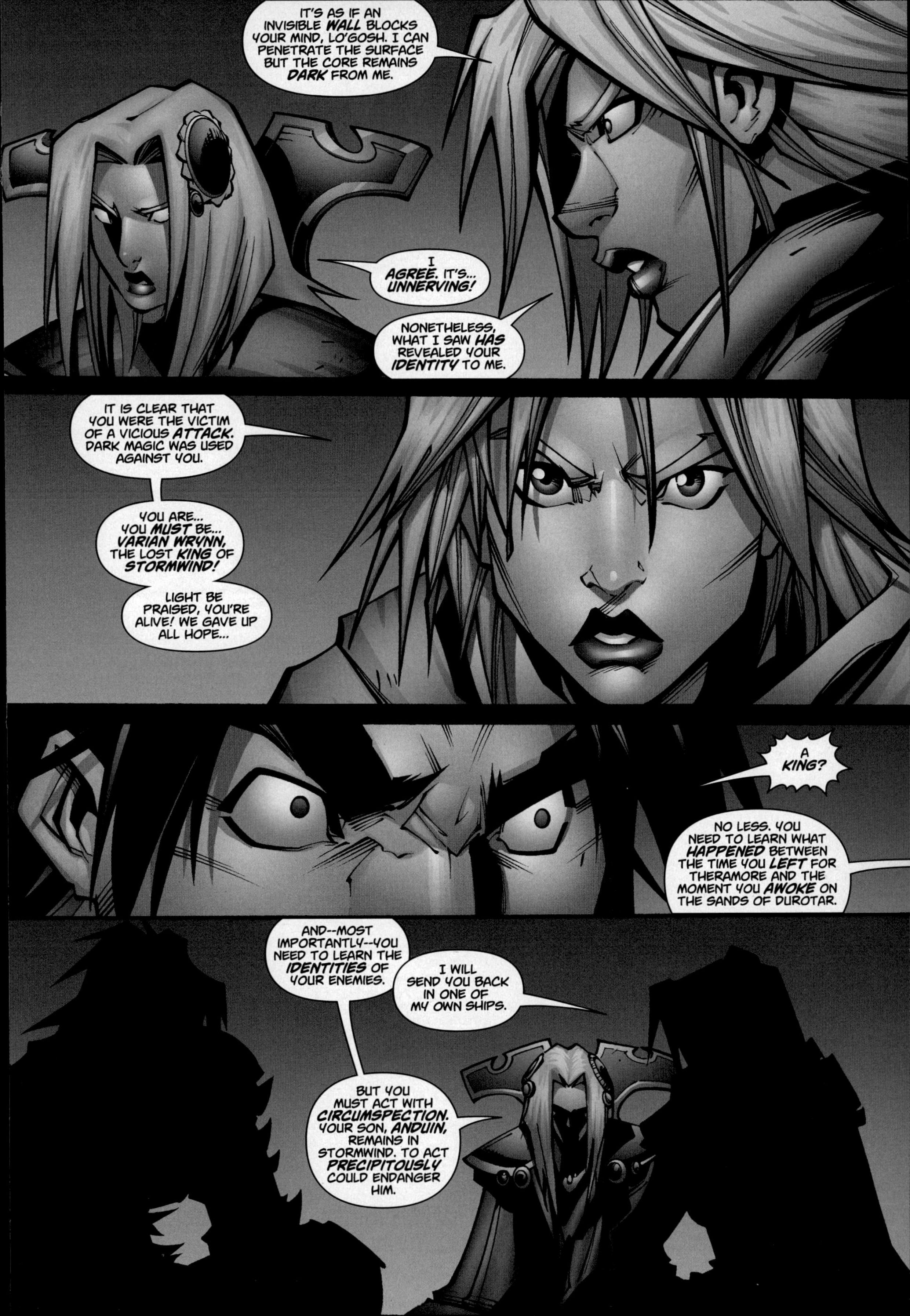
IT'S AS IF AN INVISIBLE WALL BLOCKS YOUR MIND, LO'GOSH. I CAN PENETRATE THE SURFACE BUT THE CORE REMAINS DARK FROM ME.
I AGREE. IT'S... UNNERVING!
NONETHELESS, WHAT I SAW HAS REVEALED YOUR IDENTITY TO ME.
IT IS CLEAR THAT YOU WERE THE VICTIM OF A VICIOUS ATTACK. DARK MAGIC WAS USED AGAINST YOU.
YOU ARE... YOU MUST BE... VARIAN WRYNN, THE LOST KING OF STORMWIND!
LIGHT BE PRAISED, YOU'RE ALIVE! WE GAVE UP ALL HOPE...
A KING?
NO LESS. YOU NEED TO LEARN WHAT HAPPENED BETWEEN THE TIME YOU LEFT FOR THERAMORE AND THE MOMENT YOU AWOKE ON THE SANDS OF DUROTAR.
AND--MOST IMPORTANTLY--YOU NEED TO LEARN THE IDENTITIES OF YOUR ENEMIES.
I WILL SEND YOU BACK IN ONE OF MY OWN SHIPS.
BUT YOU MUST ACT WITH CIRCUMSPECTION. YOUR SON, ANDUIN, REMAINS IN STORMWIND. TO ACT PRECIPITOUSLY COULD ENDANGER HIM.

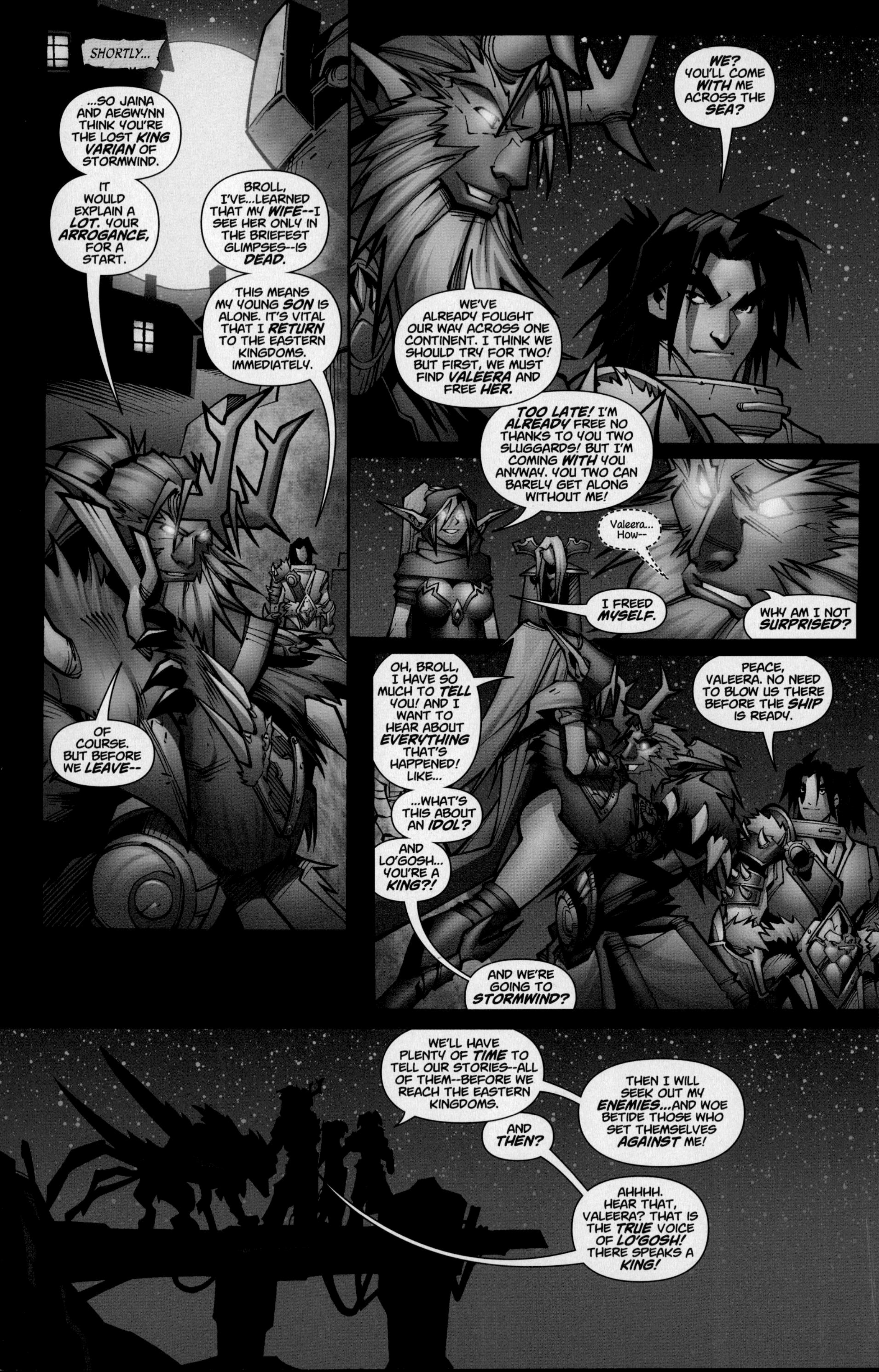
SHORTLY...
...SO JAINA AND AEGWYNN THINK YOU'RE THE LOST KING VARIAN OF STORMWIND.
IT WOULD EXPLAIN A LOT. YOUR ARROGANCE, FOR A START.
BROLL, I'VE...LEARNED THAT MY WIFE--I SEE HER ONLY IN THE BRIEFEST GLIMPSES--IS DEAD.
THIS MEANS MY YOUNG SON IS ALONE. IT'S VITAL THAT I RETURN TO THE EASTERN KINGDOMS. IMMEDIATELY.
OF COURSE. BUT BEFORE WE LEAVE--
WE? YOU'LL COME WITH ME ACROSS THE SEA?
WE'VE ALREADY FOUGHT OUR WAY ACROSS ONE CONTINENT. I THINK WE SHOULD TRY FOR TWO! BUT FIRST, WE MUST FIND VALEERA AND FREE HER.
TOO LATE! I'M ALREADY FREE NO THANKS TO YOU TWO SLUGGARDS! BUT I'M COMING WITH YOU ANYWAY. YOU TWO CAN BARELY GET ALONG WITHOUT ME!
Valeera... How--
I FREED MYSELF.
WHY AM I NOT SURPRISED?
OH, BROLL, I HAVE SO MUCH TO TELL YOU! AND I WANT TO HEAR ABOUT EVERYTHING THAT'S HAPPENED! LIKE...
...WHAT'S THIS ABOUT AN IDOL?
AND LO'GOSH... YOU'RE A KING?!
AND WE'RE GOING TO STORMWIND?
PEACE, VALEERA. NO NEED TO BLOW US THERE BEFORE THE SHIP IS READY.
WE'LL HAVE PLENTY OF TIME TO TELL OUR STORIES--ALL OF THEM--BEFORE WE REACH THE EASTERN KINGDOMS.
AND THEN?
THEN I WILL SEEK OUT MY ENEMIES...AND WOE BETIDE THOSE WHO SET THEMSELVES AGAINST ME!
AHHHH. HEAR THAT, VALEERA? THAT IS THE TRUE VOICE OF LO'GOSH! THERE SPEAKS A KING!

CHAPTER 7

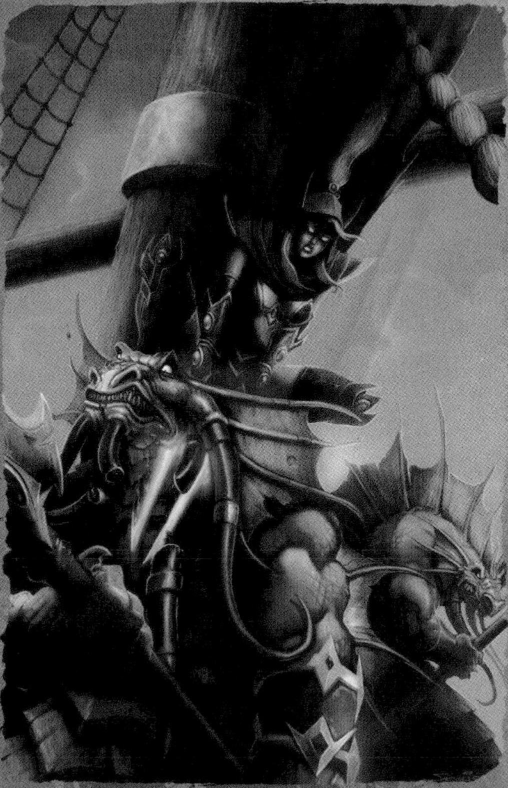

Issue #7 Cover
by Samwise Didier

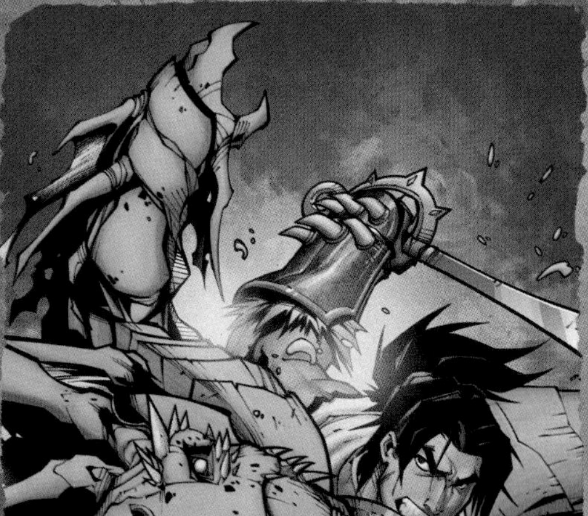

Issue #7 Cover
by Ludo Lullabi, Sandra Hope
and Randy Mayor

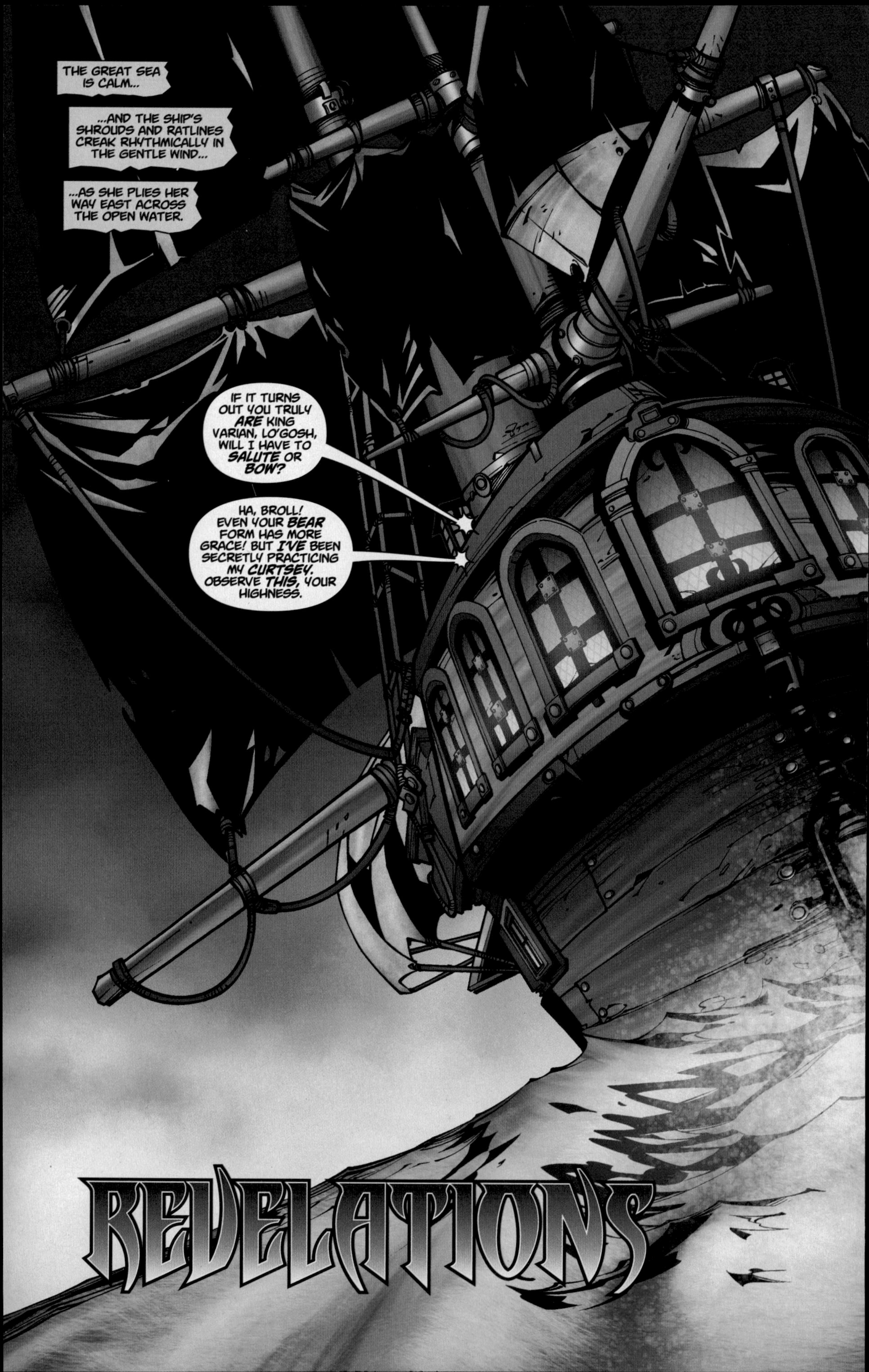
THE GREAT SEA IS CALM...
...AND THE SHIP'S SHROUDS AND RATLINES CREAK RHYTHMICALLY IN THE GENTLE WIND...
...AS SHE PLIES HER WAY EAST ACROSS THE OPEN WATER.
IF IT TURNS OUT YOU TRULY ARE KING VARIAN, LO'GOSH, WILL I HAVE TO SALUTE OR BOW?
HA, BROLL! EVEN YOUR BEAR FORM HAS MORE GRACE! BUT I'VE BEEN SECRETLY PRACTICING MY CURTSEY. OBSERVE THIS, YOUR HIGHNESS.
REVELATIONS

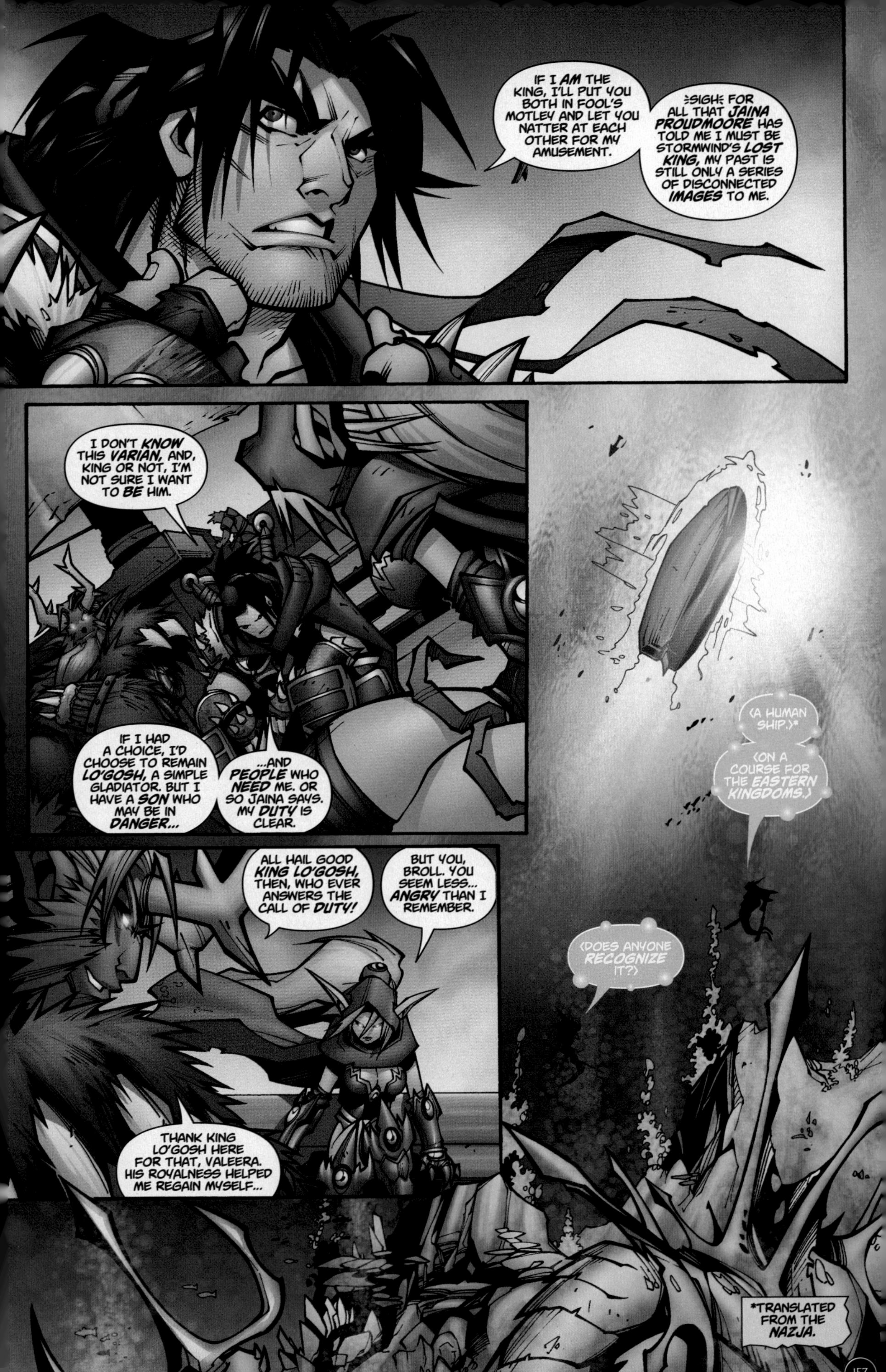
IF I AM THE KING, I'LL PUT YOU BOTH IN FOOL'S MOTLEY AND LET YOU NATTER AT EACH OTHER FOR MY AMUSEMENT.
≷SIGH≶ FOR ALL THAT JAINA PROUDMOORE HAS TOLD ME I MUST BE STORMWIND'S LOST KING, MY PAST IS STILL ONLY A SERIES OF DISCONNECTED IMAGES TO ME.
I DON'T KNOW THIS VARIAN, AND, KING OR NOT, I'M NOT SURE I WANT TO BE HIM.
IF I HAD A CHOICE, I'D CHOOSE TO REMAIN LO'GOSH, A SIMPLE GLADIATOR. BUT I HAVE A SON WHO MAY BE IN DANGER...
...AND PEOPLE WHO NEED ME. OR SO JAINA SAYS. MY DUTY IS CLEAR.
ALL HAIL GOOD KING LO'GOSH, THEN, WHO EVER ANSWERS THE CALL OF DUTY!
BUT YOU, BROLL. YOU SEEM LESS... ANGRY THAN I REMEMBER.
THANK KING LO'GOSH HERE FOR THAT, VALEERA. HIS ROYALNESS HELPED ME REGAIN MYSELF...
(A HUMAN SHIP.)*
(ON A COURSE FOR THE EASTERN KINGDOMS.)
(DOES ANYONE RECOGNIZE IT?)
*TRANSLATED FROM THE NAZJA.

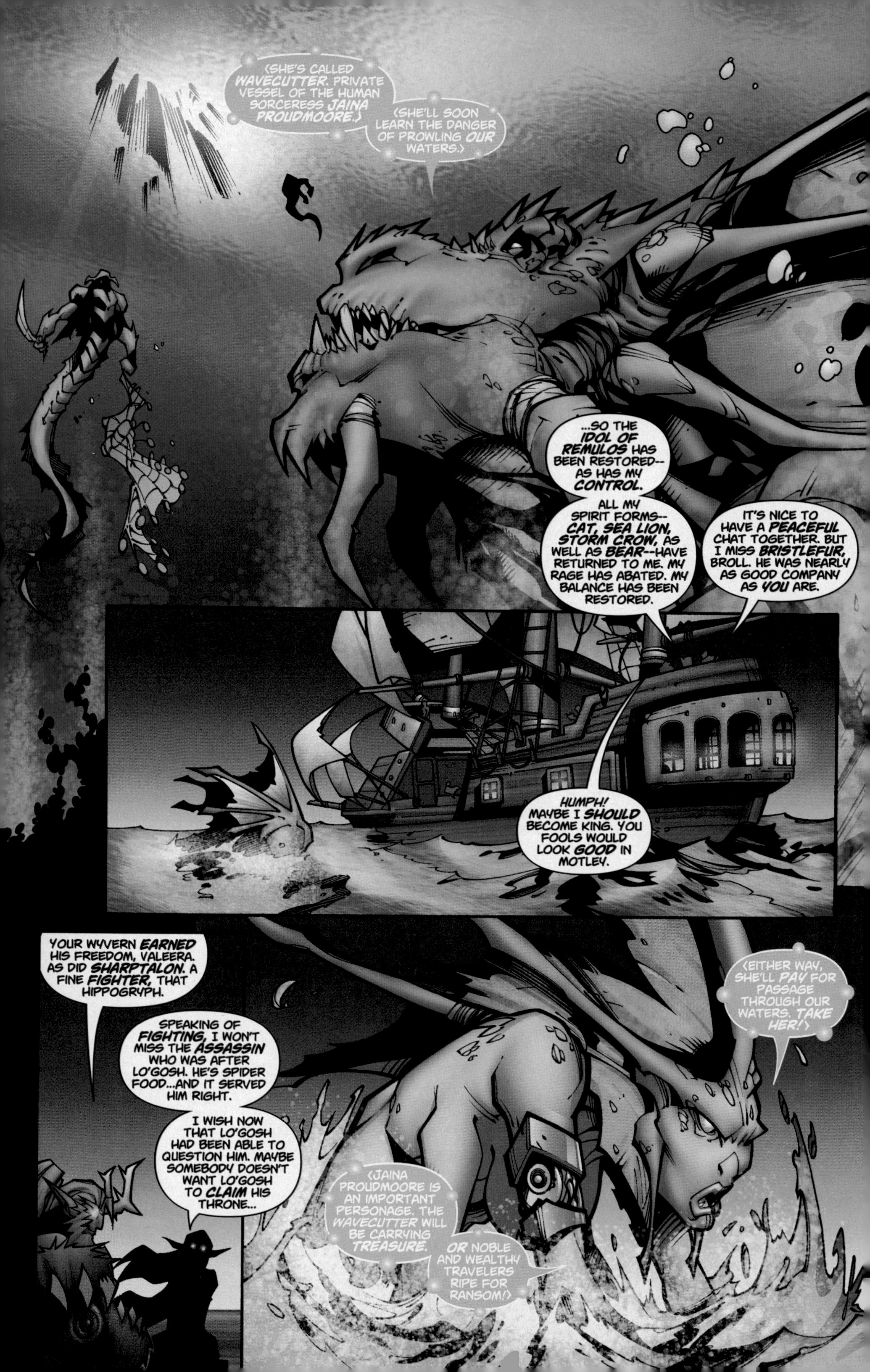
‹SHE'S CALLED WAVECUTTER. PRIVATE VESSEL OF THE HUMAN SORCERESS JAINA PROUDMOORE.›
‹SHE'LL SOON LEARN THE DANGER OF PROWLING OUR WATERS.›
...SO THE IDOL OF REMULOS HAS BEEN RESTORED-- AS HAS MY CONTROL.
ALL MY SPIRIT FORMS-- CAT, SEA LION, STORM CROW, AS WELL AS BEAR--HAVE RETURNED TO ME. MY RAGE HAS ABATED. MY BALANCE HAS BEEN RESTORED.
IT'S NICE TO HAVE A PEACEFUL CHAT TOGETHER. BUT I MISS BRISTLEFUR, BROLL. HE WAS NEARLY AS GOOD COMPANY AS YOU ARE.
HUMPH! MAYBE I SHOULD BECOME KING. YOU FOOLS WOULD LOOK GOOD IN MOTLEY.
YOUR WYVERN EARNED HIS FREEDOM, VALEERA. AS DID SHARPTALON. A FINE FIGHTER, THAT HIPPOGRYPH.
SPEAKING OF FIGHTING, I WON'T MISS THE ASSASSIN WHO WAS AFTER LO'GOSH. HE'S SPIDER FOOD...AND IT SERVED HIM RIGHT.
I WISH NOW THAT LO'GOSH HAD BEEN ABLE TO QUESTION HIM. MAYBE SOMEBODY DOESN'T WANT LO'GOSH TO CLAIM HIS THRONE...
‹EITHER WAY, SHE'LL PAY FOR PASSAGE THROUGH OUR WATERS. TAKE HER!›
‹JAINA PROUDMOORE IS AN IMPORTANT PERSONAGE. THE WAVECUTTER WILL BE CARRYING TREASURE.
OR NOBLE AND WEALTHY TRAVELERS RIPE FOR RANSOM!›

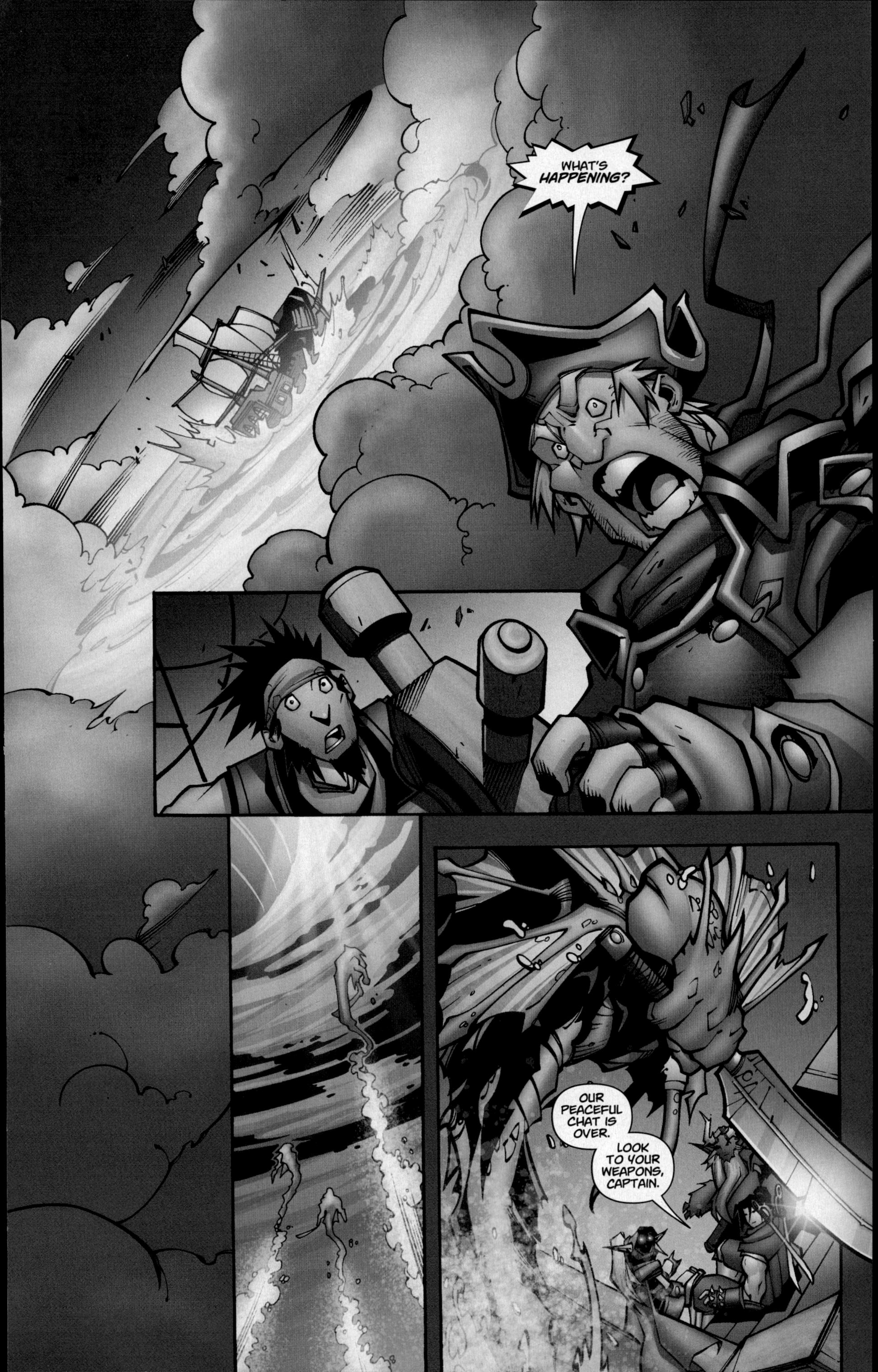
WHAT'S HAPPENING?
OUR PEACEFUL CHAT IS OVER.
LOOK TO YOUR WEAPONS, CAPTAIN.

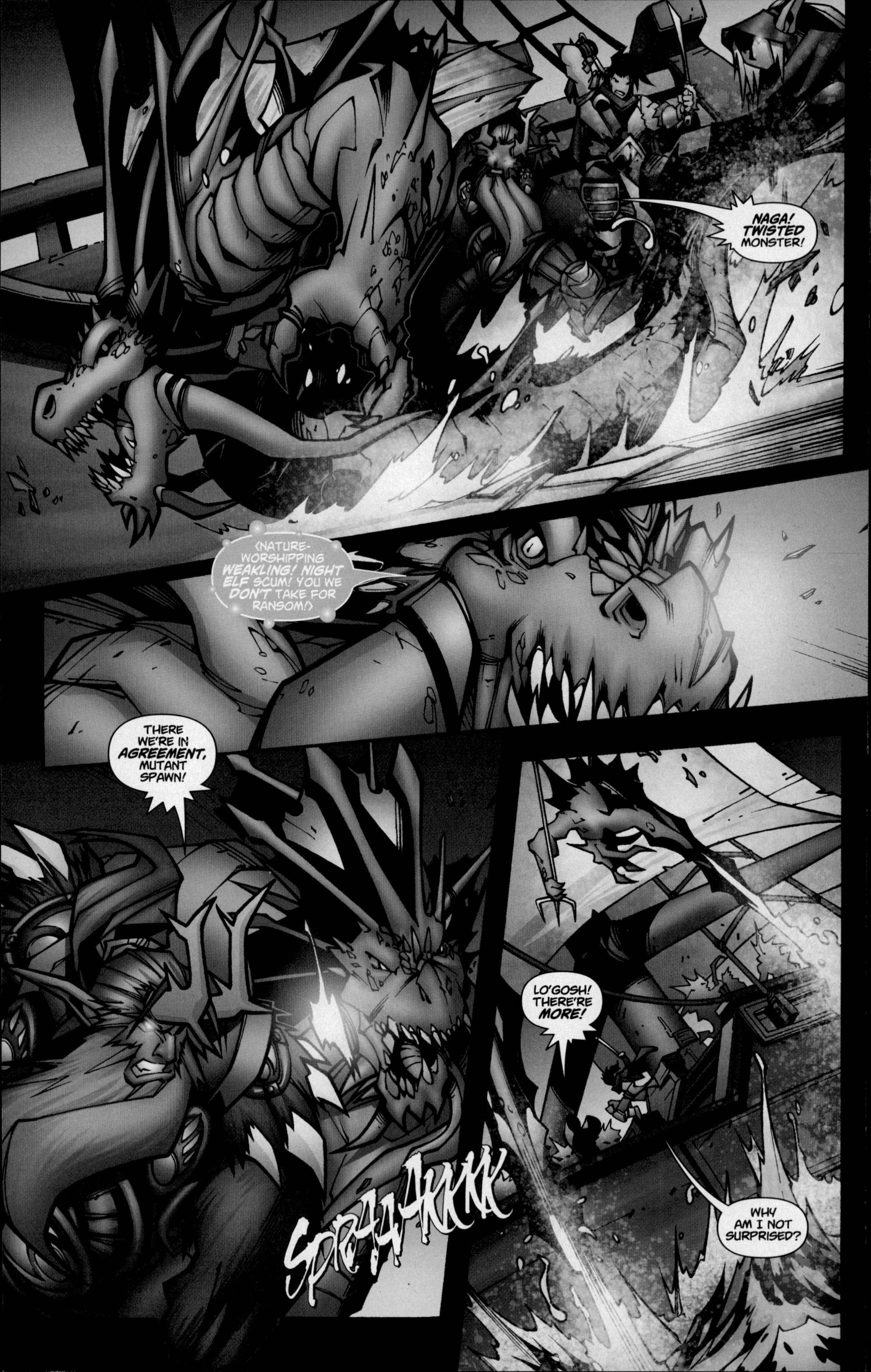
NAGA! TWISTED MONSTER!
‹NATURE-WORSHIPPING WEAKLING! NIGHT ELF SCUM! YOU WE DON'T TAKE FOR RANSOM!›
THERE WE'RE IN AGREEMENT, MUTANT SPAWN!
SPRAAAKKKK
LO'GOSH! THERE'RE MORE!
WHY AM I NOT SURPRISED?

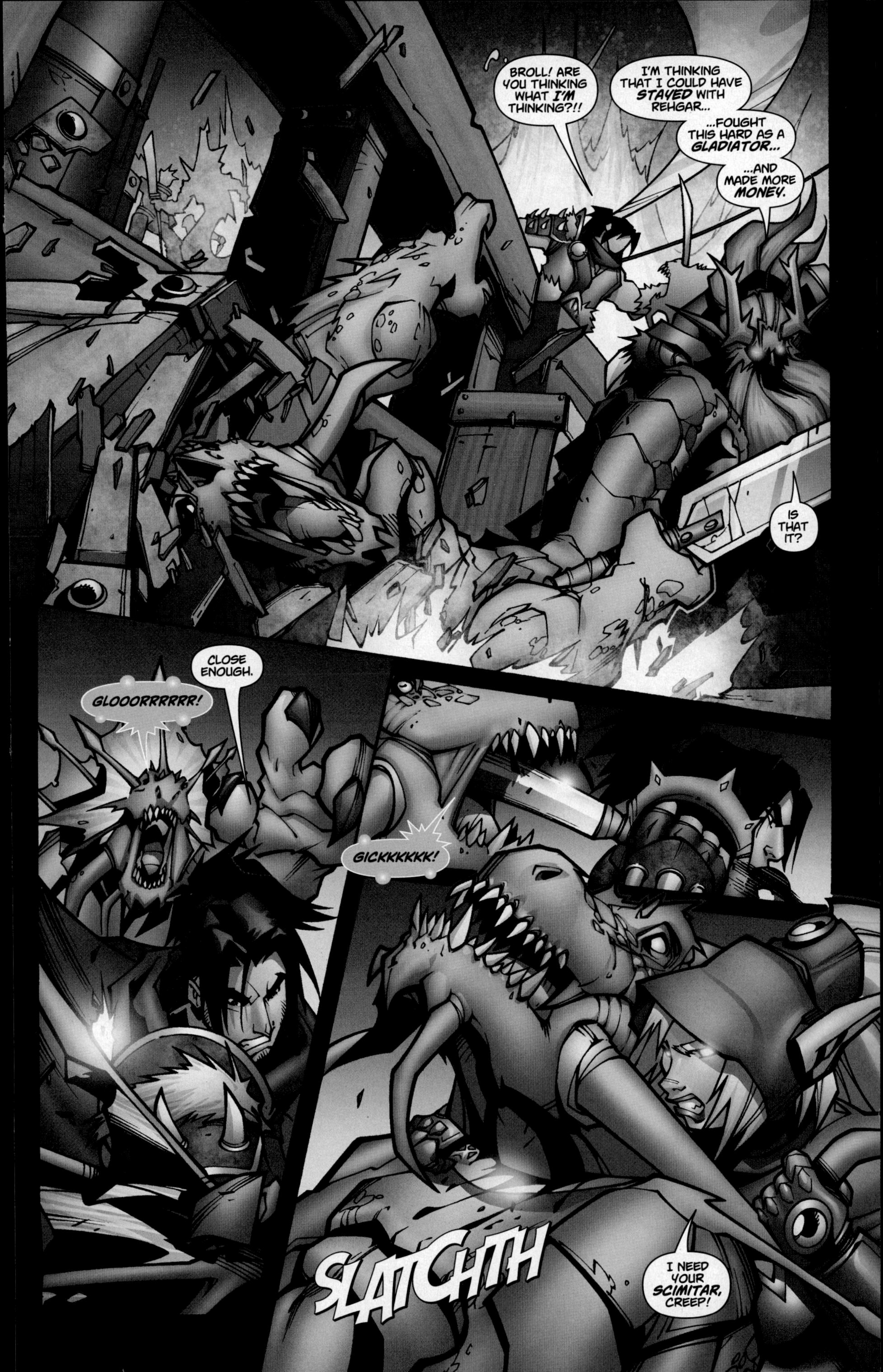
BROLL! ARE YOU THINKING WHAT I'M THINKING?!!
I'M THINKING THAT I COULD HAVE STAYED WITH REHGAR...
...FOUGHT THIS HARD AS A GLADIATOR...
...AND MADE MORE MONEY.
IS THAT IT?
CLOSE ENOUGH.
GLOOORRRRRR!
GICKKKKKK!
SLATCHTH
I NEED YOUR SCIMITAR, CREEP!

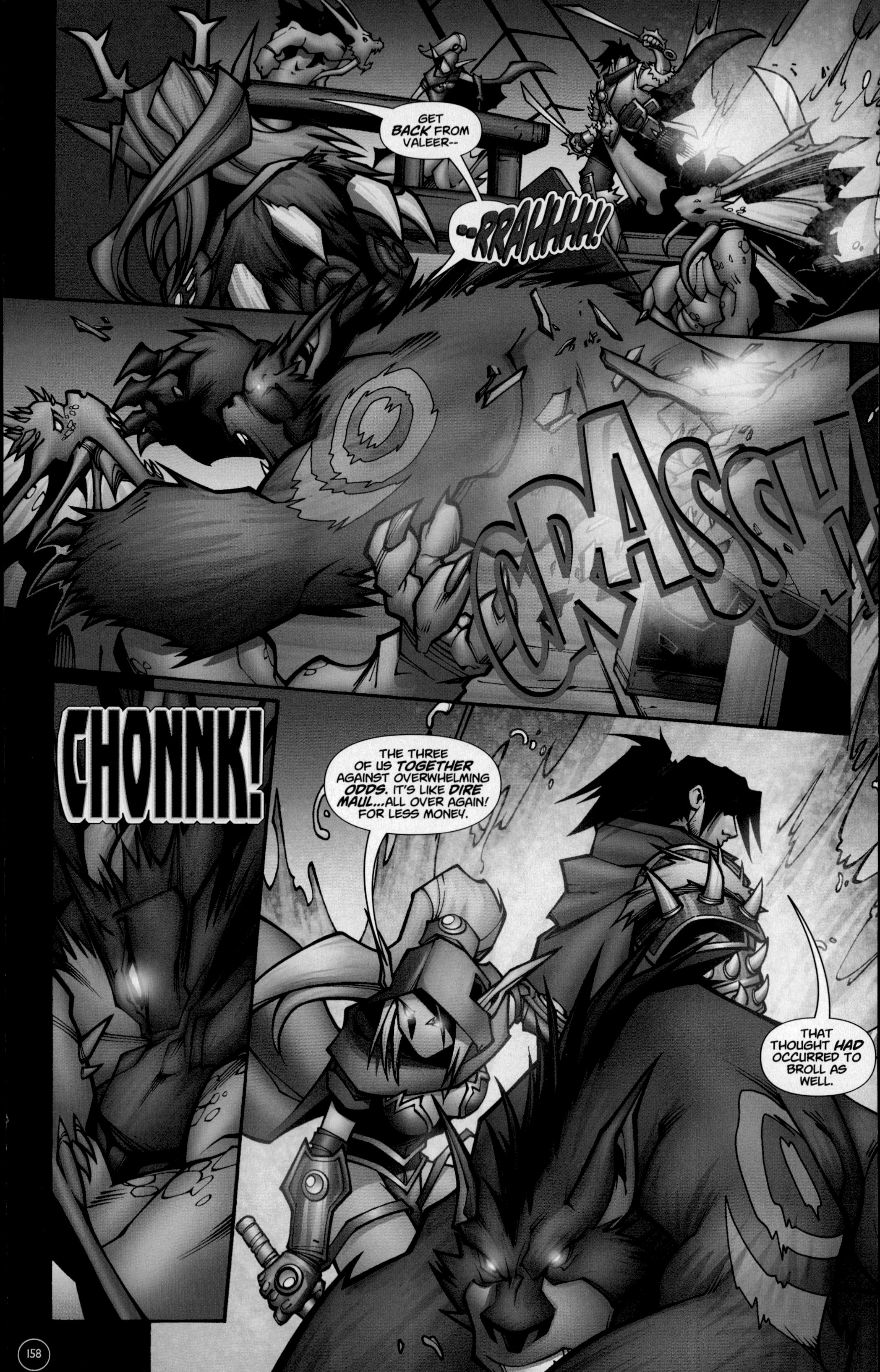

GET BACK FROM VALEER--
--RRAHHHH!
CRASSH!
CHONNK!
THE THREE OF US TOGETHER AGAINST OVERWHELMING ODDS. IT'S LIKE DIRE MAUL...ALL OVER AGAIN! FOR LESS MONEY.
THAT THOUGHT HAD OCCURRED TO BROLL AS WELL.

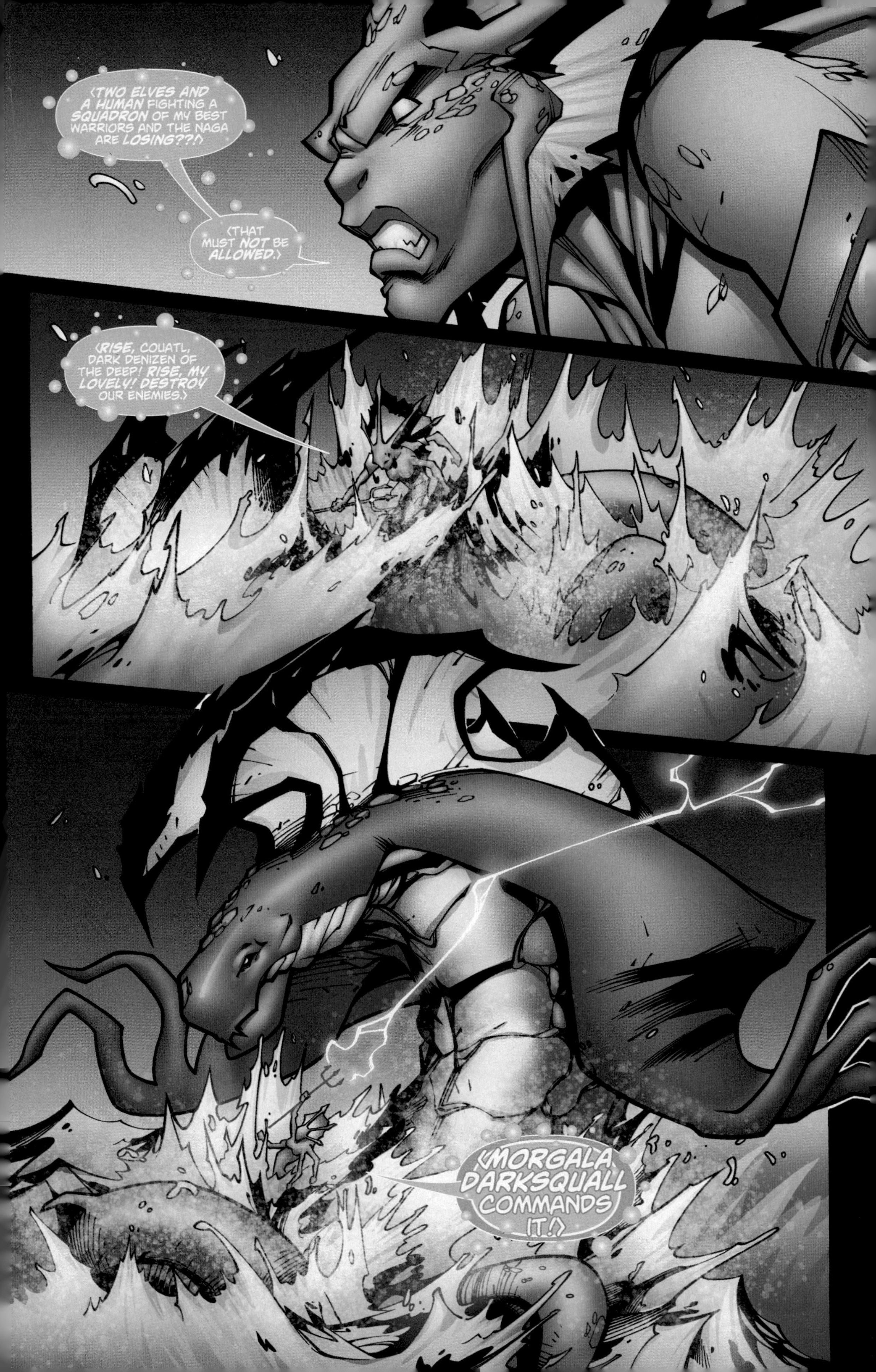
‹TWO ELVES AND A HUMAN FIGHTING A SQUADRON OF MY BEST WARRIORS AND THE NAGA ARE LOSING??!›
‹THAT MUST NOT BE ALLOWED.›
‹RISE, COUATL, DARK DENIZEN OF THE DEEP! RISE, MY LOVELY! DESTROY OUR ENEMIES.›
‹MORGALA DARKSQUALL COMMANDS IT!›

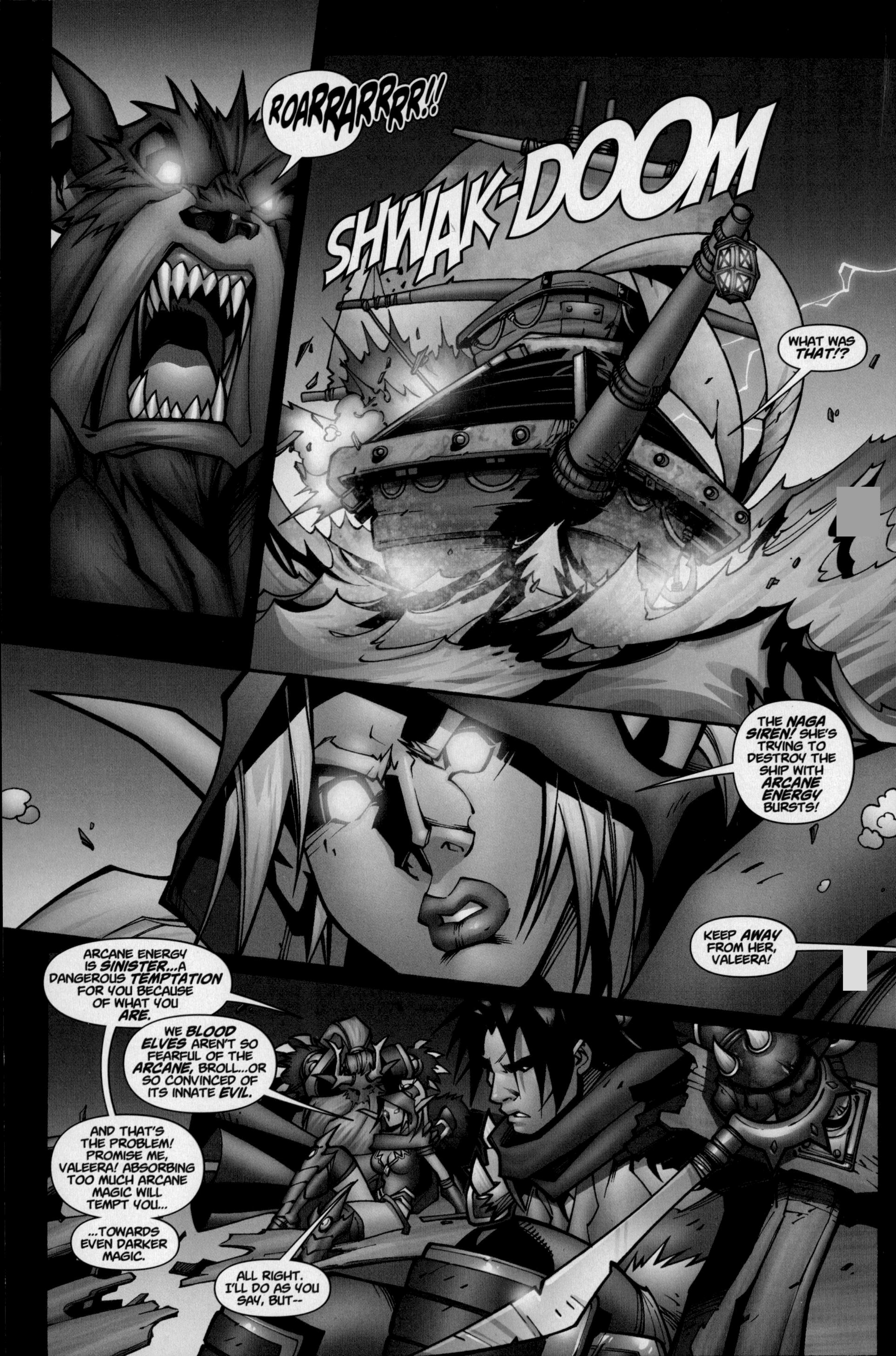
ROARRARRRR!!
SHWAK-DOOM
WHAT WAS THAT!?
THE NAGA SIREN! SHE'S TRYING TO DESTROY THE SHIP WITH ARCANE ENERGY BURSTS!
KEEP AWAY FROM HER, VALEERA!
ARCANE ENERGY IS SINISTER...A DANGEROUS TEMPTATION FOR YOU BECAUSE OF WHAT YOU ARE.
WE BLOOD ELVES AREN'T SO FEARFUL OF THE ARCANE, BROLL...OR SO CONVINCED OF ITS INNATE EVIL.
AND THAT'S THE PROBLEM! PROMISE ME, VALEERA! ABSORBING TOO MUCH ARCANE MAGIC WILL TEMPT YOU...
...TOWARDS EVEN DARKER MAGIC.
ALL RIGHT. I'LL DO AS YOU SAY, BUT--

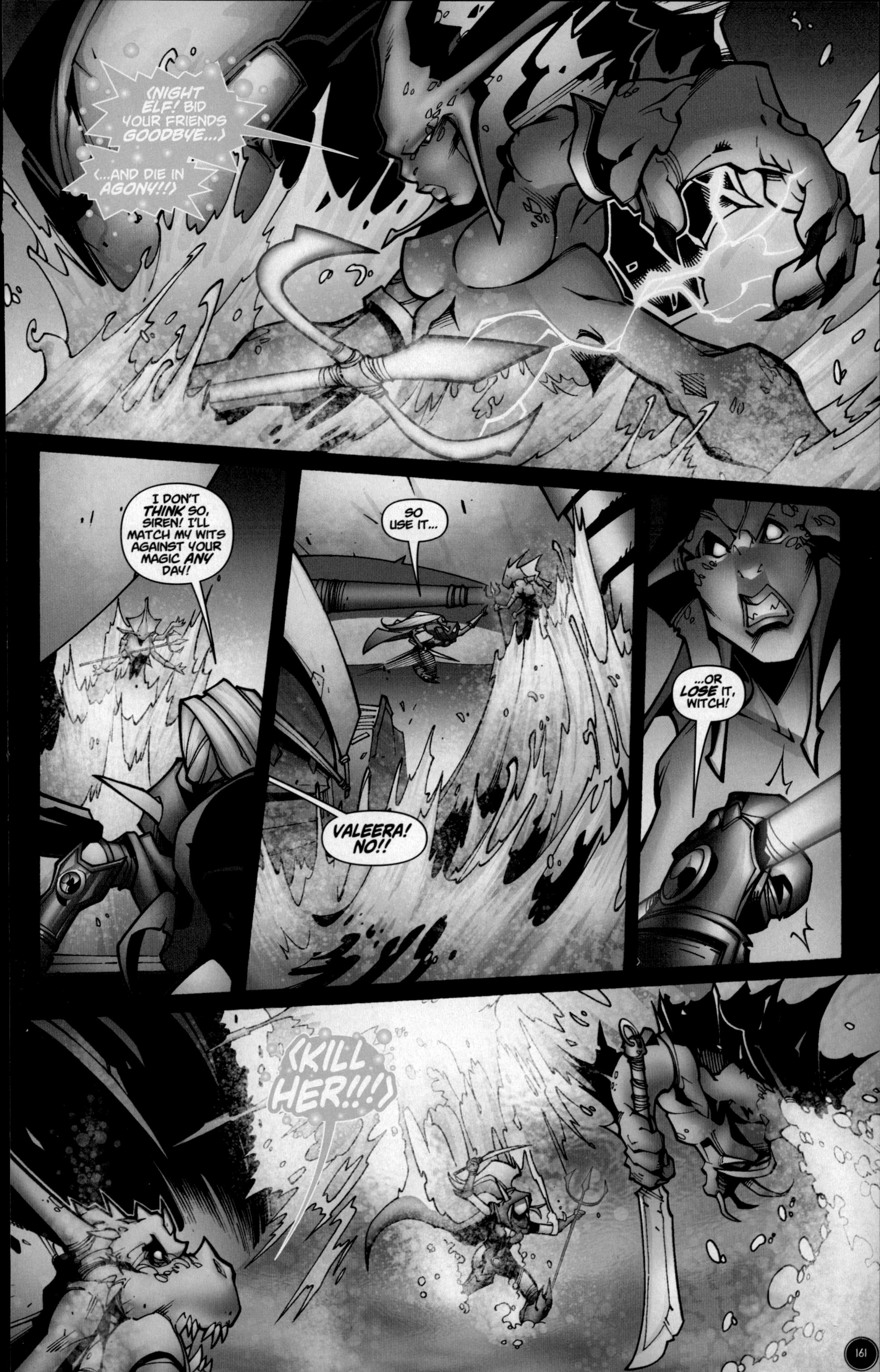

(NIGHT ELF! BID YOUR FRIENDS GOODBYE...)
(...AND DIE IN AGONY!!)
I DON'T THINK SO, SIREN! I'LL MATCH MY WITS AGAINST YOUR MAGIC ANY DAY!
SO USE IT...
VALEERA! NO!!
...OR LOSE IT, WITCH!
(KILL HER!!!)

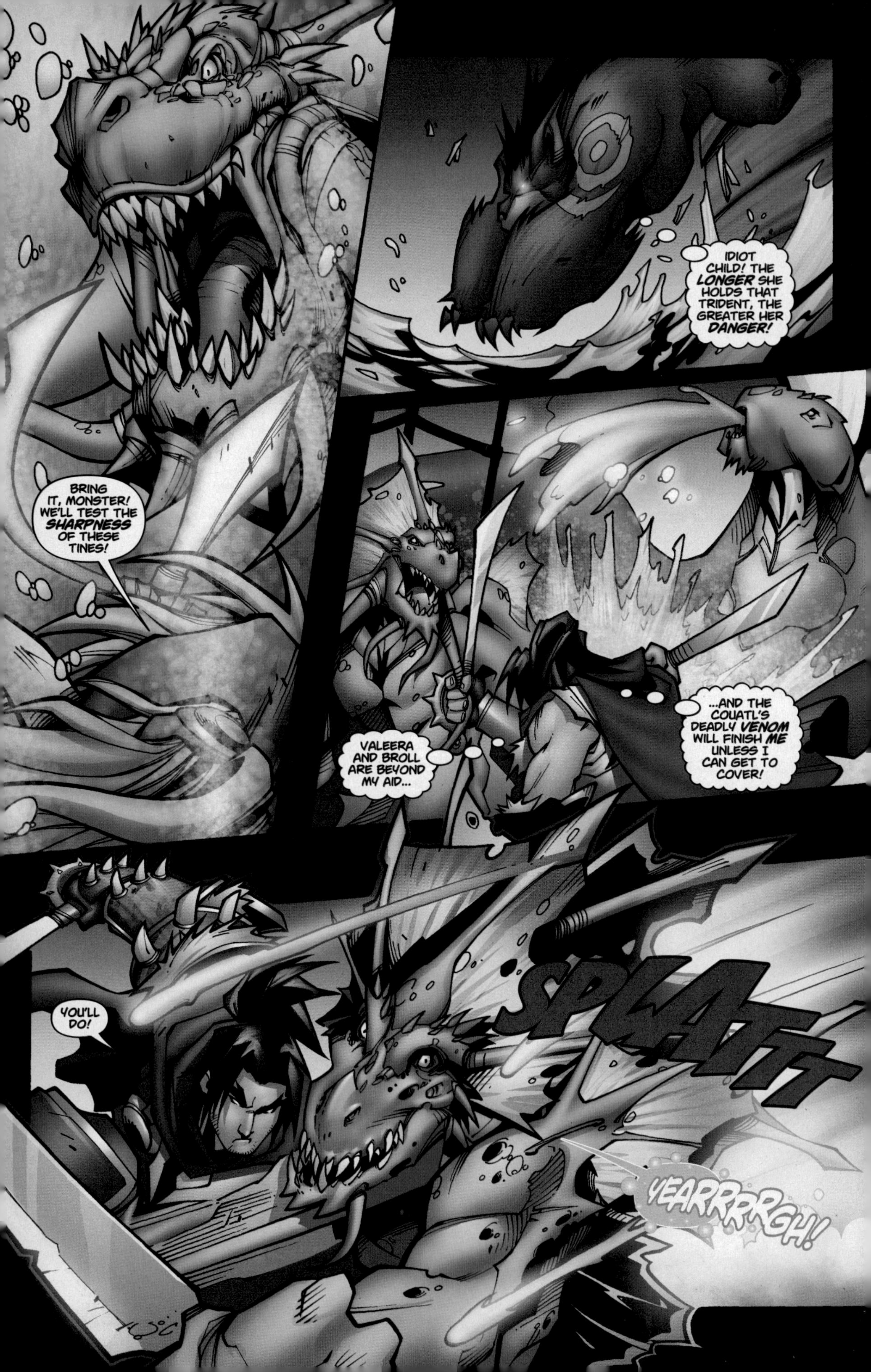
IDIOT CHILD! THE LONGER SHE HOLDS THAT TRIDENT, THE GREATER HER DANGER!
BRING IT, MONSTER! WE'LL TEST THE SHARPNESS OF THESE TINES!
...AND THE COUATL'S DEADLY VENOM WILL FINISH ME UNLESS I CAN GET TO COVER!
VALEERA AND BROLL ARE BEYOND MY AID...
YOU'LL DO!
SPLATTT
YEARRRRGH!

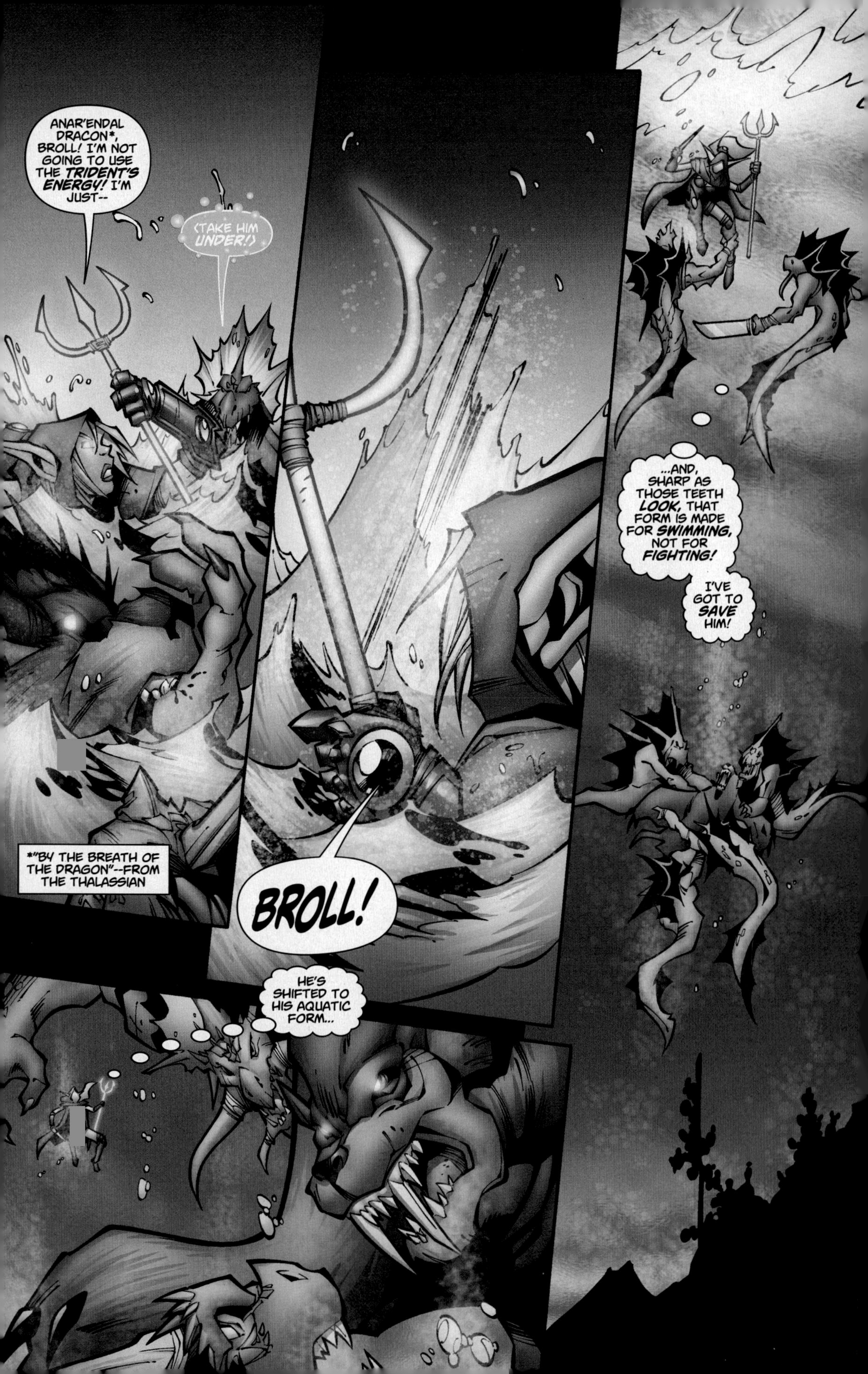

ANAR'ENDAL DRACON*, BROLL! I'M NOT GOING TO USE THE TRIDENT'S ENERGY! I'M JUST--
(TAKE HIM UNDER!)
*"BY THE BREATH OF THE DRAGON"--FROM THE THALASSIAN
BROLL!
HE'S SHIFTED TO HIS AQUATIC FORM...
...AND, SHARP AS THOSE TEETH LOOK, THAT FORM IS MADE FOR SWIMMING, NOT FOR FIGHTING!
I'VE GOT TO SAVE HIM!

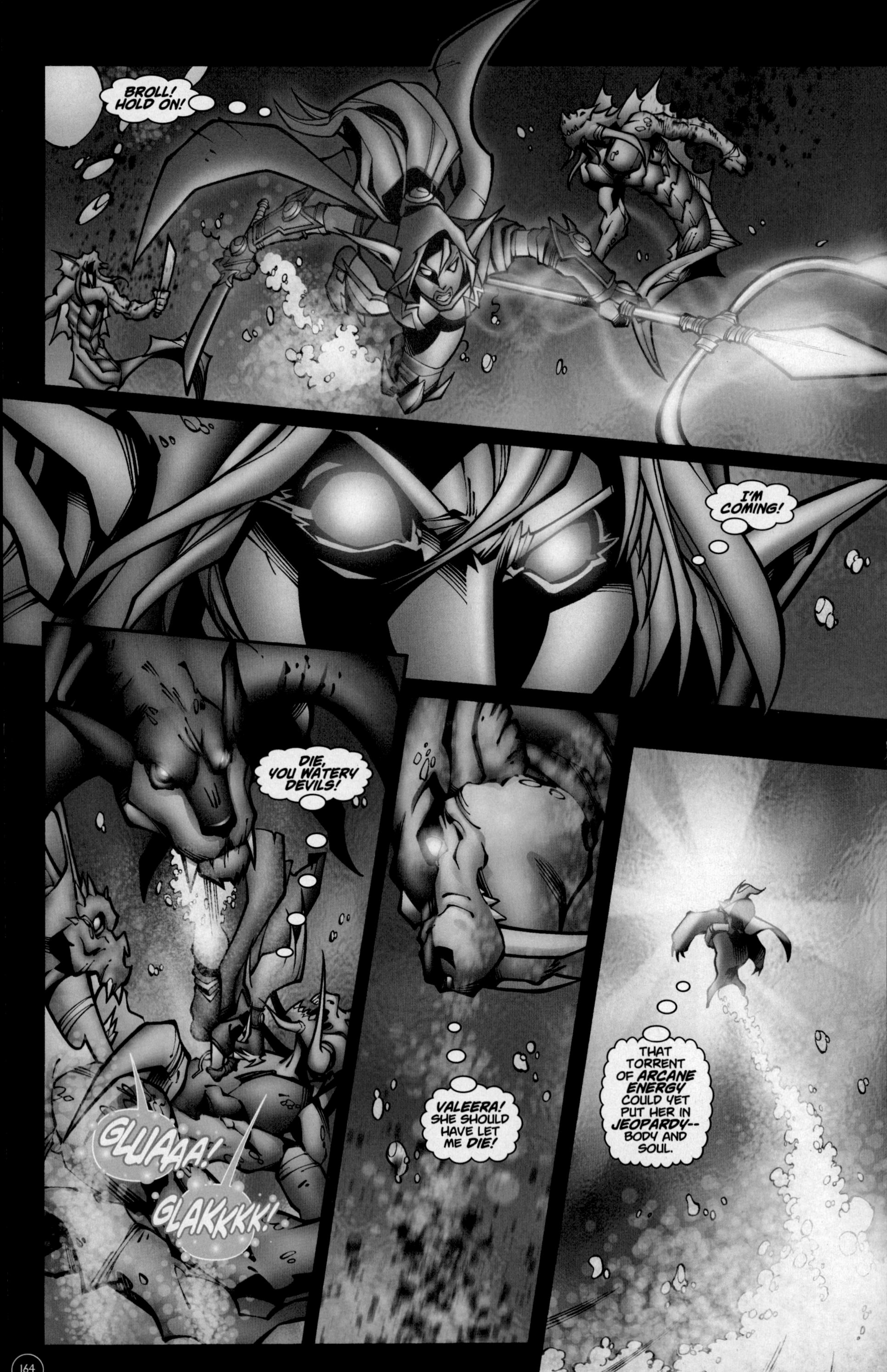
BROLL! HOLD ON!
I'M COMING!
DIE, YOU WATERY DEVILS!
GLUAAA!
GLAKKKK!
VALEERA! SHE SHOULD HAVE LET ME DIE!
THAT TORRENT OF ARCANE ENERGY COULD YET PUT HER IN JEOPARDY-- BODY AND SOUL.

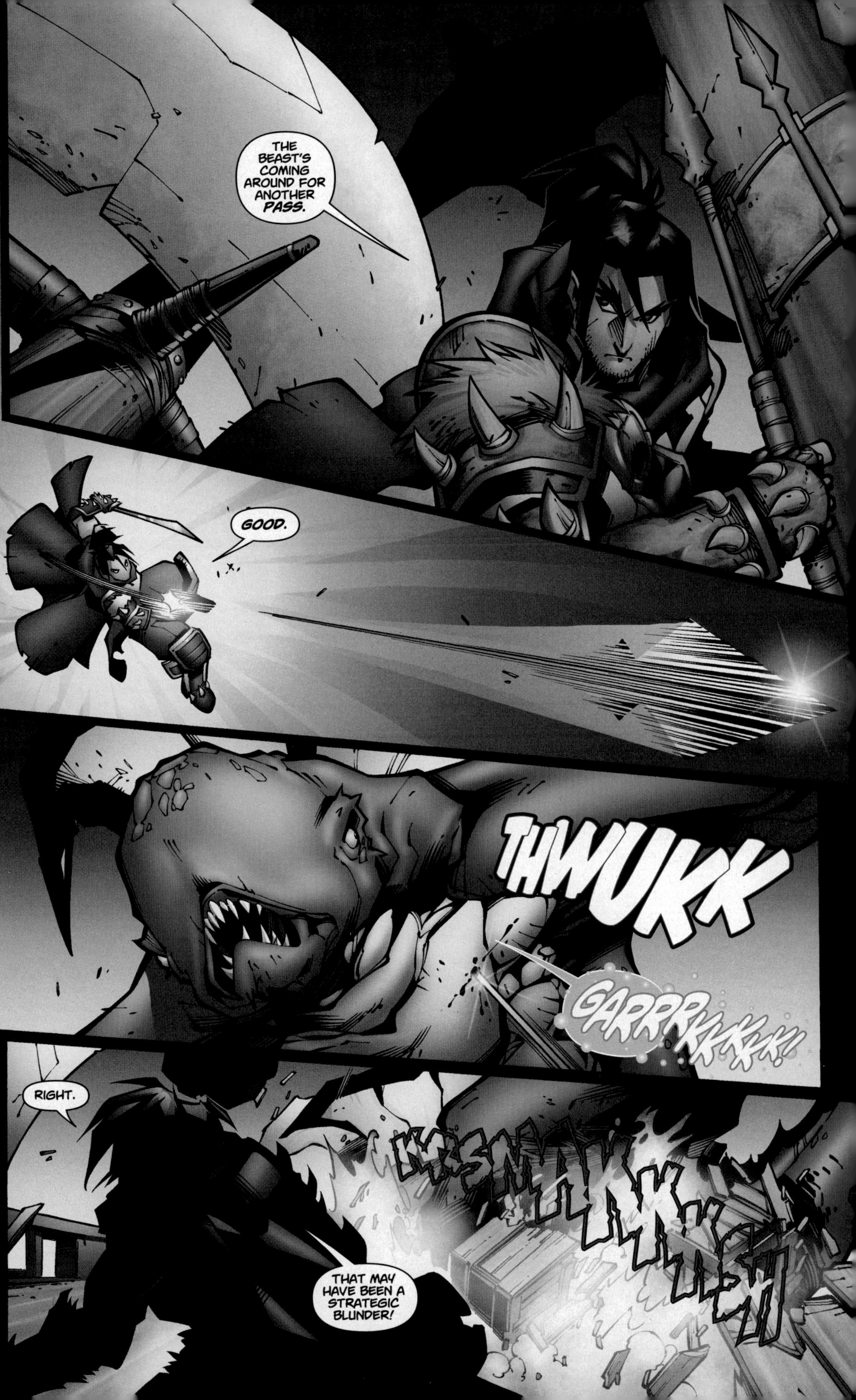
THE BEAST'S COMING AROUND FOR ANOTHER PASS.
GOOD.
THWUKK
GARRRKKKKK!
RIGHT.
THAT MAY HAVE BEEN A STRATEGIC BLUNDER!

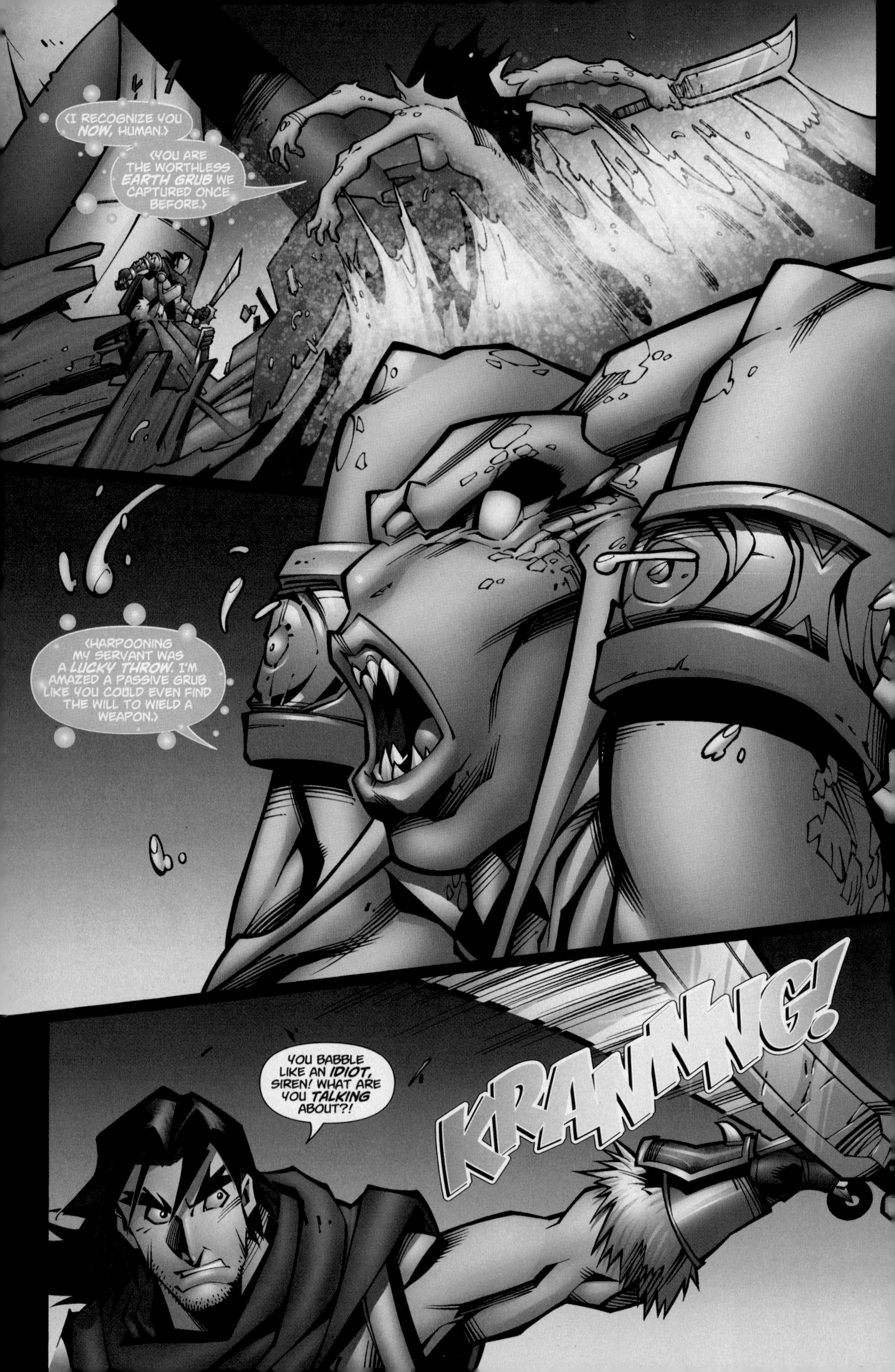
<I RECOGNIZE YOU NOW, HUMAN.>
<YOU ARE THE WORTHLESS EARTH GRUB WE CAPTURED ONCE BEFORE.>
<HARPOONING MY SERVANT WAS A LUCKY THROW. I'M AMAZED A PASSIVE GRUB LIKE YOU COULD EVEN FIND THE WILL TO WIELD A WEAPON.>
KRANNNG!
YOU BABBLE LIKE AN IDIOT, SIREN! WHAT ARE YOU TALKING ABOUT?!

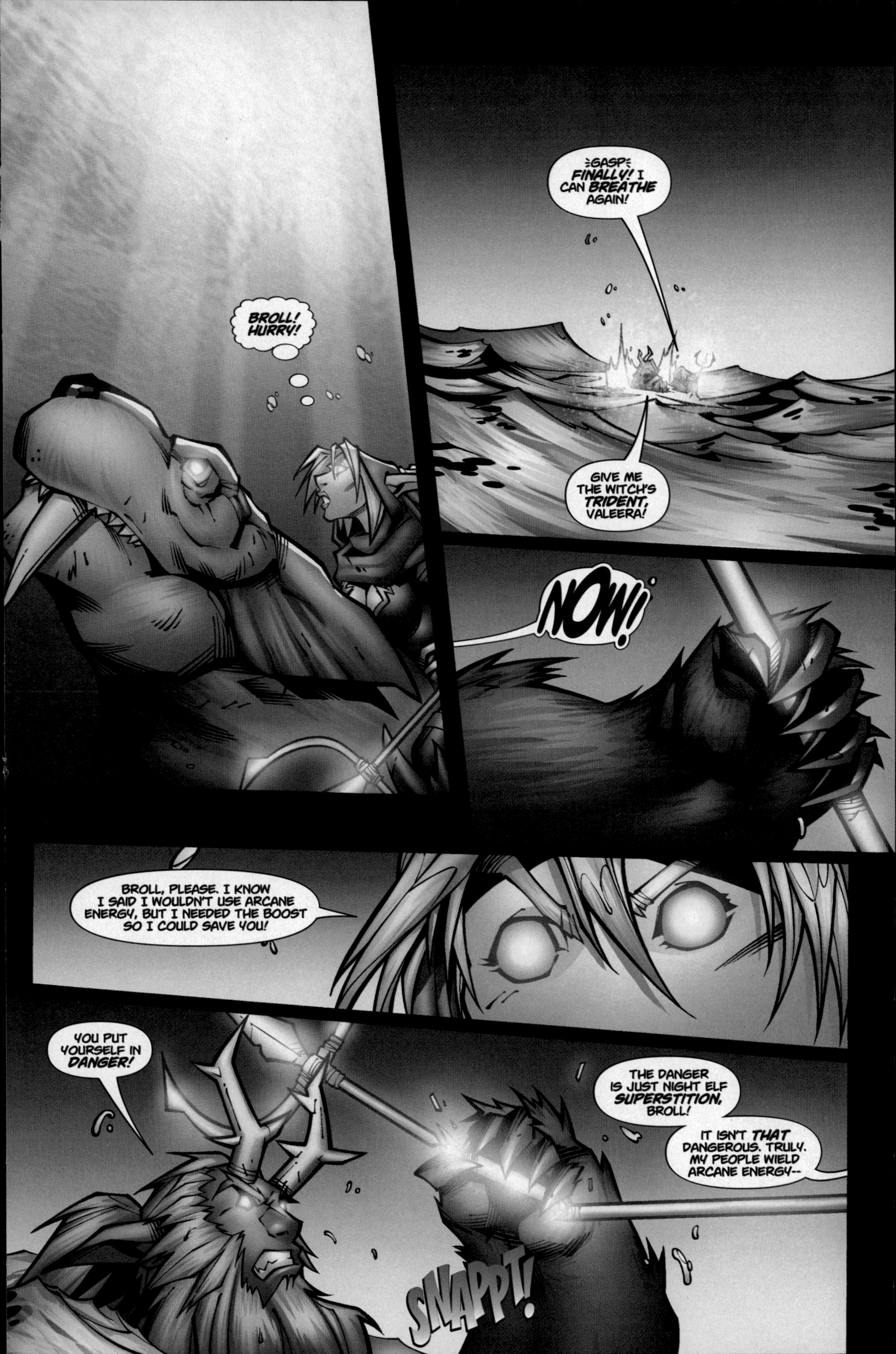
BROLL! HURRY!
GASP FINALLY! I CAN BREATHE AGAIN!
GIVE ME THE WITCH'S TRIDENT, VALEERA!
NOW!
BROLL, PLEASE. I KNOW I SAID I WOULDN'T USE ARCANE ENERGY, BUT I NEEDED THE BOOST SO I COULD SAVE YOU!
YOU PUT YOURSELF IN DANGER!
THE DANGER IS JUST NIGHT ELF SUPERSTITION, BROLL!
IT ISN'T THAT DANGEROUS. TRULY. MY PEOPLE WIELD ARCANE ENERGY--
SNAPPT!

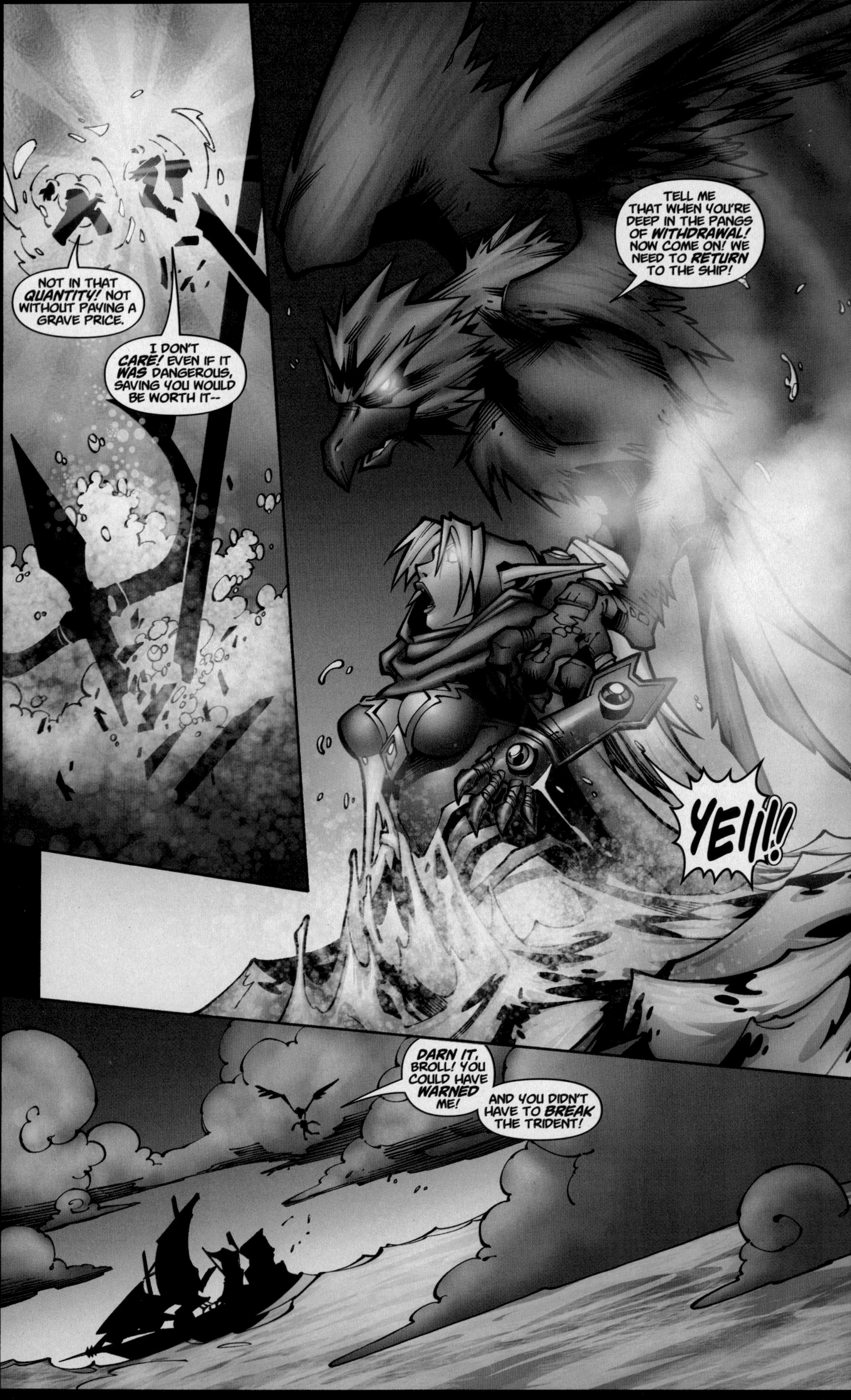
NOT IN THAT QUANTITY! NOT WITHOUT PAYING A GRAVE PRICE.
I DON'T CARE! EVEN IF IT WAS DANGEROUS, SAVING YOU WOULD BE WORTH IT--
TELL ME THAT WHEN YOU'RE DEEP IN THE PANGS OF WITHDRAWAL! NOW COME ON! WE NEED TO RETURN TO THE SHIP!
YEIII!!
DARN IT, BROLL! YOU COULD HAVE WARNED ME!
AND YOU DIDN'T HAVE TO BREAK THE TRIDENT!

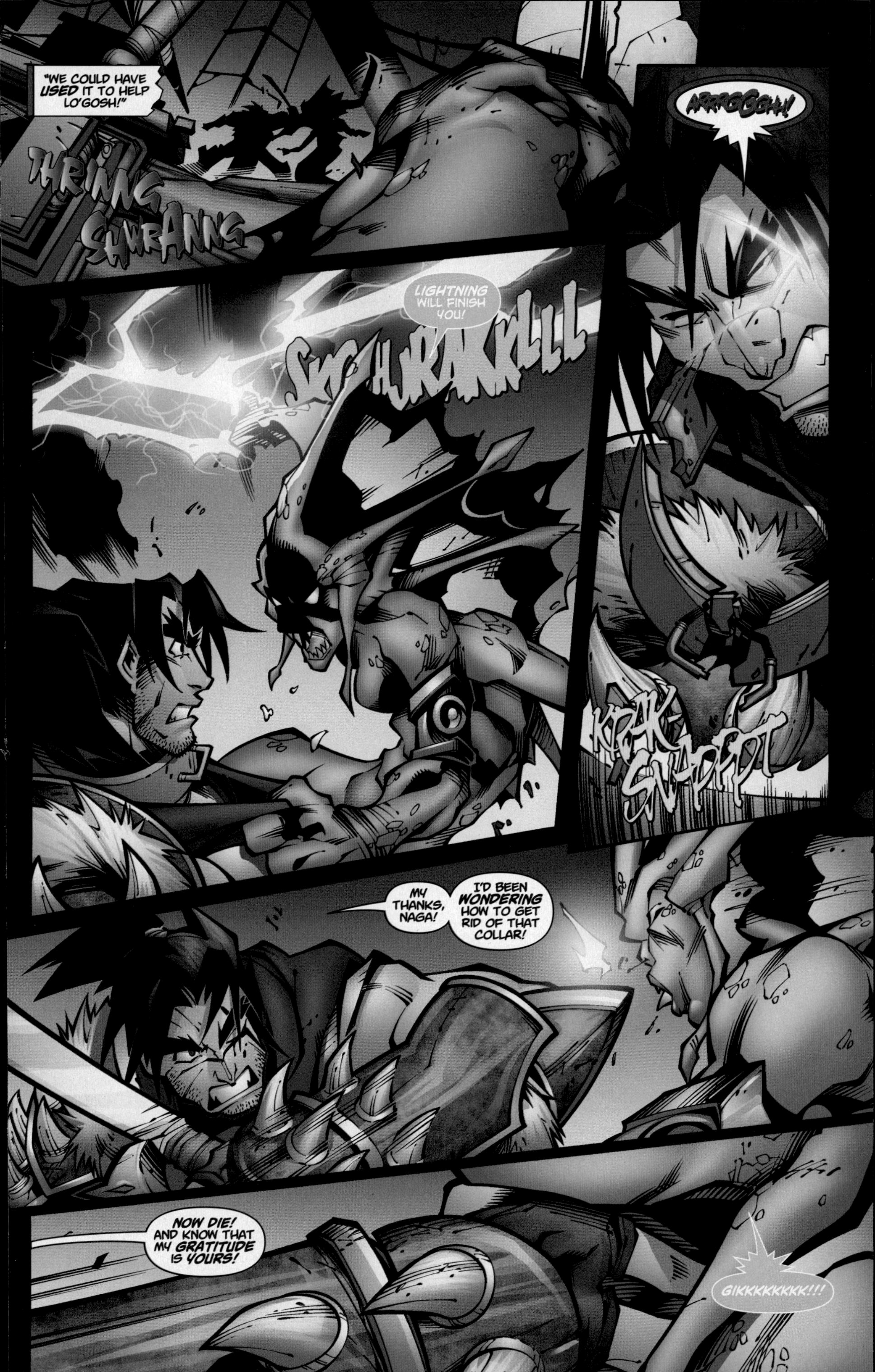

"WE COULD HAVE USED IT TO HELP LO'GOSH!"
THRINNG
SHWRANNG
ARRRGGGHH!
LIGHTNING WILL FINISH YOU!
SWSHURAKKLLL
KRAK-SNAPPPT
MY THANKS, NAGA!
I'D BEEN WONDERING HOW TO GET RID OF THAT COLLAR!
NOW DIE! AND KNOW THAT MY GRATITUDE IS YOURS!
GIKKKKKKKK!!!

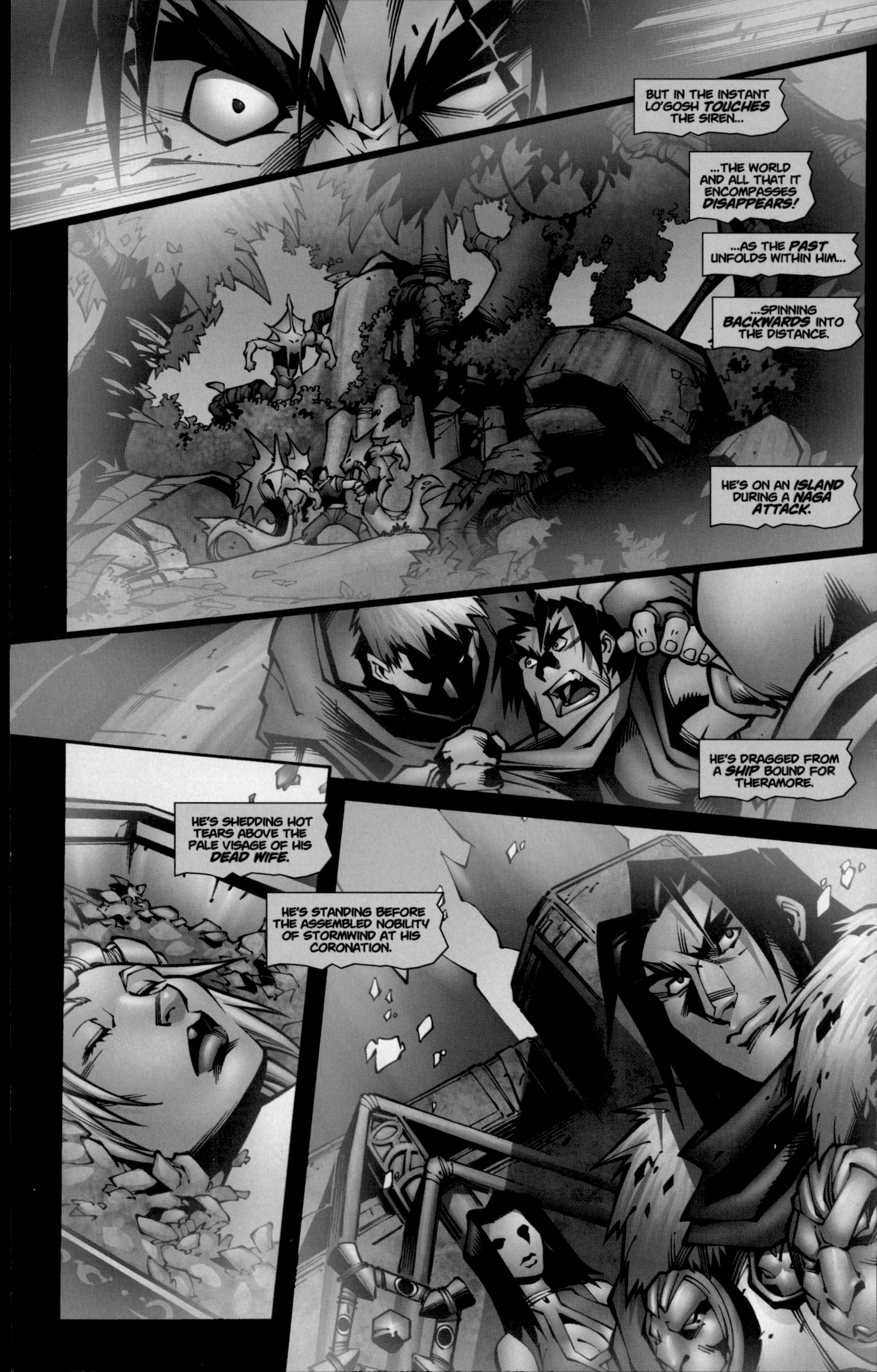
BUT IN THE INSTANT LO'GOSH TOUCHES THE SIREN...
...THE WORLD AND ALL THAT IT ENCOMPASSES DISAPPEARS!
...AS THE PAST UNFOLDS WITHIN HIM...
...SPINNING BACKWARDS INTO THE DISTANCE.
HE'S ON AN ISLAND DURING A NAGA ATTACK.
HE'S DRAGGED FROM A SHIP BOUND FOR THERAMORE.
HE'S SHEDDING HOT TEARS ABOVE THE PALE VISAGE OF HIS DEAD WIFE.
HE'S STANDING BEFORE THE ASSEMBLED NOBILITY OF STORMWIND AT HIS CORONATION.

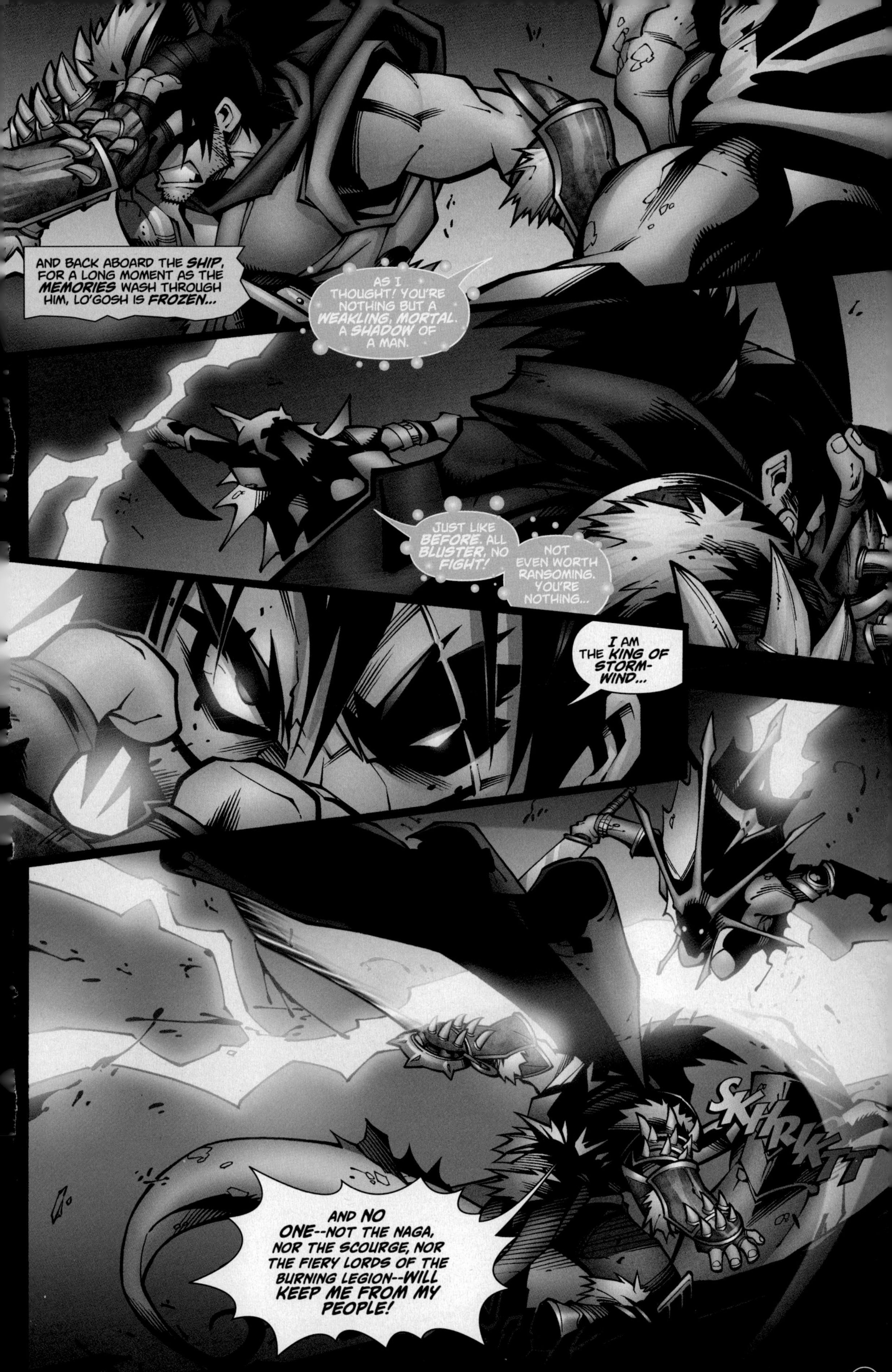

AND BACK ABOARD THE SHIP, FOR A LONG MOMENT AS THE MEMORIES WASH THROUGH HIM, LO'GOSH IS FROZEN...
AS I THOUGHT! YOU'RE NOTHING BUT A WEAKLING, MORTAL. A SHADOW OF A MAN.
JUST LIKE BEFORE. ALL BLUSTER, NO FIGHT!
NOT EVEN WORTH RANSOMING. YOU'RE NOTHING...
I AM THE KING OF STORMWIND...
SKRRKTT
AND NO ONE--NOT THE NAGA, NOR THE SCOURGE, NOR THE FIERY LORDS OF THE BURNING LEGION--WILL KEEP ME FROM MY PEOPLE!

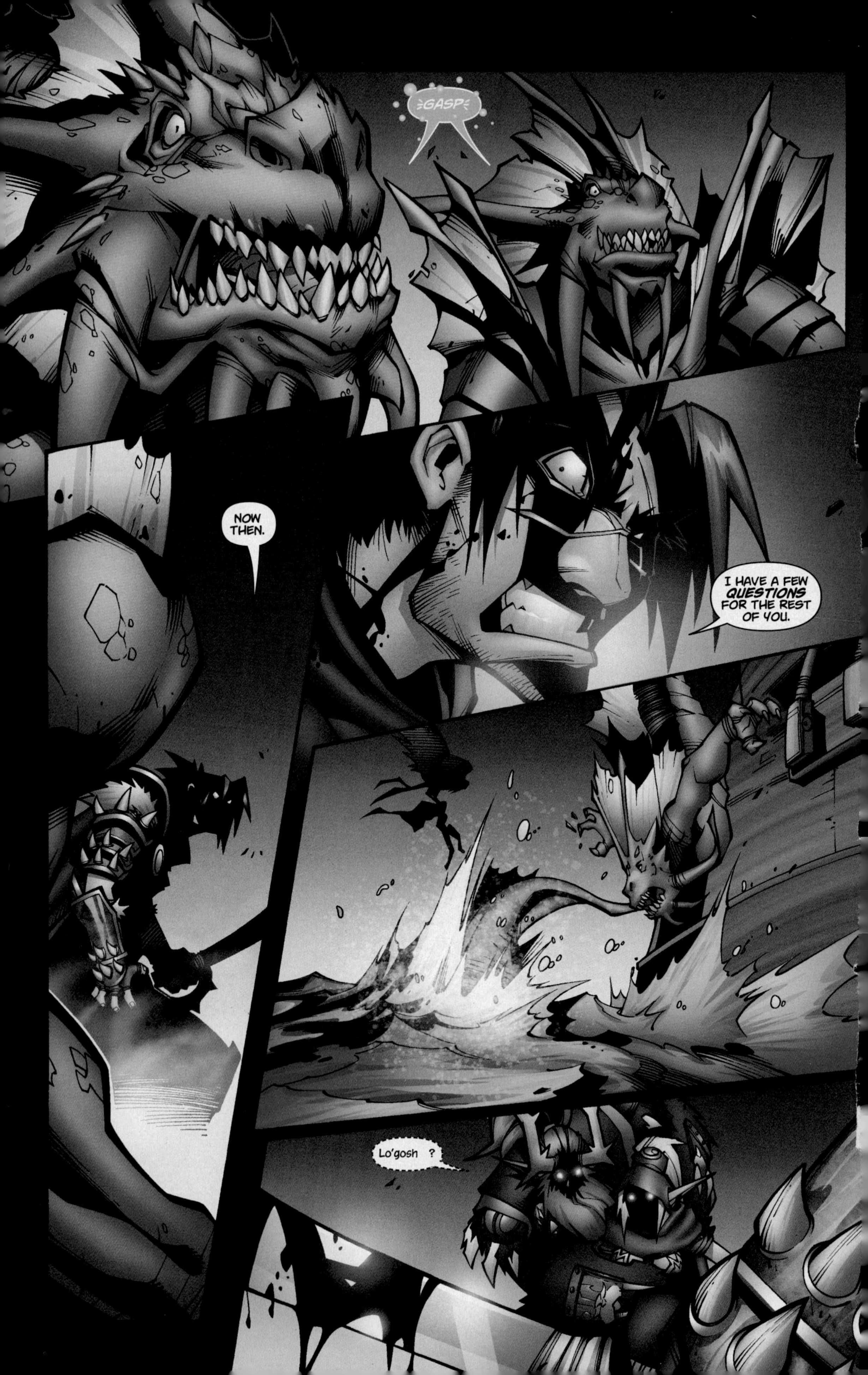
GASP
NOW THEN.
I HAVE A FEW QUESTIONS FOR THE REST OF YOU.
Lo'gosh ?

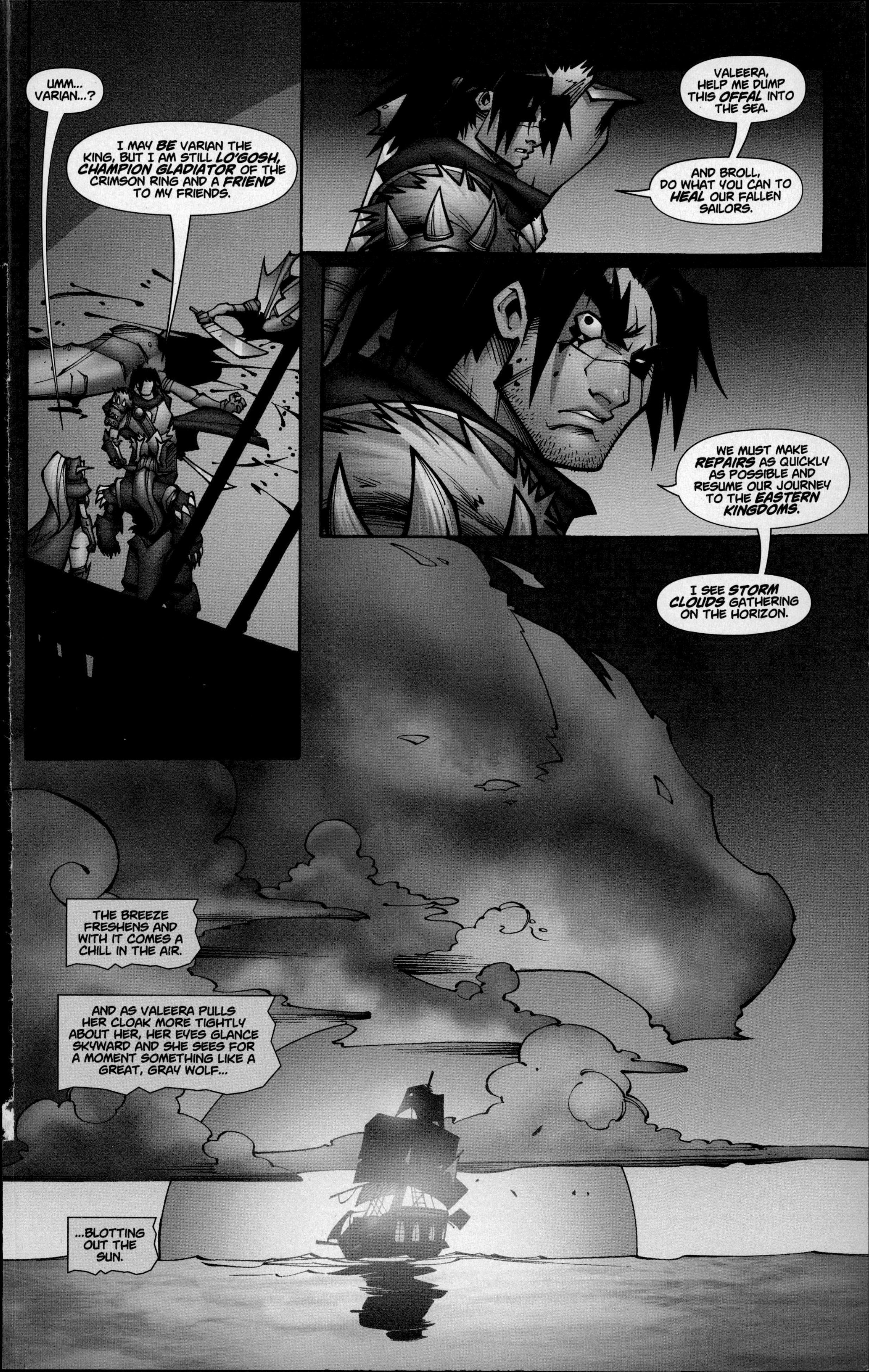
UMM... VARIAN...?
I MAY BE VARIAN THE KING, BUT I AM STILL LO'GOSH, CHAMPION GLADIATOR OF THE CRIMSON RING AND A FRIEND TO MY FRIENDS.
VALEERA, HELP ME DUMP THIS OFFAL INTO THE SEA.
AND BROLL, DO WHAT YOU CAN TO HEAL OUR FALLEN SAILORS.
WE MUST MAKE REPAIRS AS QUICKLY AS POSSIBLE AND RESUME OUR JOURNEY TO THE EASTERN KINGDOMS.
I SEE STORM CLOUDS GATHERING ON THE HORIZON.
THE BREEZE FRESHENS AND WITH IT COMES A CHILL IN THE AIR.
AND AS VALEERA PULLS HER CLOAK MORE TIGHTLY ABOUT HER, HER EYES GLANCE SKYWARD AND SHE SEES FOR A MOMENT SOMETHING LIKE A GREAT, GRAY WOLF...
...BLOTTING OUT THE SUN.

Sketches By Ludo Lullabi

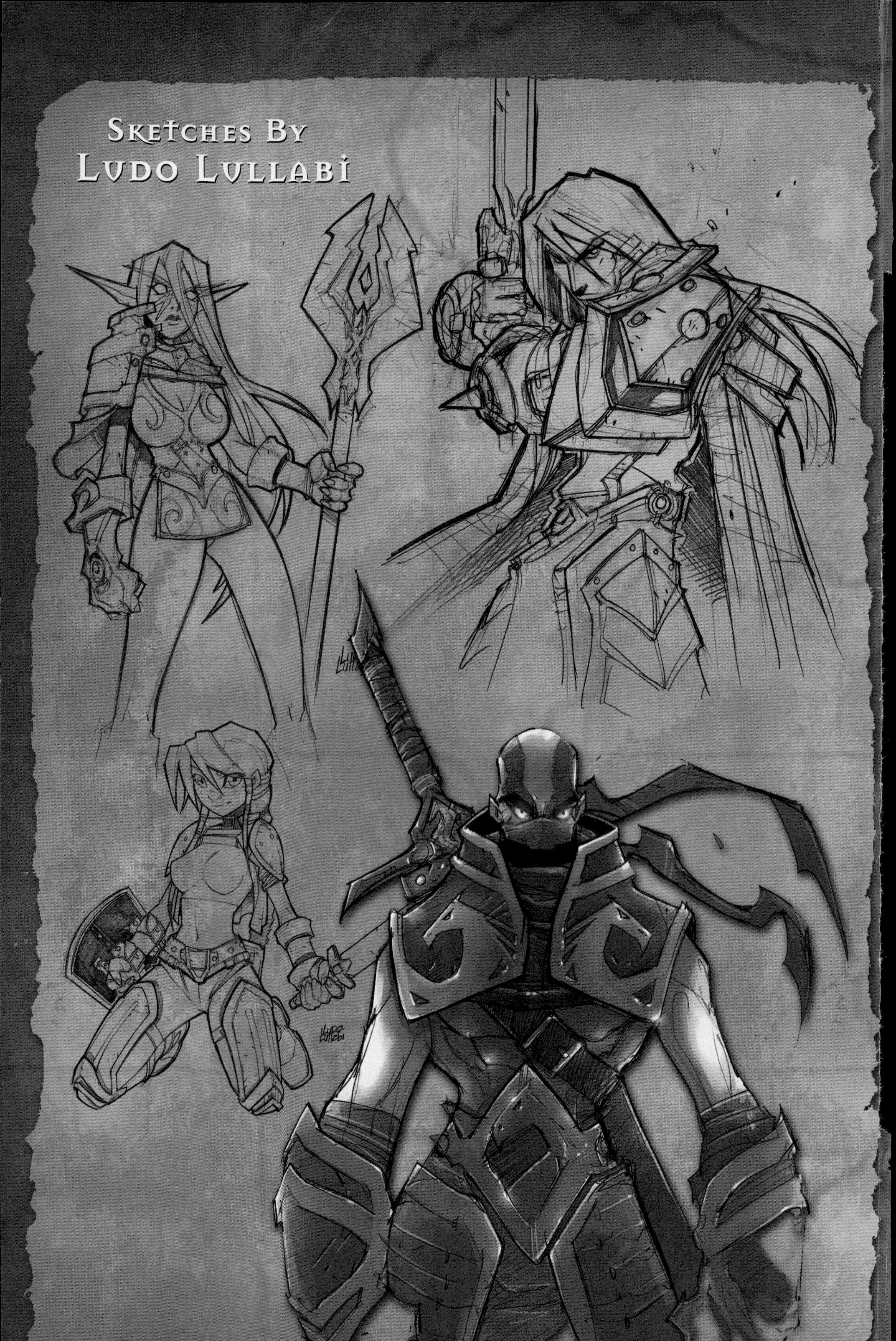

THE HIT NBC SERIES

HER○ES

GRAPHIC NOVEL

Ordinary people wake up to go to work; to go to school; to go about their ordinary lives. But what if ordinary people wake up with the ability to paint the future...or blow up the world with the power of their minds?

From the first episode of the television show, the world was introduced to people exhibiting extraordinary abilities. Secrets have been continually revealed on-screen, but further truths await. Read it all in these stories that take place between the episodes!

VOLUME ONE

MORE GREAT STORIES FROM WILDSTORM:

FREDDY VS. JASON VS. ASH

THE PROGRAMME

SUPERNATURAL: ORIGINS

KUHORIC*CRAIG

MILLIGAN*SMITH

JOHNSON*SMITH

TO FIND MORE COLLECTED EDITIONS AND MONTHLY COMIC BOOKS FROM WILDSTORM AND DC COMICS

CALL 1-888-COMIC BOOK

FOR THE NEAREST COMICS SHOP OR GO TO YOUR LOCAL BOOK STORE